FROM THE MOST TRUSTED NAME IN TRAVEL

FROMMER'S

EASYGUIDE

TO

NEW YORK CITY

2017

P9-CEX-414

Quick to Read · Easy to Carry · For Expert Advice In All Price Ranges

By Pauline Frommer

FROMMER'S STAR RATINGS SYSTEM

Every hotel, restaurant, and attraction listed in this guide has been ranked for quality and value. Here's what the stars mean:

★ Recommended
★★ Highly Recommended
★★★ A must! Don't miss!

AN IMPORTANT NOTE

The world is a dynamic place. Hotels change ownership, restaurants hike their prices, museums alter their opening hours, and busses and trains change their routings. And all of this can occur in the several months after our authors have visited, inspected, and written about, these hotels, restaurants, museums and transportation services. Though we have made valiant efforts to keep all our information fresh and up-to-date, some few changes can inevitably occur in the periods before a revised edition of this guidebook is published. So please bear with us if a tiny number of the details in this book have changed. Please also note that we have no responsibility or liability for any inaccuracy or errors or omissions, or for inconvenience, loss, damage, or expenses suffered by anyone as a result of assertions in this guide.

The Greek and Roman Art Wing of the Metropolitan Museum of Art (p. 153).

CONTENTS

The Chrysler Building.

A LOOK AT NEW YORK CITY

New York City vies with London and Paris in the variety of its attractions and the massive number of its cultural activities. It comes as close to being an indispensable visit as any other city both here or abroad. And what you come to see and experience are not only the big lures that everyone names—the Statue of Liberty, the Empire State Building, the 9/11 Memorial and Museum, the U.N. and Wall Street, the Broadway theatres and the Radio City Music Hall—but also hundreds of fascinating stores and workshops, exhibits, outlets, and clubs that attract the most enterprising and talented of our nation's most ambitious citizens. As the song goes, "If you can make it here, you'll make it anywhere." The author of our Easy Guide to New York City, my daughter Pauline, has singled out the most fascinating of these smaller attractions so that you, the reader, can have not simply a touristic experience but possibly a life-changing one. Have a great trip!

Arthur Frommer

New York City has some of the worst traffic in the nation, so take a subway! (See p. 257 for more on that.)

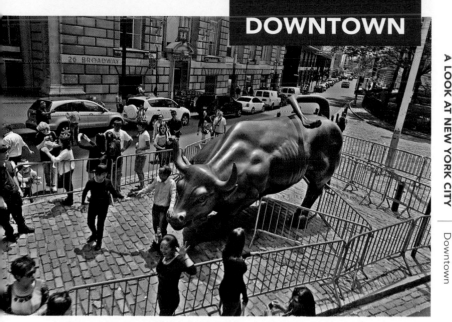

In 1987, artist Arturo di Modica surprised the city by placing his massive Charging Bull sculpture in front of the New York Stock Exchange in the middle of the night. It was eventually moved to its current location in Bowling Green Park (p. 211), and has become one of the city's icons. To this day it's owned by the artist, not the city of New York.

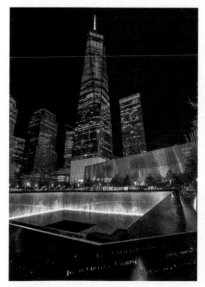

Names cut into the rim of the 9/11 Memorial fountains (p. 118) remember those who died that day. Behind them looms the new One World Trade Center, the United States' tallest building.

Leafy, serene residential streets, lined by brownstones, make up much of Greenwich Village (p. 20).

Look up: Ornate downtown fire escapes were made by 19th-century Italian immigrant artisans, trained on Old World palazzos and churches.

Kooky décor and cheap, tasty Indian food have drawn diners to the East Village for decades. See p. 75.

Washington Square Arch and Park (p. 183).

Some 1 million people attend Little Italy's Feast of San Gennaro, a raucous 10-day street festival that's held each September.

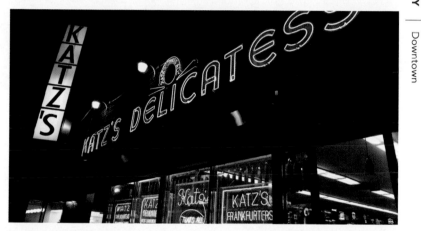

In a city where too much of the past gets bulldozed, Katz' has been dishing up pastrami, salami, corned beef and other diet-busting treats on the Lower East Side since 1888. See p. 73.

Gruesome-looking but delicious smoked ducks hang in the windows of a number of Chinatown restaurants, including one we love. See our review of New York Noodletown on p. 70.

MIDTOWN

The frenetic energy of the commuters who dash through Grand Central Terminal is counterbalanced by the soaring majesty of this Beaux Arts structure. At the center of the busy lobby is a clock valued in the tens of millions of dollars, its four faces covered not by glass but solid precious opal. See p. 141 for info on tours of the station.

At the height of the Great Depression, some 75,000 people were blessed with gainful employment, creating the "city within a city" known as Rockefeller Center (p. 147). It is one of the greatest feats of urban developments in history: 12 acres upon which stand 14 Art Deco limestone skyscrapers, each enhanced by superb works of art, like this seven-ton bronze sculpture of Atlas.

Jackson Pollock, whose work is pictured here, is just one of the titans presented by the Museum of Modern Art (p. 146), a world-class trove of late 19th- and 20th-century art.

A new kind of park, the High Line (p. 180) is set on an abandoned elevated railway trestle.

A festive window at Bergdorf Goodman department store (see p.190).

With nearly 60 million annual visitors, and 8.5 million permanent residents, the streets of Manhattan, particularly in Midtown, can get mighty crowded.

The New York Times used to have its headquarters here, hence the name Times Square (p. 149). Today, the area is synonymous with Broadway, as in Broadway shows, like the ones you see advertised in the photo.

A favorite spot in the Metropolitan Museum (p. 153), North America's largest museum, is the enclosed sculpture court of the American Wing.

Above, a cutting-edge installation at the Cooper-Hewitt Smithsonian Design Museum (p. 150). Below: The swirling architecture of the Guggenheim Museum (p. 155), designed by Frank Lloyd Wright.

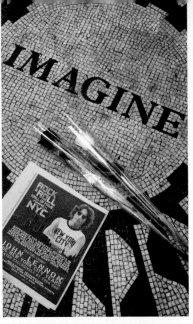

A fleet of 100 rowboats are available for rental in the heart of Central Park (see p. 172).

A tribute to John Lennon, the Imagine mosaic (p. 178) is in Central Park's Strawberry Fields garden.

At the American Museum of Natural History (p. 156), immense African elephants stand guard over the Akely Hall of African Mammals, beloved for its detailed 1930s-era dioramas.

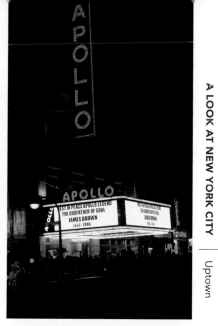

The Cloisters (see p. 159), an offshoot of the Metropolitan Museum, is dedicated to Medieval European art and architecture.

Harlem's famed Apollo Theater (see p. 234).

The Peace Fountain, at the Cathedral of St. John the Divine (p. 157), shows Archangel Michael embracing a giraffe.

Yes, this is the Little Red Lighthouse from the children's book (p. 182).

OTHER BOROUGHS

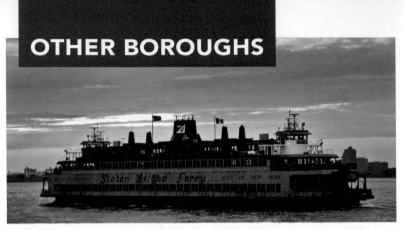

Views from the Staten Island Ferry are among the best in town, and the ride is absolutely free (p. 127).

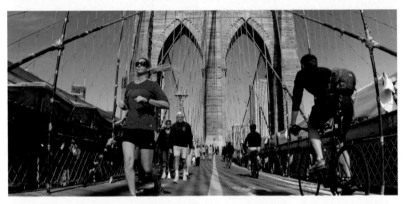

Above: Walking or biking across the Brooklyn Bridge (p. 120) is a classic Gotham activity. Below: Subways aren't always "sub": in the outer boroughs of Brooklyn, Queens, and the Bronx they often go above ground.

The wonderful-for-all-ages Museum of the Moving Image in Queens (p. 168) was the first in the world to dedicate itself to explicating the craft that goes into the creation of films, TV shows, and video games. It has now expanded into online technology as well.

A wall in hip, and politically active, Williamsburg, Brooklyn.

A lowland gorilla at the Bronx Zoo (see p. 161).

The Smorgasburg food festival (now held in several parts of Brooklyn, see p. 89) has been so influential that many products first sold here are now on grocery store shelves, and many of the booths have morphed into actual restaurants in other parts of the city. It's also a ton of fun to go and graze.

Brooklyn has likely overtaken Manhattan when it comes to live music clubs. The Music Hall of Williamsburg (pictured; p. 237) features up-and-coming bands in all genres.

THE BEST OF THE BIG APPLE

There is simply no place in the United States as brimming with opportunities as New York City. Those of us who live here open our doors to incredible options each and every day: the chance to experience the best and newest in the worlds of art, theater, dance, and music; the ability to feast on expertly prepared foods from all over the world; the belief that we can make our voices heard on political issues, in this news media capital of the nation; and the opportunity to meet today's movers and shakers. The ambitious come here because they know that if they want to achieve a certain level of prominence in their careers or in the eyes of the world, New York is the place to do it. (Are you humming "If I can make it there, I'll make it anywhere . . ." right now?)

There's a factual basis to this New Yorker's pride. Because of the density and diversity of our population; our long history as a center of commerce and ideas; our access to the United Nations, Wall Street, and the opinion makers of Madison Avenue; and endless other resources, there's simply more *more* here than in other places. And if that claim seems extreme, well, you'll just have to regard boastfulness as another unavoidable characteristic of "the Big Apple." What would we New Yorkers be without our big mouths?

In visiting New York, you, too, are opening yourself up to a world of wonderful opportunities. In fact, that's what can make New York so intimidating to visitors: There are just so many darn choices. In this chapter, I've sorted through a book's worth of options, selecting some favorites to help you hit the city's highlights.

THE MOST unforgettable NEW YORK CITY EXPERIENCES

o **Seeing the city from on high:** It doesn't really matter if you do so from the **Top of the Rock** (p. 148), the **Empire State Building** (p. 140), the **One World Observatory** (p. 125), or one of the many other venues where one can get a bird's-eye view. What's really important is that you get a feeling for the immensity of the city, with Manhattan's wonderfully orderly grid system of streets (which plays off the hubbub on the streets themselves), and the dizzying variety of building types (many of which can't be adequately seen from the sidewalk). Try to get somewhere high early in your trip—there's no better way to orient yourself.

o **Walking the Brooklyn Bridge:** The bridge, too, offers glorious views of the city. But that's not the only reason you stroll here: Walking the span allows you to see this marvel of engineering up close. (It was the longest suspension bridge in the world when it was built in 1883.) See p. 120.

o **Going to a big, splashy Broadway musical:** When they're done right—and they're not always—there are few experiences as life-affirming (no, truly!) as seeing ridiculously talented people sing and dance their hearts out in a show that makes you laugh, cry, and think about your own life story. See chapter 8.

o **Staying out late:** The city changes after dusk. All the people who were rushing by you during the day slow down and take to the city's bars, restaurants, and clubs to socialize. Even if you're not normally a nightlife person, try it while in NYC. If you're outgoing, you may be rewarded with some great conversations (despite its reputation, this is actually one of the friendliest cities on the planet); and if you're shy, well, the eavesdropping can be fascinating , too.

o **Touring Ellis Island:** You'll see the **Statue of Liberty** (p. 127) first (also a thrill) and then spend several hours in the place so many of our ancestors passed through in order to settle in the "New World." Hearing the tales of what went on here is a tremendously moving experience. See p. 120.

o **Traveling underground:** Don't be afraid of the subways! Not only will they zip you anywhere you need to go at nearly the speed of light (okay, maybe not that fast, but they're efficient), but there are few better places to feel the intense energy of this always-on-the-go metropolis. The people-watching is primo, too, and some of the musicians who perform underground are darn good, meaning you get a show with your ride.

THE best FREE NEW YORK ACTIVITIES

o **Ride the Staten Island Ferry:** The Staten Island Ferry is used daily by thousands of commuters. Ride it for a great view of the Statue of Liberty, Ellis Island, New York Harbor, and the lower Manhattan skyline. You can't beat the price: free. See p. 127.

o **Visit a museum for free (or nearly free):** A number of museums allow free entry on Fridays. The **Museum of Modern Art** (p. 146) is free from 4 to 8pm on that day, as is the **Museum of the Moving Image** (p. 168). The **Rubin Museum**'s (p. 135) free Fridays runs from 6 to 9pm, the **Whitney**'s (p. 134) from 7 to 10pm, and the **New York Historical Society** (p. 161) from 6 to 8pm. Remember that a number of museums—most prominently the **Metropolitan Museum** (p. 155), the **Brooklyn Museum** (p. 165), and the **Museum of Natural History**—charge a "suggested donation," meaning you could, without shame, pay just a nickel for entrance. See chapter 5 for more.

o **Attend a TV taping:** You'll get a behind-the-scenes peek at how Jimmy Fallon, Stephen Colbert, the SNL cast, and the other NYC-based TV stars work their magic. And you won't pay a cent more than you do to watch TV in your own home—less, if you pay for cable! See p. 232 for full details.

o **Take a tour with a Big Apple Greeter:** Volunteers who love their hometown and love showing it to outsiders lead these unique tours. You'll need to sign up well in advance, but when you do you'll be assigned a local with similar interests to yours who can show you the neighborhood of your choice. Possibly the best tours in the city, and absolutely free. See p. 21.

o **Kayak the Hudson River:** From May through October, the Downtown Boathouse organization (www.downtownboathouse.org) offers both lessons and boats, gratis, to anyone who's interested. It's a thrilling, remarkably easy-to-learn activity, and a great way to get a bit of exercise.

o **Gallery-hop in Chelsea:** Wandering through these galleries—the biggest concentration in the world—is an intellectually rich experience, as you explore the current zeitgeist of the art world, as expressed by hundreds of would-be Picassos. See p. 138.

o **Walk. Everywhere:** New York City is one of the world's greatest walking cities. Since most of Manhattan is planned on the grid system, it's hard to get lost in that borough (except below 4th Street, where getting lost is part of the fun). Avenues go north and south; streets go east and west. You can actually walk the entire length of Manhattan—a walk that, done briskly, takes about 6 hours. That's a 13½-mile hike, by the way!

THE best WAYS TO SEE NEW YORK CITY LIKE A LOCAL

o **Watch the sun set over Central Park from the roof garden of the Metropolitan Museum:** Though the museum is jammed with tourists during the day, locals take over at dusk, on Fridays and Saturdays (when the museum is open until 8:45pm). They head up to the art-filled roof—a different contemporary artist is given the commission to decorate it each year—to sip wine, socialize, and (often) pick up each other. It's a great time to look at the art downstairs, too, as the galleries are a quarter as crowded as they are during the daytime. See p. 155.

o **Ride the Roosevelt Island tram:** It may just be a 4-minute ride, but the views are spectacular, and you'll head to an island very few outsiders ever visit. A shame, especially now that the new **FDR Four Freedoms Park** has opened at Roosevelt Island's tip. See p. 142.

- **Stand in line for Shakespeare in the Park:** Shakespeare performed by stars, under the stars, in Central Park—for free! Even though you can put your name into an online lottery for tickets, every summer thousands of New Yorkers make a day out of waiting in line (and chatting, picnicking, and people-watching) for the tickets to be distributed. While you won't find a real New Yorker at Times Square on New Year's Eve, you will find lots of them on a summer's day waiting for the Bard. See p. 235.
- **Get from here to there by Citibike:** The city's bike-sharing program has shown locals just how much fun it is to get around on two wheels. Join them! The program is affordable, and thanks to all the new bike lanes in the city, getting around by bike is easier than ever. See p. 267.
- **Browse the Greenmarket:** Union Square's farmer's market has to be one of the best of its kind in the U.S. (especially on Saturdays when it's jammed with vendors). You'll meet the farmers and get to sample all sorts of treats—from jams to artisanal wines to honey from a hive on a Brooklyn rooftop—when you wander through this bustling market. See p. 182.
- **Do brunch:** After dashing around all week there's nothing we like better on the weekend than chowing down on avocado toast with poached eggs, in a restaurant with friends, and arguing about the week's news.

THE best FAMILY EXPERIENCES

- **Central Park:** With its carousel, two zoos, two ice-skating rinks and pools (depending on the season), playgrounds, and ball fields, Central Park is a children's wonderland. See p. 172.
- **Bronx Zoo:** This sprawling wildlife park is one of the great zoos in the world, and you don't have to be a kid to love it. See p. 163.
- **Coney Island:** It's far grittier than Disneyworld, but for many that's a plus. Come here to taste the vintage pleasures of what was once New York City's favorite summer playground, including the landmarked Wonder Wheel and Cyclone roller coaster. Nearby is the New York Aquarium, MCU Park (home of the minor league baseball team Brooklyn Cyclones), Nathan's Famous hot dogs, and, of course, the beach! See p. 166.
- **Museum of the Moving Image:** Make your own photo flip-book, dub your voice over Julie Andrews's in a clip from *Mary Poppins,* or play classic video games from the 1980s together. This highly interactive museum—it's dedicated to the craft of making movies, TV shows, and video games—is a blast for people of all ages. See p. 168.

best OFFBEAT NEW YORK EXPERIENCES

- **Attend a poetry slam:** The talent you'll see up on the stage, and the passion with which the spoken word is greeted here, is inspiring. See p. 243.

o **Spend the evening at Sammy's Roumanian Steakhouse:** The closest New York City comes to an old-time Catskills resort experience, you'll listen to the hoariest of jokes and songs from *Fiddler on the Roof* while eating chopped liver and downing glasses of vodka from a bottle encased in a block of ice. See p. 72.

o **Ride the International Express:** The no. 7 train is known as the "International Express." Take it through the borough of Queens (where it runs aboveground for most of its length), and you will pass one ethnic neighborhood after another, from Indian to Thai, from Peruvian to Colombian, from Chinese to Korean. See p. 169.

o **Head to a Russian nightclub:** At **Tatiana** (p. 251) or one of Brighton Beach's other supper clubs, you get a multicourse feast and a show in Russian featuring acrobats, showgirls, and lots and lots of feathers. It's a wacky way to spend the evening.

o **Visit the Mmuseumm:** The smallest museum in the city is also one of the most intriguing, filled with tiny exhibits on the oddities of modern life. See p. 133.

NEW YORK'S best MUSEUMS

o **Best all-around museum: The Metropolitan Museum of Art.** It's a case of more is more; the largest museum in the Americas is also the finest museum-going experience in New York. How could it not be, with the variety of treasures this fabled institution holds—from an actual ancient Egyptian temple to murals from a Pompeian villa, to masterworks by Rembrandt, Vermeer, van Gogh, and on and on? See p. 155.

o **Best history museum: The Tenement Museum.** Usually, historic sites tell the tales of the rich and powerful. This tiny museum recalls a more moving story: that of immigrants who made their first "New World" homes in this actual tenement. Visiting here is an emotionally powerful experience. See p. 132.

o **Best art museum that people outside New York love to tell you they love the most: The Frick.** The Frick is home to an unrivaled collection that focuses on quality over quantity, making visitors feel that they've discovered a secret art haven. See p. 150.

o **Best New York museum about New York: The New York Historical Society.** The introductory film alone is worth the cost of admission. Along with seeing the ever-changing exhibits on New York history, be sure to head to the third floor for eye-popping displays of fine furniture, Tiffany lamps, paintings, and more. See p. 161.

o **Best museum for hipsters: The Whitney.** Totally reinvented in 2015, this iconic home of American art now has a party vibe, thanks to its location (right next to The Highline, NYC's coolest park); its hours (later than the rest); and its in-your-face exhibits, which don't shy away from the raunchy or the political. See p. 134.

o **Best museum for tech fans: The Cooper Hewitt.** While many of its exhibits deal with the design of decades (and centuries) past, it displays its treasures—and as importantly, has visitors interact with them—in ways you've likely never experienced before. See p. 150.

o **Best home posing as a museum: The Louis Armstrong House Museum.** This unassuming house in Queens was Satchmo's home for almost 30 years, and it's been preserved almost exactly as it was when he died in 1971. See p. 168.

o **Most mysterious museum: The Museum of the American Gangster.** What happened to the killer who created the illegal speakeasy/alcohol smuggling operation that funneled millions of dollars through this building in the '20s and '30s? That's just one of the questions you'll explore when touring this surprisingly intriguing museum. See p. 131.

THE best NEW YORK CITY BUILDINGS

o **Best historic building: Grand Central Station.** A Beaux Arts gem, this iconic railroad station, built in 1913, was restored in the 1990s to its original brilliance. You can take a tour with the help of a smartphone once you're in the building. See p. 141.

o **Best skyscraper: The Chrysler Building.** Its sleek hood-ornament spire is as jaunty as ever, a heartening site to behold. Alas, the Chrysler has no observation deck, but this Art Deco masterpiece can be viewed from outside or from nearby observation decks, such as the Empire State Building's. See p. 136.

o **Most impressive place of worship: Cathedral of St. John the Divine.** Construction began on the world's largest Gothic cathedral in 1892—and it's still going on. This is one structure that benefits from being a work in progress. See p. 160.

o **Most fun building to "decipher": The Museum of the American Indian.** Every sculpture on this building, including four by Daniel Chester French (creator of the Lincoln Monument in Washington, D.C.), has a story to tell. See p. 124 to learn what those stories are.

THE best NEW YORK CITY PARKS

o **Central Park:** One of the world's great urban refuges, Central Park has inspired city parks across the United States and abroad. It remains a center of calm and tranquility on this clamorous island. See p. 172.

o **Prospect Park:** The *other* masterwork by Frederick Law Olmstead and Calvert Vaux (designers of Central Park), Brooklyn's great green space offers a delightful exercise in compare and contrast. See p. 180.

- **The High Line:** Located in the Meatpacking District of Manhattan, this quirky, handsome park was once an elevated structure for freight trains. It's immensely popular and a good object lesson in how New York City is constantly reinventing itself. See p. 180.

- **Battery Park:** River views, landscaping that shifts dramatically from area to area, state-of-the-art playgrounds and handsome memorials—not enough visitors decompress in this marvelously scenic string of parks along the Hudson River. See p. 178.

best NEIGHBORHOODS TO STROLL IN NEW YORK CITY

- **Brooklyn Heights:** This was the very first designated historic district in New York City, and you'll understand why when you stroll through its blocks of pristine 19th-century row houses, brownstones, and mansions. Plus there is no better view of Manhattan and New York Harbor than from the Heights' famous promenade. See p. 23.

- **Brighton Beach and Coney Island:** Explore the all-Slavic seedy but fascinating Brighton Beach first, with its stores selling Russian-nesting dolls, elaborate samovars, and all sorts of Russian food items. Then hit the boardwalk and walk half a mile to the classic, if definitely gritty, fun fest that is Coney Island. See p. 24.

- **Greenwich Village:** With its historic winding streets, cozy restaurants, and eccentric characters, Greenwich Village lives up to its reputation. See p. 20.

- **Chinatown:** You don't so much stroll here as push your way through crowds, peer in the windows of herbal medicine stores and jewelry marts, and fend off counterfeit-bag sellers. But if I've made this walk sound like a drag, I've done my job poorly; despite its teeming streets, Chinatown is fascinating to explore. See p. 19.

- **The Upper East Side:** Madison Avenue from the upper 60s to the mid-80s is still one of the best window-shopping stretches on the planet. When you get tired of staring at overpriced baubles, you can duck into the side streets between Fifth Avenue and Madison for an array of historic townhouses just as dazzling. See p. 23.

- **Harlem:** Harlem encompasses a large area where historic homes, lovingly preserved, abound. I think you'll be impressed by the architectural beauty, but beyond that, by the local spirit, which you'll experience in the area's restaurants, bars, churches, and stores. See walking tour, p. 23.

THE best FOOD

- **Best cheap eats:** "Spicy and tingly beef noodles" will set your mouth afire, but keep your vacation budget cool and collected at **Xian Famous Foods** (p. 97), a growing chain of noodle shops that serves the most authentic—and affordable—Chinese food this side of Flushing, Queens (NYC's most authentic Chinatown).

o **Most romantic restaurant:** I'll have to go classic French on this one and suggest **Daniel** (p. 104). The food is exquisite, as is the decor, and the wait-staff are veritable cupids who seem to know instinctively when to top off a glass and when *not* to interrupt a conversation.

o **Most family-friendly restaurant for those with kids over the age of 8:** Why not give your children a cultural experience along with a feeding? At **Robataya** (p. 76) they'll experience the best of cooked Japanese cuisine (almost no sushi here), while being served by a genuine Japanese chef who grills all the food in front of you with the intense concentration of a karate black belt.

o **Most family-friendly restaurant for those with kids under 8:** **John's Times Square** (p. 95) is set in a huge former church, so the tables are far enough apart that nobody gets upset when the younger folk kick up a fuss. And what kid doesn't like pizza?

o **Most fun fusion food:** How about some matzoh ball ramen? That's just one of the delectable specialties as **Shalom Japan** (p. 111), a tiny restaurant with big ambitions that serves up some mighty tasty, if mighty weird, food.

o **Best place to go with a group:** Head to **Mission Chinese** and soon the old-fashioned lazy susan in the middle of the table will be spinning as your group digs into some of the kookiest (and tastiest) riffs on Chinese food you've ever tasted. Since you'll want to try everything on the menu, the bigger the group, the better. See p. 70.

o **Best splurge:** This is a tough one, but I'll have to go with the endless, unusual, and delicious tasting menu at **Chef's Table at Brooklyn Fare** (p. 109). You'll see it all cooked in front of you, and many of the ingredients are over-the-top decadent. Dress appropriately, though; they don't let in people in jeans, sandals, or shorts.

o **Best old-school Gotham dining experience:** Still a classic, and still serving the most tender steaks in town, **Peter Luger Steakhouse** (p. 110) is the place to come when you want a taste of old New York.

o **Best new-school Gotham dining experience:** At **Marea** (p. 92) you'll be digging into astonishingly creative Italian food, in a chic and contemporary dining room filled with the biggest of bigwigs.

best CULTURE & NIGHTLIFE IN NEW YORK

o **Best for classic concerts: The New York Philharmonic.** Regular performances by the top soloists in the world, in a hall with exquisite acoustics, makes the NY Phil a must for classical music buffs. See p. 233.

o **Best children's theater: The New Victory Theater.** Savvy programmers bring in top children's productions from around the globe, from circus shows to plays and dance to performance art. See p. 228.

- **Best jazz club: The Village Vanguard.** It's the real thing. All of the greats have performed here, and because of the Vanguard's savvy bookers, this is where the current generation's stars (often up-and-coming) play, too. See p. 239.

- **Best gay bar: The Monster.** Sure, the overall scene is hotter in Hell's Kitchen than it is in the Village nowadays. But men have rediscovered this classic Village bar in the last 2 years, and are flocking to its weekend tea dances and second-floor piano bar. See p. 255.

- **Best comedy club: Upright Citizens Brigade.** The brilliance of the performers here, who are walking the tightrope of making up everything as they go along, will blow you away. See p. 241.

- **Best Off-Broadway Theater: The Public Theater.** The last two Tony-winning musicals (*Hamilton* and *Fun Home*) started life at this storied playhouse. Yeah, it's on a roll. See p. 230.

- **Best Brooklyn bar: The Shanty.** The cocktails here are made with liquors distilled on-site, along with artisanal brands from around the globe. Grab a perfectly mixed Dorothy Parker gin martini, sit back, and enjoy the nightlife of hip Williamsburg. See p. 251.

- **Best cocktail bar: Death & Company.** This one's a close race, because the bartenders at this joint, Pegu Club, PDT, The Shanty, Mace, and Employees Only are all friends and swap recipes. But I'm going out on a limb to say that the cocktails at this East Village joint are both the most balanced and the most inventive. See p. 245.

- **Best speakeasy: PDT.** Hidden behind a secret panel in the phone booth of an East Village hot dog stand, PDT (it stands for Please Don't Tell) serves some of the most expertly and creatively mixed cocktails in the city, in a hidden space that feels oh-so-exclusive. See p. 246.

- **Best Dive Bar: Dublin House.** Need a shot of whiskey at 10am in a place where no one will bat an eye? Head to this old-fashioned Irish pub that started life as a speakeasy in the 1920s (and doesn't look like it's been redecorated since the 1960s). See p. 249.

- **Best hotel bar: Bemelman's Bar in the Carlyle.** It's not a cheap experience, but enjoying an excellent jazz trio, Manhattan in hand, in this hoity-toity Upper East Side watering hole is one of those experiences that seems taken right from a Woody Allen movie. Classic. See p. 249.

Best Culture & Nightlife in New York

SUGGESTED ITINERARIES & NEIGHBORHOODS

2

How fast time flies on a visit to New York! With so many world-famous sights, the job of organizing a day of touring can be a daunting task. That's why I've placed this chapter early in the book. In it, I suggest several workable ways to organize your time. Each one hits many of the "bucket list" sights (and some of the lesser-known ones). And each one, I hope, will lead to an enjoyable New York vacation. Along the way, I'll also explain how NYC is laid out and what you'll find in the various neighborhoods, so that if you decide to skip these suggested itineraries, you'll be able to create a logical itinerary designed to satisfy your own interests.

ICONIC NYC IN 1 DAY

If you have just 1 day in New York, you have my condolences. The first thing you'll want to do is slam your shoe into your rear end for allowing far too little time to experience the city. When you're done with that, try the following itinerary: *Start: 34th Street and Fifth Avenue.*

---

1 The Empire State Building ★★★
Start your day with a King Kong's–eye view of the city. It will help you immensely to understand the layout, and is a heckuva lot of fun (especially if you can skip the lines, which you'll do by arriving first thing in the morning). See p. 140.

Walk uptown, gazing into the windows of Lord and Taylor department store between 38th and 39th streets, until you get to:

2 New York Public Library ★★
You'll recognize this building by the lion sculptures guarding its gates. Step inside to see the grand interior; usually one or two free exhibits will be on display, drawn from the library's vast collections. See p. 144 for more.

Continue walking uptown until you get to 48th Street, home to:

3 Rockefeller Center ★★

There are scores of complexes across the U.S. housing a mix of offices and arts buildings, but none have the visual wallop of Rockefeller Center. That's partly because of the harmony and grandeur of the Art Deco skyscrapers, and partly because there's always so much to see and do here. You may just have time to stroll around, or, if you're here in the right season, you could skate below the massive Christmas tree. I'd also recommend the tour of **Radio City Music Hall** ★ or the **NBC Tour** ★. Since you've just come from the Empire State Building, it doesn't make sense to go to the **Top of the Rock** ★★, the observation deck of the RCA Building in Rockefeller Center (but do so if you skipped stop #1). See p. 147 for Rockefeller Center details.

If you have time, stroll uptown on Fifth Avenue for primo window-shopping. Otherwise, hop a bus, or walk back downtown to 42nd and Fifth Avenue, then east until you get to:

4 Grand Central Terminal ★★

Before stepping into the station, take a look east toward Lexington Avenue, and up, up, up you'll see the famed scalloped spire of the **Chrysler Building** ★★★. Then enter the terminal, one of the most justifiably famous train stations in the world. If you have time, take the audio tour (see p. 142) for insights into the building's architecture and decor. See p. 141 for more.

5 Grand Central Terminal for Lunch ☕

Head downstairs to the classic Oyster Bar if you like seafood (take a peek even if you don't—it's a lovely space), to the new Nordic cuisine food court here, or to Urban Space Vanderbilt nearby on 45th St. Read up on the specialties at each court on p. 99.

In the station are the 4, 5, and 6 subway trains. Grab one of them and head uptown to 86th Street. When you exit, walk west toward Central Park and then downtown until you come to:

6 The Metropolitan Museum ★★★

Since this is the largest museum in this hemisphere, and a wondrous one at that, you're going to spend the rest of the afternoon here. See p. 155.

Return to the subway station and take a downtown train back to 42nd Street, where you'll hop the S train to:

7 Times Square ★

Try to get your first glimpse of this famed square after the sun has set, when all the lights are glittering. Otherwise it looks a bit, well, tawdry. But when it's aglow and the crowds are pulsing, it can feel like the most exciting place on the planet. Hopefully you've gotten theater tickets in advance, the perfect capper for a day on the town. See p. 149.

ICONIC NYC IN 2 DAYS

On your second day, head downtown to see where the city began, along with Lady Liberty and downtown's most sobering, but popular, sight: Ground Zero. *Start: Subway: 1 to South Ferry or 4 or 5 to Bowling Green.*

1 Statue of Liberty ★★ and Ellis Island ★★★

Whether or not you'll get to tour both depends on how early you can get to the ferry terminal and how large the crowds are. If you've scored advance tickets to go up to the crown, that's a good reason to get off at Liberty Island. But if the stars aren't aligned or you miss the first ferry of the day, take in the view of Lady Liberty from the ferry (without disembarking) so you can spend the bulk of your time at Ellis Island, the famed portal to the "New World" for millions of immigrants. It's the more compelling visitor experience of the two. See p. 127.

2 Wall Street ★

Back on the isle of Manhattan, walk uptown to the Financial District. Along the way you'll see structures such as **Castle Clinton National Monument** in Battery Park—it's what's left of a fort built in 1808 to defend New York Harbor against the British—and the impressive **U.S. Customs House,** which houses the Museum of the American Indian (p. 124). Once on Wall Street, stop for a photo op at the **Federal Hall National Memorial** (p. 214), where George Washington took the oath of office as our first President (his statue is in front), and the **New York Stock Exchange,** across the street. Unfortunately, the Exchange is no longer open for tours. See p. 130.

Walk west past Broadway to West Street and carefully cross the large, busy road for lunch at:

3 Hudson Eats at Brookfield Place

There are few decent places to eat in the Financial District. This food hall has the advantage of being right across the street from the entrance to the 9/11 Memorial; it hosts offshoots of some of the best NYC restaurants, including **Mighty Quinn's Barbecue** (p. 77) and **Parm** (p. 103).

Walk back across West Street and follow the signs to the:

4 9/11 Memorial and Museum ★★★

Be sure to get advance tickets to the National September 11 Museum, as the line for day-of-entry admission can be long (and that's on top of the 20 minutes it takes to get through security here). Still, the opportunity to pay your respects to all those who perished, and to see this moving museum and memorial, is not to be missed. Expect to spend at least 3 hours here.

Manhattan Neighborhoods

SOME THINGS not to do IN NYC

Despite what you may have heard, the following experiences are best avoided:

New Year's Eve in Times Square: You won't find any New Yorkers in this crowd. They know better than to show up in the frigid cold at 6am (get there any later and you won't see the ball drop), and stand around all day long in a massive crowd of people, with few eating options nearby and even fewer bathroom facilities. Did I mention they don't allow open champagne or other alcoholic drinks EVER on the streets of New York (and definitely not in Times Square that night)? 'Nuf said.

Chain Restaurants: Yes, we have them. But why would you eat at a place you can find in your hometown when right next door to these chains are restaurants lovingly created by some of the most talented chefs in the nation? And I'm not just speaking of haute cuisine! We have some of the most wonderful cheap eats, too, so don't resort to Mickey D's. You're missing a great opportunity if you do.

Driving: Most New Yorkers don't own cars. They know that the traffic is impossible, finding affordable parking even more so, and one can get anywhere, much quicker, on the subway. So don't drive yourself crazy by bringing your own car to Gotham. If you must get around in a private car, hail a cab or get an Uber (see p. 260). Even with the recently increased rates, getting around that way will be cheaper than paying for parking.

Exit the site and head east toward Broadway and Fulton Street, to the Fulton Street subway stop. There, you'll hop a 4 or 5 train to 14th Street/Union Square, where you'll get off and walk downtown 7 blocks to:

5 Washington Square Park ★★

As the sun starts to set, head to this carnival of a park, where street musicians are always performing and crowds of Villagers and NYU students gather. Spend some time relaxing here before heading somewhere in the vicinity for a terrific dinner (the restaurants downtown and in Brooklyn are the best in the city). See chapter 4 for suggestions.

ICONIC NYC IN 3 DAYS

If you've followed the first 2 days' suggested itineraries, you've experienced a slice of the best of Manhattan, but there's still plenty to see (more than can be done in just 3 days, sadly). Note that this day should only be attempted if the weather is nice. If not, head inside to one or two of the city's great museums. *Start: Subway B or C to 72nd Street.*

---

1 The Dakota

The day begins in front of this 1884 French Renaissance–style apartment building (corner of 72nd Street and Central Park West). Besides being used for several films, the Dakota is in many ways a shrine for visitors, as this is where musician John Lennon lived (and where his widow Yoko Ono still lives), and where he was shot and killed in 1980. After seeing the building, head across the street to Central Park and **Strawberry Fields** ★, named in honor of the former Beatle; fans gather to leave flowers, play music, and commune together. See p. 178.

2 Central Park ★★★

Wander deeper into the park. If you keep walking straight from Strawberry Fields, you'll hit the park's grand promenade area and boat pond. Another option is to take one of the Central Park Conservancy's terrific tours; you'd head toward **The Dairy** (p. 176) if that's your plan. For more on what else to see in the park—which will easily occupy the rest of your morning (unless the weather is bad)—see p. 172.

Make your way back to the west side of the park and exit at 81st street. Walk west to Columbus Avenue and walk downtown one block to:

3 Shake Shack ☕

Time is short, so you'll want to just grab a burger and perhaps one of the Shack's famed milkshakes. See p. 91 for more.

4 American Museum of Natural History ★★★

Head across the street to one of the country's greatest science museums. I highly recommend the tours led by well-trained docents of the museum's highlights. If you'd rather do it on your own, don't skip the Fossils Hall, which has the world's largest dinosaur collection. See p. 158 for more.

Exit the museum and walk west to Amsterdam Avenue to catch an uptown M11 bus. Get off at 110th Street.

5 Cathedral of St. John the Divine ★

On the east side of Amsterdam Avenue is the world's largest Gothic cathedral and a sight that's overlooked by too many tourists. Construction began in 1892, but because the builders are using medieval techniques, it's still unfinished. Tours are offered of the spectacular interior, or you can see it on your own (p. 160). If you have a bit of extra time, head to 116th and Broadway where you'll see the gated entrance to **Columbia University**. It's a handsome campus, with celebrated neoclassical buildings and a stunning statue by Daniel Chester French (the man you did the Lincoln Monument in Washington, D.C.) of a seated woman, called *Alma Mater.* For insight into what you're seeing, go to www.columbia.edu to download the free podcast walking tour of the campus.

Walk to the subway at 116th street and Broadway and take the 1 train down to 66th street, which will put you right in front of:

6 Lincoln Center ★★

Attending a performance at this iconic arts complex is always a grand experience, whether you're going to the opera, seeing ballet, listening to a symphony, or heading slightly downtown to Columbus Circle for Jazz at Lincoln Center. See p. 231 for a description of your many options here. You should have time to grab dinner at one of the Upper West Side restaurants (see p. 101) before the show.

AN ITINERARY FOR FAMILIES

The key to enjoying NYC with kids is to take it easy and choose a hotel outside of the overcrowded Times Square area. Many youngsters find the incessant bustle of midtown, and the city in general, tiring (as do adults!). So choose a hotel in a more residential area (the Upper West Side is a good choice). Also, build a lot of free time into your itinerary, especially if the kids are under the age of 8. Here's what this mom recommends for a 3-day visit.

Day 1: Park and Museum

Once the sun is up, **Central Park** is open, so if you have an early-rising tot, grab a bagel and explore the park over breakfast. With its zoo, playgrounds, and boating ponds (both for rentable toy boats and ride-able row boats), this should account for the entire morning. See p. 172 for more on visiting the park. Right before lunchtime, head out of the park on the east side near 59th Street and hop the subway (the N, Q, or R train at 59th and Fifth avenues) to 36th Avenue in Astoria, Queens. Your ultimate goal is **The Museum of the Moving Image** (p. 168), but right opposite it is **5 Napkin Burger** (35-01 36th St. at 35th Ave.; ☏ **718/433-2727;** Mon–Fri 11:30am–midnight, Sat–Sun 11am–midnight), where you can have lunch. After lunch, head to this incredibly fun, interactive museum (people of all ages love it) and spend the afternoon there learning about how film, TV, and video games are created.

Day 2: Boats, a Big Statue, and Another Boat

What kid doesn't love a boat ride? You'll start day 2 on the very first ferry of the day (to avoid the lines) heading across the Hudson River to visit the **Statue of Liberty** (p. 127). Get advance tickets, so you can climb up to the crown (it's a narrow, winding staircase that most kids will find to be a great adventure). If your young ones are over the age of 8, continue to **Ellis Island** (p. 120); it was the point of entry for millions of immigrants, and older children will find the stories of how they were processed, with some turned away, both fascinating and moving. Once back on the isle of Manhattan, walk to **Stone Street** (p. 213) for lunch and then grab the A, C, or E subway nearby to 42nd Street. Then hop the M42 bus west to the **Intrepid Sea, Air and Space Museum** (p. 145). Set on a 40,000-ton aircraft carrier, it has all kinds of fun flight simulators, as well as an actual space shuttle, a submarine (for kids over the age of 6 only), and lots more neat hardware and gizmos to view.

Day 3: A Museum and a Show

You may need to do this itinerary on day 1 or 2, as matinees are only on Wednesdays, Saturdays, and Sundays. But before you get to the theatrical part of your day, head to the **American Museum of Natural History** (p. 158), one of the finest science museums in the country. A terrific

SUGGESTED ITINERARIES & NEIGHBORHOODS | An Itinerary for Families planetarium show, the massive dinosaur exhibit, and the huge whale that hangs from the ceiling of one gallery enthrall most children, as does the interactive Discovery Center. Eat lunch at the cafeteria here before heading downtown to see the matinee of either a Broadway show (p. 224, there will be a few that are appropriate for children) or a very fine kids' show at the **New Victory Theater** (p. 228). After the show, explore all the sights of Times Square (most kids LOVE the **M&M Store** on Broadway between 48th and 49th streets), including all the costumed characters. (*Note:* you'll be expected to tip them if you take a photo with them.)

A WEEKEND FOR ROMANTICS

Friday: A Stroll, a Gallic Lunch, Shopping, and a Cabaret

Sleep in—you're on vacation! Then grab a bagel and head to the Manhattan side of the **Brooklyn Bridge** (see p. 120). Saunter over it to Brooklyn, where you can catch some rays in the **Brooklyn Bridge Park** (p. 178), a masterwork of landscape architecture that's always bustling. Stop next at the **Jacques Torres Ice Cream Shop** at 62 Water St. Here the famous chocolatier sells scrumptious sundaes as well as chocolates (peek at the factory to see it all being made). With treats in hand, hop the C subway at High Street to the Spring Street stop so that you can have lunch at the oh-so-French **Balthazar** (p. 74) in SoHo. Spend the rest of the afternoon shopping (or window-shopping) in SoHo (see p. 188 for suggestions), and then head to midtown for a cabaret performance with dinner at the swank **Feinstein's/54 Below** (p. 240).

Saturday: Picnic in the Park, a Matinee, and a Museum

Head to **Eataly** (p. 89) or **Zabar's** (p. 201) to purchase the ingredients for brunch in Central Park (go to p. 172 to pick a spot). Then sightsee in the park for a few hours before heading to a **Broadway matinee** (p. 225). After the show, hop the S subway to Grand Central and the 4, 5, or 6 uptown to the **Metropolitan Museum** (p. 155). It's open until 9pm on Friday and Saturday nights, and there are few better places to watch the sun set over Central Park than the terrace here (cocktails are served!). Then head across the park to **Marea** (p. 92) for one of the cushiest, most delicious seafood meals of your life.

Sunday: Gospel, Brunch, and a Step Back in Time

Attend a **gospel service in Harlem** (p. 163), then head to *Top Chef Masters* champion Marcus Samuelson's **Red Rooster** (p. 108) for lunch. For your last few hours in the city, head uptown even further to the exquisite **Cloisters Museum** (p. 161), which features art and artifacts from the Middle Ages in a setting that seems airlifted from Europe.

CITY LAYOUT

Lots of people travel to New York, plop themselves down into Time Square, and never go anywhere else. They seem to fear venturing into neighborhoods that exist for purposes other than tourism.

You don't have to be among them. By devoting just a few minutes to learning the basic geography of New York and its distinctive neighborhoods, you can immensely enhance your enjoyment of this multifaceted city. And once you absorb the highly logical organization of New York's transportation system, you'll find that you can zip from place to place with minimal fuss.

The Grid Plan of Manhattan

The city is comprised of five boroughs on four different pieces of land, only one of which is on the North American continent! When most people talk about "New York City," however, most are referring to the borough of Manhattan, which is a narrow island between New Jersey and Long Island, bordered by the Hudson and East rivers.

Finding your way around Manhattan is easier than in almost any other city because of the careful plan that was adopted for laying out the city's avenues and streets. In the areas above 14th Street, the city fathers imposed a strict and unnatural grid upon Manhattan, leveling hills and tearing down existing homes to create straight, evenly spaced thoroughfares in all but a few places. The grid consists of numbered streets and avenues that cross each other at right angles. If you can count up to 100 you can get around this surprisingly compact island.

Streets in Manhattan are numbered and run from east to west. So if you're on 23rd Street and wish to get to 42nd Street, you simply go 19 blocks north. To get from 80th Street to 75th Street, walk 5 blocks south. **The avenues of Manhattan run north to south,** with some bearing numbers and others names (which does complicate the picture, but only a bit). Those that are numbered go from east to west, with First Avenue being close to the East River and Twelfth Avenue on the far west side of the island near the Hudson River. Interspersed between these numbered avenues are several named avenues, including Park (the uptown name for Fourth Avenue), Lexington, and Madison on the east side. On the west side above 59th Street, Seventh, Eighth, and Ninth avenues turn into Columbus Avenue, Central Park West, and Amsterdam Avenue, respectively.

The exceptions to the grid rule (all found below 14th Street) are the Financial District, Chinatown, Little Italy, the Lower East Side, Greenwich Village, SoHo, and TriBeCa. These southern parts of Manhattan were the first to be settled, and therefore follow a haphazard nonsystem of streets and alleys that curve and twist, sometimes doubling back on themselves (most famously in Greenwich Village, where West 4th Street goes rogue, angling north to cross West 10th, 11th, 12th, and 13th streets). Because most of these southern-section streets bear names rather than numbers (Delancey Street, Wall Street,

Church Street), orienting yourself can be tricky. It's important to carry a good map and ask for directions when necessary. Even native New Yorkers can get lost down there.

New York City Neighborhoods in Brief

It never fails to amaze. I'm strolling along a pleasant street of small brownstones, I come to the corner, and suddenly, the landscape morphs. I'm a small ant in a canyon of skyscrapers, or else I'm a visitor to India, surrounded by cumin-scented restaurants and men with strong accents beckoning me into their curry joints. New York is a city of multiple personalities, and they can shift on a dime, within the space of 1 block going from elegant to seedy, from industrial to chic, from ethnic to all-American.

It's this quicksilver quality, this constant metamorphosis, that endows even a simple stroll in New York with real excitement. I urge you to spend at least part of your vacation simply ambling around, window-shopping, eavesdropping on passing conversations, and exploring places beyond the heavily touristed areas.

Here's what you'll find in the various—and strikingly different—neighborhoods of New York City.

DOWNTOWN

THE FINANCIAL DISTRICT

Best for: Museums, historic sites, architecture, and access to Ellis Island, the Statue of Liberty, and the Brooklyn Bridge

What you won't find: Great dining, much evening entertainment

Parameters of the neighborhood: Everything south of Chambers Street

This is where New York City—then New Amsterdam—was born. The area packs the same historic punch as colonial sections of Boston and Philadelphia. It was on Wall Street that George Washington took the oath of office as America's first president. It was here, at Fraunces Tavern, that the Sons of Liberty gathered to plot the overthrow of the British. It was at Castle Clinton and then Ellis Island that millions of immigrants flooded the city in the 19th and 20th centuries to get their first glimpse of a "promised land." The great financial movers and shakers also stalked the area (and continue to do so today), and a visit to these "canyons of greed" at the beginning of the day or at 5pm, when those men and women in suits and trader's smocks pour onto the streets, is an exciting sight. Recent history has overshadowed other sights, and for many visitors this has simply become the place to pay respects at **9/11 Memorial and Museum.**

CHINATOWN (& LITTLE ITALY)

Best for: Affordable dining and shopping

What you won't find: Top museums, streets without gridlock

Parameters of the neighborhood: Chinatown is roughly bordered by Broome Street to the north, Allen Street to the east, Worth Street to the south, and Lafayette Street to the west.

At points, Chinatown takes on the aspects of Shanghai or Beijing: the dense crowds on the streets, the awnings with Chinese characters, the pinging sound of Chinese conversation everywhere. It's a fun, truly transporting area to visit and one that's been voraciously swallowing up other neighborhoods—Little Italy, the Jewish Lower East Side—for the past few decades. In fact, except for 2 blocks of Mulberry Street (from Canal to Broome), strung with colored lights, Little Italy has ceased to exist and is really only a tourist-trapping shadow of its former self. There are a handful of worthwhile places to shop for Italian food, eat gelato, or get Italian coffee, but no noteworthy restaurants and very few real Italian-Americans around anymore. For great, cheap eats (and shopping), stick with Asian restaurants and marts, for the most part.

TRIBECA, NOLITA & SOHO

Best for: Dining, bars, star sightings, architecture, shopping

What you won't find: Cutting-edge galleries (they're now mostly in Chelsea), museums

Parameters of the neighborhood: Let's explain the names first. **SoHo** means "south of Houston Street." This fashionable neighborhood extends down to Canal Street, between Sixth Avenue to the west and Lafayette Street (1 block east of Broadway) to the east. **Nolita** is the area just *no*rth of *Li*ttle *Ita*ly (Mott Street, Mulberry Street, and Elizabeth Street north of Kenmare Street). Bordered by the Hudson River to the west, the area north of Chambers Street, west of Broadway, and south of Canal Street is the *Tri*angle *Be*low *Ca*nal Street, or TriBeCa. To get here, take the 1 subway to Chambers Street.

Now that we've gotten *that* out of the way, we're left with the harder task of figuring out what it is about former factories and tenements that the ultra-rich find so appealing. They certainly wouldn't have wanted to work or live in this area back in the 19th and early 20th centuries, but these formerly industrial areas have been drawing a lot of boldfaced names lately. And with these *arrivistes* has come a welcome wagon of hot new restaurants, boutiques, spas, and boîtes. Which means simply wandering these often-cobblestoned streets, by the cast-iron buildings (SoHo has the most of any area in the world) can be a hoot.

THE LOWER EAST SIDE & EAST VILLAGE

Best for: Dining, bars, dance and music clubs, innovative theaters, local designer-clothing shops, cheeky art galleries

What you won't find: Museums (with the exception of the very fine **Tenement Museum, The Museum of the American Gangster,** and the **New Museum of Contemporary Art**)

Parameters of the neighborhood: Between Houston and Canal streets east of the Bowery

For millions, these areas were once the portal to America. In fact, the buildings you see on the Lower East Side were built expressly to house the teeming masses of immigrants who flooded into New York between roughly 1840 and 1930. At the turn of the last century, this was the most densely populated area in the world, with a dozen people to an apartment and pushcarts jamming the streets. While there are some remnants of that life in the old-world fabric and luggage stores along **Orchard Street,** these areas are mostly known today for bars, lounges, art galleries, and music clubs. It's in these two neighborhoods that you're most likely to find young designers opening their own tiny stores and protégés of the town's great chefs trying out their own first restaurants. I may be prejudiced because I live in the East Village, but I find it one of the most vibrant areas of Manhattan, though many blocks have lost their gritty edges thanks to ever-rising real estate prices.

GREENWICH VILLAGE

Best for: Strolling, dining, historic sites, lovely architecture, specialty food shops, theater, live music clubs, star sightings

What you won't find: Museums, many hotels

Parameters of the neighborhood: From Broadway west to the Hudson River, bordered by Houston Street to the south and 14th Street to the north

Greenwich Village has always been where the city's outsiders and oddballs have found a haven. In Dutch Colonial times, it was farmland set outside the walls of the city, and a number of slaves were given conditional freedom in return for providing the burghers with food (and fighting off the Native Americans). At the turn of the 20th century, the area became known as a bohemian enclave, where artists of all sorts (Mark Twain, Edgar Allan Poe, Henry James, and Winslow Homer, to name a few) could find cheap lodging and companionship. In the 1950s it was at the center of the Beat movement; in the '60s and '70s the area around Christopher Street became the hub of a burgeoning gay rights movement (in the '80s it was a hotbed of AIDS-related activism).

Today, high real estate prices have dulled the Village's edge, and you're more likely to see moms with strollers than long-haired poets walking these streets. And that mom might be Sarah Jessica Parker or Uma Thurman, two of the many celebs who now call the tree-shaded brownstones of the Village home sweet home. But the charms of the area are still intact, as is the illusion that you've entered another city altogether. Very few buildings in the neighborhood reach ten stories (most are lower than that) and small shops elbow out chain stores. It's a wonderful place to simply come and get lost.

If you'd like to tour a specific neighborhood with an expert guide, contact **Big Apple Greeters** (✆ **212/669-8159;** www.bigapplegreeter.org). For 25 years this non-profit group has been pairing volunteers with visitors for free and highly personal looks at the city. The guides are not expected to be able to spout history or talk in detail about the architecture of the places you'll be visiting. Instead, they introduce tourists to the city they know and love deeply, taking them to areas that few outsiders see. The 4-hour tours are for individuals and couples (the largest group they accept is five people) and are hugely popular, so book 4 weeks in advance of arrival (or more) as many would-be participants are turned away.

MIDTOWN
CHELSEA & THE MEATPACKING DISTRICT

Best for: Art galleries, nightlife, shopping, the Highline, gay bars

What you won't find: Theaters, museums (other than The Whitney)

Parameters of the neighborhood: *Chelsea* lies roughly west of Sixth Avenue from 14th Street to 30th Street; the *Meatpacking District* extends south to 12th Street west of Greenwich Avenue.

Manhattan's Chelsea neighborhood is today what SoHo was 10 years ago, and what Greenwich Village was 20 years ago. The major art galleries have moved here, as has Greenwich Village's large gay population. This makes for a lively cultural scene with many bars and clubs (dance clubs are in abundance from 22nd and 29th streets between Tenth and Eleventh avenues). The so-called Meatpacking District, named for the slaughterhouses that once filled the area west of Greenwich Avenue, has also become an extremely popular nightlife destination (and a shopping mini-mecca for its handful of super-trendy stores). It's NYC's adult Disneyland, filled with late-night clubs, bars, and restaurants that are unhindered by the city's zoning laws (as there are no schools or churches in this part of town). Two final reasons to come here: the fab Whitney Museum, which moved here in 2015 (see p. 134), and the High Line Park, a marvel of urban reclamation (see p. 180).

THE FLATIRON DISTRICT, UNION SQUARE & GRAMERCY PARK

Best for: Dining, historic sites, architecture, Off-Broadway theater

What you won't find: Museums, nightlife (with a few exceptions)

Parameters of the neighborhood: The *Flatiron District* runs south of 23rd Street to 14th Street, between Broadway and Sixth Avenue; *Union Square* is the hub of the district from 14th Street to 18th Street; the *Gramercy Park* neighborhood lies between 16th and 23rd streets, from Park Avenue South to Second Avenue.

As you meander through these three bustling, adjoining (and overlapping) areas, you're likely to see brown street signs proclaiming LADIES MILE. It was on this stretch, mostly on Broadway and Park Avenue South, that the first wave of department stores transformed the lives of New Yorkers in the 1850s. Instead of hopping from a dry-goods shop for fabric to a milliner for hats to a cobbler for shoes, women from all over the city came here to outfit themselves and their homes in stores that, wonder of wonders, had everything they needed under one roof. Notice the large plate-glass windows on many of the facades, another department store innovation. Above, the windows are much smaller and point to a second element of the "Ladies Mile": brothels. When the stores closed for the day, the establishments upstairs opened. And where there's prostitution, theater often follows. The area around Union Square was New York's first show district. Interestingly, it has become an important Off-Broadway theater district again in recent years. The dining scene is also hot here.

For the best strolling, head directly to the **Gramercy Park** area, named for the only privately owned park in the city (the keys go to those apartment owners whose windows overlook the park). Around the park are a number of beautifully preserved historic homes and clubs, including the wisteria-clad home of former Mayor James Harper (4 Gramercy Park S.), the Players Club (16 Gramercy Park S; its members included Edwin Booth and Mark Twain), and the National Arts Club (15 Gramercy Park S., a hangout for Woodrow Wilson and Theodore Dreiser).

TIMES SQUARE & MIDTOWN WEST

Best for: Theaters and entertainment of all sorts, the *Museum of Modern Art, Rockefeller Center, Macy's*

What you won't find: Serenity

Parameters of the neighborhood: From 34th Street to 59th Street west from Fifth Avenue to the Hudson River

Midtown West, a vast area, encompasses several famous places: Madison Square Garden, the Garment District, Rockefeller Center, the Theater District, and Times Square. It's the area most people think of when they think of New York, and the reason why so many visitors say with a smirk, "Well, it's a nice place to visit, but I couldn't ever live there." And because they're basing their judgments on crowded, loud, pushy midtown, they're absolutely right: It's unlivable . . . which is why so few *New Yorkers* actually live in this area. In certain parts of Midtown there's no residential housing whatsoever, and it's only the tourists who attempt to get a good night's sleep in this bustling neighborhood.

MIDTOWN EAST & MURRAY HILL

Best for: Great architecture, shopping (and window-shopping), historic sites, the United Nations, the Empire State Building

What you won't find: Museums, nightlife (again, with some exceptions)

Parameters of the neighborhood: East from Fifth Avenue to the East River, north from 34th Street to 57th Street

In the 1950s, Madison, Park, and Lexington avenues started to sprout skyscrapers and were soon rivaling the Wall Street area for office space. That's primarily what you'll find here: people in suits, looming glass towers, and lots of traffic. Among all that are some spectacular architectural sights like **Grand Central Station** (p. 141), **St. Patrick's Cathedral** (p. 144), the **Chrysler Building** (p. 136), and the **Seagram Building** (52nd and Park Avenue). Go closer to the East River and the area becomes largely residential, with little to recommend it to visitors beyond Bloomingdale's and the UN. A tremendously popular stretch of Fifth Avenue runs from 57th Street down to the Empire State Building at 34th Street, where you'll find some of the best window-shopping on the planet.

UPTOWN
UPPER WEST SIDE

Best for: Museums (like the *American Museum of Natural History* and the *New York Historical Society*), Central Park, bars, kid-friendly restaurants, classical music and dance at *Lincoln Center* and elsewhere

What you won't find: Great shopping (with some exceptions), edge

Parameters of the neighborhood: Starts at 59th Street and encompasses everything west of Central Park

In some ways, the Upper West Side has the most suburban vibe of any of Manhattan's neighborhoods. National chain stores line the major thoroughfares and the sidewalks swarm with strollers. It's a popular area for families thanks to its proximity to Central Park, the American Museum of Natural History, and the Children's Museum of Manhattan.

It wasn't always this way. When I was growing up on the Upper West Side, and even before that, the neighborhood had a reputation for being an intellectual hotbed, a place where highly political New Yorkers planned protests. No more. But it's still an extremely pleasant place to visit with good, if chain-oriented, shopping; a handful of top-notch museums; New York's famous performing arts hub, Lincoln Center; and, of course, access to the glories of Central Park. And the

Time Warner Center gives the neighborhood the dubious distinction of having one of the priciest food malls in the world.

UPPER EAST SIDE

Best for: Museums, architecture, window-shopping, Central Park

What you won't find: Fine dining (although I list some exceptions to that), theater, music clubs

Parameters of the neighborhood: Starts at 59th Street and encompasses the area east of Central Park

10021 is the richest zip code in the world, and it belongs to the Upper East Side; in particular, the swank swatch of pavement that runs from 61st to 80th streets. Also known as "The Gold Coast" and "Millionaire's Mile," this is the stomping grounds for New York's high society: the Prada-clad women and old-money men who sit on the boards of the neighborhood museums, go to a lot of cocktail parties, and endow scholarships for kicks. Their mansions and marble-faced townhouses make for nifty sightseeing for those interested in architecture, and the shops along **Madison Avenue** offer a peek into the extravagant fashions adopted by the 1% and the top designers who serve them.

Museums also play a key role on the Upper East Side, and there's a greater concentration of top-flight museums here than anywhere else in the country, with the exception of the Mall in Washington, D.C. You'll want to spend at least 1 day exploring **Museum Mile**—the **Metropolitan, Guggenheim, Cooper-Hewitt,** and more are all in the area.

HARLEM

Best for: Dining, bars, clubs, historic sites

What you won't find: Theaters, shopping, museums (except for the *Studio Museum* and the *Museo del Barrio*)

Parameters of the neighborhood: *Harlem proper* stretches from river to river, beginning at 125th Street on the West Side, 96th Street on the East Side, and 110th Street north of Central Park. East of Fifth Avenue, *Spanish Harlem (El Barrio)* runs between East 100th and East 125th streets.

Perhaps the most rapidly transforming neighborhood in the city, Harlem is safer and cleaner than it's been in decades . . . but may be losing some of its intrinsic character. A largely African-American neighborhood since the 1920s—and home to some of the greatest black writers, politicians, and artists of the 20th century—the neighborhood is now drawing an increasing number of non-black residents, lured here by lower real estate prices and the beauty of a brownstone-lined community. My recommendation: Visit here soon before the authentic soul and Caribbean joints disappear, the gospel churches lose their swing, and the rhythm of the streets changes its beat. There's much to see, including the Studio Museum, dozens of well-preserved Beaux Arts brownstones, and hopping clubs.

THE OUTER BOROUGHS
BROOKLYN

Best for: Museums, parks, lovely architecture, innovative galleries, dining, the city's hottest club and bar scene, great views of Manhattan

What you won't find: You find pretty much all the same types of attractions in Brooklyn that you will in Manhattan. It deserves a visit!

If Brooklyn had not traded its sovereignty to become a borough of New York City in 1898, it would be the fourth-largest city in the United States, just after New York City, Los Angeles, and Chicago. With 2.6 million residents (according to the last census), it certainly is the most populous borough of the city, and at 71 square miles, it's also the largest. Which is all a long way of saying it's very difficult to pin down the nature of Brooklyn, as it's just too darn big to be summarized in a nutshell.

The two most affluent neighborhoods are **Brooklyn Heights,** which is right off the Brooklyn Bridge, boasting spectacular views of Manhattan; and **Park Slope,** the area surrounding Frederick Law Olmstead's *other* great work of landscape architecture (after Central Park), Prospect Park. Both are stellar strolling areas, filled with lovely Beaux Arts brownstone buildings (Brooklyn Heights was the first neighborhood in the city to be landmarked). In 2015, the *New York Times* discovered that apartments in these neighborhoods, for the first time, were selling for more than apartments in many areas of Manhattan.

The borough's artists tend to live in Red Hook, Greenpoint, Gowanus, Williamsburg (though many are getting priced out here), and a few holdouts still live in DUMBO (the area "Down Under the Manhattan Bridge Overpass"). You can pop by all for afternoons of gallery or artist-studio-hopping. **Williamsburg** has a split personality. Part of it houses one of the largest Hasidic Jewish communities in the world. Walk the streets peopled by this sect and you may feel as if you've stepped back into an old country Shtetl (an illusion only somewhat ruined by the incongruous but ever-present cellphones). The other half is hipster heaven, a neighborhood of art galleries, bustling boîtes, and soignee boutiques. Rumor has it that men who move here must sign a pledge to grow a beard within 3 months of signing their lease.

Eastern Europe also makes an appearance in **Brighton Beach,** which has the largest ex-pat Russian community in the world. It's not the friendliest area, but fascinating to visit nonetheless, with stores selling endless rows of nesting dolls and Lenin T-shirts, and small-scale nightclubs that out-glitz and out-crass Vegas. Just up the shore from Brighton Beach, famed **Coney Island** (see p. 166) still holds an amusement park, though one with less panache than in its heyday.

Among the touristic highlights of the borough are the view from the **Brooklyn Heights** promenade; **Peter Luger,** an iconic steakhouse in Williamsburg; the shows at the **Brooklyn Academy of Music;** and in **Park Slope,** a constellation of sights including the **Brooklyn Museum,** the **Brooklyn Botanical Gardens,** and **Prospect Park.**

THE BRONX

Best for: Baseball, Italian restaurants, zoos, and gardens

What you won't find: Museums, nightlife, other types of noteworthy food, hotels, theaters

I may be condemned for this assessment, but to my mind there are only four reasons a tourist should even think of going to the Bronx: **Yankee Stadium,** the **Bronx Zoo,** the **New York Botanical Gardens,** and the Italian restaurants and stores of **Arthur Avenue.** If you have no interest in any of these sights or facilities, you can skip this giant borough without too much regret.

QUEENS

Best for: Museums, ethnic dining, affordable hotels

What you won't find: Theaters, great shopping, top architecture

Archie Bunker no longer lives in Queens. In fact, the grouchy, bigoted xenophobe at the center of the famed 1970s sitcom *All in the Family* probably wouldn't recognize the borough today. In just the past 50 years it's gone from being a somewhat insulated community of Irish- and Italian-Americans to the most international community in the United States. It's this ability of tourists to tourists to globe-trot in an afternoon that makes Queens appealing, despite the dreary, industrial look of much of it. Whether you're downing samosas or shopping for saris in very Indian **Jackson Heights,** breaking plates at a Greek restaurant in **Astoria,** or buying miracle water and tacos at a Mexican *botanica* in **Corona,** there's much to taste, smell, and experience.

Museums are another big draw, and the borough now ties Brooklyn for its cultural attractions, boasting four great ones: the **Museum of the Moving Image, PS 1 Museum of Contemporary Art, Isamu Noguchi Galleries,** and the **Louis Armstrong House.**

STATEN ISLAND

Best for: Views of Manhattan from the ferry

What you won't find: Notable museums, nightlife, hotels, theaters, truly great restaurants, interesting architecture

And I'll again be blunt: Except for the fun and free ferry ride here, there's no reason a tourist should visit here. Yes, there are a handful of cultural and historic sites, but none that justify the commute.

WHERE TO STAY

Time now for a change of mood. In a book that celebrates the fun and attractions of New York, it's necessary for just a short while—the length of this chapter—to deal with a far less pleasant topic: the overpriced accommodations of New York. By and large, hotels in Gotham charge more than hotels anywhere else in the U.S. (an average of $291 per night) for rooms that often aren't nearly as spacious or full of amenities. Why? A record 58.3 million people visited NYC in 2015, keeping occupancy rates at over 85% for much of the year. Hotels can charge pretty much whatever they darn please . . . and most do.

Though I admit this unpleasant fact, I'm not discouraged by it. Bargains can be found in all price categories. Values exist. And this chapter will introduce you to the very best of them, as well as to a few worthy splurges, for those willing to splash out.

Furthermore, the hotels in this book are hotels that could only exist in the Big Apple. They will give you a more authentic experience than staying in a place chosen randomly over the Internet—and that, in the end, will make up for the high cost of lodgings here. I promise.

PRACTICAL MATTERS: THE HOTEL SCENE

In the following listings, I'll give you an idea of the kind of deals that may be available at particular hotels. But there's no way of knowing what the offers will be when you're booking, so also consider these general tips:

o **Choose your season carefully.** Room rates can vary dramatically—by hundreds of dollars in some cases—depending on what time of year you visit. Winter, from January 4 through mid-March, is best for bargains, with summer (especially July–August) second best. Fall is the busiest and most expensive season except for Christmas, but November tends to be quiet and rather affordable, as long as you're not booking a parade-route hotel on Thanksgiving weekend. All bets are off at Christmastime, New Year's, and the weekend of the NYC marathon—expect to pay top dollar then.

Bizarrely enough, when the city fills up, lesser-quality hotels will often charge prices that are equal to or even higher than what the luxury hotels are asking. So it's important to NEVER try and assess the quality of a hotel by the price it's asking. Instead, read the reviews carefully and compare the prices you're being quoted to make sure you're not getting taken.

o **Go uptown, downtown, or to Jersey City or an outer borough.** The advantages of a Midtown location are overrated, especially when saving money is your object. The subway can whisk you anywhere you want to go in minutes; even if you stay on the Upper West Side, you can be at the ferry launch for the Statue of Liberty in about a half-hour. You'll not only get the best value for your money by staying outside the Theater District, in the residential neighborhoods where real New Yorkers live, but you'll have a better overall experience: You won't constantly be fighting crowds, you'll have terrific restaurants nearby, and you'll see what life in the city is really like. Lodgings in Jersey City, Brooklyn, and Queens offer particularly good savings, and they're easier to get to than you'd think.

o **Visit over a weekend.** If your trip includes a weekend, you might be able to save big. Business hotels tend to empty out, and rooms that go for $300 or more Monday through Thursday can drop dramatically, as low as $150 or less, once the execs have headed home. These deals are prevalent in the Financial District, but they're often available in Midtown, too. Sunday nights are the least expensive, with prices peaking on Tuesdays.

o **Buy a money-saving package deal.** A travel package that combines your airfare and your hotel stay for one price may just be the best bargain of all. In some cases, you'll get airfare, accommodations, transportation to and from the airport, plus extras—maybe an afternoon sightseeing tour or restaurant and shopping discount coupons—for less than the hotel alone would have cost. Most airlines and many travel agents, as well as the usual booking websites (Priceline, Expedia) offer good packages to New York City.

o **Shop online.** There are so many ways to save online and through apps, I've devoted an entire box to the topic. See p. 28.

o **Choose a chain.** With some exceptions, I have not listed mass-volume chain hotels in this chapter. In my opinion, they tend to lack the character and the local feel that most independently-run hotels have. And it's that feel, I believe, that is so much a part of the travel experience. Still, when you're looking for a deal they can be a good option, particularly if you have reward points or can access some type of corporate discount. And every single major chain has hotels in the city, so go where you have the most points.

o **Avoid excess charges and hidden costs.** Use your own cellphone instead of dialing direct from hotel phones, which usually have exorbitant rates. And don't be tempted by minibar offerings: Most hotels charge through the nose for water, soda, and snacks. Finally, don't forget to factor in local taxes and service charges, which can increase the cost of a room by 15% or more.

o **Make multiple reservations.** This strategy is only necessary in high season. But often then, as the date of the stay approaches, hotels start to play "chicken" with one another, dropping the price a bit one day to try to lure customers away from a nearby competitor. Making this strategy work takes vigilance and persistence, but since your credit card won't usually be charged until 24 hours before check-in, little risk is involved.

Alternative Accommodations

o **Consider private B&B accommodations.** Alas, it is now illegal to rent vacation apartments in New York City for less than 30 days. So though **AirBnB.com**, **HomeAway.com**, **VRBO.com** and others list dozens of apartment rentals around the city, often going for far less than a hotel room, there is a risk to booking one. In November of 2015, the Mayor's office announced that it would be allotting $10 million to root out illegal rentals. Since that announcement, we haven't *heard* of any visitors showing up and finding they had no place to sleep, but since it could happen, we're nervous about recommending rentals. However, you can legally rent a room in an apartment, if the owner remains in residence. Think of it as a private B&B (though often breakfast is not included). This type of stay is usually much cheaper than a hotel room, it allows you to meet a friendly local, and it will most likely place you in a residential neighborhood where you live like a local, rather than a visitor. Some of the companies that offer these types of stays include **Affordable New York City** (www.affordablenewyorkcity. com; © **212/33-4001**), **New York Habitat** (www.nyhabitat.com; © **212/255-8018**), **Wimdu.com** and **AirBnB.com**. Be sure to get all details in writing and an exact price for the stay, including applicable taxes and fees, before booking.

o **Stay at a guesthouse affiliated with a religious order or at a military hotel.** Around Manhattan are a number of specialty lodgings operated by the U.S. military, churches, and other organizations. In some cases they're open to all, in others you must be a member to stay here, but they all are clean, friendly, well-located hotels, offering private rooms for as little as $90/night for a single, rarely more than $160 for a double with private bathroom. In the case of the religious hotels, there's no required attendance at services, though at some, unmarried couples are not allowed to share the same room. Here are four I heartily recommend:

The Seafarers and International House (123 E. 15th St., just off Irving Place; www.sihnyc.org; © **212/677-4800**; 4, 5, 6, N, R, or L to Union Sq.). Open to all, run by the Lutheran Church.

Soldiers', Sailors', Marines' & Airmens' Club (283 Lexington Ave., between 36th and 37th sts.; www.ssmaclub.org; © **800/678-8443** or 212/683-4353; 6 to 33rd St.). Open to active military and veterans from the U.S. and its allied nations, as well as first responders.

TURNING TO THE internet or apps FOR A HOTEL DISCOUNT

Before going online, it's important that you know what "flavor" of discount you're seeking. Currently, there are three types of online reductions:

1. **Extreme discounts on sites where you bid for lodgings without knowing which hotel you'll get.** You'll find these on such sites as Priceline.com and Hotwire.com, and they can be money-savers, particularly if you're booking within a week of travel (that's when the hotels resort to deep discounts to get beds filled). As these companies use only major chains, you can rest assured that you won't be put up in a dump. For more reassurance, visit the website **BiddingTraveler.com**. On it, actual travelers spill the beans about what they bid on Priceline.com and which hotels they got. I think you'll be pleasantly surprised by the quality of many of the hotels that are offering these "secret" discounts.

2. **Discounts on the hotel's website itself.** Sometimes these can be great values, as they'll often include such nice perks as free breakfast or parking privileges. And in 2016, Hyatt and Marriott announced they'd be reserving special discounts for travelers who booked directly through the hotel. Before biting, though, be sure to look at the discounter sites below (because even with those promises, the rates are sometimes lower through online travel agencies).

3. **Discounts on online travel agencies such as Hotels.com, Booking.com, Expedia.com, and the like.** Some of these sites reserve rooms in bulk and at a discount, passing along the savings to their customers. But instead of going to them directly, I'd recommend looking at such dedicated travel search engines as **Hipmunk.com**, **HotelsCombined.com**, **Momondo.com**, and **Trivago.com**. These sites list prices from all the

The House of the Redeemer (7 E. 95th St. off Fifth Ave.; www.houseoftheredeemer.org; ✆ **212/289-0339;** 6 to 96th St.). Open to all, run by the Episcopal Church.

The Leo House (332 W. 23rd St., between Eighth and Ninth aves.; http://leohousenyc.com; ✆ **800/732-2438** or 212/929-1010; E or C to 23rd St.). Open to all, run by the Catholic Church.

o **Look into hostels.** Open to people of all ages as well as families, the following hostels have a mix of dorm accommodations and private rooms. Rates range between $35 and $60 per person at these facilities, varying by date and type of room. Private doubles start at $120. Here are NYC's best-maintained (and amenity-laden) hostels:

Hosteling International New York (891 Amsterdam Ave., at the corner of 103rd St.; www.hinewyork.org; ✆ **212/932-2300;** 1 to 103rd St., or 1, 2, or 3 to 96th St.).

NY Loft Hostel (249 Varet St., Williamsburg, Brooklyn; www.nylofthostel.com; ✆ **718/366-1351;** L to Morgan Ave.).

discount sites as well as the hotels directly, meaning you have a better chance of finding a deal.

Note: Sometimes the discounts these sites find require advance payment for a room (and draconian cancellation policies), so double-check your travel dates before booking.

Tingo.com is another good source, especially for luxury hotels. Its model is a bit different: users make a pre-paid reservation through it, but if the price drops between the time of booking and the date of arrival, the site refunds the difference in price.

4. **Chain loyalty discounts.** Another option is **Roomkey.com**, a site founded by the massive hotel chains (some 60-plus brands are represented). As of May 2015, it started aggregating discounts for loyalty club members wiling to book directly with the hotels, rather than through online agencies such as Orbitz and Priceline. Sometimes the savings are puny ($5 less than the best Expedia rate, for example), but I've found substantial discounts on it for pricier properties, and for hotels in off-season (up to $55 a night off the lowest online rate from other sources).

5. **Last-minute discounts**. Try the app **Hotel Tonight** (www.hotel tonight.com). It works best for day of bookings though it now allows users to book a few days in advance of travel. And it can get great prices for procrastinators (up to 70% off if you book on the day of travel, 40% on average if you book a few days in advance or for a multi-night stay). A possible strategy: Make a reservation at a hotel, then on the day you're arriving, try your luck with HotelTonight. Many hotels allow cancellations without penalty, even on the date of arrival.

It's a lot of surfing, I know, but in the hothouse world of Big Apple hotel pricing, this sort of diligence can pay off.

Q4 Hotel/Hostel (29-09 Queens Plaza North, Long Island City, Queens; www.q4hostel.com; ✆ **718/706-7700;** E, M, N, R, or 7 to Queensborough Plaza).

Vanderbilt YMCA (224 East 47th St. between Second and Third Aves.; www.ymcanyc.org; ✆ **212/902-2504;** 6, N, or R to 51st St.)

THE FINANCIAL DISTRICT

In this part of downtown, you are far away from the bustle of midtown. Busy during the day, the Financial District empties out at night. Some enjoy the after dark serenity, while others find it too deserted (and a bit spooky).

Best for: Visitors doing business in the Financial District during the week, and people who like things quiet (as quiet as they get in Manhattan) at night. Plus, there are some substantial savings to be found when staying at a Financial District hotel on a weekend.

Drawbacks: It's a fairly long cab/subway/bus ride to many attractions.

Inexpensive/Expensive

Andaz Wall Street ★★★ The Andaz is a wonderfully chic haven from the bustle of Manhattan. Designed by David Rockwell with a comfy, loft sensibility, the rooms are larger-than-the-norm, with floor-to-ceiling windows that let in scads of light (but are soundproofed for serenity). Filled with plush yet minimalist furnishings and designed for usability (love how the full-length mirror pops into and out of the built-ins), these may be among the most livable rooms in the city. Another perk: complimentary wine and coffee in the lobby.

75 Wall St. (at Water St.). www.andazwallstreet.com. ✆ **212/590-1234.** 253 units. $154–$530 double. Subway: 2 or 3 to Wall St. **Amenities:** Restaurant, bar, fitness center (and spa), room service, complimentary snacks and nonalcoholic-beverage minibar, free local calls, free Wi-Fi.

Riff Hotel Downtown ★ Riff is rough—around the edges, that is. Its hallways look like they're still under construction, rooms have floors of unpolished concrete and walls of unsealed brick, and if you put a couple of liquor bottles on the check-in desk, passersby might mistake the lobby for a dive bar. But all that, and construction across the street, keep prices below the NYC norm. To be fair, guest rooms do have bright white private bathrooms, area rugs here and there to keep the chill off the floors, and beds that are just fine (they can be squeaky). Bizarrely, the prices are the same whether you get a room off the noisy (during the daytime) street, or one with a balcony facing the quiet back courtyard. Ask for the latter (a "balcony loft" room).

102 Greenwich St. (btw. Rector and Carlisle Sts.). www.riffhotels.com. ✆ **877/827-6969** or 212/244-7827. 36 units. $116–$254 double. Subway: 1 or R to Rector St., 4 or 5 to Wall St. **Amenities:** Free loaner Atari and board games, kitchenettes in each room, free Wi-Fi.

The Wall Street Inn ★★ Gracious. That's the first word that comes to mind when one walks into this frilled little inn, a place so old-fashioned it still has a payphone nook in the lobby (though it now just holds a house phone) and only art from the colonial era adorn its walls. But the staff are cheery and helpful, the rooms decent-sized (those ending in 01 are smallest) and quiet (with the exception of those overlooking the raucous outdoor party on Stone Street in the warm weather months; see p. 213). As for the beds: they only *look* lumpy because real feathers are used in the comforters. Best of all: Prices plunge on weekends by a good $100 (in mid-season, you might pay just $199 on a Sunday night but $299 on a Tuesday).

9 S. William St. (at Broad St.). www.thewallstreetinn.com. ✆ **800/747-1500** or 212/747-1500. 46 units. $106–$345 double. Continental breakfast included. Subway: 2 or 3 to Wall St.; 4 or 5 to Bowling Green. **Amenities:** Babysitting, exercise room w/sauna and steam, communal guest kitchen w/ microwave, free Wi-Fi.

Price Categories

I list double room rates only. Please assume that suites will be pricier, and those few hotels that offer single rooms will do so for less than the rate listed in this guide.
Inexpensive: $175 and under
Moderate: $175–$300
Expensive: $300 and up

Downtown Accommodations

Andaz Wall Street **3**
The Bowery Hotel **14**
Cosmopolitan
  Hotel–Tribeca **5**
Crosby Street Hotel **12**
Duane Street Hotel **6**
The Greenwich Hotel **4**
The James **7**
The Jane **18**
Larchmont Hotel **17**
The Marlton Hotel **15**
NobleDen **9**
Nolitan Hotel **11**
Riff Hotel Downtown **1**
The Sago Hotel **13**
Sohotel **10**
Solita Soho **8**
The Wall Street Inn **2**
Washington Square
  Hotel **16**

TRIBECA, THE LOWER EAST SIDE, CHINATOWN & NOLITA

Both TriBeCa and the Lower East Side offer a taste of New York neighborhood living with lots of street life.

Best for: A taste of life Downtown with a capital "D." The Lower East Side, in particular, boasts some of the city's most vibrant clubs and hippest restaurants.

Drawbacks: Both neighborhoods are a little off the beaten track in terms of sightseeing, and the LES is hard to get to via public transportation.

Expensive

The Greenwich Hotel ★★ Named for the street it's on, this plush hotel could as easily be named for Greenwich, CT. It has that same sort of "old money" feel to it: While elegant, it's not overdesigned. Walls tend to be cream-colored, with just a few pieces of art on them (many created by co-owner Robert DeNiro's father). The couches are velvety and squashy, like you might find at an English manor house. Touches such as a fireplace in one suite and a real sauna in another tell you you've entered the upper strata of NYC hotels. Need more evidence? Room service comes from one of the best Italian restaurants in town (Locanda Verde, p. 69), and guests have their own private lounge and garden in which to eat and drink (when I was there, Heidi Klum and her four children were enjoying a meal). The basement spa, with a swimming pool topped with the beams of an ancient Japanese farmhouse, is understated, yet unmistakably luxe. Final touch? If you need to travel anywhere below 34th Street, the hotel's limo will sweep you there at no extra charge.

377 Greenwich St. (at Franklin St.). www.thegreenwichhotel.com. ℂ **212/941-8900.** 88 units. $525–$686 double. Subway: 1 to Chambers St. **Amenities:** Fitness club, indoor heated pool, spa, limo service, restaurant, free in-room snacks, free Wi-Fi.

Moderate/Expensive

Duane Street Hotel ★★ Not that it matters (ahem), but the Duane may well have the handsomest staff in Manhattan: suave young fellows with vaguely European accents and just the right amount of stubble. The rooms in this slim hotel (just 26 ft. wide) are just as dashing, if petite at the lower price categories, with high ceilings and shiny black walls offset by sleek blond wood built-ins (all designed to maximize the space) and cool pieces of art here and there. Such niceties as rainfall showers and iPod docking stations add to the plush vibe. Other pluses: workable desks and cookies 24 hours at reception.

130 Duane St. (at Church St.). www.duanestreethotel.com. ℂ **212/964-4600.** 45 units. $189–$395 double. Subway: A or C to Chambers St. **Amenities:** Free passes to nearby Equinox Gym, restaurant, free Wi-Fi.

WHAT YOU'LL really PAY

You'll notice that the rates listed in this chapter are more than a little bit odd. A typical hotel listing will state that rates start at $199 per night but can go up to $399—for the same room category. That's not a typo. Unfortunately, getting a bed in this city is a bit like playing roulette: You never know what number will come up. It's all based on occupancy rates. And in high season, that means hotels charge whatever they feel they can get away with (see more about that below).

I've calculated the rates in this chapter by looking at what discounters are offering in three different seasons and then showing you the range, from low to high. But the sad truth is, **rates can change at any time,** meaning you may find even higher rates than those listed in this guide. I've tried to list the averages, for high and low season, for these hotels, but nothing's average here. Alas, that's the nature of NYC, the city that not only never sleeps, it never stops gouging. Good luck!

Nolitan Hotel ★★   "Hello There" reads the carpet in the elevators, an obvious sign—not needed—that this is one of the friendliest hotels in the city. Guests can already tell, thanks to the free, nightly happy hour in the living room–like lobby; the offers of multiple loaners to guests (laptops, iPads, and bikes); and the gracious service. Rooms, too, have a happy air, with bright splashes of color on a blanket or chair, which contrast nicely with the shabby -chic concrete ceilings (this was once a parking garage). Some rooms even have that rare-for-NYC amenity: a balcony. For really great views—at slightly more expense—ask for a "cityscape" rather than a "neighborhood" room.

30 Kenmare St. (btw. Elizabeth and Mott sts.). www.nolitanhotel.com. ✆ **212/925-2555.** 55 units. $159–$483 double. Subway: 6 to Spring St. Pets accepted. **Amenities:** Restaurant, bar, free use of nearby full-service gym, 24-room service, bicycle and skateboard loans, free Wi-Fi.

Moderate

NobleDen ★★   Mostly Europeans book this sleek new hotel, which sits on the porous border between Chinatown and Little Italy. My guess is they're drawn by the clean Scandinavian-style design (lots of neutral colors offset by pops of red, hidden drawers that double your storage space, angular lamps, and two-room bathrooms). I like the king units best, as they have floor-to-ceiling windows that open to a Juliet balcony overlooking the action on Grand Street below. But the Queen-bedded rooms, the cheapest on property, are a bit quieter as they face a courtyard rather than the street (that being said, Grand Street isn't particularly busy at night, just during the day). One note: the beds, though high quality, are firmer than many Americans are used to (perhaps because the hotel's owner is Malaysian and that's the style there).

196 Grand St. (btw. Mulberry and Mott sts.). www.nobleden.com. ✆ **212/390-8988.** 54 units. $198–$284 double. Subway: B, D to Grand St. or N, Q, R, 6 to Canal St. **Amenities:** Restaurant, free use of nearby full-service gym, free Wi-Fi.

The Sago Hotel ★ The Sago hasn't yet lost that "new hotel" smell, not surprising as the property opened in the spring of 2016. Standard rooms are diminutive but feel airy thanks to large picture windows and uncluttered décor. The look is a trendy mix of rustic (a burlap stool, hardwood floors, wood-slatted shower floors, a cork backboard on the bed) and industrial chic (painted cinderblock walls, exposed steel beams and bolts). For those who want to splash out a bit there are rooms with daybeds—really a large window seat that can be made up with sheets and a blanket—plus king rooms with kitchenettes and full-floor suites that can hold up to 6. An onsite, farm-to-table resto provides room service.

120 Allen St. (at corner of Delancey St.). www.sagohotel.com. ℭ **212/951-1112.** 20 units. $250–$262 double. Subway: J, Z to Bowery, F to Second Ave. **Amenities:** Restaurant, room service, free use of nearby full-service gym, free Wi-Fi.

Inexpensive/Moderate

Cosmopolitan Hotel–Tribeca ★ George Washington never slept here, but the staff at the Cosmopolitan swear that Abraham Lincoln did, back when the building was Hotel Girard. Built in the 1840s, it's always been a hotel of some sort or another, and the Lilliputian dimensions of the cheaper rooms reflect how much smaller people were back then. Still, it's often a great value, with sleek dark-wood furnishings, Frette linens, and a crack housekeeping staff that keep everything extremely tidy (no fraying carpets or telltale signs of the last guest here).

95 W. Broadway (at Chambers St.). www.cosmohotel.com. ℭ **888/895-9400** or 212/566-1900. 105 units. $143–$281 double. Subway: 1, 2, 3, A, or C to Chambers St. **Amenities:** Free Wi-Fi.

Sohotel ★ One of the oldest hotels in the city (built in 1822), Sohotel housed Union soldiers during the Civil War. They wouldn't recognize it today—in fact, people who visited just 5 years ago wouldn't recognize it, as the hotel has input major improvements. Flatscreen TVs and handsome bureaus now grace rooms, and walls are chic exposed brick or painted a cheerful shade of yellow or blue. Along with standard doubles are massive family rooms with three to four beds. There are some lapses still, especially in the mattress department: If you get a stony one, ask to be moved (they vary by room). Also move if you're placed in one ending in the numbers 21, 23, or 25, which overlook a noisy bar. *Warning:* This is not the place for people with mobility impairments, as there are stairs to the lobby and many of the rooms.

341 Broome St. (near Bowery). www.thesohotel.com. ℭ **800/737-0702** or 212/566-1900. 105 units. $121–$279 double. Subway: 1, 2, 3, A, or C to Chambers St. **Amenities:** Restaurant, bar, free Wi-Fi.

SOHO

Despite numerous chain stores moving into SoHo, the area still has great charm, due to its proliferation of cast-iron buildings. In terms of hotels, the neighborhood is strictly high-end.

Best for: A stay in the SoHo area offers close proximity to Chinatown, designer-name shopping, and some very fine restaurants.

Drawbacks: You won't find much in the way of budget/value accommodations in the neighborhood. Also, because of the downtown arts scene, SoHo has two high seasons: May/June and the fall months. So you'll find fewer deals here than in other areas during those times.

Expensive

Crosby Street Hotel ★★★   As much gallery as hotel, the Crosby Street is true eye-candy. Designed by co-owner Kit Kemp, every room and every public area features quirky, often funny, and always compelling works of sculpture and painting. This includes the guest rooms, each of which has a different look from the next (mine was all done in black and white, but others are saturated with colors, perhaps taking on the ambience of a garden, or the vibrant color palette of Morocco). Floor-to-ceiling warehouse-style windows light up the rooms, and the deluxe bathrooms feature such niceties as heated towel racks and bidets. None of this comes cheap, but with an on-site movie theater, fabulous location, and very good restaurant, the Crosby Hotel is perfect for a special-occasion stay.

79 Crosby St. (btw. Prince and Spring sts.). www.crosbystreethotel.com. ✆ **212/226-6400.** 86 units. $625–$675 double. Subway: N or R to Prince St. **Amenities:** Restaurant, bar, fitness center, room service, screening room, free Wi-Fi.

The James ★★   Welcome to the "locavore" hotel. Everything at the James is meant, in some way, to celebrate and reflect New York City, a concept that works in spades. So, the luxurious sheets on the beds are bought from a local manufacturer, as are the chocolates placed on the pillows. The hallways are a gallery to New York City artists; simply train your cellphone at the barcodes on the walls to learn more about each one. Best of all, this skyscraper hotel, custom-built in 2010, is all glass, so every guest room has spectacular floor-to-ceiling views, bringing NYC directly into your bedroom. Other perks include a plunge pool and hip rooftop lounge called **The Jimmy,** an urban garden on the second floor for more outdoor lounging, and room service from star chef David Burke, whose restaurant is on the first floor.

27 Grand St. (at Thompson St.). www.jameshotels.com. ✆ **888/526-3778.** 114 units. $259–$502 double. Subway: 1 to Canal St. Pets accepted. **Amenities:** Restaurant, bar, rooftop pool, fitness center with complimentary training sessions, room service, free Wi-Fi.

Moderate/Inexpensive

Solita Soho ★   Don't worry: The Solita isn't under construction, though the odd squares of sheet metal and plywood latticework in the lobby make it look that way. Rooms, too, have an unfinished appearance, thanks to their weird color scheme of purple, gray, and black (it looks like an accident), and the way the furniture seems to just barely fit into the tiny bedrooms. But I'm guessing that the poor design choices are what keeps a hotel with this terrific a location in the realm of the affordable. And that's good news because it means you can stay, in high quality beds and with a private bathroom, in the heart of the action for what you will often pay for a room in the "wilds" of New Jersey.

159 Grand St. (Btw. Centre and Lafayette Sts). www.solitasoho.com. © **212/925-3600.** 42 units. $119–$292 double. Subway: 6, J, Z, N, Q, R to Canal St. **Amenities:** Room service from Restaurant Le Perigot next door, free Wi-Fi.

THE VILLAGE

Greenwich Village, despite the influx of big-name stores, still has that romantic appeal with its winding, narrow streets, brownstones, and intimate dining spots.

Best for: People who love to explore classic/historic old neighborhoods; close to shops, restaurants, bars, and clubs.

Drawbacks: Can be noisy and crowded, particularly on weekends. While it's got its residential streets, Downtown (with the exception of the Financial District) is where New York (and the surrounding area) goes to party.

Expensive

The Bowery Hotel ★★★ The "wow" factor is high at the Bowery Hotel, which channels the kind of grand mansions E. M. Forster would have inhabited (ultra-luxurious colonial outposts). The lobby—which you should visit for a drink, even if you don't stay here—is decorated with fine pieces of woodwork and furniture salvaged from European churches and historic homes; the tile floors and walls, too, speak of long journeys from abroad (Morocco, most likely). But though the hotel looks old, it was actually built in 2007 by nearby New York University as a dorm. Oddly, no two guest rooms are alike, but all are light-bathed, with antique furnishings, fine linens, and a teddy bear (dressed as one of the bellmen), gracing each bed.

335 Bowery (at 3rd St.). www.theboweryhotel.com. © **212/505-9100.** 135 units. $375–$555 double. Subway: 6 to Bleecker St. **Amenities:** Restaurant, bar, room service, gym, free Wi-Fi.

Moderate/Expensive

The Marlton ★★ Owned by Sean MacPherson, the hotelier behind the Jane (see p. 38) and the Bowery Hotel (see above), among others, the Marlton has the same swellegant, if miniaturist, sensibility. Its rooms look like they were airlifted from one of the Grand Dame hotels of Paris . . . and shrunk. Sadly, as with MacPherson's other properties, the rooms are lilliputian (150 square feet is the standard size). But if you're not claustrophobic, they offer a good dose of old-fashioned glamor, with aqua-blue velvet headboards, fake fur throws at the end of the beds, crown moldings on the ceilings (a nice contrast to the chandeliers, which look like Calder mobiles), and coy brass hands holding up the sconces that serve as reading lights. Plus the lobby, which looks like the anteroom of a British men's club, is a charming place for lounging and dining (there's an on-site coffee bar and good restaurant). You won't be the first to have squeezed yourself into one of these tiny rooms: the

PLENTY OF room AT THE INN

Don't assume that all NYC hotels are in skyscrapers. This is a diverse city, and that diversity can be found in its accommodations, too. If you want an alternative to the quintessential huge Gotham hotel, and (often) lower prices, try the following options.

The first home of the Gay Men's Health Crisis, an 1850 brownstone in the heart of Chelsea, is now the quirky **Colonial House Inn**, 318 W. 22nd St. near Eighth Ave (www.colonialinn.com; 212/243-9669). This 20-room four-story walk-up caters to a largely LGBT clientele, but everybody is welcome. Some rooms have shared bathrooms; deluxe rooms have private bathrooms, and some have working fireplaces.

For another genuine New York brownstone experience, head to Harlem. It's anything but a flophouse, but that's what they call **Harlem Flophouse**, 242 W. 123rd St., between Adam Clayton Powell and Frederick Douglass boulevards (www.harlemflophouse.com; 347/632-1960). Owner René Calvo has restored the historic row house to Harlem Renaissance splendor, when the "flophouse" was frequented by top musicians and artists of that era. If you visit in the summer, you just might get invited to one of Calvo's impromptu barbecues.

In a lovely area of Brooklyn's Park Slope, the **Sofia Inn** (p. 61) offers up two family-friendly, floor-wide suites, and four very affordable rooms that share bathrooms. Nearby is the oh-so-Victorian and quite charming **Leffert's Manor Bed and Breakfast** (www.leffertsmanor bedandbreakfast.com; 347/351-9065), part of a set of row houses, which has such niceties as elaborately molded ceilings and fireplaces. As at the Sofia Inn, some rooms do share bathrooms, but heck, you'll never pay more than $149/night here (and sometimes as little as $89). A third choice—with a longer commute into Manhattan and not near any tourist sights—is the very friendly and super-affordable **Honey's B&B** (www.honeysbedandbreakfast.com; 917/973-9493).

Finally, consider two inns with very similar names—the **Chelsea Pines Inn** ★★ (p. 39), and the **Chelsea Inn** ★ (p. 42)—but very different characters. The Pines is run by a charismatic owner and is service-heavy, while the "Inn" is the choice for budgeteers, thanks to very reasonable prices and plain furnishings.

building started as a hotel in 1900, and in the course of its many iterations was home to Jack Kerouac, who wrote a few novellas here.

5 West 8th St. (nr Fifth Ave.). http://marltonhotel.com. 212/321-0100. 107 units. $225–$285 double. Continental breakfast included. Subway: A, C, D, E, N, R to 8th St. **Amenities:** Restaurant, lounge and coffee bar, free Wi-Fi.

Washington Square Hotel ★   This hotel has always had a top location, right off graceful Washington Square Park, but today has a decor to match, filled with Art Deco paintings, murals, and photos that pay homage to the many stars who have stayed here over the years. Built in 1904, it served as a second home for many top vaudeville and Broadway performers until the '50s, when it devolved into a rather seedy apartment hotel housing a number of struggling artists including Joan Baez, Bob Dylan, Barbra Streisand, and Phyllis Diller. Legend has it that the Mamas and the Papas wrote "California Dreamin'" at the Washington Square. The rooms, though small, are smartly designed with cushy duvets, rich jewel-colored walls, and space-saving features (such as the wall-mounted TV) that make the rooms appear *slightly* bigger than they actually are.

103 Waverly Place (btw. Fifth and Sixth aves.). www.wshotel.com. ℂ **800/222-0418** or 212/777-9515. 160 units. $215–$264 double. Continental breakfast included. Subway: A, B, C, D, E, or F to 4th St. (use 3rd St. exit). **Amenities:** Restaurant and lounge, exercise room, free Wi-Fi.

Inexpensive

The Jane ★★ In 1912, when the survivors of the *Titanic* were brought back to New York by the SS *Carpathian,* many stayed that first night at this hotel. It seems appropriate, therefore, that most of the Jane's rooms have the look of a ship's cabin (or perhaps a railway sleeping car)—highly compact with a shelf above the bed for luggage. Let me go a bit further in explaining what I mean by "compact": These may well be the smallest rooms in NYC (which says a lot). When I was standing in one recently, I spread out my arms and came within about 5 inches of touching both walls at once. Rooms for two have bunk beds, making the space seem even smaller. Most rooms share bathrooms, though larger, pricier rooms do have private facilities. That being said, these dollhouse-size digs have every luxury: The walls are paneled with burnished anigre wood, a marble counter at the window doubles as a tiny desk and boasts an iPod docking station, and a flatscreen TV is attached to the wall at the foot of the bed. Two bars—one on the roof and one in the massive lounge area in the lobby—are true scenester haunts, and the public areas are fab, looking like they were lifted from a movie about opium dens in the "Gay 90s."

114 Jane St. (at West St.). www.thejanenyc.com. ℂ **212/924-6700.** 170 units. $99–$135 rooms with shared bathroom, more for rooms with private facilities. Subway: A, C, or E to 14th St. **Amenities:** Restaurant, 2 bars, free loaner bikes, free Wi-Fi.

Larchmont Hotel ★★ Situated on one of the prettiest tree-lined streets in the Village, a block of historic brownstones a short stroll from top dining, shopping, and the subway, the location here can't be beat. What the Larchmont doesn't have (because the hotel is housed in a historic Beaux Arts–era brownstone) are private bathrooms for the guest rooms—it simply doesn't have the plumbing to support multiple loos. Instead, travelers share two toilets and two showers per floor (with either six or seven other rooms). Should this keep you from choosing this hotel? I hope not, because this is a charming, extremely well-maintained hotel in which the owners have striven to keep the period feel throughout, filling the rooms with rattan furniture, bookshelves brimming with hardcover books, and good, firm beds. There are also some high-class amenities, such as portable sacks of nice toiletries and cotton robes and slippers.

27 W. 11th St. (btw. Fifth and Sixth aves.). www.larchmonthotel.com. ℂ **212/989-9333.** 62 units, all with shared bathrooms. $90–$125 single; $125–$149 double. Continental breakfast included. Children 12 and under stay free. Subway: A, B, C, D, E, or F to W. 4th St. (use 8th St. exit). **Amenities:** Communal kitchenette, free Wi-Fi.

CHELSEA

A center for both contemporary art and nightlife, Chelsea is home to the High Line Park and many galleries and restaurants, and it's an easy walk to Herald Square.

Best for: People who want to be close to the action but not in the center of it; a good range of accommodations from high-end to moderate.

Drawbacks: Can be noisy at night along the main drags (especially the avenues and along 23rd Street).

Moderate/Expensive

Chelsea Pines Inn ★★   The most welcoming hotel in the Chelsea area is owned and run by Jay Lesiger, a native Brooklynite who seems intent on dispelling the myth that New Yorkers are unfriendly. Jay bends over backward to make sure guests enjoy their visit, along with personally baking a different loaf of bread for each morning's breakfast (it's served amidst an ample spread of bagels, fruits, and cereals). He and his staff publish a daily newsletter for guests covering walking tours, concerts, and other events happening that day. Jay also serves as concierge and is happy to make dinner reservations (he's worked out a 10% discount at some of the best local restaurants), book limousines, and get theater tickets, for which he takes no commission (in fact, he scours the Web for cheaper seats). He and his partner opened the guesthouse in 1985 when it was a rundown boardinghouse. To hide the scarred walls (since renovated), Jay covered them with his large collection of movie posters, and the tradition stuck: Now each room is named after a different star and filled with movie memorabilia. Rooms are cozy and pretty, the beds topped with 300-thread-count sheets. I'd recommend a room on the second or third floor, where the ceilings are higher. Single rooms are available for a lesser amount than the doubles. *One final note:* Though 70% of the guests at Chelsea Pines are gay, everyone is made to feel comfortable here.

317 W. 14th St. (btw. Eighth and Ninth aves.). www.chelseapinesinn.com. ℂ **212/929-1023**. 22 units. $179–$309 double. Continental breakfast included. Subway: A, C, or E to 14th St., L to Eighth Ave. **Amenities:** Snacks available around the clock, free Wi-Fi.

The High Line Hotel ★★★   Very few NYC hotels deserve the high price tag they wear. This one just may. Set in a former ecclesiastical building (a beaut of a red brick Victorian that was once the dormitories of a seminary), the Highline Hotel looms like a castle over Tenth Avenue. Its interior is as grand, though delightfully quirky, with rooms that look like they could have been inhabited by a Gatsby type in the 1920s. The drapes are a luxurious midnight-blue velvet, oriental rugs cover areas of the handsome wood floors, and unique works of art hang here and there. Each room is a different size, but all have high ceilings, often with the original plaster moldings, and beds swathed in feather-top mattresses. As you might guess from the name, the hotel is quite near to the super-cool High Line Park (p. 180) and fulfills its

Midtown Accommodations

PARK

Center Dr.

East Dr.

South

E. 63rd St.

UPPER
EAST SIDE

Lexington Av/
63 St
F

E. 62nd St.

E. 61st St.

Roosevelt Island Tram

E. 60th St.

5 Av/59 St
N-R

59 St
4-5-6

Lexington Av/
59 St
N-R

E. 59th St.

Queensboro
(59th St.) Bridge

57 St
F

E. 58th St.

E. 57th St.

E. 56th St.

Lexington Av/
53 St
E-M

E. 55th St.

E. 54th St.

5 Av/53 St
E-M

51 St
6

E. 53rd St.

E. 52nd St.

E. 51st St.

ROCKEFELLER
CENTER

E. 50th St.

E. 49th St.

47-50 Sts
Rockefeller Ctr
B-D-F-M

MIDTOWN
EAST

E. 48th St

E. 47th St.

E. 46th St.

E. 45th St.

42 St Bryant Pk
B-D-F-M

Grand
Central
Terminal

E. 44th St.

5 Av
7

E. 43rd St.

E. 42nd St.

Bryant
Park

Grand Central
42 St
S-4-5-6-7-Metro North

E. 41st St.

New York
Public Library

E. 40th St.

E. 39th St.

E. 38th St.

MURRAY
HILL

E. 37th St.

E. 36th St.

34 St
Herald
Square
B-D-F-M-
N-Q-R

Empire
State
Bldg.

E. 35th St.

E. 34th St.

W. 32nd St.

33 St
6

E. 33rd St.

E. 32nd St.

E. 31st St.

E. 30th St.

E. 29th St.

28 St
N-R

28 St
6

E. 28th St.

E. 27th St.

E. 26th St.

Madison
Square
Park

E. 25th St.

E. 24th St.

23 St
F-M

23 St
N-R

23 St
6

E. 23rd St.

E. 22nd St.

E. 21st St.

Gramercy Park

E. 20th St.

FLATIRON
DISTRICT

GRAMERCY
PARK

E. 19th St.

E. 18th St.

E. 17th St.

14 St
F-M

6 Av
L

14 St-Union
Square
L-N-Q-R-4-5-6

3 Av
L

E. 16th St.

E. 15th St.

E. 14th St.

1 Av
L

Mitchell
Place

United
Nations

East River

ROOSEVELT ISLAND

Queens-Midtown Tunnel

Upper
Manhattan

Uptown

Midtown

Downtown

M Subway stop

0   1/4 mi

0   0.25 km

WHERE TO STAY | Chelsea

3

41

own hipster quotient by parking a food truck in one of its outdoor gardens (there are three).

180 Tenth Ave. (at 20th St.). www.thehighlinehotel.com. © **212/929-3888.** 60 units. $209–$489 basic double. Subway: C to 23rd St. **Amenities:** Cafe, use of nearby gym, free local and international calls, free Wi-Fi.

Inexpensive

Chelsea Inn ★ Straddling the border between Chelsea and Union Square, the Chelsea Inn's prices are low because many rooms share a bathroom (never more than two rooms to a toilet; you'll have a shower and sink in your room). It has a lived-in ambience, thanks to a decor of mismatched antique bedsteads, old wooden armoires, and patchwork quilts on the hard beds—kind of like what you'd find in the home of an elderly aunt. A nice touch: All rooms have small fridges and coffeemakers. Bad news: street noise and loud plumbing.

46 W. 17th St., near Fifth Ave. www.chelseainn.com. © **800/640-6469** or 212/645-8989. $110–$178 double. Subway: Q, N, R, L, 4, 5, 6, or L to Union Sq. **Amenities:** Free Wi-Fi.

UNION SQUARE, FLATIRON DISTRICT & GRAMERCY PARK

Farmer's markets, top-notch restaurants, an active street life, and pockets of charming brownstones and historic buildings—what's not to like about this tri-partite district? I think it's probably the best place in the city to base yourself, partially because Union Square is one of the most useful hubs in the subway system, hosting a crosstown train (the L), several that go from east to west (the N, Q, and R) and the green line that runs up the east side (4, 5, and 6).

Best for: People who like a centrally located neighborhood that's not dominated by skyscrapers, but still has great lodging, shopping, theater, and dining options.

Drawbacks: Not the cheapest neighborhood in Manhattan, plus no museums or major tourist sights are here.

Expensive

Gramercy Park Hotel ★★★ One of the most coveted status symbols in NYC is a key to Gramercy Park, the city's only private park (only apartments overlooking the park get keys). Stay in this 1925-built gem, though, and you can join the elite in more ways than just park access. Few hotels in the city, or anywhere for that matter, are as luxurious or as riotously artistic. The public spaces are *de facto* galleries, where the art changes every other month and features such heavy-hitters as Damien Hirst and Andy Warhol. The rooms are aglow with the colors of a Tiffany lamp and filled with fine photography plus an exquisite mix of Edwardian and modern furnishings—an embroidered chair here, a velvet headboard there, DVD players hidden in mahogany English drinking cabinets. One of the best Italian restaurants in the city,

Maialino (p. 85), not only resides in the lobby but is responsible for the 24-hour room service. A true original, and sometimes it even discounts (try Booking.com).

2 Lexington Ave. (at 21st St.). www.gramercyparkhotel.com. ℭ **212/920-3300.** 185 units. $299–$599 double. Subway: 6 to 23rd St. **Amenities:** 2 restaurants, 2 bars, fitness center and spa, room service, rooftop lounge, key to Gramercy Park, free Wi-Fi.

The New York Edition ★★ The ultra-rich—whether they be rich in cash or in Marriott reward points—apparently are a scatterbrained lot. Or so one would think seeing the amenities that the Edition has seen fit to stock the mini-bar area with. Along with the usual little bottles and snacks is a very good quality, one-size-fits-all thong—you know, just in case you, er, forget your panties somewhere. And that could happen in this ultra-sexy hotel, I suppose, the latest from Studio 54 impresario Ian Schrager. The sensuality isn't overt— no red walls or lava lamps here; in fact the room decor is strictly neutrals (lots of light oak). But then you look up at the 14-foot ceilings with their oceanlike waves, down at the bed with its faux fur throw, and out the windows at the spectacular views (this is one of the tallest hotels in the city), and it's clear that this is a place for adult romance. You can start your evening at the "gold bar" (so called because it's coated in 24-karat gold leaf), which peeks into the former Metropolitan Life Insurance boardroom (now a so-so resto). That's the company that built this 1909 beaut, styled after Venice's famed *campanile* (bell tower), overlooking Madison Square Park. As I implied at the start, you can use points here to lessen the sting of the nightly rate.

5 Madison Ave. (at 24th St.). www.editionhotels.com/new-york. ℭ **212/413-4200.** 273 units. $550–$750 double. Subway: 6, N, R to 23rd St. **Amenities:** Restaurant, 2 bars; 2 fitness rooms with free yoga classes; small spa; room service; loaner iPads, laptops, and cellphones; free Wi-Fi.

The NoMad ★★★ Imagine if Gustav Klimt and Edward Gorey were to collaborate on the design of a hotel, and you'll have a good sense of the whimsical elegance of the NoMad. (It was actually designed by Jacques Garcia, a well-known Parisian architect.) Klimt-like touches abound in the lobby, with its elaborate painted panels and movie-set–like spaces (such as the two-story library that serves as an anteroom to the bar, or the wondrous, massive skylight that hovers over the dining room). Gorey's territory, the guest rooms, look like a humorous if elegant take on an English nobleman's abode. Huge fabric dressing screens serve as the barrier between bedroom and bathroom; a dozen paintings hang, gallery-style, on the white walls; and fine pieces of wooden furniture are paired (in some rooms) with a free-standing, old-fashioned bathtub that sits right in front of the large windows! *Some tips:* Be sure to ask for a room on the second or third floor, as the ceilings are highest there. And eat in one night: Room service is from the fab NoMad Restaurant (p. 85).

1170 Broadway (at 28th St.). www.thenomadhotel.com. ℭ **212/796-1500.** 168 units. $295–$575 double. Subway: N, R, 6 to 28th St. **Amenities:** Restaurant, 2 bars; gym, room service, free Wi-Fi.

A surreal STAY IN THE ARTFUL APPLE

The Carlton Arms Hotel ★★ is not a place for everyone. If you get worried when you notice that your room is listing a bit to the right, or if you expect a maid to change your sheets daily, then this is not the hotel for you. But if you're the type who wants to try something really different, and who finds the idea of being cocooned in art interesting, then choose this 160-year-old hotel with the soul of William Blake in all of its wacky, joyous excess.

Over the years, the Carlton Arms (160 E. 25th St. at Third Ave.; www.carltonarms. com; ℂ **212/679-0680**) has invited artists to paint murals and create unusual environments in their guest rooms, which many have done with wild glee. There's the Egyptian Hallway, with mummy portraits of staff members; the Japanese Room, with its elaborate dragons and Buddhas; and the Goth Room, where "she-male" portraits leer down at the queen-sized bed. Even the now-famous Banksy added murals to the stairwell.

Pricing? Comfortable but not luxurious double rooms with private facilities go for a low $90–$160 year-round and singles for $80–$130. Share a bathroom (an option in about a third of the rooms) and you'll save $20 to $30 a night. Affordable triples and quads are available, too. To get here, take the N, R, or 6 subway to 28th Street.

Moderate/Inexpensive

The Paul ★   In just the past 5 years, what had been a gritty no-man's land of wholesale clothing and accessory stores has been transformed into a chic hotel corridor. And a stay at the Paul allows visitors to stay in this (now) restaurant- and nightlife-rich 'hood for far less than what you'd pay at the Nomad (see p. 85) or the New York Edition (p. 43). The Paul also has taken some style cues from its neighbors, creating chic (if small) spaces for guests with kicky window treatments, textured wallpapers, Keurig coffeemakers, handsome framed paintings of the city, workable desks, and pillowtop beds swathed in white duvets. For families there are bunk-bed rooms, with attached queen-bedded rooms. Though there's no on-site gym, guests get free passes to the very well-equipped Blink gym down the street. Heck, the hotel even gives discounts to people whose names include some derivation of Paul (something I personally appreciate!). The only downer here is the air freshener that's sprayed into hallways above the elevators (luckily that ugly chemical smell doesn't make it into the guest rooms). 32 West 29th St. (near Broadway). www.thepaulnyc.com.

ℂ **212/204-5750.** 122 units. $118–$296 basic doubles, more for larger rooms. Subway: N, R, 6 to 28th St. **Amenities:** On-site restaurant, fridges upon request, use of nearby gym, free Wi-Fi.

Inexpensive

Hotel 17 ★   Fans of Charles Dickens will feel right at home at this very old-fashioned and spotless if somewhat cheerless hotel (think "Bleak House"). The rooms are done in Edwardian fashion, the beds tend to squeak, and most rooms share a bathroom. But when all is said and done, this is a *very*

Union Square, Flatiron District & Gramercy Park

WHERE TO STAY

well-located, affordable place to stay in a city that has few such options. Along with doubles are single and triple rooms. And the crowd who stay here—mostly young European backpackers—seem to be having a fine time. The hotel's sister property, **Hotel 30,** is identical in pricing and looks.

225 E. 17th St. (off Third Ave.). www.hotel17ny.com. ℰ **212/475-2845.** 150 units. $98–$149 double w/shared bathroom. Subway: 4, 5, 6, N, Q, R, or L to Union Sq. **Amenities:** Free Wi-Fi.

Hotel Deauville ★   This tidy tourist-class property was erected in 1912 as a luxury apartment building; consequently, there are rooms of all different sizes, but most have a tad more space than their competitors do, with gloriously high ceilings to boot. Furnishings are worn but serviceable, with mass-produced art on the walls, carpets on the floors, and old wood furniture (often chipped, but dust free). Mattresses range from just fine to softly sagging, so ask to move if you have back issues. The hotel has one of the last few staffed elevators in the city, an elaborate birdcage-like beauty in service 24 hours a day. That speaks to the service here, which is unusually solicitous and kindly for a cheaper hotel. Hidden perk (or problem depending on your point of view): the Deauville is a favorite of jazz musicians so it is not unusual to hear a little concert in the afternoons, emanating from the on-site rehearsal/piano room, as guests practice for that evening's gigs.

103 E. 29th. St., just off Park Ave. www.hoteldeauville.com. ℰ **800/333-8843** or 212/683-0990. 54 units. $119–$159 double, more for junior suites with cooking facilities. Subway: 6 to 33rd St. **Amenities:** Fridge and microwave available on request, free Wi-Fi.

TIMES SQUARE & MIDTOWN WEST

Times Square might be the heart of Manhattan, but it's also the city's most congested neighborhood (if you can really call it a neighborhood). Corporate Midtown West is centrally located, but as a result, high in demand for both business and leisure travelers. Hotels here almost always fill up fast, thus prices tend to be substantially higher than most other areas.

Best for: People who want to be in the center of "the city that never sleeps"; steps from Broadway theaters, and both high-end and affordable restaurants.

Drawbacks: Staying here puts you among tourists rather than locals and keeps you from experiencing more of the "real" New York. It's also the most frenetic, exhausting, loud neighborhood in the city (so not great for sleeping).

Expensive

Bryant Park Hotel ★★   The Bryant Park Hotel is set in the landmark Radiator Building, a 1924 skyscraper that, with its jet-black brick facade, spiky towers, and gold trim, looks like a building Lord Voldemort would have designed. But no villains work here: in fact, the hotel has one of the friendliest, most helpful staffs in NYC (just whisper that it's a special occasion, and you're guaranteed to return to cupcakes or a balloon bouquet in your room).

Their cheeriness is mirrored by the chipper bedrooms, which are unusually spacious and attractive, with blond-wood floors, scads of air and light, and a vibe that's distinctly Californian. The gym is also unusually well-equipped and pleasant. And you can't beat those Bryant Park views!

40 W. 40th St. (btw. Fifth and Sixth aves.). www.bryantparkhotel.com. ⓒ **212/642-2200** or 212/861-0100. 128 units. $225–$545 double. Subway: B, D, F, or M to 42nd St. **Amenities:** Restaurant, bar, fitness center, room service, screening room, free Wi-Fi.

The Chatwal ★★ What a surprise it is to walk off 44th Street into the Great Gatsby-esque splendor of the Chatwal! Built as a theater in 1905 by architect Stanford White (a movie about his life plays on continuous loop in the elevators), it was converted to a church in the 1960s and most recently into a hotel. That last transformation took a full 9 years as the owner wanted to get every luxe detail right, from the burnished Art Deco wood fittings of the lobby to the round caps and white gloves of the bellmen. The rooms, though small for this price point, are swanky, with all-leather desks, superior beds, and suede walls (it takes an hour to clean each room between guests, as every inch of the walls must be brushed down to remove handprints). Bathrooms contain TVs hidden behind mirrors and Japanese toilets (like bidets but much more, er, interactive). Butler service is part of the deal, as are a spa and gym.

130 W. 44th St. (btw. Sixth and Seventh aves.). www.chatwalny.com. ⓒ **212/764-6200.** 76 units. $403–$547 double. Subway: 1, 2, 3, 7, N, R, Q, or S to 42nd St./Times Sq. **Amenities:** Restaurant, bar, butler service, gym, lap pool, room service, spa, free Wi-Fi.

The Knickerbocker ★★★ First things first: no, the doormen do not get hazard pay for having to wear knickers and knee-socks on 42nd Street. That odd (and cruel) uniform choice is really the only misstep at this suave, relatively new (it opened in 2015) hotel, aimed squarely at the 1 percent. Set in a landmarked 1902 Beaux Arts knockout of a skyscraper, the hotel makes smart use of the building's grand bones: Guest rooms all have soaring ceilings and massive windows. The latter are set off by diaphanous, silvery curtains, allowing daylight to pour onto the Zen furnishings: smoky blue and gray velvet pillows, upholstered chairs, and bedspreads; smooth white oak built-ins, hiding closets, minibars, and safes; and marble bathrooms, with separate bath and toilet areas. On-site are two gyms (one for cardio, one for weights) and two Charlie Palmer Restaurants. Right outside is the mad scrum of Times Square, where you'll be able to get a selfie with Elmo or Batman in 5 seconds flat (for all the good, and bad, that implies).

6 Times Square (right on 42nd St., near Broadway). www.theknickerbocker.com. ⓒ **212/204-4980.** 230 units. $225–$565 double. Subway: 1, 2, 3, 7, N, R, Q, or S to 42nd St./Times Sq. **Amenities:** 2 restaurants (1 on the roof), bar, 2 gyms, room service, free mini-bar soft drinks, free Wi-Fi.

Le Parker Meridien ★★ Sometimes, the out-of-room extras are more important than the rooms themselves. Take the Parker Meridien, which boasts a stellar location (2 blocks from Central Park in one direction, the stores of Fifth Avenue in the other), and a host of amenities. Not only does it feature a

Times Square & Midtown West

WHERE TO STAY

17,000-square-foot fitness center (with basketball and racquetball courts, a spa, and rooftop pool), but it's also the site of two of the most unique restaurants in midtown, **Norma's** (p. 94) and **the Burger Joint** (p. 95) As for rooms, they're respectable, if nowhere near as creative as the rest of the hotel, featuring feather-top mattresses, workable desks with fancy Aeron chairs, a good amount of elbow room, and comfy armchairs. The hotel's a favorite among families for the large suites, that pool, and the cartoons that play in the elevators.

119 W. 56th St. (btw. Sixth and Seventh aves.). www.parkermeridien.com. © **800/543-4300** or 212/245-5000. 726 units. $229–$589 double. Subway: F, N, Q, or R to 57th St. Pets accepted (extra charge). **Amenities:** 2 restaurants, bar, fitness center, spa, rooftop pool, room service, sun deck, free Wi-Fi.

Sofitel New York ★★   You'll feel like you're sleeping in a Fortune-500 company boardroom here. And I mean that in the very best way. The walls and furnishings are covered with the most burnished of woods, the rooms are huge, and the art is of a quality that's usually guarded by hidden security cameras (and rarely placed in private rooms). Beds, as you might expect, are covered with the finest linens and are very comfortable. Bathrooms are downright splendid, with separate showers and soaking tubs. The hotel has every amenity and service you could want, from a workout room that would please Arnold Schwarzenegger to a polished, unflappable staff.

45 W. 44th St. (btw. Fifth and Sixth aves.). www.sofitel.com. © **212/354-8844.** 398 units. $279–$512 double. 1 child stays free in parent's room. Subway: B, D, F, or M to 42nd St. Pets accepted. **Amenities:** Restaurant, bar, exercise room, room service, free Wi-Fi.

Moderate/Expensive

The Blakely Hotel ★★   The name tells the story: this is a hotel that's adopted country club aesthetics. So the dignified, larger-than-usual rooms—duded up in leather, Nantucket blues, and big, cushy armchairs—have prints of racehorses on the walls, and the hall carpeting is a jaunty tartan. Best of all: each room has a mini-kitchen, with a small fridge, microwave, and coffeemaker. The hotel doesn't scream "Big Apple" but it's a pleasant conceit nonetheless, and the staff bend over backwards to make guests feel like they're members of the club. The best deals here are the one-bedroom suites, which come with a very sleepable daybed as a couch, and only cost $40 more per night than the regular doubles—good news for traveling threesomes.

136 West 55th (btw. Sixth and Seventh aves.). www.blakelynewyork.com. © **212/245-1800.** 48 units. $219–$395 double. Subway: B, D, E to Seventh Ave, N, Q, R to 57th St.–Seventh Ave, F to 57th St. **Amenities:** Restaurant, room service, gym, kitchenettes in each unit, free Wi-Fi.

Casablanca Hotel ★★   Yes, this hotel is an homage to that famous movie. So the breakfast room, which doubles as a wine-and-cheese lounge in the evenings (and offers free treats all day), is called **Rick's Café.** Some nights there's free piano music ("Play it again, Sam!"). Rooms (small, but what else is new in New York?) are equipped with rattan furniture, ceiling fans, and wooden blinds for that 1940s hideaway-in-Morocco atmosphere. And the building offers two outdoor areas, a rooftop deck and a second-floor courtyard, so that you can enjoy the sunshine without having to deal with the madding crowds of Times Square (which is just down the block). Did I mention that most of the staff seem to have as sweet a temperament as Ingrid Bergman? (Translation: Service is top-notch).

147 W. 43rd St. (just east of Broadway). www.casablancahotel.com. © **888/922-7225** or 212/869-1212. 48 units. $225–$417 double. Continental breakfast included. Subway: N, R, 1, 2, or 3 to 42nd St./Times Sq. **Amenities:** Free access to New York Sports Club, room service, all-day cappuccino, nightly wine and cheese reception, free Wi-Fi.

Citizen M Times Square ★★★   And here's where the cool kids stay. Especially the tech-savvy ones, because you're going to have to know your way around an iPod to enjoy a sojourn at this groovy Dutch chain. You'll use that device to self check-in; and then once you get to your pod (I'll explain), you'll be tapping away to open the curtains, program the gazillion-channel TV, even change the artworks in electronic frames that decorate your temporary abode. It's an unapologetically pre-fab room to be sure, shiny white, with a modular shower/toilet enclosed unit, lots of hidden storage space, hip orange chairs, a plug adaptor for foreign guests, and a huge bed that pushes right up to a wall-to-wall window, with bright red pillows bearing notes encouraging pillow fights. No need to worry that your neighbor has swanker digs: every room in the hotel is exactly the same (no suites) and rents for the same price each night—unless you sign up for the Citizen M Club, which will net you a 15% discount off the cheapest Internet rate and a free drink upon arrival. Outside your room are the hippest lounging areas in Times Square: a rooftop bar (only open to guests); a high-tech, light- and view-flooded gym; and a whimsical lobby, with a soaring ceiling and a 24-hour bar/resto.

218 W. 50th St. (btw. Seventh and Eighth aves.). www.citizenm.com. No phone. 230 units. $149–$313 double. Subway: C, E to 50th St., B, D to Seventh Ave or N, R to 49th St. **Amenities:** 24-hr. restaurant, 2 bars, gym, free Wi-Fi.

Novotel New York ★   A little over 3 years ago, the Novotel completed an $85-million renovation that transformed its lobby into the set for *Star Trek*. Okay, not really, but your first vision of the hotel, a pulsing purple hall that looks like the entrance to a Disney ride, is, er, a stunner. Rooms are almost as whiz-bang, with a TV entertainment system that you can control from your cellphone; truly soundproofed windows (you can't hear the city at all); and a lighted frame on the backboard of the bed that gives the room an eerie glow. Other than that, they're not all that odd, but quite comfortable and spacious, with excellent views, good desk space, and even better beds. Families can easily share the rooms with two double beds. The breakfast room has one of the city's best views of Times Square.

226 W. 52nd St. (at Broadway). www.novotel.com. © **212/315-0100.** 480 units. From $159–$429 double. 2 children 16 and under eat for free (with adults) and stay free in parent's room. Subway: B, D, or E to Seventh Ave. Pets accepted. **Amenities:** Restaurant, bar, fitness room, room service, free Wi-Fi.

The Quin ★★ Thoughtful touches abound at The Quin. Like the in-room espresso machines, which come with both porcelain cups and to-go paper cups. And super-deluxe Duxian beds topped with an easily-removable featherbed layer for those who like their sleeps firmer (there are also foam pillows in the closet for guests who prefer them). As for the rooms themselves, they have a pin-striped vibe—think chic corporate with lots of dignified grays and taupes, angled lamps, and a bedside panel that controls lights, TV, curtains, you name it. Room service is provided from the topnotch on-site restaurant; the gym has machines that were invented about 10 minutes ago, plus a wide selection of free weights, along with refrigerated towels and loaner headphones.

101 W. 57th St (at Sixth Ave). www.thequinhotel.com. ℭ **212/245-QUIN (7846).** 210 units. $249–$521 double. Subway: F to 57th St or N, Q, R to Fifth Ave. **Amenities:** Restaurant, bar, gym, room service, laundry facilities, free Wi-Fi.

The Refinery ★★ This sophisticated hotel pays homage to the manufacturing roots of its Garment Center building (an installation behind the front desk is made of old millinery tools, appropriate since this 1912 edifice was once a hat factory, one of many such factories in the area). Rooms come in a range of sizes, starting at 250 square feet, but feel bigger than they are thanks to the 12-feet-high ceilings and large windows. Original abstract artwork, oak hardwood floors, and custom furniture up the design ante. Bathrooms feature marble mosaic floors, polished brass fixtures, and rainfall showers.

69 W. 38th St. (btw. Fifth and Sixth aves.). www.refineryhotelnewyork.com. ℭ **646/664-0310.** 197 units. $239–$439 double. Subway: N, Q, R, B, or D to 34th St. **Amenities:** Restaurant, bar, oversized gym, pool, free Wi-Fi.

Inexpensive/Moderate

Ameritania ★★ In a city where each hotel room looks like the next (trust me, I've visited all of them), it's refreshing to come to a hotel with its own aesthetics, in a price range that's not outrageous. Guest rooms are unusually stylish, with handsome works of art on the walls, mod clocks, and textured wallpapers. They come in all shapes and sizes, so ask to switch if you're not happy with the one you get. Included in the room price is a large breakfast, and while Wi-Fi incurs an extra fee, let's just say that if you ask some of the staff members in an unobtrusive way, they'll share the password with you. (You didn't hear that from me, though).

230 W. 54th St. (right off Broadway). www.ameritanianyc.com. ℭ **212/247-5000.** 249 units. $129–$319 double. Continental breakfast included. Subway: 1 to 50th St. **Amenities:** Gym, free lounge/bar, Wi-Fi ($10/night).

Herald Square Hotel ★ Yin and yang—that's probably the most polite way to comment on the bizarrely mixed looks of this classic, if (sometimes) poorly renovated, Belle Epoque building. The outside is promising, a lovely Beaux Arts facade complete with gold-leaf cherub, but the low-ceilinged lobby and cheaply-tiled hallways look like what they are: a holdover from the bad old days when this was a welfare hotel. Of course, first impressions aren't everything, and the solicitous staff and spiffy rooms should soon dispel any lingering worries. Today, in guest rooms, the handsome wrought-iron beds have pillowtop mattresses, room floors are a shiny hardwood, and a fancy dream-maker clock radio/iPod dock wakes you in the mornings. By the way: the reason there are framed *Life* magazine covers everywhere is that the building was erected in 1894 to house the magazine's offices and staff.

19 W. 31st St. between Fifth Ave. and Broadway. www.heraldsquarehotel.com. ℂ **800/727-1888** or 212/279-4017. 100 units. $134–$244 double. Breakfast included. Subway: N, Q, R, B, or D to 34th St., Herald Sq. **Amenities:** Free passes to nearby gym, free Wi-Fi.

Hotel Wolcott ★   The digs here are a real mixed bag. Some rooms have nice period touches such as high ceilings with intricate plaster designs (the building was erected in 1904), others are swathed in dreary, mud-colored wallpaper, made even more dingy-looking by light-trapping, wall-facing windows. Though the rooms vary wildly in size, those in the same category are priced identically, so you could end up paying a premium for a closet-sized room or very little for a very nice one. So be proactive when you check in; I recommend the place because often, it's the best value in town for hotel rooms with private bathrooms. And the lobby is one of the most impressive of any budget hotel, with its giant columns and fake Louis XIV plasterwork all installed by John Duncan, the architect who designed Grant's Tomb uptown (see p. 181).

4 W. 31st St. (off Fifth Ave.). www.wolcott.com. ℂ **212/268-2900.** 175 units. $95–$243 double. Continental breakfast included. Subway: 6 to 34th St. **Amenities:** Fitness center, Wi-Fi ($10/night).

Mayfair Hotel ★   Just west of Times Square, on a block that also houses the Majestic Theater and Eugene O'Neill Theater (and the crowds that descend on them eight times a week), the Mayfair Hotel bills itself a "European-style, boutique hotel," which I've found to be the code phrase for "Our rooms are very, very small, but they sure do look pretty." That's certainly the case here, with rooms that are oddly shaped, usually opening into a tiny alcove with a doorway to the bathroom, behind which is wedged a full, queen, or king-size bed and a small desk. Pretty comes into the equation with the toile–like bedspreads and curtains, white with either baby-blue or pink scenes of peasants at play. As with many Theater District hotels, rates rise sharply on the weekends. Penny-pinching couples can rent single rooms to share, but this is only recommended for very loving twosomes (it's a tight fit).

242 W. 49th St. (btw. Broadway and Eighth Ave.). www.mayfairnewyork.com. ℂ **800/556-0300** or 212/586-0300. 78 units. $95–$189 double. Subway: N, Q, or R to 49th St. **Amenities:** Bar, free Wi-Fi.

Room Mate Grace ★   The lobby here is the sexiest in Midtown and the rooms among the oddest. But let's start with the pluses: a purple-lit swimming pool is the centerpiece of the ground floor, and right off it a bar, so that drinkers can watch their compatriots frolic and those in the pool can swim up for a tipple. It's a fun party scene most nights. (The hotel also features a steam room, sauna, small gym, and breakfast room.) Now, ahem, on to the problematic rooms. First off, those too near the pool/bar area can be noisy and smell of chlorine; and while the configuration of the rooms is very different from one to the next, the majority mount the beds on high, often wide platforms, requiring the agility of a gymnast to climb into for the night. And heaven forbid you drop acid here because the narrow, striped hallways and clashing prints on the walls and coverlets are straight out of a Kubrick film (read: bad trip). In short: this isn't the hotel for everyone.

125 W. 45th St. (btw. Sixth Ave. and Broadway). www.room-matehotels.com. © **212/354-2323.** 139 units. $123–$257 double. Subway: B, D, F, or M to 47th–50th sts./Rockefeller Center. **Amenities:** Bar, breakfast ($12), gym, indoor pool, sauna, free Wi-Fi.

Row NYC ★ Will wonders never cease? The weary, old Milford Plaza Hotel has not only gotten a new name, it's been flipped. And that doesn't mean the staff has gone nuts. Highgate Hotels stepped in and gave it a thorough makeover. Today when you check in, no longer does a tiny room with chipped and aged furniture await you. Now, your tiny room (well, they couldn't move walls) has a jaunty look, with a fresh white duvet on the bed, two curtains in front of the window (one for daytime and one for night), and a cheery tangerine-colored wall. And off the lobby is a fab gourmet food court (see p. 88). Alas, prices seem to be rising, though on many nights you can still catch 40 winks here for just $169, even in the busy season.

700 Eighth Ave. (btw. 44th and 45th sts.). www.rownyc.com. © **888/352-3650** or 212/869-3600. 1300 units. $95–$296 double plus $25 facilities fee. Subway: A, C, or E to 42nd St./Port Authority. **Amenities:** Restaurant, fitness center, free Wi-Fi.

The Salisbury Hotel ★ A church-owned hotel, the Salisbury often seems to take a, well, more charitable view of pricing than its brethren. When most every property nearby is charging $249, it's often possible to get a $179 room here. Alas, the Salisbury has discovered high season, and during those periods, prices can jump to $287. Built by Calvary Baptist (located next door), the hotel has the sort of decor you'd expect in a church-sponsored place: a bit bland and not recently refreshed, but spotlessly clean. What's *unexpected* here is the size of the rooms—massive (the hotel was originally designed as an apartment building)—and the fact that a number of units come with kitchenettes at no additional cost. All of that, combined with the (sometimes) lower prices, makes this an excellent choice for families. Rooms with two double beds will comfortably house a family of four. And the location is unbeatable.

123 W. 57th St. (btw. Sixth and Seventh aves.). www.nycsalisbury.com. © **888/NYC-5757** or 212/246-1300. 201 units. $141–$287 double. Subway: B, D, F, or M to 42nd St. Pets accepted. **Amenities:** Kitchenettes (in most rooms), Wi-Fi ($5 and up).

Skyline Hotel ★ Really a motel, set in an area of Manhattan that could be best described as "Siberia," the Skyline does its best to offset its dreary far-west location with a cluster of amenities that can only be replicated at one other hotel in the city. First off, the Skyline has that rarest of all luxuries: an indoor swimming pool, and a nice one at that, on the roof. Guests can store cars or vans for a mere $10 per day in the hotel's basement parking lot. And

FAMILY-FRIENDLY hotels

Lugging the kids to New York City can be a daunting experience. Finding a hotel that makes that experience a bit less overwhelming (whether in the accommodations themselves or via amenities) can be a huge help. Here are some of the city's best accommodations for families:

Affinia Dumont (Midtown east; p. 55)   Real kitchens in which to cook for picky kids, plus rooms of a size that allows all the family members to spread out.

Hotel Beacon (Upper West Side; p. 56)   In-room kitchenette, on-site Laundromat, and spacious rooms in a kid-friendly neighborhood—what more do you want?

Le Parker Meridien (Midtown West; p. 46)   Cartoons playing in the elevators, a great swimming pool, a kid-friendly burger joint in the lobby, and spacious rooms and suites.

The Lowell (Upper East Side; p. 59)   Total *luxe*, but with the feel of a residential dwelling. Most units are equipped with a kitchenette or full kitchen.

Novotel New York (Midtown West; p. 48)   Kids 16 and under stay free in their parent's room and eat free at the hotel's Café Nicole.

Pod 39 (Midtown West; p. 55)   Bunkbed rooms plus Ping-Pong and pool tables in the lobby. Can you say kiddie heaven (and at an affordable rate)?

Salisbury Hotel (Midtown West; p. 51)   Large, clean rooms and kitchenettes in many of the units make this a smart choice for families.

Skyline Hotel and Travel Inn (Midtown West; p. 51)   Inexpensive ($10) to free parking at the Skyline and Travel Inn, respectively, oversize rooms, and swimming pools (a rarity in affordable hotels).

---

the rooms, enormous by New York standards (particularly the luxury rooms, which cost only 10% more than normal), are bright and comfortable, and come with such nice extras as Nintendo games and fridges. In the front wing (slightly smaller rooms), rates start at $153 a night, but can soar to nearly $300. Usually they hover in the mid-$200s, and I wouldn't pay more than that.

725 Tenth Ave. (at 49th St.). www.skylinehotelny.com. © **800/433-1982** or 212/586-3400. 232 units. $139–$265 standard; extra person $20. Children 14 and under stay free in parent's room. Subway: A, C, or E to 50th St. **Amenities:** Restaurant, fitness center, Internet access in lobby, indoor pool, Wi-Fi ($3/night).

Travel Inn ★   The Travel Inn is a dead ringer for the Skyline (see above), but with a few important differences. Like the Skyline, it has a pool, a gym, and parking facilities, but it one-ups its rival with the size of its pool (a summer-only facility about twice as large as its rival's), its gym (also a hair bigger), and the fact that it gives guests free parking—a very rare perk in this parking-poor city. Rooms are renovated each year and are therefore immaculate, with good, firm mattresses and a standard motel look, but they're markedly smaller than Skyline's, though the prices are similar. Location? Though it's as far west as the Skyline, in this area of town Off-Broadway theaters line 42nd Street all the way to Tenth Avenue, so it feels less remote.

515 W. 42nd St. (just west of Tenth Ave.). www.thetravelinnhotel.com. © **888/HOTEL58** [468-3558], 800/869-4630, or 212/695-7171. 160 units. $138–$250 double. Extra person

$10. Children 15 and under stay free in parent's room. Subway: A, C, or E to 42nd St./ Port Authority. **Amenities:** Coffee shop, fitness center, outdoor pool, room service, Wi-Fi ($6/night).

Inexpensive

Americana Inn ★ Hard-core budgeteers would do well to consider the Americana, another bathless wonder. But here just three to four rooms share a bathroom with shower (rooms do come with sinks) and some of those rooms are very low-cost singles. Families may want to look into the rooms that have three twin beds. As for decor, it's hostel-like in its plainness and the sheets can be scratchy. Plus those rooms in the front get street noise (ask to bunk in the back). Still, prices are usually reasonable, and there's a kitchenette on each floor for guest use, helpful when you're pinching pennies.

69 W. 38th St. (at Sixth Ave.). www.theamericanainn.com. ℰ **888/HOTEL-58** [468-3558] or 212/840-6700. 50 units, all with shared bathroom. $102–$169 double. Extra person $20. Subway: B, D, F, or M to 34th St. **Amenities:** Communal kitchen, Wi-Fi ($6/night).

Park Savoy Hotel ★ Try to ignore the fact that this little hotel just about defines the saying "Well, it ain't the Savoy." For a hotel this well located (just 1 block from Central Park), I'm willing to overlook beds that are a bit rocky (though not lumpy), scuff marks on the walls, and chipped furniture. Yes, the hotel needs refreshing, but the staff keeps what it has clean. And it's nearly impossible in Manhattan to do better than these prices, which include a coupon for breakfast at the pizzeria next door. (No joke—they also make eggs and waffles, apparently.)

158 W. 58th St. (btw. Sixth and Seventh aves.). www.parksavoynyc.com. ℰ **212/245-5755.** 50 units. $123–$156 double. Subway: N, Q, or R to 57th St. **Amenities:** Breakfast coupon, Wi-Fi ($10/night).

MIDTOWN EAST & MURRAY HILL

This is *Mad Men* territory, where the barons of advertising and big business reside. As a result, you'll find some of the grandest hotels—and also the most expensive.

Best for: People who like to stay in a more residential area, with a wide variety of (more high-end) accommodations.

Drawbacks: There's not a lot of variety in the dining options, and most attractions are farther west or further uptown.

Expensive

Andaz Fifth Avenue ★★ How's this for luxury: They'll even clean your feet for you at the Andaz on Fifth Avenue. No, there are no handmaidens on call, but each massive, slate-faced shower has a ledge seat, along with knee-height spigot and bowl, so that you can sit and soak your tootsies at the end of a long day of pavement-pounding. That spigot is one of three shower heads (rain shower head above, handheld in the middle) in this swank bathroom. Other sniffy touches include panels on either side of the bed that control every single light in the oversized room, blackout curtains (along with regular ones), wonderfully high ceilings, and a complimentary snack and beverage bar (excluding alcohol), that sits in all-glass cases that look like they were lifted from Saks Fifth Avenue. The pièce de résistance? Splendid views of the New York Public Library (see p. 144) across the street.

485 Fifth Ave. (at 41st St.). www.andaz5thavenue.com. ℂ **212/601-1234.** 194 units. $265–$725 double. Subway: B, D, F, or M to 42nd St. **Amenities:** Restaurant, bar, over-sized fitness center, room service, free Wi-Fi.

Langham Place ★★ Half hotel, half apartment building, and formerly known as the Setai, this ultra-exclusive skyscraper is expert at coddling its guests. What that means is free shoeshines when guests arrive (can't have dusty tootsies in a place this fancy), a town car available at all hours, complimentary access to the minibar, and rooms that feel like they're the dimension of a squash court (the smallest start at 700 square feet). Bathrooms feature soaking tubs and TVs hidden behind the mirrors. Not enough? On-site is a celeb-helmed restaurant (Ai Fiori from Michael White), a massive spa and gym, and the Julian Farel salon. Those who ante up for suites get even more luxury, including full and state-of-the-art kitchens (in the larger ones), and espresso machines. While the immediate area of the hotel is rather grungy, it's just a few short blocks from Bryant Park and the Empire State Building.

400 Fifth Ave. (btw. 36th and 37th sts.). www.langhamplacehotels.com. ℂ **212/695-4005.** 214 units. $485–$892 double. Subway: B, D, F, M, N, R, or Q to 34th St. **Amenities:** Restaurant, bar, fitness center, personal assistants, 24-hr. room service, spa, salon, complimentary pressing service upon arrival, free Wi-Fi.

The Plaza Hotel ★★★ Everything is as you would expect it to be at the glamorous, glorious Plaza Hotel. Rooms are simply dripping with gold leaf, crystal chandeliers, and crown molding. The furnishings are French Empire, including pieces with fine inlaid woods. And though half the building is now private apartments, the Fairmont chain has taken over the other half and is keeping standards high. A state-of-the-art gym is in the basement and a spa inhabits the fourth floor. And in some ways, the Plaza is more fun than ever, thanks to a wonderfully gourmet food court/restaurant in the basement (see p. 88), which co-exists alongside the classic Palm Court (still the best place in New York to go for high tea). *Some tips:* Only eight rooms now have a Central Park view in the hotel (the rest went to the apartment units), so request it if having that is important to you. As well, Fairmont loyalty members get free Wi-Fi, so join the club (also free), before checking in. Is there a more ideal place for a honeymoon? I can't think of many.

768 Fifth Ave. (at Central Park S.). www.theplazany.com. ℂ **888/850-0909** or 212/759-3000. 282 units. $645–$685 double. Subway: N or R to Fifth Ave. **Amenities:** 2 bars/lounges, food court, 3 restaurants, fitness room, spa, butler service for suites, Wi-Fi ($15/night).

Moderate/Expensive

Affinia Dumont ★ Many hotels claim they have kitchenettes, but the Affinia truly delivers (great news for families). Each of their suites—and this is an all-suite hotel—features a kitchen that would make many native New Yorkers jealous, with a four-burner stove, full-size fridge, microwave, and full complement of flatware and cookware. The large on-site gym/spa is the Affinia's other lure (the hotel will even provide you with a "fit kit" if you wish to work out in your room). Rooms themselves are very livable, with huge desks, armchairs, multiple beds (with multiple pillow options, through the pillow menu), and lots of closet space. Again, an excellent choice if you're going to be sharing the room with several generations.

150 E. 34th St. (btw. Third and Lexington aves.). www.affinia.com. (✆ **212/481-7600.** 241 units. $197–$396 studio suite (smallest unit here). Subway: 6 to 33rd St. **Amenities:** Restaurant, health club and spa, room service, grocery-shopping service, full kitchens, Wi-Fi ($15/night).

Hotel Elysée ★★★ You would expect to find a hotel like this on a side street in the Marais in Paris. It has that sort of gentility. But no, this little brick 1926 gem sits where it always has, as glass skyscrapers have sprouted all around it. This is the famed hotel that was once a haunt for such artists as Tennessee Williams, Maria Callas, and Vladimir Horowitz (the piano he donated still sits in the Piano Suite). In it is the Monkey Bar, with its iconic murals. Unchanged (though refreshed) are the gracious Gallic furnishings in the rooms, which include heavy embroidered curtains draping the windows, fine mahogany dressers, and unexpected touches like a chinoiserie vase here, a fine marble-based lamp there. Rooms vary greatly; some have fireplaces, others have kitchens or solariums, and some (the cheapest ones) are just good-sized, elegant places to sleep. A generous breakfast (fruit, bagels, pastries) is included, as is wine and cheese nightly from 5 to 8pm.

60 E. 54th St. (btw. Park and Madison aves.). www.elyseehotel.com. (✆ **800/535-9278** or 212/753-1066. 103 units. $237–$434 double. Continental breakfast included. Subway: E or M to Fifth Ave. **Amenities:** Restaurant, bar, free access to nearby gym, room service, nightly wine-and-cheese reception, free Wi-Fi.

Inexpensive/Moderate

The Pod Hotel ★★ **and The Pod 39** ★★ Two of the most unusual hotels in the city, both the original Pod and its offshoot on 39th Street, offer high style, and even high jinks, at low, low prices. As you might have guessed from the name, most of the rooms are pretty small—combining and enlarging them would have forced the owners to raise prices—and some at the original location (on 51st St.) do share a bathroom. But even these negatives don't detract too much. The designer has done a bang-up job of making savvy use of the space, building dressers into the bases of the beds, for example; attaching small TVs at each level of the bunk beds (yes, some doubles have bunk beds); and covering the beds with sofa-like covers in primary colors, so that they can be used as couches during the day. All this in rooms that have a smart

Scandinavian look, with clean-lined light-wood-and-brushed-metal furnishings, fine modern prints on the walls, and such non-budget touches as flat-screen TVs, free Wi-Fi, CD players, and iPod-recharging stations in each room. In addition, both properties go out of their way to make stays fun for their guests, with rooftop bars, bustling on-site restaurants, and lobbies that double as lounges (the downtown one offers a Ping-Pong and pool table for guests). Though most of the guests are in their 20s and 30s, people of all ages will enjoy staying at these cheery and affordable hotels (including families; a number of rooms are perfect for them).

www.thepodhotel.com. **Pod Hotel:** 230 E. 51st St., off Third Ave.; ℂ **800/742-5945** or 212/355-0300; 348 units; subway 6 to 50th St. **Pod 39:** 145 E. 39th St., off Lexington Ave.; ℂ **855/POD-5700** or 212/865-5700; 360 units; subway 4, 5, 6, or S to Grand Central. Both hotels: $115–$190 double. **Amenities:** Roof bars, on-site restaurants, free Wi-Fi.

UPPER WEST SIDE

Families and chain stores are the chief residents of the Upper West Side, though it also has some significant sights (including Lincoln Center, Central Park, and the Museum of Natural History).

Best for: Visitors who want a more residential neighborhood, not as congested and noisy as Midtown, and who are comfortable on the bus or subway; rooms are often larger and have a better value than in Midtown.

Drawbacks: Midtown attractions are a bus/subway/taxi ride away, and downtown ones even more so.

Moderate/Expensive

Hotel Beacon ★★ Comfort comes well before style at the Beacon and that's just fine. I'm not saying the rooms are ugly; with their olive-green and white furnishings, last refurbished in 2013, they're actually kind of handsome in a "college town parent's hotel" sort of way. But what gives the Beacon two stars are its creature comforts: Each room comes with a fully usable kitchenette and is a generous 340 square feet or more, not including a good-sized bathroom and roomy closet. And because most of the standard rooms come with two double beds, they're ideal for families. Up one level, but still affordable, are big one- and two-bedroom suites, each with a pullout sofa (families of five and six, take note). The two-bedroom suites have a second bathroom and are almost big enough for the Duggar family.

2130 Broadway (at 75th St.). www.beaconhotel.com. ℂ **800/572-4969** or 212/787-1100. 265 units. $209–$349 double. Extra person $15. Children 12 and under stay free in parent's room. Subway: 1, 2, or 3 to 72nd St. **Amenities:** Gym, kitchenettes, free Wi-Fi.

Moderate

The Empire ★ You're paying for the location at the Empire, but frankly that location is both a blessing and a curse. Yes, the hotel is right opposite Lincoln Center, but that puts it on one of the busiest strips in Manhattan, so

Hosteling International
New York **11**
Hotel Beacon **3**
Hotel Newton **10**
The House
of the Redeemer **9**
Le Belleclaire **4**
The Lowell **2**
The Riverside Towers **5**
The Surrey **7**

3

WHERE TO STAY | Upper West Side

The Empire **1**
Excelsior Hotel **6**
The Franklin Hotel **8**
Harlem Flophouse **12**

the symphony you're likely to hear—all night—is that of car horns. Rooms vary greatly: Some have a feeling of real luxury, with Rothko-like paintings on the walls, handsome leather and dark-wood furnishings, and cushy beds. Others are overdue for an update, and feature rusted shower fixtures and chipped furnishings. Plus the hotel, annoyingly, charges for items that are free elsewhere, like use of the in-room coffee-maker and Wi-Fi (it's free in the lobby, not rooms). Still, this is that rare NYC hotel to have a rooftop pool (it's small, but usable) and a fun sun-tanning deck with cabanas. A mixed bag.

44 W. 63rd St. (btw. Broadway and Columbus Ave.). www.empirehotelnyc.com. ✆ **212/265-7400.** 420 units. $176–$337. Subway: 1 to 66th St.; A, B, C, D, or 1 to 59th St./Columbus Circle. **Amenities:** Restaurant, 2 bars, fitness center, spa, pool, Wi-Fi ($10/night).

Excelsior Hotel ★ It's the Excelsior's stupendous location, down the block from Central Park and across the street from the Museum of Natural History, that keeps it in this guide. Other than that plus—and it's a major one—this is your standard bus-tour hotel (when I was last there, signs for

Cosmos Tours were all over the lobby). So the rooms have the kind of art and furnishings that one expects in a mass-volume tourism joint. Not that they're uncomfortable—actually the rooms are roomy and feature quality bedding. But they're the sort of digs that you forget what they look like the minute you get out the door. Rooms with a park view are pricier; those overlooking the courtyard are a bit dark, but very quiet.

45 W. 81st St. (btw. Columbus Ave. and Central Park West). www.excelsiorhotelny.com. ℂ **212/362-9200.** 198 units. $148–$275 double. Extra person $20. Children 12 and under stay free in parent's room. Subway: B or C to 81st St./Museum of Natural History. **Amenities:** Restaurant, daily breakfast buffet, exercise room, free Wi-Fi.

Hotel Belleclaire ★★ Built in 1903 as one of the first "skyscrapers" on the Upper West Side, the Belleclaire has housed such notables as Babe Ruth and Mark Twain. Its ambiance is old-fashioned, both in its self-consciously "historic" lobby (the front desk looks like a library card catalogue cabinet—for no apparent reason) and in the twisting, narrow hallways that lead from small guest room to even smaller guest room. Once inside your room, you'll find that the digs are contemporary and comfortable, but take their design cues from art deco, with tufted red-leather headboards and classic wooden blinds on the (often) bayed windows. Overall: a good value in a great location (the subway is just 2 blocks away, Central Park is near), though lower-floor rooms that face Broadway can be loud.

250 W. 77th St. (at Broadway). www.hotelbelleclaire.com. ℂ **877/HOTEL-BC** [468-3522] or 212/362-7700. 189 units. $161–$281 double. Subway: 1 to 79th St. **Amenities:** Gym, lobby coffee bar, free Wi-Fi.

Inexpensive

Hotel Newton ★ Cheery if motel-like decor is the norm here but prices can be VERY good. Along with more expensive "superior" rooms and suites, two rooms per floor share a bathroom; these go for $85 to $165 depending on the date (*hint:* ask for a third-floor shared bathroom as there's only one room on that floor without private bathroom, meaning you get it to yourself). The good-sized suites are a smart choice for families (they have sofa beds).

2528 Broadway (btw. 94th and 95th sts.). www.thehotelnewton.com. ℂ **888/HOTEL58** [468-3558] or 212/678-6500. 180 units. $127–$189 standard double. Extra person $25. Children 14 and under stay free in parent's room. Subway: 1, 2, or 3 to 96th St. **Amenities:** Room service, free Wi-Fi.

The Riverside Towers ★ The floor coverings are industrial rugs, the rooms cramped and old, the mattresses covered with plastic (below the sheets), the sinks are chipped, and woe betide you if you get a room near the elevators because it emits a whine that would startle a dog in heat. So why even bother to write about the Riverside Towers as an option? Because New York City is so crazy expensive, and commuting from New Jersey such a vacation-buster, that some travelers will put up with this hotel's (many) deficiencies for the ability to stay in a lovely Manhattan neighborhood at a reasonable price (and all rooms do have private bathrooms). Are you among those who don't mind indoor camping? If you are, the Riverside Towers may be your cup of tea.

80 Riverside Dr. (at 80th St.). www.riversidetowerhotel.com. ✆ **888/724-3136** or 212/877-5200. 110 units. $90–$139 double. Subway: 1 to 86th St. **Amenities:** Cafe on main floor, free Wi-Fi (not always working, though).

UPPER EAST SIDE

Beautiful townhouses, world-class museums, and the shops of Madison Avenue define the Upper East Side. It's a tony, quiet area to use as a base.

Best for: Visitors who like an upscale residential neighborhood, close to Central Park and Museum Mile, with luxury shopping and some fine dining.

Drawbacks: It's not the best-served by public transportation, and can be one of the more expensive areas of town.

Expensive

The Lowell ★★★   The Lowell is the only hotel in New York City that puts actual wood-burning fireplaces in some of its rooms. That may seem like an odd fact to point out first, but for me it sums up the very special ambience of the place, which somehow manages to be quite homey despite being outrageously elegant. Rooms and suites are divided into two categories. The "traditional" ones have a chicly cluttered look, with antique rugs and bookshelves brimming with books. Contemporary rooms are just as lovely, but with bigger bathrooms, a dusty pastel color palette (of browns, grey-blues, tans, and greens), and slightly more modern couches and chairs. All feature exquisite works of art on the walls (a Chinese watercolor in one, a French print in another) and lovely pieces of porcelain here and there. The location is also swell, just 1 block from Central Park on a quiet, brownstone-lined street.

28 E. 63rd St. (btw. Madison and Park aves.). www.lowellhotel.com. ✆ **212/838-1400.** 70 units. $516–$664 double. Subway: F to Lexington Ave./63rd St. Pets under 15 lb. accepted. **Amenities:** 2 restaurants, tearoom, babysitting, fitness room, room service, video library, free Wi-Fi.

The Surrey ★★   In 2009, the Beaux Arts Surrey was literally gutted and rebuilt at a cost of $60 million. In the process it was transformed into the sort of hotel that one usually sees downtown rather than up. By which I mean: It now has edge. On the walls are contemporary art by such big names as Chuck Close, Richard Serra, and Jenny Holzer; and the decor, instead of consisting of tastefully tassled couches and velvet chairs (like so many other Upper East Side hotels), is proudly contemporary. That's not to say rooms aren't comfortable: They are—in the extreme. Spacious, well-appointed, and wow, each has a Duxiana mattress, an amenity that alone costs about $15,000 per room. The one disappointment here: The walls could be thicker (they're not always fully soundproof). Even if you don't end up staying, drop by for a drink at the comely rooftop garden bar; a treatment at the state-of-the-art Cornelia Spa; or a meal at Café Boulud. (It supplies the room service here.)

20 E. 76th St. (btw. Fifth and Madison aves.). www.thesurrey.com. ✆ **212/288-3700.** 189 units. $354–$762 double. Subway: 6 to 77th St. Pets accepted. **Amenities:** Restaurant, 2 bars, fitness center, spa, room service, rooftop garden, free Wi-Fi.

Moderate

The Franklin Hotel ★ The Franklin is making its first appearance in this guidebook series because the management used to charge just a hair too much for what visitors got (small rooms—so what else is new?). Oh, what a bit of construction can do! From now through mid-2018, a massive building is going up next to the Franklin, creating a wall of noise from 9am to 5pm . . . and forcing the hotel to drop its rates. But if you're not a late sleeper, who cares? It means you'll be able to afford one of the genteel rooms here, with their crystal chandeliers lighting raw-silk gray wallpaper, polished wood antiques, and Egyptian linen-swathed poufy beds with all their poufy pillows. Room rates include a generous Continental breakfast, and a wine and cheese reception each evening, both served in two stately lounges. The staff couldn't be a sweeter bunch and the location is within walking distance of Museum Mile.

164 E. 87th St. (btw. Lexington and Third aves.). www.franklinhotel.com. ✆ **212/369-1000.** 15 units. $134–$260 double. Continental breakfast included. Subway: 4, 5, 6 to 86th St. Pets accepted. **Amenities:** Nightly wine and cheese reception, complimentary shoe shines, free local calls, free Wi-Fi.

BROOKLYN, NEW JERSEY & QUEENS

I'm not a fan of commuting while on vacation, especially considering how maddening the traffic into and out of New York City can be. And since most of what visitors come to New York City for is in Manhattan, I've only chosen properties that are convenient to that famed isle. For me, that means *only* hotels that have access to the subway or PATH train—you don't want to spend your vacation stuck in a slow-moving bus going to the outer reaches of New Jersey, or paying too much for transportation. To make it into this book, they also had to offer substantial savings compared to what you would pay across the river in Manhattan. Some are in vibrant neighborhoods, others in areas that are just beginning the gentrification process, and one in a shiny "office park"-type setting. All are safe and convenient to NYC's sights.

Best for: Visitors who are planning on outer borough as well as Manhattan activities; people comfortable with public transportation; foodies who want to be close to some of NYC's and New Jersey's most interesting restaurants.

Drawbacks: You'll be taking a cab/train/bus ride to Manhattan and its various attractions, activities, and restaurants.

Brooklyn

Dazzler Brooklyn ★★ And what's most dazzling about this hotel is its gym. Since the hotel is part of a high-rise that's half apartments (from floor 7 and up), the fitness rooms were built for the residents and they're top quality and BIG, with brand new weight machines, free weights, and lots of exercise machines. After you're done sweating off the vacation calories, you can repair to your roomy room, where large windows let in scads of light. The dignified décor (Scandinavian-style furnishings, polished wood floors, tan-and-black geometric-patterned wallpaper above the bed) has some fun surprises, like a peek-a-boo panel into the bathroom (you can pull it back or keep it shut), swank C.O. Bigelow bath products, and wacky nature prints on the walls. The location is a bit dull, but it's not far from Brooklyn Bridge Park. *Two warnings*: About half the rooms overlook the hotel's beer garden, which can get noisy in the warm weather months; and the hotel's a bit of a walk to the nearest subway.

85 Flatbush Ave. Extension (right off Tillary St.), Brooklyn. www.dazzlerhotels.com. © **718/329-9537.** 72 units. $141–$235 double. Subway: 2, 3, 4, 5 to Borough Hall, A, C to High St., R to Court St. **Amenities:** Gym, restaurant, bar, beer garden, room service, business center, sunning terrace, free Wi-Fi.

Sofia Inn ★★ You'll understand why so many people want to live in Prospect Heights after visiting this handsome little inn. First lure is the quiet, tree-shaded street, which despite its serenity, is within easy walking distance of boutiques, restaurants, the Brooklyn Museum, Prospect Park, the Botanical Gardens, and subways into Manhattan (about a 20- to 25-minute ride). Next is the style of the place, which is oh-so-Brooklyn. Owner Billy Tashman, a former public school math teacher (he's a very sweet guy), salvaged massive school science posters from the 1950s (on such topics as "Symbiosis" and "Evolution"); these give each room a quirky charm, which is further enhanced by the antique chandeliers, carved wooden bedframes, and lovely armchairs he and his designer bought, mostly on Craigslist. The final appealing element: the prices, which come in well below Manhattan rates, both for the rooms with bathrooms (and kitchens) and those without.

288 Park Place (off Vanderbilt Ave.), Brooklyn. www.brooklynbedandbreakfast.net. © **917/865-7428.** 6 units. $95–$135 double. Extra guests $25. Subway: 2 or 3 to Grand Army Plaza. **Amenities:** Kitchens in some rooms, free Wi-Fi.

Union Hotel ★ Set on a funky (but very safe) street near the historic Boerum Hill area of Brooklyn, this colonial-looking brick hotel features cheery contemporary rooms at excellent prices. So what if you won't be able to walk around your bed once you've laid your suitcase next to it? The bed is a highly comfortable one, and you're getting digs with a private bathroom at prices some places charge for rooms with shared facilities. The included breakfast consists of a coupon to a nearby diner. And it's just 2 short blocks from a subway that will zoom you into Manhattan. *Tip:* Ask for a room *away* from the next-door indoor skating rink, as it can be noisy when open.

611 Degraw St. (btw. Third and Fourth aves.), Brooklyn. www.unionhotelbrooklyn.com. © **917/865-7428.** 40 units. $99–$164 double. Breakfast included. Subway: R to Union St. **Amenities:** Free Wi-Fi.

Jersey City

Candlewood Suites Jersey City ★★   Set in an area of Jersey City that's a dead-ringer for Dallas, Texas (huge boxy skyscrapers, streets that are empty of pedestrians, malls galore), the Candlewood offers the types of perks that are standard in many parts of the U.S.A. but rarely seen in the NYC-area at this reasonable a price. (Note that the other hotels in the immediate area have rates that are no lower than Manhattan's.) I'm talking Texas-sized rooms with usable kitchenettes (including ranges, fridges, every kitchen gadget you could need, even dishwashers!), and pleasant, on-trend decor featuring a huge desk (for business travelers), comfy beds, and spacious bathrooms. The only downside to staying here is the third-of-a-mile walk to the PATH train (but the hotel runs a shuttle). So you don't forget where you are, ask for a room with a view of the Freedom Tower, across the river.

21 Second St. (at Hudson St.), Jersey City. www.candlewoodsuites.com. © **800/496-7630** or 201/659-2500. 230 units. $125–$199 double. PATH: Exchange Pl or Pavonia/Newport. **Amenities:** Fitness room, laundry room with free machines, full kitchens in rooms, 24-hr. pantry, self-parking $10/day, area shuttle, free Wi-Fi.

Haiban Inn ★   I think visitors will enjoy exploring the immediate area around this hotel, as it's New Jersey's festive "Little India," with flag-draped streets, dozens of South Indian restaurants, and Ayurvedic health centers and grocery stores. Alas, the Haiban isn't nearly as lively as its neighborhood (though its all-Indian staff couldn't be a more kindly crew). Instead, visitors will find rooms that are Edward Hopper-esque in their bleakness: industrial rugs, hard beds, scratchy sheets, and a color scheme that isn't. That being said, the price here is reasonable year-round, the location is a 3-minute walk from the PATH train (which will whisk you into Manhattan in 15 minutes for $2.75) and rooms, which have double the amount of space you'd find in Manhattan, are kept spotlessly clean. Each comes equipped with a microwave, fridge, and brand-new bathroom (also sparklingly tidy).

799 Newark Ave. (entrance on Herbert Pl.), Jersey City. www.haibaninn.com. © **201/685-7770.** 21 units. $80–$100 double. PATH Train: Journal Sq. **Amenities:** Free breakfast, fridges and microwaves in all rooms, free Wi-Fi.

Holland Hotel ★   Despite its forbidding exterior, not to mention its bizarre location right at the mouth of the Holland Tunnel into Manhattan, the Holland is a pleasant, efficiently-maintained motel. You know the type: generic furnishings, generic paintings of flowers on the wall, small bathroom. But a warm welcome and a complimentary breakfast make up for its lack of character. It's about a 10-minute walk from the PATH train (oddly, you walk through a mall for 5 of those minutes).

175 12th St. (right near the tunnel entrance), Jersey City. www.thehollandhotel.com. © **201/590-2186.** 55 units. $75–$149 double. PATH Train: Pavonia/Newport. **Amenities:** Free breakfast, in-room fridges and microwaves, free parking, free Wi-Fi.

Queens

Country Inn and Suites ★   Just 1½ blocks from a subway stop that's one stop from Manhattan—that's the main attraction of this Queens cookie-cutter chain motel. Oh, and the prices are excellent, the rooms are clean and big, and a continental breakfast is part of the deal. As for the neighborhood, it's on its way up, so though it looks industrial, it's very safe.

40-34 Crescent St. (near 41st Ave.), Queens. www.countryinns.com. © **800/830-5222** or 718/729-2111. 48 units. $80–$124 double. Subway: N or Q to 39th Ave. **Amenities:** Free breakfast, garden, free Wi-Fi.

La Quinta Inn ★   Free parking, a friendly staff, and a commute that's just two-subway stops into Manhattan—so what's wrong with staying in Queens? Okay, the elevated subway that passes right by the front of the hotel can be disruptive to sleep patterns. But those who choose a room in the back—MAKE SURE you get a room in the back—won't hear it at all. Other than that odd requirement, this is like any other La Quinta on the planet, by which I mean bland in decor but comfortable and tidy.

37-18 Queens Boulevard (at 37th St.), Queens. www.lq.com. © **718/729-8775.** 45 units. $125–$160 double. Subway: 7 to 40th St. **Amenities:** Free breakfast included, free local calls, fitness room, free Wi-Fi.

Nesva Hotel ★★   Churches and hotels are the main tenants of this little corner of Queens; I counted half a dozen of each on my last visit. But the hotel that bestows the most blessings—I can't comment on the churches—would have to be the Nesva. Its prices are consistently lower than its neighbors'—and the thoughtful staff promises to beat any internet rate by 10% if you call direct!—and the hotel is buffered from the sound of a nearby above-ground subway by another hotel standing between it and the tracks. Plus the rooms are just as pleasant as those of its rivals, with quality beds and non-cookie-cutter contemporary décor (lots of brown with orange patterning, nice wood furnishings). The nearby subway stop is just a two-stop hop from Midtown Manhattan.

39-12 29th St. (at 39th Ave.), Long Island City, Queens. www.nesvahotel.com. © **917/745-1000.** 36 units. $140–$154 double. Subway: N, Q to 39th Ave. **Amenities:** Free breakfast, free Wi-Fi.

The Paper Factory Hotel ★★   What a piece of eye-candy this place is! Opened in 2014 in a (you guessed it) converted paper factory, rooms here look like film sets, an illusion enhanced by the use of actual movie lights (massive round ones) as lamps. The ceilings are soaring, the furniture like something you'd see at a design museum—desks inlaid with thousands of rectangles of different colored woods; old-fashioned steamer trunks out of which flatscreen TVs rise; and in some rooms, retro stoves in bright colors and curvaceous shapes. I like the guest rooms on the fifth level best, as the floors are wood rather than concrete (which also means this is the quietest floor), but even in the concrete rooms, handsome area rugs cover the floors. In the lobby is a restaurant; the subway is half a block away, and in two stops you're in Manhattan. As for the prices, they're less than what you'd pay for a hotel of comparable quality in Manhattan (if high for Queens).

37-06 36th St. (off 37th Ave.), Queens. www.paperfactoryhotel.com. © **718/392-7200.** 122 units. $159–$194 double. Subway: F, M, or R to 36th St. **Amenities:** Café, restaurant, fitness room, free Wi-Fi.

WHERE TO EAT

ts competitors are Hong Kong and Paris, Brussels and San Francisco, and Rome and New Orleans. But I'll argue hard that none of these other great restaurant cities has quite the same number of serious, satisfying eateries as New York, nor its amazing variety of cuisines in every price range . . . and quirk. Would you believe there are restaurants that serve only mac 'n' cheese or peanut butter concoctions—and flourish doing so?

How did the surprising volume and variety of NYC restaurants come about?

- New York has a larger and more varied immigrant population than any of the other foremost restaurant cities—and that means ethnic specialties of every sort.
- New York has an unprecedented number of top-notch cooking schools, the offices of international magazines devoted to the art of cooking, and the headquarters of the Food Channel.
- The pace of life here is more hectic and pressured than in other famous restaurant cities, creating a vast population with "no time to cook."

Mix all these reasons together, sauté them over the bright flame of the city's celebrity, and you have a mecca for foodies, a place where people obsess over the gratification of their taste buds without anyone thinking it is odd. In China, one way of saying "hello" is to ask, "Have you eaten?" In Gotham, we say, "Where have you eaten—and do you need a reservation?"

PRACTICAL INFORMATION

Sad but true, sometimes a restaurant that's crowded one week will be closed by the next. So though I've done my best to only recommend the ones I think have staying power, I don't have psychic abilities. Do call in advance to make sure the place you're intending to dine is still in business. It likely will be, but better safe . . .

Reservations

Reservations are always a good idea in New York, and a necessity for popular restaurants. Call *far* ahead for any special meal you don't want to miss. Most top places start taking reservations 30 days in advance. If you're booking a holiday dinner, call even

Price Categories
Meal per person, not including drinks or tip:
Inexpensive: $20 and under
Moderate: $20–$40
Expensive: $41 and above

earlier, or head to **OpenTable. com,** a reservations site that handles more than 30,000 restaurants worldwide, as soon as you decide on the date of your dinner.

But if you didn't call well ahead, don't despair. Often, early or late hours—between 5:30 and 6:30pm or after 9pm—are available, especially on weeknights. And most restaurants have bar seating, for which one needs no reservations. Or go for lunch, which is usually much easier to book without advance notice. If you're staying at a hotel with a concierge, don't be afraid to use him or her—a well-connected concierge can often get you into hot spots.

Tipping

Tipping is easy in New York. The way to do it: Double the 8.75% sales tax and *voilà,* happy waitstaff. Don't forget to tip: Waiters make less than minimum wage and are taxed on what the government expects them to make in tips. So when you stiff the waiter, he not only loses that extra bit of income, he still has to pay taxes on it.

Leave $1 per item, no matter how small, for the checkroom attendant. You don't need to tip the host who escorts you to your table.

Note: A scattering of restaurants in this chapter instituted "no tipping allowed" policies in late 2015. In those cases I've listed the cost of entrees and added the words "including gratuities."

FINANCIAL DISTRICT & TRIBECA

Finding decent food near the 9/11 Memorial and Museum has gotten a bit easier, thanks to the 2014 opening of the Brookfield Place Dining Gallery in the World Financial Center (which is just across the street from the 9/11 Memorial, p. 118). It contains a number of local chains, including an outpost of the terrific **Mighty Quinn's Barbecue** (p. 77). In Tribeca, the hippest place for brunch and/or cocktails is the Aussie-run **Two Hands** ★★ at 251 Church St. (near Leonard St., www.twohandsnyc.com). Toasts with eggs and "smashed" veggies on top (avocado or peas) are a specialty, as are the spiky salads. Service is by a squadron of chiseled men with charming accents.

Expensive

Bâtard ★★★ GOURMET AMERICAN   Bâtard was named the best new restaurant in the United States in 2015 by the James Beard Association—the culinary equivalent of winning an Oscar. You'll understand why once you've dined here. Just like some of the recent Oscar winners—Julianne Moore pops to mind—Bâtard is both accomplished and surprising. It's a place where you're taken on a journey, told a story, with foods the likes of which you

Downtown Restaurants

10 Below **9**
Adrienne's Pizza
  Bar **3**
Alfanoose **4**
Balthazar **29**
Bâtard **8**
Baz **15**
Big Gay Ice
  Cream **52**
Boqueria **30**
Brushstroke **6**
Chikalicious **43**
Contra **18**
Dominique Ansel **31**
Dirt Candy **17**
El Rey Coffee Bar **20**
EN Japanese
  Brasserie **55**
Gato **32**
Great New York
  Noodletown **10**
Hampton Chutney **14**
Hecho en Dumbo **34**
Hudson Eats at Brookfield
  Place **5**
Huertas **36**
Jack's Wife Frieda **28**
Jing Fong **11**
Katz's Delicatessen **22**
Keste Pizza & Vino **53**
Locanda Verde **7**
Lombardi's **26**
Lumpia Shack Snack Bar **49**
Mighty Quinn's Barbecue **39**
Mile End Sandwiches **33**
Mission Chinese **12**
Momofuku Ssäm Bar **46**
Morgensterns **24**
Nix **48**
Noreetuh **37**
Nyonya **13**
Oiji **38**
Panna II **35**
Parisi's Bakery **25**
Pearl Oyster Bar **54**
Prime & Beyond **42**
Rice to Riches **27**
Robataya **40**
Sammy's Famous Romanian
  Restaurant **23**

Shabu Tatsu **44**
Smorgas Chef **2**
Spotted Pig **50**
Strip House **47**
Tertulia **51**
Tre **21**
Two Hands **16**
Ulysses **1**
Venieros **45**
Veselka **41**
Wildair **19**

4

WHERE TO EAT | Financial District & TriBeCa

history written in **STONE STREET**

Just off Hanover Square is the oldest street in Manhattan (it's thought to be the only one still in the place the Dutch put it). Lined by 15 lovely Greek Revival industrial buildings—all built right after the great fire of 1835—this happens to be a splendid place to dine, especially when the weather's nice. That's when the cute-as-kittens restaurants that now fill these historic structures place tables right on the cobblestone street, which is closed to traffic to allow for some of the most picturesque al fresco dining in Manhattan. The best of them are:

Smorgas Chef ★ SCANDINA-VIAN   A sunny yellow and sea-blue Scandinavian restaurant that exposes its customers to all the greatest hits of the region: Norwegian smoked salmon (on top of eggs, chives, and bread), salty herring from Denmark, and, yes, Swedish meatballs as light as beach balls and carrying a nice smattering of lingonberry sauce.

53 Stone St. www.smorgaschef.com. 🄲 **212/422-3500.** Main courses $16–$25. Daily 11am–4:30pm and 5–11pm. Subway: 2, 3 to Wall St., R, Q to Whitehall.

Ulysses ★ IRISH/GREEK   Ulysses bills itself as a Greco-Gaelic pub, if you can imagine that. More Irish than Greek (though there are tributes to the Greek hero on some of the walls), it's huge but divided adroitly into intimate "snugs" and furnished with several tons of County Clare shale (forming oh-so-Irish country walls). Food is standard pub grub, though the lunchtime carvery (heaping platefuls of meat and veggies) tends to be fresh and tasty.

58 Stone St. www.ulyssesnyc.com. 🄲 **212/482-0400.** Main courses $10–$26. Daily 11am–4am. Subway: 2, 3 to Wall St., R, Q to Whitehall.

Adriennes Pizza Bar ★ PIZZA   Square instead of round, this isn't your usual pizza joint—and that's just fine. The sauce is well spiced and the cheese high quality.

54 Stone St. www.adriennespizzabarnyc.com. 🄲 **212/248-3838.** Main courses $8–$15. Mon–Sat 11am–midnight, Sun 11am–10pm. Subway: 2, 3 to Wall St., R, Q to Whitehall.

haven't tasted before. Octopus "pastrami" is one "supporting character" of note, as is crispy sweetbreads, given a kapow by tangy lemon curd. That being said, Bâtard's menu changes with the seasons so I can't guarantee these dishes will be on offer when you visit. The fare is accompanied by vino from one of the most intriguing wine lists in the city; and the casual yet classy atmosphere (bare wood tables but fine flatware, zen ochre walls etched with a bas relief, a hum rather than a roar from surrounding tables) is ideal for a date night or a business outing. Many congratulations to Bâtard: well deserved!

239 West Broadway (nr North Moore St.). www.batardtribeca.com. 🄲 **212/219-2777.** Two courses $58, three $72, four $82. Mon–Sat 5:30–10:30pm. Subway: 1 to Franklin St.

Brushstroke ★★ JAPANESE   There are three ways to dine at Brushstroke, all of them pretty, well, splendid. Those with advance planning skills and a dash of luck call many months ahead for the chance to sit at the sushi bar in front of master chef Eiji Ichimura and try his *omakase* or tasting menu ($195). Ichimura is one of the few people in the U.S. to practice the Edo-mae style of sushi making, which substitutes fish cured in salt, soy sauce, or vinegar for fresh fish, with spectacular results.

But even if you don't get a reservation with that master, you can try the tasting menus devised by the *other* on-site guru, owner David Bouley. He's been working with the Japanese Culinary Institute to create the *kaiseki* experience here—a meal created from many exquisite small plates. When we were there recently that included such delicacies as summer vegetables and squash blossoms in a vinegar geleé, softshell crabs with fresh uni (sea urchin), and tender sashimi (from Ichimura). Even the wasabi was the tastiest I've ever tried (my husband finished the entire little pile *after* he was done with his sashimi). The final way to dine is from the a la carte menu (introduced in 2016), but frankly, you might end up paying less with one of the tasting menus (unless you just want a small snack). The service is almost kabuki-like in its formality (I've never before had a waiter walk me to the bathroom, open the door, and say gravely "Enjoy"). But that, too, is part of the fun.

30 Hudson St. (btw. Duane and Reade sts.). www.davidbouley.com. (℃ **212/791-3771.** Kaiseki menu $135; Omakase menu $195; vegetarian tasting menu $120; a la carte entrees $28–$155 (less at lunch for tasting menus and a la carte). Tues–Sat 11:30am–2:45pm; Mon–Thurs 5:30–10:30pm, Sat–Sun 5:30–11pm. Subway: 1 to Franklin St.

Locanda Verde ★★ ITALIAN   I have a single girlfriend who comes here whenever she's feeling blue. She claims the sheep's-milk ricotta crostini is a picker-upper like no other. But the real reason may be she always gets picked up here. Darkly lit, with plush leather booths, a handsome Art Deco–ish decor, and a bar populated by eligible bachelors, Locanda Verde completes the neat trick of making Grandma's cooking seem as sexy as George Clooney. That's due to chef Andrew Carmellini, who must have had quite the talented ancestors if the recipe for "My Grandmother's Ravioli" was actually passed down to him. Fabulous food and that handsome decor make this the perfect date place.

377 Greenwich St. (at N. Moore St.). www.locandaverdenyc.com. (℃ **212/925-3797.** Reservations highly recommended. Main courses $22–$37. Mon–Thurs 7:30–11am, 11:30am–3pm, 5:30–11pm; Fri 7:30–11am, 11:30am–3pm and 5:30–11:30pm; Sat 8am–3pm and 5:30–11:30pm; Sun 8am–3pm and 5:30–11pm. Subway: 1 to Franklin St.

Inexpensive

Alfanoose ★ MIDDLE EASTERN   This long-time Fi-Di (Financial District) fave moved in 2014 to brighter-looking, if smaller, digs near South Street Seaport. It still serves the best falafel in town, fried to order, so be ready for a wait, as this place is always jam-packed with local office workers.

64 Fulton St. (btw. Gold and Cliff sts.). www.alfanoose.com. (℃ **212/528-4669.** Main courses $6–$14. Daily 11:30am–9:30pm. Subway: 4, 5 to Fulton St.

CHINATOWN & LITTLE ITALY

Do what the locals do, and have done since 1903: Line up for a lunchtime sub at **Parisi's Bakery** ★★ (198 Mott St. at Kenmare; www.parisibakery.com, (℃ **212/226-2378**). The family-owned bakery/deli is famous for its smoked turkey, imported provolone, and house-roasted red peppers combo, but I have the sauce-stained shirts to prove that the meatball sub is a messy winner, too. **Baz** ★ (p. 90) is a fun to-go option for bagel fans.

Moderate

Mission Chinese ★★★ CHINESE/FUSION   When the first version of Mission Chinese was forced to close (a migration of rats from a next-door construction site earned it a failing grade from the health department), it was a huge blow to the foodies of NYC—myself included. Which is why I'm thrilled to announce that wonder-chef Danny Bowien's creation is back and even better (and far more hygienic) than before. With a dining room that looks like it could have been designed by Austin Powers (love the '60s-era chandeliers, the tin foil "forest," and all the pudgy ceramic Buddhas), and a menu as groovy, Mission's again one of the hottest restaurants in town. Happily it now accepts reservations, which means 2-hour waits for tables are a thing of the past (use the app on their odd website). Bowien's signature dishes—Kung Pao pastrami and thrice-cooked bacon—are explosions of flavor (rivers of spice, the tenderest of meats, surprising veggies). New additions to the menu, like the refreshing papaya, banana blossom, and chicken salad, and the velvety noodles with matcha (green tea) sauce, are just as scrumptious, if more subtle. The menu even coddles less-courageous eaters with a fried chicken that is at once wonderfully crisp and moister-than-moist, thanks to a fermenting agent used on the skin. Cocktails are supplied by not one but two groovy on-site lounges.

171 E. Broadway (near Rutgers St.). www.mcfny.com. ℂ **212/432-0300.** Main courses $13–$37. Tues–Sun 5:30pm–midnight, Sat–Sun noon–4pm and 5:30–midnight. Subway: F to East Broadway.

Inexpensive

Great New York Noodletown ★★ CHINESE   It ain't much to look at: The lighting's too bright and the seats are crowded together, but there are few finer dining experiences to be had in this restaurant-crammed city. In fact, in the years I've been coming here, I've seen chefs from far pricier places, still in their chef's whites, dining here after their shifts were over. I couldn't see what they ordered, but I always go for the sautéed pea shoots, a delicate, very green taste sensation; the salt-baked squid (the seafood equivalent of potato chips, they're that light and crunchy); some slices off one of the ducks that hang in macabre style in the window; and the heat-packing Singapore mai fun, an al dente, spicy mix of thin pasta, vegetables, and pork. No reservations accepted.

28½ Bowery (at Bayard St.). http://greatnynoodletown.com. ℂ **212/349-0923.** Main courses $4–$16. No credit cards. Daily 9am–4am. Subway: N, R, or 6 to Canal St.

Jing Fong ★ DIM SUM   The classic Chinatown meal is the dim sum brunch or lunch. For those who've never tried it, dim sum is a meal made up of many small dishes, primarily different sorts of dumplings and buns, a tradition that started in the tea houses that lined China's Silk Road many centuries ago (scholars believe the custom began shortly after A.D. 300, when the long-held notion that tea should not be accompanied by food fell out of favor).

And the top place for dim sum in Chinatown today is this cacophonous, massive, always-jammed restaurant, where the clientele is often entirely Chinese, and the dishes range from the expected to the un: chicken feet, stinky durian pastries. Since many of the servers don't speak English, you'll have to point at what interests you. If you make a mistake (hard to do, as it's all tasty), it's no big deal, as most dishes cost just a few bucks.

20 Elizabeth St. (btw. Canal and Bayard Sts). http://jingfongny.com. © **212/964-5256.** Daily 10am–10pm. Meals $6–$12 per person on average. Subway: N, R, or 6 to Canal St.

Nyonya ★ MALAYSIAN   The menu is a good 10 pages long at Nyonya, reflecting the broad mélange of influences that go into Malaysian cuisine. From India, there are rich curry dishes, such as roti canai, light-as-air fried bread that you use to scoop up a bright yellow, chunky curry sauce. The oyster omelet with chili sauce speaks of China in its flavor profile, and has a delightful texture, as do the crabs with dried shrimp and chilis. Wash it all down with excellent house-made juices (my daughters' fave is the green apple/kiwi concoction). Don't come if you're in a hurry or want a romantic atmosphere: The decor is nonexistent and there's always a line to get in.

194 Grand St. (btw. Mulberry and Mott sts.). www.ilovenyonya.com. © **212/334-3669.** Main dishes $6–$23. Sun–Thurs 11am–11:30pm; Fri–Sat 11am–midnight. Subway: 6 to Spring St.

LOWER EAST SIDE

In addition to the choices below, consider **Tre** ★★ at 173 Ludlow St. near E. Houston (www.trenewyork.com; © **212/353-3353;** main courses $14–$22; Mon–Wed 5–11pm, Thurs–Fri 5pm–midnight, Sat noon–midnight, Sun noon–11pm), a locals' fave that serves mouthwatering and affordable Neapolitan food in a casual but pretty setting.

Expensive

Contra ★★ GOURMET AMERICAN   The dress code at Contra is hoodies and uncreased brows, which is unusual for a tasting menu-only joint. But the 20-somethings are flocking here for very good reason: The music on the soundtrack is by musicians who debuted yesterday, and the food tastes like something that could only be created today. Just a list of ingredients tells the tale: walnut butter encased in knotweed, green strawberries bathed in almond milk atop fluke, kale vichyssoise, or an olive oil mousse with elderflower granita, pickled celery, and pistachio. So yes, you're going to try some things you've never put in your mouth before—or at least have never put in your mouth in that particular combination—and I'm betting you'll be blown away. The only downside to dining here, for us old folks, is the noise level (high) and the bench seating (hard).

Tip: If you can't get a reservation at Contra, head to its off-shoot wine bar **Wildair** ★★ at 142 Orchard St. (www.wildair.nyc). It's walk-in only, with stools instead of benches, but the food is of the same high standard and inventiveness as at Contra.

138 Orchard St. (at Rivington St.). www.contranyc.com. $\mathcal{C}$ **212/466-4633.** Tasting menu $67. Tues–Sat 6–11pm. Subway: F to Delancey St., J, M, Z to Essex St.

Sammy's Famous Roumanian Restaurant ★★ ROMANIAN At some point in their lives, nearly every New Yorker makes his or her way to Sammy's, a nightly bar mitzvah masquerading as a steak joint. Set in a basement on the Lower East Side, its decor is gloriously tacky: business cards stuck all over the ceiling, balloons at the tables, and photos of patrons cramming the walls. Completing the ambience is an aged fellow at an electric keyboard who regales the crowd with Yiddish songs, selections from *Fiddler on the Roof,* and the hoariest Jewish jokes you've ever heard. Diners dance in the aisle (especially if they've ordered the house special drink: a bottle of vodka encased in a block of ice). The crusty, gruff waiters will try to push you into ordering too much food: Resist them. There's no reason whatsoever to order the prix-fixe menu; and the steaks are a foot long and overhang the plate, so order one for every two people with just one side of fried potatoes. You have to start with a helping of the chopped liver, a heart attack in a bowl, which the waiter mixes tableside, combining the liver with fried onions, plain onions, and literally a cup and a half of schmaltz (for the uninitiated, that's liquefied chicken fat). One order of liver is enough for four people. Bring a group, as there are few better places in the city for a blowout party.

157 Chrystie St. (at Delancey St.). www.sammysromanian.com. $\mathcal{C}$ **212/673-0330.** Main dishes average $22–$37. Tues–Thurs 4–10pm; Fri–Sat 4–11pm; Sun 3–9pm. Subway: F to Delancey St., B, D, Q to Grand St.

Moderate

Dirt Candy ★★★ VEGETARIAN Please excuse the fact that I'm going to start this restaurant review by discussing its bathroom. But when you walk in there, after dining to the alternative music that's the standard aural fare in many restaurants, it's startling to suddenly be greeted by the sound of tweeting birds and the hum of insects. If you were to close your eyes, you'd swear you were in a meadow in midsummer. That soundtrack upends expectations, as does the food. Sure, like most vegetarian restaurants, Dirt Candy takes some inspiration from dishes that are usually made with meat, but once you start digging into, say, the kale matzo ball soup, and marveling at how the poached egg in it somehow translates the flavor into the chicken soup realm, you realize it's the unexpected tastes that make the dish special—the smoky thump of the shisito peppers, the herbaceous broth, the snap of okra chunks. The soup becomes an utterly unique sensation. The same delightful transfiguration occurs with the broccoli stuffed hot dogs, which will take you back to childhood ballpark pleasures; and the decadent chocolate tart that looks pretty standard, until you remember the crunchy bits are caramelized onion (who knew chocolate and onion would meld so well together?). An elegant setting and discreet service brings this even further into the realm of a restaurant that will have a much wider audience than just vegetarians. *Note:* All dishes can also be made vegan.

86 Allen St. (btw. Broome and Grand Sts.). www.dirtcandynyc.com. © **212/228-7732.** Main courses $21–$24, including gratuities. Tues–Fri 5:30–11pm, Sat 11:30am–2pm and 5:30–11pm, Sun 11:30am–2pm. Subway: F to Delancey St., B, D to Grand St.

Inexpensive

El Rey Coffee Bar & Luncheonette ★★ MIDDLE EASTERN/ FUSION   Just as there's no better way to understand the Lower East Side's history than by tasting it at nearby Katz's (see below), you head to this sunny, always jammed hole-in-the-wall to understand the area's current zeitgeist. El Rey's menu is at once militantly healthy and absolutely delish, the better to attract the slim young things who crowd nearby boutiques and bars. That means extraordinarily satisfying salads (love the kale with a lush dressing made from almond milk); vegetarian entrees like charred radicchio with ricotta; and a finger-licking "deconstructed" falafel sandwich, that has a hint of the real taste thanks to za'atar spices, warm pita bread, and raw chickpeas (but without the calories that frying brings). In the evening, artisanal wines and beers come out. Guests order at the front and perch on high stools at counters.

100 Stanton St. (at Ludlow St.). www.elreynyc.com. © **212/260-3950.** Reservations not accepted. Mains $6–$17. Mon–Fri 7am–10:30pm, Sat–Sun 8am–10:30pm. Subway: F, J, M or Z to Delancey St.

Katz's Delicatessen ★ DELICATESSEN   One of the city's longest-running success stories, Katz has been in business since 1888. You may feel a sense of déjà vu as you enter, as this is where Meg Ryan, ahem, made a scene in *When Harry Met Sally,* and it looks just as it did in the flick: a cavernous, loud space with linoleum-topped tables, celebrity photos and testimonials plastering the walls, and curtains of hanging salami in the window. Though its menu is varied and long, only the uninitiated bypass the corned beef sandwich—the best in the city—a towering stack of meat cured for as long as 30 days, which gives it a richness and depth that you simply don't find with commercially prepared corned beef (which is "pressure injected" to cure in a mere 36 hours).

205 E. Houston St. (at Ludlow St.). www.katzsdelicatessen.com. © **212/254-2246.** Reservations not accepted. Sandwiches $5–$18. Sun–Wed 8am–10:45pm; Thurs 8am–2:45am; Fri–Sat 24 hr. Subway: F to Second Ave.

SOHO, NOLITA & NOHO

For a quick, non-sit-down bite in these areas, I have two recommendations. First is **Mile End Sandwiches** ★★ (53 Bond St. off Bowery; www.mileend deli.com; © **212/529-2990;** Mon–Fri 8am–10pm, Sat 10am–10pm, Sun 10am–4pm), which brings Montreal-style deli to the Big Apple (see box, p. 98). In SoHo, **Hampton Chutney Company** (68 Prince St. near Broadway; © **212/226-9996;** daily 11am–9pm) is a close second, serving *dosas,* southern Indian pancakes rolled up with all sorts of fillings, both Indian and not. Nearby, **Jack's Wife Freda** (224 Lafayette St. near Spring St.; ✆ **212/510-8550;** Mon–Sat 10am–midnight; Sun 10am–10pm) specializes in hearty Israeli food in a cramped but cheery cafe, where the service is speedy.

Expensive

Balthazar ★★ FRENCH Walt Disney's imagineers couldn't do a better job than restaurateur Keith McNally has of re-creating the quintessential Parisian brasserie. But not only does Balthazar look picture-perfect with its zinc bar, smoked mirrors, soaring ceiling, and serious, vest-wearing waiters, the food hits the mark as well. Open for breakfast, brunch, lunch, and dinner, it's the place to come for delectable pastries, perfectly executed French classics (like *steak au poivre* or *moules frites*), and tiptop cocktails. The whole concept should feel phony, but instead the effect is charming.

80 Spring St. (btw. Broadway and Crosby St.). www.balthazarny.com. ✆ **212/965-1414.** Main courses $26–$43. Mon–Fri 7:30am–5pm; Sat–Sun 9am–4pm; Mon–Wed 6pm–midnight; Thurs–Sat 6pm–1am; Sun 5:30pm–midnight. Subway: 6 to Spring St., N, R to Prince St.

Gato ★★★ MEDITERANNEAN My favorite member of the Bobby Flay empire, Gato is very different from the American food eateries where this celebrity chef made his name. But in mastering Med fare, Flay seems to have gotten his mojo back: this is one of the best restaurants in town. The setting is magnificent, a former warehouse with soaring, barrel-vaulted ceilings and ornate cast-iron columns. And what you'll eat here is different from any other place in the city, thanks to the chef's creative, and spot-on, food combos. That might mean a small "bar starter" of artichoke hearts with sea urchin and tenderly poached quail egg; or a paella that's a mélange of kale, mushrooms, and crispy artichokes; or grilled duck liver slathered with melted red grapes.

324 Lafayette St. (just off Houston St.). www.gatonyc.com. ✆ **212/334-6400.** Main dishes $29–$39. Sun–Thurs 5:30–10:30pm; Fri–Sat 5:30–11:30pm. Subway: C or E to Spring St.

Moderate

Boqueria ★★ SPANISH/TAPAS The music thumps, the seats are all high stools (though with backs, so you're comfortable), and the din of happy voices around you make you feel like you're at a bar rather than a restaurant. Then the food arrives, and it's clear: You're definitely at a fine-dining establishment, and one that's at the top of its game. Traditional tapas are superb (such as the creamy croquettes and perfectly crisped *patatas bravas*), while the creative tapas are downright exhilarating (who would ever have guessed that raw scallops with yogurt, hazelnuts, and pomegranate seeds would be such a sublime combo?). The paella, artisanal cheese and meat plates, and sangria are top-notch, too. Boqueria now has two more outlets, one in Chelsea (p. 81) and one on the Upper East Side (p. 104)

171 Spring St. (btw. Thompson and W. Broadway). www.boquerianyc.com. ✆ **212/343-4255.** Reservations for groups of 6 or more. Tapas $5–$14; *raciones* (main courses) $19–$29. Sun–Thurs noon–11:30pm; Fri–Sat noon–midnight. Subway: C or E to Spring St.

THE EAST VILLAGE

Kids, and anyone who likes to do their own cooking, love **Shabu Tatsu ★** (216 E. 10th St. off Second Ave.; ✆ **212/477-2972**; Mon–Thurs 5–11pm; Fri–Sat noon–3pm and 5pm–1:30am, Sun noon–3pm and 5–11pm), where diners dip meats, noodles, and vegetables into a pot of boiling water before immersing them in scrumptious dipping sauces.

Moderate

Huertas ★★★ SPANISH   "There is no way any of us could ever make this," one of my dining companions, an avid home cook, said in awe and respect on a recent visit to Huertas, as we tucked into one of the best trout that has ever swum my way. In this case, it had been baked encrusted in salt and was accompanied by three different sauces. We had already oohed and aahed over a mound of shoestring potatoes that had been cooked for just 7 seconds (according to the waiter) so that it resembled pasta, and then tossed with chorizo sausage and sauce. We laughed aloud when some of our food came accompanied by an extra beverage that acted as Astaire to the Ginger Rogers on the plate: *boquerones* (marinated sardines) and olives accompanied by the perfect sherry, followed by house-smoked salmon washed down with just the right sour beer. All of this ambrosial grub comes from the Basque region of Spain and it's served by a staff who make guests feel like they're not just out to dinner, but have stumbled into an exclusive dinner party. Sorry to gush, but my husband and I love this place so much, we've given out certificates for a meal as gifts to friends and colleagues.

107 First Ave. (btw. 6th and 7th sts.). www.huertasnyc.com. ✆ **212/228-4490.** Pinxto plates (assorted tiny tapas) $20, main courses $16–$37 including gratuities. Mon–Thurs 5:30–11pm; Fri 5:30pm–midnight; Sat 11:30am–midnight; Sun 11:30am–10pm. Subway: 6 to Astor Place, F to Second Ave.

Momofuku Ssäm Bar ★★★ ASIAN   It's hard to decide which of the Momofukus—the name means "lucky peach," and it's become a small chain here in the city—is best. All of them (others include Momofuku Noodle Bar, Momofuku Nishi, and Momofuku Ko) are casual restaurants—think long counters and shared tables—with decidedly elegant Asian food. Ko, a tasting-menu-only place, is near impossible to get into, so it drops off the list; the noodle bar, while good, has been upstaged by Ippudo (p. 95); and the newest, Momofuku Nishi, is a bit more western and frankly, less compelling tastewise. So that leaves Momofuku Ssäm, where chef/owner/culinary savant David Chang pays homage to pork in many, many forms. There's the delightful Asian-style burrito the restaurant is named after; the artisanal ham plate; and the pork steak (which comes with blue cheese, beets, and shisito peppers, yet works amazingly well). The *pièce de résistance:* a whole pork butt for 6 to 10 people (this must be ordered in advance). Beyond pig, Chang is a master with vegetables and fish and . . . well, everything he serves.

207 Second Ave. (at 13th St.). www.momofuku.com. ✆ **212/777-7773.** Main courses $10–$29. Daily 11:30am–3:30pm; Sun–Thurs 5pm–midnight; Fri–Sat 5pm–1am. Subway: N, Q, R, L, 4, 5, 6 to Union Square.

Noreetuh ★★ HAWAIIAN   I'd go back in a millisecond to Hawaii for the snorkeling, the warming sun, the petroglyphs, orchids, welcoming people, and lava flows. For the food? Not so much. Luckily for me, in my native city of New York, an ambitious young chef named Chung Chow is serving the best Hawaiian fare I've ever tasted, here or across the Pacific. The food is crafted with the sophistication Chow learned from his time in the kitchens of Per Se, but doesn't shy away from favored Hawaiian ingredients—like tripe and Spam—that often turn off mainlanders. The results? Like a rainbow over Haleakala. Of the many, many superb dishes are a melange of house-made silken tofu and sea urchin that tastes like luxury on a plate; a decadent torchon of monkfish liver with passionfruit gelée that you smear on coconut bread imported from the islands; and a spaghetti tossed in marinated roe and butterfish that will knock your flip-flops off. For those who really want to "go native" there's ravioli-encased spam and a garlic shrimp dish that tastes just like the stuff you'd get from one of the Honolulu food trucks. I also have to say *mahalo* for the prices, which are quite reasonable by NYC standards. Main courses start in the teens and rarely go over $22. The only bummer here is the restaurant's space—two cramped, railcar-shaped rooms with little élan (or space between tables). But that's what might be keeping the prices sane.

128 First Ave. (btw. 7th St. and St. Marks Pl.). www.noreetuh.com. © **646/892-3050**. Main courses $17–$25. Tues–Thurs. 5:30–10pm, Fri 5:30–11pm, Sat noon–2:30pm and 5:30–11pm, Sun noon–2:30pm and 5:30–10pm. Subway: 6 to Astor Place or L to First Ave.

Oiji ★★★ KOREAN   As with so many East Village restos, this one is a real labor of love. It was created by two young Korean ex-pats, Tae Kyung Ku and Brian Kim, who developed their mad skills toiling in some of the city's most high-status kitchens, before deciding to team up and follow their own culinary dreams. And after wolfing down the scintillating fare here, I can only imagine what a gloomy day it must have been when these rising stars gave notice at their former places of employment. Because these two are magicians. Who knew, for example, that the skin on chicken would turn into crisp bubbles simply by being dredged in tapioca before frying? Or that cold buckwheat noodles could be elevated to a sublime realm by a broth of preserved ramps? And you may find yourself planning a return trip to NYC just for another tasting of Oiji's silky mackerel (served on a bed of smoking pine needles) or its ice cream embedded with honey-chili potato chips.

119 First Ave (btw. 7th St. and St. Marks Pl.). www.oijinyc.com. © **646/767-9050**. Main courses $14–$22. Tues–Thurs 6–10:30pm, Fri–Sat 6–11pm, Sun 5–10pm. Subway: 6 to Astor Pl. or L to First Ave.

Robataya ★ JAPANESE   This is where we take out-of-town guests because it is, quite literally, dinner and a show. Ask for space in the front room when you make your reservations, so you can sit at the squared bar, in the center of which two Japanese chefs kneel. In front of them is a grill, onto which, with gestures that are as delicate as a ballerina, they flip seafood, meats, and vegetables, gathering the ingredients they need with a 10-foot-long paddle. That paddle is later used to serve you your dishes, hot off the grill. Kids love this place, too, not just for the experience but for the food, which is scrumptious but straightforward (there aren't a lot of sauces or spices used).

231 E. 9th St. (btw. Second and Third aves.). www.robataya-ny.com. © **212/777-7773.** Main courses $7–$35. Daily noon–2:45pm and 6–11pm. Subway: 6 to Astor Place.

Inexpensive

Hecho en Dumbo ★★ MEXICAN   Originating as a pop-up in Brooklyn (the Dumbo in the title refers to its former "Down Under Manhattan Bridge Overpass" neighborhood), Hecho now thrives in Manhattan, where it continues to serve a slow food version of Mexican fare. All of the ingredients are organic, many are locally sourced, and all breads, salsas, and even cheeses are made in house, a fact that elevates even the simplest quesadilla. But you don't come here for simple fare; the food is more complex and original than that, incorporating such ingredients as roasted bone marrow or huitlacoche mushrooms into the tacos. All of this yummy, healthy stuff is served in an airy, industrial-chic space on the Bowery.

354 Bowery (at Great Jones St.). www.hechoendumbo.com. © **212/937-4245.** Main courses $10–$27. Mon–Thurs 5:30–11:30pm; Fri 5:30pm–midnight; Sat 11:30am–4pm and 5:30pm–midnight, Sun 11:30am–4pm and 5:30–11pm. Subway: 6 to Bleecker St.

Mighty Quinn's Barbecue ★★ BARBECUE   Meet Texalina BBQ: that's Texas spices (and some of the dishes here are fiery) with that Carolina vinegar-based taste. It's a mighty fine combination, so good that owner Hugh Magnum was able to parlay his popularity as a vendor at an outdoor Brooklyn market into this indoor Manhattan restaurant, one of a small chain now (see p. 66). The decor is pure Southern roadhouse, and the BBQ isn't simply "good for NYC," it would hold its own against any 'cue down south. Best on the menu: the meltingly tender brisket, which is slow cooked for 22 hours before hitting your cardboard plate.

103 Second Ave. (at 6th St.). www.mightyquinnsbbq.com. © **212/677-3733.** Main courses $6–$9. Sun–Thurs 11:30am–11pm; Fri–Sat 11:30am–midnight. Subway: 6 to Astor Place.

Panna 2 ★ INDIAN   The Village Voice newspaper once called Panna II the "best unintentional art installation" in the city, which seems right. It's a wacky-looking place. Over the years, the owners have covered every possible inch of this small restaurant with Christmas lights, chile lights, hanging beach balls, Hawaiian leis and other kitsch, packing it so tightly that those over 5'8" have to duck to get a seat. Once inside you dine on solidly tasty and very affordable Indian food (it's better than Milon next door, which stole the décor idea). And if you're an Instagrammer, you'll be in heaven here. Fun, fun, fun!

93 First Ave. (upstairs, near 6th St.). www.panna2.com. © **212/598-4610.** Main courses $11–$15. Daily noon-midnight. Subway: 6 to Astor Pl or F to Second Ave.

Veselka ★ UKRAINIAN   A popular spot for East Village hipsters, families, businesspeople, and anybody who's ever had a deep need for cold borscht at 3am in the morning. When Veselka debuted in 1954 the area was awash in Ukrainian diners, but most have since gone belly-up (or have upgraded to the point of assimilation), leaving this crowded, tall-windowed eatery the standard-bearer for pierogi, kielbasa, and other Eastern European fare.

144 Second Ave. (at 9th St.). www.veselka.com. © **212/228-9682.** Main courses $10–$17. Daily 24 hr. Subway: 6 to Astor Place.

GREENWICH VILLAGE

Expensive

EN Japanese Brasserie ★★★ JAPANESE   EN has something very few other restaurants in New York have: elbow room. Set in a space as large and high ceilinged as an old-fashioned train station, the restaurant has a serenity that most lack. That's not why you come here, of course. It's for the food, creative *Izakaya* cuisine (meaning Japanese small plates) that is exquisite and hearty by turns. On the delicate side is the house-made tofu, creamy as a cloud and sided with a tart vinegar soy sauce that adds just the right bit of oomph. On the hearty side are toothsome noodles in duck broth, fabulously ungreasy fried chicken, and plates of root vegetables in rich sesame sauce. But that's just the beginning of the menu, which serves Japanese food of a complexity one rarely gets outside of Japan itself. It also has one of the widest selections of fine sakes and *shochus* (a vodka-like liquor) in the city.

435 Hudson St. (at Leroy St.). www.enjb.com. © **212/647-9196.** Main courses $14–$35; *kaiseki* (tasting menu) $70–$140 per person. Mon–Thurs noon–2:30pm and 5:30–10:30pm; Fri noon–2:30pm and 5:30–11:30pm; Sat 11am–2:30pm and 5:30pm–11:30pm; Sun 11am–2:30pm. Subway: 1 to Houston St., A, C, E to West 4th St.

Moderate

Nix ★★ VEGETARIAN   And what is "nixed" here is meat. But this newbie's chefs cook in such a happily indulgent fashion, even the dedicated flesh-eaters leave satisfied. That may be because Nix has one menu for the vegetarians and another for the hardcore vegans, and the first is awash in milk products, particularly creamy cheeses and actual cream. So a dish of mushroom *caccio e pepe* has silky heirloom polenta and lots of melted parmesan, and tastes as rich as marrow scooped from a shank; and Nix' beets (with yogurt, pistachio, and endive) are roasted overnight in a clay oven, which takes the edge off their beetiness and transforms them into succulent, meaty hunks. The dips, a favored appetizer, are equally extravagant, especially the spiced eggplant with pine nuts and the rich red pepper and walnut spread. All of these are served with bread charred in a real tandoori oven—the space belonged to an unsuccessful Indian joint previously. And speaking of that space: it's elegant in its simplicity, with mysterious venetian blinds providing a peekaboo window into the kitchen and lots of sleekly unadorned wood throughout. An excellent addition to an already restaurant-blessed neighborhood.

72 University Place (btw. 9th and 10th sts.). www.nixny.com. © **212/498-9393**. Main courses $12–$19. Daily 5–11pm. Subway: 4, 5, 6, N, Q, R, L to Union Square.

Pearl Oyster Bar ★★ SEAFOOD The Big Apple equivalent of your favorite Maine clam shack, Pearl serves the best lobster roll in the city (big chunks of lobster meat, just enough mayo, sided by a nice pile of shoestring fries) and can't be beaten on its clam roll, either. But even the seafood that doesn't come in a bun is darn tasty, from the buckets of steamers to excellent pan-roasted and grilled fish of all sorts. If you want to get in quickly (they don't take reservations), you may have to hunker down at the marble-topped bar up front, though tables do turn over relatively fast, and Cornelia Street is a lovely place to linger.

18 Cornelia St. (near Bleecker St.). www.pearloysterbar.com. © **212/691-8211.** Main courses $15–$25 (lobster and oysters at market price). Mon–Fri noon–2:30pm and 6pm–11pm; Sat 6pm–11pm. Subway: A, B, C, D, E to West 4th St.

Tertulia ★★ SPANISH/TAPAS An Irish guy from Vermont, Seamus Mullen, runs this place, yet in atmosphere and food Tertulia is the quintessential Iberian taberna. The food is cooked (mostly) in a roaring, wood-fired oven (copied from one Mullen saw in a small Basque town, near Bilbao); try to get a seat near the stove, as it's mesmerizing to watch the chefs work it, creating food that's perfectly charred and just a touch smoky. I highly recommend the tasting menu, but if you don't want to shell out for that, build a meal around tapas (the *tosta matrimonio,* which "marries" black and white anchovies with sheep's mild cheese, is a stunner) and the chef's crunchy yet succulent chicken paella.

359 6th Ave. (at Washington St.). www.tertulianyc.com. © **646/559-9909.** Tapas $6–$12; raciones (larger dishes) $12–$19; paella (for several people) $45. Lunch Mon–Fri 11:30am–3pm, Sat–Sun 11:30am–3:30pm; dinner Sun–Thurs 5:30–11:30pm, Fri–Sat 5:30pm–midnight. Subway: A, B, C, D, E, F to West 4th St.

Inexpensive

Keste Pizza & Vino ★★★ PIZZA Used to be that John's (see p. 95 for the Times Square outlet) was the one restaurant on Bleecker Street that saw lines out the door. Alas, foodies are fickle, and now this upstart, which serves Neapolitan-style pizzas created by an actual Neapolitan (Roberto Caporuscio), has all the glory, and the waits to get in. Deservedly so, I must say. Topped by house-made mozzarella, with a perfectly balanced sauce and a whole raft of ingredients to play with (Keste offers 40 options), this is, hands down, the best pizza I've had in the U.S. and may be a very close second to what I gorged on in Naples. Full pies only are sold, but they're so delish, even single diners are able to put them away. Keste means "this is it" in the Neapolitan dialect, by the way.

271 Bleecker St. (near Cornelia St.). www.kestepizzeria.com. © **212/243-1500.** Pies $12–$23; gluten-free pizza available. Mon–Thurs noon–3:30pm and 5–11pm; Fri–Sat noon–11:30pm; Sun noon–10:30pm. Subway: 1 to Christopher St.

Lumpia Shack Snackbar ★★ FILLIPINO The *lechon kawali* fries here are gonna kill you. These pork belly "french fries," a warm and gourmet version of pork rinds (set atop a bracingly fresh salad of herbs, lettuce, and celery,

SWEETS FOR THE sweet

Dessert is given a place of honor on the NY restaurant scene, with venues ranging from beloved bakeries to all-dessert restaurants. Here are some of the best:

10 Below ★ Thai ice cream is created before your eyes here, with staff pouring liquid and fixings (chocolate sauce, peanut butter, berries and more) onto a frigid round plate where it hardens and then is vigorously chopped (think a Benihana chef) and rolled into finger-shaped nuggets. It's a fun show.

10 Mott St. (near Canal St.). www.10belowicecream.com. No phone. Sun–Thurs 11am–10pm; Fri–Sat 11am–11:30pm. Subway: J, R, Z, or 6 to Canal St.

Big Gay Ice Cream ★★ Vanilla is the basis of most of the treats here, but that's the only "vanilla" thing about this ice cream shop, which serves up outrageously decadent treats like "Salty Pimp" (ice cream with dulce de leche, sea salt, and chocolate dip) and "Mexican Affo'Gay To" (ice cream with spicy hot chocolate, cayenne pepper, and shaved chocolate).

61 Grove St. (at Seventh Ave. S.). www.biggayicecream.com. ✆ **212/414-0222.** Sun–Wed noon–10pm; Thurs–Sat noon–midnight. Subway: 1 to Christopher St. Also at 12 E. 7th St. (btw. First Ave. and Avenue A), subway L to First Ave.

Chikalicious ★★★ A dessert-only restaurant, it's owned by a diminutive pastry chef named Chika Tillman (hence the name) who presides from behind the central counter in this glossy, all-white restaurant (think: the "Milk Bar" in the movie *A Clockwork Orange*). All customers get a three-course tasting menu for $16. And what desserts they are! Ms. Tillman, who has baked at some of the top restaurants in the city, has a rich imagination when it comes to food, and though the pairings she makes seem weird—molten chocolate tart with red peppercorn ice-cream and red wine sauce is one—they're right on. If you're not up for a sit down "dessert meal," head across the street to Chika's fab takeout place.

203 E. 10th St., off Second Ave. www.chikalicious.com. ✆ **212/995-9511.** Wed–Sun 3–10:45pm. Subway: 6 to Astor Place.

Dominque Ansel ★★★ Thankfully the cronut craze—celebrating the unholy union of the donut and the croissant—has passed, and sugarholics can enjoy the better pastries at this oh-so-Gallic little bakery without waiting on line for 5 hours. These include "Paris-New York," a jester's cap of a pastry teaming choux dough with peanut butter, rich chocolate, and caramel; and

and sided by the perfect vinegar dipping sauce), will literally make your face explode with flavor. And if you were foolish enough to eat just these for, say, ten meals in a row, likely the fat in them would make your arteries explode, too. But heck, you're on vacation, and how likely is it that you'll ever make it to the Philippines? These fries will show you what you're missing. The rest of the menu—which includes shrimp-cracker-like garlic chips, *lumpia* (a type of spring roll), shaved ice desserts, and a number of noodle and fried rice dishes—is almost as good. Alas, the place really does look like a shack, which means the space is cramped and the seating limited to a few high stools, so pop by to get food for a picnic or grab a chair for a quick meal.

50 Greenwich Ave. (at Perry St.). www.lumpia-shack.com. ✆ **917/475-1621.** Main courses $8–$13. Tues–Sat noon–9pm. Subway: A, C, E, B, D, F to West 4th St.

4

Greenwich Village | WHERE TO EAT

wonderfully crumbly cinnamon rye shortbread.

189 Spring St. (btw. Thompson and Sullivan sts.). www.dominqueansel.com. *C* **212/219-2773**. Mon–Sat 8am–7pm, Sun 9am–7pm. Subway: C, E to Spring St. or N, R to Prince St.

Lady M Cake Boutique ★★★
The specialty here is the crepe cakes, particularly the green tea cakes, which are so well balanced they win over even those who don't usually like sweets. There's a small, usually crowded seating area, or you can get your slices to go and have a picnic in Central Park.

41 E. 78th St. (near Madison Ave.). www.ladym.com. *C* **212/452-2222**. Mon–Fri 10am–7pm; Sat 11am–7pm; Sun 11am–6pm. Subway: 6 to 77th St. Also a take-out-only shop at 36 W. 40th St. (btw. Fifth and Sixth aves.).

Morgensterns ★★★
Nicholas Morgenstern, the surprisingly slim gentleman behind this ice cream parlor sensation, was a pastry chef at a number of big-name restaurants before he found his chilly calling. Between baking sessions he experimented with different techniques for crafting ice cream—eliminating eggs, using an old fashioned French machine that employed paddles rather than spinners, adding more salt and less sugar. The result is mind-bendingly good. Favorite flavors: salt and pepper pinenut, pistachio green tea, and Vietnamese coffee.

2 Rivington St. (near Bowery). www.morgensternsnyc.com. *C* **212/209-7684**. Sun–Thurs 8am–11pm, Fri–Sat 8am–midnight. Subway: 6 to Spring St., F to Second Ave.

Rice to Riches ★★★
A delightful one-trick pony, it serves only rice pudding. This isn't the rice pudding your mom made, however; it's tarted up with all sorts of exotic flavorings and unfortunately cutesy names such as "Sex, Drugs and Rocky Road" and "Surrender to Mango." I have yet to discover a flavor that wasn't ambrosial.

37 Spring St. (btw. Mott and Mulberry sts.). www.ricetoriches.com. *C* **212/274-0008**. Sun–Thurs 11am–11pm; Fri–Sat 11am–1am. Subway: N, R to Prince St.

Venieros ★★
A beloved Italian bakery, Venieros has been in business since 1894, with an attached cafe for those who'd like an aperitivo or café with their cannoli. Though the cannolis are legendary, I'm a particular fan of their pignoli cookies which are, in a word, scrumptious.

342 E. 11th St. (at First Ave.). www.venierospasty.com. *C* **212/674-7070**. Sun–Thurs 8am–midnight; Fri–Sat 8am–1am. Subway: N, R to Prince St.

CHELSEA & THE MEATPACKING DISTRICT

In addition to the choices below, there are swell eateries both on the **High Line** (mostly food stands) and within **Chelsea Market** (p. 81). The Chelsea branch of **Boqueria** (see p. 74) at 53 West 19th Street, near Sixth Avenue, is another nice choice.

Expensive

Santina ★★ MEDITERRANEAN   Santina is the restaurant equivalent of Sofia Vergara: sexy, exuberantly Latin, and just bursting with fun. As it should be: it's an eatery in a goofy glass box that's directly under the uber-hip High

Line Park, and everyone who comes to the Meatpacking District is here for a party. Santina fulfills that "mandate" with its looks and sound (lots of salsa music, full-sized palm trees instead of flower arrangements, bubblegum-colored chandeliers) and with a menu that's built for large groups. This is one of the few restaurants in town where the sharing plates are truly shareable, though they're so tantalizing, you may not want to give up a morsel. The most successful dishes include the *ceccina* (chickpea-flour pancakes, almost like Indian dosas, topped with mounds of avocado and nuts, or peppery tuna tartar), fab rice dishes (which aren't risotto, but steamed rice soaked in butter and studded with such goodies as fine *guanciale* sausage or shrimp), the crisp fried seafood, and the unexpected mix of fried artichokes with grapes and cream.

820 Washington St. (at Gansevoort St.). www.santinanyc.com. ℭ **212/254-3000.** Main courses $19–$30. Daily 10am–midnight. Subway: A, C, L to 14th St.

Scarpetta ★★★ ITALIAN   The word "scarpetta" means "little shoe" in colloquial Italian. But it's not the type of shoe one puts on one's foot. Instead the "shoe" referred to is a bit of bread, like what people use after they've finished their plate of pasta to scoop up every last bit of sauce from the plate. It's therefore an apt name for this restaurant, helmed by celebrity chef Scott Conant (you may recognize him from *Chopped* and *Top Chef*), as you're going to want to get every morsel off these plates. Conant is cooking up unusually flavor-packed food, perhaps because he's not afraid to use rich ingredients— like ravioli stuffed with duck and foie gras, or agnoletti containing brisket and bone marrow. But even when the dish is slightly less fat-laden—like the tuna *susci* (raw tuna wrapped around preserved truffles and pickled vegetables) or the seared diver scallops with morels and spring peas—somehow he manages to make every single taste bud sing. My only beef with the place: It's too darn loud. But that's the case in many NYC restaurants nowadays.

355 W. 14th St. (at Ninth Ave.). www.scarpettanyc.com. ℭ **212/691-0555.** Main courses $24–$49. Mon–Thurs 5:30–10:30pm; Fri–Sat 5:30pm–11:30pm; Sun 5:30–10pm. Subway: A, C, E, or L to 14th St.–8th Ave.

Moderate

High Street on Hudson ★★★ GOURMET AMERICAN   Paleo dieters beware: you're going to be sorely tested here. The linchpins of the menu are breads and they are the kind of divine treat Oprah Winfrey gushes about in her overwrought Weight Watchers commercials: Crafted from locally milled flour and non-commercial yeasts, they're moist, often complex, with satisfyingly crusty crusts. But the grain-a-palooza doesn't end with breads: there's a range of fabulous pastas on the menu (special kudos to the bucatini with squid and mussels that's flavored with seaweed); and, often, the sauces on the proteins will have the crunch of soured oats (a perfect accompaniment to the tender roast Long Island duck) or other grains. Chef/owner Eli Kulp has long been a star in Philadelphia and so specialties of that town sometimes make an appearance, like the chow chow relish that gives a happy zip to the tempura broccoli. High Street isn't glamorous looking—with its unadorned

THE prime cut: STEAKS! STEAKS!

Though NYC is no longer famous for its cheesecakes, or even its deli fare (with some exceptions), for red meat it still reigns supreme. The city is brimming with top-notch steak joints—doable for those on expense accounts, a little daunting for the rest of us. Still, if you're in the mood for a perfectly aged rib-eye with a side of creamed spinach and crisped potatoes, one of the following places will do you right:

Peter Luger Steakhouse ★★★ is the original and still in many ways, the best, though because of its Brooklyn locale it's not as convenient as some others listed below. But I'd argue that the commute's worth it. See p. 110.

Ben & Jack's Steakhouse ★★ has two locations in Manhattan: 219 E. 44th St. between Second and Third avenues (www.benandjackssteakhouse.com; *📞* **212/682-5678**) and 255 Fifth Avenue between 28th and 29th streets (*📞* **212/532-7600**). Opened by two former Peter Luger staffers, it shows they learned their trade well.

Prime and Beyond ★★, located at 90 E. 10th St. near Third Avenue (www.primeandbeyond.com; *📞* **212/505-0033**), is proving that scallion salad is just as tasty a condiment on steaks as A-1. This Korean-helmed steakhouse is very proud of their aging facilities (meats are aged an unusually long 7 to 9 weeks for intense flavor); ask, and they'll take you on a tour while your food cooks.

Quality Meats ★ (www.qualitymeatsnyc.com; *📞* **212/371-7777**) is set in a stunning, bi-level space designed by the famous team of AvroKO at 57 W. 58th St. between Fifth and Sixth avenues. The quality of the food matches the quality of the design. It has some nontraditional steakhouse menu items such as pan-roasted lamb T-bones with figs and mint, and a flatiron steak with blackberries.

Sparks ★★, at 210 E. 46th St. near Third Avenue (www.sparkssteakhouse.com; *📞* **212/687-4855**), reputedly used to be a Mafia favorite. With its "ye olde steakhouse" decor, crammed into a low-ceilinged modern building, it has that Cosa Nostra air, part of the fun of coming here. The other part (along with the perfect hollandaise sauce and aged meats) is the wise-cracking waitstaff, with their thick outer-borough accents. They typify the type of service that used to be de rigueur in NYC, but alas, rarely exists anymore. Take a look at the wall of cigars before you head out; you can't legally smoke them in here, but they're apparently still big sellers.

Strip House ★, at two locations— 15 W. 44th St. off Fifth Avenue (www.striphouse.com; *📞* **212/336-5454**) and 15 E. 12th Street near University Place (*📞* **212/328-0000**)—merges steaks with strippers, placing photos of noted ecdysiasts from the '40s and '50s on the walls in an all-red, leather-and-wood interior that's sexy and fun. And the beef? It's like buttah.

wooden chair and tables, and minimal art, it looks like the type of straightforward cafe where you'd grab a quick breakfast or lunch (both of which you can have here)—but the food is far more dazzling than it will be at many of the fancier joints in town.

637 Hudson St. (at Horatio St.). www.highstreetonhudson.com. *📞* **917/388-3944.** Main courses $12–$28. Mon–Fri 8am–3pm, Sat–Sun 8am–2:30pm; dinner 5:30pm–10:30pm daily except Tues. Subway: A, C, E, or L to 14th St.–8th Ave.

Inexpensive

Co. ★★ PIZZA   Yes, this is a chic pizza joint, with a sleek, woodsy look, but don't hold that against the place. The pies are first class (and you can order only pies, no slices, from traditional tomato-and-cheese ones to delicious creations with leeks and sausage or shitake mushrooms with a caramelized onion-walnut puree). Co.'s salads, cheese plates, and soups are darn impressive, too, as is the wine list.

230 Ninth Ave. (btw. 24th and 25th sts.). www.co-pane.com. © **212/243-1105.** Pizzas $9–$20. Mon 5–10pm; Tues–Thurs 11:30am–10pm; Fri–Sat 11am–11pm; Sun 11am–10pm. Subway: C, E to 23rd St.

Coppelia ★★ LATIN AMERICAN   The sign outside reads DINER but the Caribbean colors inside (down to the teal faux shutters on the walls), the long marble bar, and the salsa and samba soundtrack, let you know this ain't your usual NYC greasy spoon. As does the menu, which ranges across the Caribbean and Latin America, offering up perfect renditions of such regional stars as *lomo saltado* (a toothsome tomato and ginger beef stir-fry from Peru), Cuban roast pork with crispy chicharons, and Brazilian sweet-corn empanadas. Open 24 hours, Coppelia also offers breakfast items, day and night, and these, too, have a Latin flair (like the *Pan Francese*, a take on French toast, which is topped with creamy *dulce de leche*). A fun place, night or day.

207 W. 14th St. (near Seventh Ave.). www.ybandco.com. © **212/858-5001.** Main courses $7–$18. Daily 24 hr. Subway: 1, 2, 3 to 14th St.

UNION SQUARE, FLATIRON DISTRICT & GRAMERCY PARK

In addition to what's below, try the gourmet food court **Eataly** (see p. 89).

Expensive

Cosme ★★ MEXICAN   Believe the hype. Cosme opened in NYC with nothing less than the media-equivalent of air force jets flying in formation over the Statue of Liberty, as it is the first U.S. restaurant from Enrique Olvera, owner of the iconic Pujol Restaurant in Mexico City (named the 20th best restaurant in the world by the 1000 members of the Diner's Club Academy). For once the PR whirl is merited: Cosme is bringing to New York the kind of contemporary, deeply luxurious Mexican food that it had yet to experience. This includes *pibil*, a rich Yucatecan dish usually made with shredded pork, done here with lobster and delicate mâche lettuce; exquisite *ceviches* with just the right hint of heat and tang from fermented Serrano peppers; *uni* (sea urchin) tostado with a creamy salsa of bone marrow; and a "corn husk" dessert that tastes like summer and sunshine. I'm knocking off one star from this review for dignified-but-boring décor and the miniscule portions (you'll have to order a lot to leave full). *Note:* It's often difficult to get reservations here, but the restaurant has a large bar and communal table for walk-in diners.

35 E. 21st St (btw. Broadway and Park Ave. South). www.cosmenyc.com. ℂ **212/913-9659.** Main courses $28–$59. Mon–Thurs noon–2:30pm and 5:30pm–11pm, Fri noon–2:30 and 5:30–midnight, Sat 11:30am–2:30pm and 5:30–midnight, Sun 11:30am–2:30pm and 5:30–11pm. Subway: 6, N, R to 23rd St.

Maialino ★★★ ITALIAN Though its website says this restaurant is inspired by the *trattorias* of Rome, I'd be more specific than that. To me, Maialino takes its cues from the Roman neighborhood of Testaccio, which was for many years the slaughterhouse area of that city, and is known for its hearty, expert preparations of all the cuts of meat we in the U.S. discard. So, when you come to Maialino and you see the menu item "pig face salad," know that you will get a plate of food that looks just like what it was in life (and is spectacularly delicious). Salami plates, a tortellini stuffed with liver, and spicy tripe also shine. But you don't have to be adventurous to enjoy the fare here; even such standards as *spaghetti a la carbonara* or *spaghettini alle vongole* are done in a way that's a cut above the usual. And as at other restaurants owned by Danny Meyer (he's also behind Santina, see p. 81), the waitstaff are genuinely friendly and well trained in the art of hospitality.

2 Lexington Ave (at 21st St. in the Gramercy Park Hotel). www.maialinonyc.com. ℂ **212/675-7223.** Main courses $23–$52 including gratuities. Mon–Thurs 7:30–10am, noon–2pm, 5:30–10:30pm; Fri 7:30–10am, noon–2pm, 5:30–11pm; Sat 10am–2:30pm and 5:30–11pm; Sun 10am–2:30pm and 5:30–10:30pm. Subway: 6 to 23rd St.

Maysville ★★ AMERICAN REGIONAL It's named for the birthplace of Kentucky bourbon, and the bar is a big part of the experience at Maysville—it stretches the length of the restaurant, its bartenders churning out brown cocktail after brown cocktail (they're terrific, by the way, especially the Manhattans). But the appeal of Maysville isn't strictly alcoholic; there's real artistry in the food here, too. Chef Kyle Knall gives a creative spin to the Southern classics—for example, grits, which he fries in cubes and tops with sliver-thin pieces of pork as an appetizer. The result is a wonderful mélange of creamy, crunchy, and salty, unlike anything I've ever tasted before. He smokes an entire trout and then serves it as part of a perfectly dressed salad. Other highlights include the nettle *agnoletti* and duck breast with a hunk of almost-frozen foie gras (it gives the dish an ice-cream–like appeal). So why two stars instead of three? That goes back to the bar, which attracts such a large, noisy crowd that diners have to shout to be heard in other parts of this handsome high-ceilinged restaurant.

17 W. 26th St. (near Broadway). www.maysvillenyc.com. ℂ **646-490-8240.** Main courses $28–$34. Mon–Thurs 11:30am–3pm and 5:30–11pm; Fri 11:30am–3pm and 5:30pm–midnight; Sat 11am–3pm and 5:30pm–midnight; Sun 11am–3pm and 5:30–11pm. Subway: N, R to 28th St.

The NoMad ★★ AMERICAN Forgive them for the cutesy spelling; the name is the only part of this restaurant that isn't sophisticated in the extreme. Set in the NoMad Hotel (p. 43) and "chef-ed" by rising star Daniel Humm,

Midtown Restaurants

4

WHERE TO EAT | Union Square, Flatiron District & Gramercy Park

FOODIE food courts

Sorry Auntie Anne, in New York City food courts are out of your league. Dedicated to non-chain, gourmet fare, their booths are being claimed by some of the city's most celebrated chefs. And the number of these multiple-venue eateries has exploded in just the last three years. From uptown to down and over to Brooklyn, here are the top ones, and their specialties. They're all ★★★ experiences to my mind, so I haven't rated them individually. **Note:** All have seating and serve alcohol along with the food.

NEAR CENTRAL PARK:

The **Plaza Food Hall** in the Plaza Hotel, at Fifth Ave. and Central Park South (www.theplazany.com/dining/foodhall). **Specialties:** Exquisite desserts from **Lady M Confections** (see p. 81), crunchy, lightly vinagery broccoli tacos from Brooklyn's **no. 7 sub,** and caviar from **Olma.**

Turnstyle in the Columbus Station subway stop at Columbus Circle, entrance at 57th and 58th sts and Broadway (www.turn-style.com). **Specialties:** Triple pork sandwiches from **Bolivian Llama Party** (pork shoulder, bacon and crackling!), and the best grilled cheese sandwiches ever from **Meltkraft** (the owners have a dairy farm, graze their stock on grass, and make their own sensational cheeses.)

IN AND NEAR GRAND CENTRAL STATION:

Great Northern Food Hall In Grand Central Station on 42nd Street between Lexington Ave. and Vanderbilt Ave. **Specialties:** Curated by Claus Meyer, co-founder of the renowned Copenhagen restaurant Noma, the food features such Scandinavian treats as sweet and savory porridges at **GrainBar** and open-faced Danish sandwiches at **Open Rye.**

Urbanspace Vanderbilt at 45th St. and Vanderbilt Ave., across from Grand Central Terminal (www.urbanspacenyc.com). **Specialties:** Pizza with house-made mozzarella from Brooklyn's own **Roberta's** (p. 109), hummus from another Brooklyn legend, **Mimi's Hummus,** and tinned seafood snacks (they taste better than they sound, especially sided by beer) from **Maiden Lane.**

NEAR TIMES SQUARE

City Kitchen at 700 Eighth Ave at 44th St., 2nd floor (http://citykitchen.rownyc.com). **Specialties:** Roasted duck schwarma pita wrap from **Box** (an offshoot of **ilili,** see p. 90), ramen soup from **Kuro Obi** (from the fab **Ippudo** company, see p. 95), and passion fruit doughnuts from **Dough.**

NEAR-ISH TO THE JAVITS CONVENTION CENTER

Gotham West Market at 600 11th Ave. between 44th and 45th streets (http://gothamwestmarket.com). **Specialties:** Spanish tapas at **El Colmado** (run by acclaimed chef Seamus McManus of Tertulia, see p. 79), toothsome ramen noodles from **Ivan Ramen,** and Ooey Gooey Buttercake ice cream from **Ample Hills Creamery.**

it's a primo date restaurant, with a sexy *Belle Epoque* design; "kiss me now" cocktails, including one made with absinthe; and food that is wonderfully colorful as well as scrumptious. The menu changes constantly, but when I was last there, the spring garlic velouté was swoon-worthy, and the poached lobster was just as luxurious as it should have been. The only thing I don't like about the NoMad is how maddening it is to try to get a reservation here

NEAR MACY'S & PENNSYLVANIA STATION

The Pennsy at 33rd St. and Seventh Ave (above Penn Station; www.thepennsy. nyc). *Specialties:* Black Angus steak sandwich at renowned butcher **Pat La Frieda's** first restaurant, chef Marc Forgione's wacky but worthwhile pressed lobster sammy with dipping sauce from **Lobster Press,** and craft beers at the **Pennsy Bar.**

NEAR THE HIGHLINE & MEATPACKING DISTRICT

Chelsea Market 75 Ninth Ave. between 15th and 16th sts (www.chelseamarket. com). *Specialties:* Authentic, Tijuana-style tacos from **Los Tacos no. 1,** halvah (sesame candy) from **New York Seed + Mill,** brown butter rice cakes with bacon and *kimchi* (a spicy Korean relish) from **mo kbar,** and curry sausage from **Berlin Currywurst.**

NEAR THE FLATIRON BUILDING

Eataly 200 Fifth Ave. between 23rd and 24th streets (www.eatalyny.com). *Specialties*: All the food here is by celebrity chefs Mario Batali (Babbo, Del Posto) and Joe and his mother Lydia Bastianich, and it is uniformly excellent from the vegetarian resto to the pasta place to the rooftop Italian beer garden. Unlike other food courts, much of the space here is given over to uncooked foods, many imported from Italy (some of the jarred and dried goods make excellent souvenirs and gifts). Also now at 101 Liberty St., 3rd floor (near the 9/11 Memorial).

NEAR THE 9/11 MEMORIAL AND MUSEUM

Hudson Eats/Le District at Brookfield Place Dining Gallery 200 Vesey St. across the street from the 9/11 Memorial. *Specialties:* Brisket from **Mighty Quinn's Barbecue** (see p. 77), Montreal-style bagels from **Black Seed** (p. 90), and veal parmigiana at **Parm** (see p. 103).

IN BROOKLYN

In the winter months, Brooklyn's **Smorgasburg ★★★** (www.brooklynflea. com; Sat–Sun only 11am–6pm) can count as a food court, as it's held indoors. Come spring, Smorgasbord's 100 or so food vendors take their stands outdoors to both Brooklyn Bridge Park, near Pier 5, and East River State Park, which you enter at Kent Street and North 7th Street. *Specialties:* You pick, I can't. With dozens of vendors, the variety of foods is staggering and the quality incredibly high. On a recent visit, my group noshed on curried hot dogs with a slaw of kimchi apples; oysters with three delightful mignonette sauces; fried eggplant with yogurt sauce; root beer–flavored macaroons; fab barbecue; and El Salvadorean *pupusas* (like a tortilla, with a variety of stuffings).

(call weeks in advance) and the separate, and not as good, menu for the major bar area.

Inside the NoMad Hotel, 1170 Broadway (at 28th St.). www.thenomadhotel.com. ℭ **212/796-1500.** Main courses $26–$42. Mon–Thurs 7–10am, noon–2pm, 5:30–10:30pm; Fri 7–10am, noon–2pm, 5:30–11pm; Sat 7–10am, 11am–2:30pm, 5:30–11pm; Sun 7–10am, 11am–3pm, 5:30–10pm. Subway: N, R to 28th St.

THE hole TRUTH: NEW YORK'S BEST BAGELS

Not many things are more "New York" than a bagel, and New Yorkers are loyal to their favorite bagel stores. In fact, discussions about who makes the best bagel can lead to broken friendships. Following are the top contenders:

Absolute Bagels   2708 Broadway between 107th and 108th streets (✆ **212/ 932-2052**). The egg bagels, hot out of the oven, melt in your mouth, and their whitefish salad is perfectly smoky, not overpowering.

Black Seed Bagels   170 Elizabeth St. near or 176 First Ave. between 10th and 11th Sts. (www.blackseedbagels. com). All hail the Montreal-style bagel, which is chewier and sweeter than its NYC cousin (before baking, the bagels are parboiled in honey water and the oven is wood-fired). I approve, and like the range of creative toppings.

Baz   189 Grand St. near Mulberry St. (www.bazbagel.com; ✆ **212/335-0609**). Home to the "Flagel," a flat bagel aimed at those who prefer the crust. It won't save you any calories, though, as it has a larger circumference than usual. Top it with one of the fab house-made cream cheeses, such as horseradish and beet or cucumber and dill.

Ess-A-Bagel   831 Third Ave. between 50th and 51st streets (www.ess-a-bagel. com; ✆ **212/980-1010**). When it comes to size, Ess-a-Bagel's are the best of the

biggest; plump, chewy, and oh so satisfying.

Kossar's Bialys   367 Grand St. at Essex Street (www.kossarsbialys.com; ✆ **877/4-BIALYS** [424-2597]). Bialys—flat, yeast rolls with savory fillings—are the star offerings here, but don't ignore Kossar's bagels. Also hand-rolled, the result is a slightly crunchy exterior with a tender, moist middle. Sure, you came for the bialys, but you will leave with both.

Murray's Bagels   500 Sixth Ave. between 12th and 13th streets (✆ **212/ 462-2830**), and 242 Eighth Ave. at 23rd Street (http://murraysbagelschelsea.com; ✆ **646/638-1335**). There's nothing like a soft, warm bagel to begin your day, and Murray's does them beautifully. Their smoked fish goes perfectly on their bagels.

Sadelles   463 W. Broadway near Prince St. (www.sadelles.com; ✆ **212/254-3000**). High-gluten flour, and a pre-baking parboil in barley-malt syrup, give these bagels just the right amount of yeastiness and crunch. The glamorous Soho setting, in which the bagels are stacked on dowels and placed as centerpieces on the tables (this is a sit-down restaurant, though there is a take-away counter), announce the gentrification of this once humble bread product. The smoked fish toppings are ethereally soft and tasty.

Moderate

ilili Restaurant ★★★ LEBANESE   Boxes inside of boxes inside more boxes. That's the phrase I'd use to describe the decor of ilili, which is a ravishing, Escher-like jumble of wooden squares set along the walls of a huge room with cathedral-height ceilings. That complexity also marks the food, with each forkful unlocking another taste or texture. Lebanese in origin, the food is sophisticated and surprising, whether you're digging into a plate of musky chicken livers cut by a brightly tart tamarind syrup and sided by creamy yogurt, or tasting one of the traditional spreads, which take the usual hummus and baba ganoush to another level. Do know, however, that most of the *mezes* (appetizers) are the same portion size as the main dishes and yet cost half as much. So make a meal of those and leave feeling satisfied, rather than broke.

236 Fifth Ave. (at 28th St.). www.ililinyc.com. © **646/683-2929.** Average meals $26–$32. Mon–Wed noon–3pm and 5:30–10:30pm; Thurs–Fri noon–3pm and 5:30–11:30pm; Sat noon–11:30pm; Sun noon–10:30pm. Subway: N, R to 28th St.

Pure Food and Wine ★★ VEGETARIAN   At this elegant restaurant—with one of the nicest garden dining areas in the city—the food is not just vegetarian, it's vegan and raw. So the "cheeses" are made from fermented nuts, the "pasta" in the lasagna is thin sheets of zucchini, and the breads are made from sprouted grains. Sounds weird, I know, but the meal proceeds a bit like a magic show, as you try each substitution and realize "wow, this works." I'm a dedicated carnivore, but I don't miss meat when I come here. Instead I realize that I've rarely tasted tomatoes as, well, tomatoey as those in the lasagna here, or "cheeses" as creamy. An experience.

54 Irving Place (btw. 16th and 17th sts.). www.purefoodandwine.com. © **212/477-1010.** Main courses $19–$23. Daily noon–4pm and 5:30–11pm. Subway: N, Q, R, L, 4, 5, 6 to Union Square.

Inexpensive

Shake Shack ★★ BURGERS   Yes, it's now an international chain (I just stumbled on a Shake Shack at the Dubai Airport!) but this was the original, the only actual "shack," set in lovely Madison Square Park, and still attracting hordes of diners. When the weather's good (there's no indoor seating here), there are few more delightful places to dine in Manhattan. And though many will argue, I think they serve the best burger in Manhattan: always juicy, high-quality meat, with the perfect bun-to-patty ratio. The shakes are pretty orgasmic, too. If you have kids, grab a burger, some fries, a shake, and then head to the nearby playground for dinner.

In Madison Square Park (near 23rd St. and Madison Ave.). www.shakeshack.com. © **212/889-6600.** Burgers $5–$8. Daily 11am–11pm. Subway: 6, N, R to 23rd St. Other locations dotted around the city, including one behind the Museum of Natural History (p. 158).

TIMES SQUARE & MIDTOWN WEST

For an extraordinary sandwich, I recommend **City Sandwich** in Hell's Kitchen (649 Ninth Ave. near 45th St.; http://citysandwichnyc.com; © **646/684-3943;** Mon–Fri 9am–9pm; Sat–Sun 10am–8pm) which serves Portuguese fare—salt cod, blood sausage, roasted eggplant, or less exotic ingredients—all between two slices of excellent Portuguese bread. At lunch, the line for this place can snake down the block, but the staff is quick, so add yourself to the back. Not sure what you want? The gourmet food courts

CityKitchen, Gotham West Market and **The Pennsy** (all p. 89) have many primo offerings.

For a more elegant sit-down meal, beyond the selections below, you might consider **The Modern ★★** (at the Museum of Modern Art, 9 W. 53rd St. between Fifth and Sixth aves.; www.themodernnyc.com; ✆ 212/331-1220; daily 11:30am–2:30pm and 5–10:30pm), which serves primo contemporary American fare; or that temple of seafood helmed by celeb-chef Eric Ripert, the expensive **Le Bernardin ★★** (155 W. 51st St. near Seventh Ave.; www.le-bernardin.com; ✆ 212/554-1515; Mon–Thurs noon–2:30pm and 5:15–10:30pm; Fri noon–2:30pm and 5:15–11pm; Sat 5:15–11pm).

Expensive

Benoit ★ FRENCH Celeb chef Alain Ducasse is behind this old-school bistro, which means that the service is flawless, the atmosphere (with its burnished wood walls and velvet banquettes) *très* Gallic, and the food is, for the most part, *parfait*. Benoit doesn't try to be creative, but that's part of the charm of eating here: What's served is a paradigm of classic French cuisine. The cheese soufflé is an old-fashioned high-calorie treat (it's an appetizer), the French onion soup is one of the best in the city, and the roasted chicken can't be improved upon (it's simple and utterly delicious).

60 W. 55th St. (near Sixth Ave.). www.benoitny.com. ✆ **646/943-7373.** Main courses $28–$46. Mon–Sat 11:45am–3:30pm and 5:30–11pm; Sun 11:30am–3pm and 5:30–11pm. Subway: N, Q or R to 57th St.

Keens Steakhouse ★ STEAK For a taste of Olde New York—and some of the best chops in the city (lamb chops, mutton chops, short ribs)—head to this iconic restaurant, established in 1885 and still going strong. The portions are humongous, so don't be afraid to share. Spend some time simply wandering around this museum-like eatery, with its collection of ceramic pipes on the ceiling (some of the regulars who had their own pipes here include Albert Einstein and Babe Ruth), its working fireplaces, memorabilia-laden walls, and plush leather banquettes.

72 W. 36th St. (at Sixth Ave.). www.keens.com. ✆ **212/947-3636.** Main courses $28–$59. Mon–Fri 11:45am–10:30pm; Sat 5–10:30pm; Sun 5–9:30pm. Subway: B, D, F, N, Q, R, or M to 34th St./Herald Square.

Marea ★★★ ITALIAN/SEAFOOD The *New York Times* critic wrote, when awarding Marea its three stars, that trying the restaurant's *ricci* (sea urchin roe with lardo and sea salt on toast) was like "kissing an extremely attractive person for the first time—a bolt of surprise and pleasure combined." The metaphor holds for the entire experience of dining here, I'd say. There are few restaurants anywhere as attractive (or as comfortable to dine in, thanks to their tremendously cushy leather chairs); and the pleasure quotient is high. A lot of the credit goes to chef Michael White, who has an extraordinary talent for coaxing every last bit of flavor from a fish, whether he's serving it raw (*crudo*) with some delightful sauce, or simply grilled, again with a fab sauce.

DINNER PARTY: A MEAL AT THE james beard foundation

For chefs, the James Beard Awards (named for the notable culinary critic) are the equivalent of the Oscars. Win one and you can write your own ticket.

The second biggest honor in the industry is being invited to cook a meal at the **James Beard Foundation** (www.jamesbeard.org). When the call comes, rising and established chefs across the US drop everything and fly to New York City to work their magic. And since chefs need mouths to feed, pretty much anyone can attend these ambitious, "look-what-I-can-do" culinary showcases (if they pay the entrance fee that is; see below).

Most of these special meals take place in the former home of James Beard, an elegant Greenwich Village townhouse (look out for the ceiling mirror in a nook of the dining room; it used to be over his bed!). The evening will start with cocktails and passed hors d'oeuvre in the garden, weather permitting, followed by a no-holds-barred multi-course meal. For non-members, the full experience costs $170, members pay $130—that includes alcohol. A list of upcoming chefs and their impressive menus is on the website. You cannot get in without advance reservations; many dinners sell out, so make your plans early.

He also knows his way around noodles, creating inventive dishes (such as tiny gnocchi with ruby red shrimp, chilies, and rosemary). And keep your eyes peeled, as this place is a celebrity magnet.

240 Central Park S. (near Columbus Circle). www.marea-nyc.com. ✆ **212/582-5100.** Main courses $29–$57. Mon–Thurs noon–2:30pm and 5:30–11pm; Fri noon–2:30pm and 5–11:30pm; Sat 11:30am–2:30pm and 5–11:30pm; Sun 11:30am–2:30pm and 5–10:30pm. Subway: N, Q, R to 57th St.

Molyvos ★ GREEK Within easy walking distance of both Carnegie Hall and City Center, Molyvos has long been the go-to place for a quick but distinguished meal before a show. Though it's one of the grandfathers in this always-changing neighborhood, it has kept its standards high, meaning that its *mezes* (appetizers, such as cold spreads or grilled octopus) are among the tops in town, its *spanakopita* (spinach pie) is cloud light, and its *moussaka* (a sort of lasagna with ground lamb), will make you feel like you're tasting the dish for the first time. Service can be brusque, but they know how to time the meal so that you get to the curtain on time.

871 Seventh Ave. (btw. 55th and 56th sts.). www.molyvos.com. ✆ **212/582-7500.** Main courses $22–$42. Daily noon–11pm. Subway: N or R to 57th St.; B, D, or E to Seventh Ave.

Moderate

Cho Dang Gol ★★★ KOREAN I knew immediately I was in the right place the first time I walked into Cho Dang Gol. It wasn't its looks, which are pleasant but unmemorable: wooden tables, tan walls, a few Korean musical instruments hung here and there as decoration. Nor was it the smells issuing from the kitchen or the look of the food going by. No, it was the realization, as I entered, that not a word of English was being spoken. The restaurant was jammed, and every guest was of Korean origin. As soon as I tasted the food I knew why: This was far and away the best Korean food I'd ever had, each dish better than the last, from the home-made tofu (some crafted from black sesame seeds, some from white), to the piping hot and savory *bulgogi* (a beef and rice stew), to the parade of small plates, which included fried seaweed as addictive as crack. The *pièce de résistance* was the kimchi, a dish that I sometimes find overpowering. Here it was just fiery enough, with a citrus zing that was downright refreshing. My only worry in sending you here, dear reader, is that it will spoil you for all other Korean restaurants. Yes, it's that good.

55 W. 35th St. (off Avenue of the Americas). www.cdgnyc.com. © **212/695-8222.** Shareable casseroles and entrees $13–$43. Daily 24 hr. Subway: N, Q, R to 34th St.

Danji ★★ MODERN KOREAN   The hipster counterpoint to Cho Dang Gool (see above), Danji reinvents Korean classics in odd but very tasty ways. That might mean a kimchi, bacon, and Spam paella (weird, but delish) or tofu infused with ginger before being flash-fried. The young chef Hooni Kim got his chops cooking for such master chefs as Daniel Boulud. At this point, he's starting small, so his little restaurant, while serving superb food and looking chic, isn't the most comfortable. To amortize the space, most everyone has to perch on high stools, elbow to elbow. And he keeps it hopping with a "no reservations" policy, which means you just might miss the curtain if you try to dine here before a show.

346 W. 52nd St. (btw. Eighth and Ninth aves.). www.danjinyc.com. © **212/586-2880.** Main courses $13–$26, with most in the teens. Mon–Thurs noon–2:30pm and 5:15pm–midnight; Fri noon–2:30 and 5:15–1am; Sat 5:15pm–1am. Subway: C, E to 50th St.

Gyu Kaku ★ JAPANESE   Think of Gyu Kaku as a do-it-yourself Benihana. In front of you is a grill; you're served meats, vegetables, and/or fish (your choice), and you get to cook it yourself—no fancy knife skills required. Kids love the experience, as it is interactive, but adults do too, because the quality of the ingredients is high and the dipping sauces are phenomenal.

321 W. 44th St. (btw. Eighth and Ninth aves.). www.gyu-kaku.com. © **646/692-9115.** Average meal $17–$21. Mon–Thurs 11:30am–11pm; Fri–Sat 11:30am–midnight; Sun 11:30am–10pm. Subway: A, C, E to 42nd St.

Norma's ★ AMERICAN   The schtick here are what I'd call "stunt breakfasts," dishes so huge and overloaded with ingredients, they'd make a trucker faint. I'm not saying these humongous concoctions—like chocolate waffles with peanut butter and toffee crunch filling, or omelets stuffed with lobster and asparagus—aren't delicious. They are. But don't expect to have room for lunch, or even dinner, after your meal. Which is good, since the prices are pretty darn high for breakfast. An over-the-top experience.

In Le Parker Meridien hotel, 118 W. 57th St. (btw. Sixth and Seventh aves.). www.normasnyc.com. © **212/708-7460.** Main courses $17–$35. Mon–Fri 7am–3pm; Sat–Sun 7:30am–3pm. Subway: N, Q, or R to 57th St.

Toloache ★★ MEXICAN   It speaks to the sophistication of New Yorker's taste buds that this very authentic Mexican eatery (hey, they've got crickets on the menu!) has become such a hit that it now has three locations in the city. You can get standard Mexican food here, but I'm partial to their more creative fare like tacos with succulent brisket, or ceviche with lobster, strawberry, avocado, truffles, and red onions. They're also expert at getting you to the theater on time; service is brisk but friendly. Make a reservation, as they book up well in advance. Also at 166 E. 82nd St. (✆ **212/861-4505**, subway 4, 5, 6 to 86th St.) and 205 Thompson St. (✆ **212/420-0600**, subway A, B, C, D, E, F to West 4th St or 6 to Bleecker St.).

251 W. 50th (at Eighth Ave.). www.toloachenyc.com. ✆ **212/581-1818.** Main courses $12–$32. Sun–Mon 11:30am–10pm; Tues–Thurs 11:30am–11pm; Fri–Sat 11:30am–midnight. Subway: C, E to 50th St.

Inexpensive

Burger Joint ★ AMERICAN   A greasy spoon among silver spoons, Burger Joint is hidden behind a curtain in the lobby of the ultra-swank Parker Meridien Hotel (see p. 46). Pull back that curtain and you enter a hidden diner that looks like it was yanked off some side street in Detroit. And it serves up the juiciest, most perfectly charred burgers in the western half of Midtown— order them with "the works" (red onions, lettuce, tomato, pickles, mustard, and mayo) for not a cent extra.

In Le Parker Meridien hotel, 118 W. 57th St. (btw. Sixth and Seventh aves.). www.burgerjointny.com. ✆ **212/245-5000.** Burgers $8.50. Sun–Thurs 11am–11:30pm; Fri–Sun 11am–midnight. Subway: B, N, Q, R to 57th St.

Ippudo NY ★★★ JAPANESE   Ever see that Japanese film *Tampopo*? The one about the couple who spent their time tramping from one ramen place to another, searching for the perfect noodle? I didn't realize I, too, was on that quest until I tried Ippudo, and understood for the first time just how life-changing sublime ramen could be. That will sound hyperbolic until you try the silky soups here, made from the finest Berkshire pork and filled with toothsome noodles. The only shortcomings? I'm not the only one who feels this way, so the waits can be long (go at lunch). It also is not the place for quiet conversation, as a full-throated Japanese greeting is hurled at each guest who enters. Also try New York's original Ippudo, downtown at 65 Fourth Ave (btw. 9th and 10th sts., subway 6 to Lafayette, R to Eighth St.).

321 West 51st St (btw. Eighth and Ninth aves.). www.ippudony.com. ✆ **212/974-2500.** Reservations not accepted. Main courses $15–$18. Mon–Thurs 11am–3:30pm and 5–11:30pm; Fri–Sat 11am–3:30pm and 5pm–12:30am; Sun 11am–10:30pm. Subway: C, E to 51st St.

John's Times Square ★★ PIZZA   About a half block west of Broadway, John's has the top pizza in Times Square, served in a soaring, elegant space that was once a church (you can still see the lovely stained-glass windows in places). But come hungry! John's serves only large full pies big

THE pizza CAPITAL OF THE UNITED STATES

No city in the U.S. has better pizza than New York. And in recent years, with the emergence of many new, authentic Neapolitan places, it's gotten even better. Here I've separated the old-school New York pizzerias from the new kids on the block. You won't go wrong with any of the choices below.

OLD SCHOOL

DiFara Pizza ★★ 1424 Avenue J, Brooklyn, at E. 15th Street (✆ **718/258-1367;** subway Q to Avenue J/16th St.). DiFara's lives up to its reputation for having the best traditional NY pizza in the city (worth a commute from Manhattan), thanks to the zeal of owner Dominic DeMarco, who, for over 40 years, has made every pizza himself. That means service can be slow (expect to wait an hour for a pie, maybe a bit less for a slice). But it's worth it!

John's Times Square ★ See p. 95. Full pies only, with brick-oven goodness.

Juliana's ★ The *real* original Grimaldi's. See p. 131.

Lombardi's 32 Spring St. between Mulberry and Mott streets (www.firstpizza.com; ✆ **212/941-7994;** subway 6 to Spring St.). Claiming to be New York's first "licensed" pizzeria, Lombardi's opened in 1905 and still uses a generations-old Neapolitan family pizza recipe. The coal oven kicks out perfectly cooked pies, topped with ingredients such as pancetta, homemade sausage, and even fresh-shucked clams. Garden seating during warm weather.

Totonno's Pizzeria Napolitano ★★★ 1524 Neptune Ave. between West 15th and West 16th streets, Coney Island, Brooklyn (✆ **718/372-8606;** subway D to Stillwell Ave./Coney Island). This unassuming little pizzeria has been at the same spot since 1924, and it makes pizzas almost exactly as it did 80 years ago—thin crust, fresh sauce, mozzarella, what more do you need?

NEW SCHOOL

Co. ★ See p. 84. A more upscale experience than your average pizzeria, with top-notch pizzas and exceptional salads to boot.

Keste Pizza & Vino ★★★ See p. 79. Pizza so fresh, so authentically Neapolitan, that many have abandoned nearby classic slice joints in its favor.

Marta ★★ 29 E. 29th St. near Madison Ave. (www.martamanhattan.com; ✆ **212/651-3800**). Roman-style pizza that's cooked over open embers, making the crust thin and crackly. Some pies are classics, others feature such nouveau adds as English peas, mint, and leeks. Salads are great here, too. All are served in a chic loungey space, with a ceiling so high, there's a second floor balcony for some tables.

Trattoria Zero Otto Nove ★★ 2357 Arthur Ave. at 186th Street, the Bronx (www.roberto089.com; ✆ **718/220-1027**). Taking its name from the Salerno, Italy, area code, you'll think you're on "The Boot" when you bite into one of Roberto Paciullo's Neapolitan pizzas. The mozzarella is made at nearby Casa de Mozzarella, the tomatoes are San Marzano, the pies are cooked in a wood-burning brick oven, the basil is from the Arthur Avenue Market across the street—the result: pure pizza perfection. Good news for people who can't make the trip up to the Bronx: The pizzeria has opened a branch at 16 W. 21st Street in Manhattan.

enough for two—no slices—and they are potently tomatoey, charred, thin-crusted circles of delight. You can also order salads and pastas, but it's the pizza that's exceptional.

260 W. 44th St. (btw. Broadway and Eighth Ave.). www.johnspizzerianyc.com. ℂ **212/391-7560.** Pies $15–$22. Daily 11:30am–11:30pm. Subway: 1, 2, 3, N, Q, R, S to 42nd St.

Larb Ubol ★ THAI   Thought you knew what to expect at a Thai restaurant? Larb Ubol's talented chef/owner, Ratchanee Sumpatboon, will make you think again. She's bringing "Isaan" food to midtown, a cuisine from the Laotian border of Thailand that's as different from the coconut milk-drenched creations most of us have tried as ice cream is from pickles. Instead of sweet, soupy stews, here one dines primarily on salads and dry dishes: Along with noodles and a few grilled items, there are 8 types of refreshing papaya salads, and as many "larbs"—a spicy and happily tart salad of cilantro, meats, scallions, shallots, mint, and lime dressing (my favorite is the crispy pork; in fact, pork stars in a lot of the best dishes here). While not fancy, Larb Ubol is quite cheery, festooned in bright plaids, with a wall full of colorful umbrellas at the back, the kind of homemade decor that shows someone cares (the friendly service telegraphs the same message).

380 Ninth Ave. (btw. 38th and 39th sts.). www.larbubol.com. ℂ **212/564-1822.** Reservations not accepted. Main courses $6–$16. Sun–Thurs 11:30am–10:30pm; Fri–Sat 11:30am–11:30pm. Subway: A, C, E, 7 to 42nd St.

Sapporo ★ JAPANESE   While the ramen here isn't as sublime as it is at Ippudo (p. 95), sumo-sized portions and a right-at-Times Square location make this a great before-theater pick. It's also authentically Japanese: You'll be dining among Midtown's many ex-pats, who make this place their unofficial canteen. My favorite noodle soup/meal: the *tantan-men,* which is topped with a spicy sesame paste.

152 W. 49th St. (btw. Sixth and Seventh aves.). www.sapporo-nyc.com. ℂ **212/869-8972.** Reservations not accepted. Main courses $10–$16. No credit cards. Mon–Sat 11am–11pm; Sun 11am–10pm. Subway: N or R to 49th St.

Xian Famous Foods ★★ CHINESE   If this restaurant were a laboratory—and it looks very much like one, with its sterile white-tiled walls and stools for chairs (casually pulled up to counters built into the wall)—the scientists working here would be studying just how much spice the human tongue can take before it explodes. Yes, this is a restaurant for chili heads, and its menu doesn't lie: "Spicy and tingly beef with hand-ripped noodles," the house specialty ($6), will make your entire body heat up. This is truly authentic Sichuan food, family recipes of a caliber rarely tasted in the U.S. For those who can't take the heat, there are less fiery choices that are nearly as delish. Brave the line to get in: It moves quickly.

24 W. 45th St. (btw. Fifth Ave. and Avenue of the Americas). Reservations not accepted. http://xianfoods.com. Main courses $5–$10. Daily 11am–8:30pm. Check website for other branches around the city. Subway: 4, 5, 6 or S to Grand Central, or B, D, F, or M to Rockefeller Center.

THE NEW YORK deli NEWS

Alas, New York delicatessens are a dying breed. Few are left and few are worth going to anymore. With the following exceptions:

Barney Greengrass, the Sturgeon King 541 Amsterdam Ave. between 86th and 87th streets on the Upper West Side (℃ **212/724-4707**). This unassuming, daytime-only deli has become legendary for its high-quality salmon (sable, gravlax, Nova Scotia, kippered, lox, pastrami—you choose), whitefish, and sturgeon.

Carnegie Deli 854 Seventh Ave. at 55th Street (www.carnegiedeli.com; ℃ **800/334-5606** or 212/757-2245). It's worth subjecting yourself to surly service, tourist-targeted overpricing, and elbow-to-elbow seating for some of the best pastrami in town. But do share: No one person can down one of the meat Cadillacs they call sandwiches here. Open 8am to midnight.

Katz's Delicatessen ★
205 E. Houston St. at Ludlow Street (℃ **212/254-2246**). It's rightly famous for its corned beef and remains fabulously old-world despite its hipster-hot Lower East Side location. For more on Katz's, see p. 73.

Mile End Sandwiches ★★
53 Bond St. at Bowery (www.mileenddeli. com; ℃ **212/529-2990**). Mea culpa! But I prefer the Montreal-style deli sandwiches at this spiffy, white-tiled little takeout place to any of the delis above. Portions are reasonable, and the deli meats—pastrami, salami, corned beef (all cured in Brooklyn)—are first-rate. Some sandwiches are topped with unusual items, such as fried capers or poached eggs, which enhance their flavors immensely.

Russ & Daughters ★★
Uptown and downtown outlets now, but both have uptown sensibilities. See p. 106 for more.

MIDTOWN EAST & MURRAY HILL

If none of the choices below appeal, head to the two superb gourmet food courts area (see p. 88). Otherwise, try Le Relais de Venise L'Entrecote (590 Lexington Ave. at 52nd St.; www.relaisdevenise.com/newyork; ℃ **212/758-3989;** Mon–Fri 11:30am–2:30pm and 5–10:30pm; Sat–Sun 12–3pm and 5–10:30pm) a very traditional Parisian import that serves one meal and one meal only: excellent steak frites (you also get salad).

Expensive

Aquavit ★★ SCANDINAVIAN When Aquavit opened in 1987, the concept behind it seemed radical: a cuisine no one in New York knew (Scandinavian), served in a setting far more elegant than obscure ethnic foods usually enjoyed. Of course, today founding chef Marcus Samuelsson is world famous (as the winner of *Top Chef: Masters;* his replacement Emma Bengtsson is a rising star) as are the pleasures of Nordic cuisine. They're on parade here, on a menu that offers some tasty curveballs (like kelp or dandelion as a side dish) along with such classics as the light-as-light Swedish meatballs with lingonberries, expertly grilled fish dishes, and excellent imported herring. Frankly, I prefer the food here to that at **Agern**, the extremely trendy new resto in Grand Central Station from the founders of Copenhagen's Noma Restaurant.

65 E. 55th St. (btw. Park and Madison aves.). www.aquavit.org. © **212/307-7311.** Lunch mains $26–$38; dinner tasting menus $95, $115, or $145. Mon–Fri noon–2:30pm; Sun–Thurs 5:30–10:30pm; Fri–Sat 5:15–10:45pm. Subway: E or F to Fifth Ave.

Sushi Yasuda ★★★ JAPANESE   Pure Japanese sushi, as it's been made for centuries (that is, no mayonnaise or other fusion touches), cut, dabbed with soy sauce, and patted into shape by master chefs. That's the Zen formula here, and it works so well that the *New York Times* has twice awarded this little restaurant three stars. My advice: Sit at the sushi bar so that you can consult with the small army of white-coated sushi ninjas about which of the 60 fish on offer you should try. And go for the nigiri sushi rather than rolls: With fish this meltingly tender, you don't want it buried in a lot of rice.

204 E. 43rd St. (btw. Second and Third aves.). www.sushiyasuda.com. © **212/972-2001.** Sushi $5–$15 per piece, including gratuities. Mon–Fri noon–2:15pm; Mon–Sat 6–10:15pm. Subway: 4, 5, 6, 7, S to 42nd St.–Grand Central.

Inexpensive/Moderate

Chola ★★ INDIAN   Normally, I'd be suspicious of a restaurant that attempted to serve foods from pretty much every region of the vast country of India. But somehow Chola makes it work, whether sending out perfectly crisp yet supple *dosas* (a Southern Indian pancake, often wrapped around other ingredients); chicken tikka masala that's both moist and flavorful; and the Calcutta dish of lamb and okra cooked in a sweet and sour sauce (a knockout). The lunch buffet is especially recommended; beyond the lunch buffet, waiters walk around with a number of freshly cooked specialties, at no extra charge.

225 E. 58th St. (btw. Second and Third aves.). www.fineindiandining.com. © **212/688-4619.** Main courses $12–$25; lunch buffet $15. Daily noon–3pm and 5–11pm (closes 10:30pm on Sun). Subway: 4, 5, 6, N, or R to 59th St.

Oyster Bar and Restaurant ★ SEAFOOD   Opened in 1913, this Gilded Age holdover in Grand Central Station has changed very little in nearly a century, and the architecture—a series of swooping tiled vaults that always remind me of the grand crypts of some European cathedrals—still impresses. Don't bother going to the restaurant side; you want to be able to see the handwritten menu above the shelling station (on the right as you enter), where the best choices will be laid out. There will be fresh oysters and clams, flown in from all parts of North America; shellfish pan-roasts and stews; and chowders of all kinds (from $5). Ignore the paper menu entirely (for some reason, everything that comes out of the kitchen is overcooked and tepidly sauced); confine yourself to the list of foods that is prepared right at the bar, and you'll have a real old-fashioned feast.

Lower level, Grand Central Station (42nd St. btw. Vanderbilt and Lexington aves.). www.oysterbarny.com. © **212/490-6650.** Average meal $15–$30. Mon–Sat 11:30am–9:30pm; closed Sun. Subway: 4, 5, 6, 7, S to Grand Central Station.

APRIL bloomfield: TRAILBLAZER

Read through this chapter, and you'll see me mention a battalion of chefs, all of whom have made their names cooking up a storm in the Big Apple. I'm chagrined to say there's hardly a woman among them (which I hope says more about the world of NYC cooking than any sort of myopia on my part). But their ranks have been breached in the last decade by a chef who, arguably, serves cuisine that's more testosterone-laden than any of the guys'. April Bloomfield is her name, and heavy, fatty, absolutely scrumptious fare is her game. I find that I can't go to her restaurants too often because the scale scolds me the next morning. But when I do, boy, do I enjoy the experience.

Being from the U.K., her first venture in New York was a British gastropub, called the **Spotted Pig** ★★ (314 W. 11th St. at Greenwich Street; www.thespottedpig. com; ☎ **212/620-0393**). It was the first of its kind in the city, a triumphant announcement to us Yanks that British food didn't have to be, well, awful. Like the gastropubs of London, which have taken classic fare and settings and made them cool, she serves items like crispy pigs' ear salad and squid with roasted fennel to great acclaim.

Her next successful outing was **The Breslin** ★★★ (16 W. 29th St. off the lobby of the Ace Hotel; www.thebreslin. com; ☎ **646/214-5780**), which went even further with the Brit grub, serving up such iconic dishes as Scotch eggs, beef and Stilton pie, blood sausage, and even pigs' foot for two (romance is *not* dead on the NYC dining scene). Once again, huge cheers and huge crowds.

Then Ms. Bloomfield took a new direction—two, actually. First she opened a fish restaurant, the **John Dory Oyster Bar** ★★ (1196 Broadway at 29th St. in the Ace Hotel; www.thejohn dory.com; ☎ **212/792-9000**), which serves the heartiest fish dishes I've ever tasted. And then she turned her attention to Mexican food, with **Salvation Taco** ★★ (inside the Pod 39 Hotel, 145 E. 39th St. between Lexington and Third aves.; www.salvationtaco.com; ☎ **212/865-5800**). I should note that though she's serving tacos and other classic south-of-the-border dishes, she gets creative with them: Those tacos are as likely to be filled with Moroccan lamb or crispy sweetbreads as shredded pork.

Bloomfield's only misstep so far has been 2016's **Salvation Burger** (230 E. 51st St. between Second and Third aves; www.salvationburger.com; ☎ **646/277-7900**), where a cramped space, surly staff, and insanely high prices take the pleasure out of chomping into one of these admittedly good burgers. Bottom line: you can get burgers that are just as good, for less money and in nicer surroundings, elsewhere.

Inexpensive

Luu's Baguette ★ VIETNAMESE   The "Curry Hill" neighborhood may be known for its Indian restaurants, but it's this plain-looking hole-in-the-wall that consistently has a line out the door come lunchtime. Most of those folks are here for the *pho*, arguably the city's best version of that noodle soup dish. It features a complex, rich broth, studded with al dente rice noodles, slivers of onion, bean curd, and scallions. The *pho tai* (my favorite) has the addition of paper thin slices of beef, which are added raw to the broth and cook in about a minute and a half. Luu's also serves *bahn mi* sandwiches and decent dumplings, but it's the *pho* that is (forgive me!) photastic. *Note:* You'll order at the counter and the food will be delivered to your table.

134 East 26th St. (just off Lexington Ave.). www.luusbaguette.com. ℭ **212/679-8881.** Meal-size pho soups $8. Sun–Fri 11am–7:45pm.

UPPER WEST SIDE

The Time Warner Center (at 10 Columbus Circle) holds some of the most celebrated—and pricey—restaurants in the nation. Of those, only the Japanese restaurant **Masa** (www.masanyc.com; ℭ **212/823-9800;** Tues–Fri noon–1pm and 6–9pm; Mon and Sat 6–9pm) is potentially worth the jaw-dropping price tag (hello $1000 meals!). Reserve a month to the day of your intended meal. The iconic restaurant **Tavern on the Green** (in Central Park at 67th St., just off Central Park West; www.tavernonthegreen.com; ℭ **212/877-8684;** daily 11am–11pm) re-opened in May 2014; the food, sadly, is just so-so, but eating in Central Park is a treat, and happily, all of the tables on the open-air terrace are reserved for walk-ins, so you can have a memorable spur-of-the-moment meal here. If good food is more important to you than a bucolic setting, try **The Mermaid Inn ★★** (570 Amsterdam Ave. at 88th St.; www.themermaidnyc.com; ℭ **212/674-5870;** open Sun–Mon 5–10pm, Tues–Fri 5–10:30pm, Sat–Sun 4–10:30pm, and Sun 4–10pm), a seafood specialist with fab lobster rolls, raw bar fare, and grilled fish with all sorts of lovely sauces.

Expensive

Boulud Sud ★★ MEDITERRANEAN   Though Lincoln Center has its own forgettable restaurant on site, this is really the only place in the immediate vicinity of that performance complex where one can have a meal as celebratory as the show is likely to be. That's because the food is downright operatic here, a masterful take on Mediterranean fare, from the south of France to North Africa. You might have octopus grilled *a la plancha* with just the right amount of jerez vinegar, or lamb loin sided by creamy *tzatziki* (a yogurt spread) and dusted with wonderfully sunny harissa spices. The room is elegant enough to wear your concert-going duds to, and the service is friendly and helpful.

20 W. 64th St (near Broadway). www.bouludsud.com. ℭ **212/595-1313.** 3-course pre-theater meal $60; main courses $32–$52. Mon–Fri 11:30am–2:30pm and 5–11pm; Sat 11am–3pm and 5–11pm; Sun 11am–3pm and 5–10pm. Subway: 1 to 66th St.

Moderate

Fishtag ★★ SEAFOOD   Forgive Fishtag for having the most complicated menu in Manhattan, with appetizers mixed willy-nilly with entrees, and certain dishes for no apparent reason on another sheet of paper altogether. The waiter will explain, you'll say "huh," and then you'll sit back in this cozy brownstone restaurant and order what will likely be one of the most satisfying meals you have in the city. That's because Fishtag not only sources wonderfully fresh ingredients, it pairs them in imaginative ways. A platter of cheese or smoked fish, for example, will come with three or four lovely jams and sauces, so that you can build your own taste sensations. Branzino isn't just grilled, but stuffed with headcheese for an over-the-top rich dish. Smoked octopus, another highlight, is served with a puree of hearts of palm, dates, and olives. Or you can have any fish on the menu simply grilled with a touch of lemon. Chef Michael Psilakas, also of **Kefi** (see below), understands the appeal of simple preparations.

222 W. 79th St. (btw. Broadway and Amsterdam). www.fishtagrestaurant.com. © **212/362-7470.** Main courses $10–$30. Sun–Thurs 5–10pm; Fri–Sat 5–11pm; Sat–Sun noon–3pm. Subway: 1 to 79th St.

Inexpensive

Flor de Mayo ★ CUBAN/CHINESE   When Cubans of Chinese heritage came to the city after the Cuban revolution, they brought this hybrid "Chino-Latino" cuisine with them. It's an interesting concept, but the Latino side of the menu is far better than the Chinese here—whether you order the chopped beef with yellow rice, the excellent avocado salad, or Dominican chicken with rice. Solid food and wonderfully affordable.

2651 Broadway (btw. 100th and 101st sts.). www.flordemayo.com. © **212/663-5520** or 212/595-2525. Main courses $9–$24 (most under $18). Daily noon–midnight. Subway: 1 to 103rd St. Also at 484 Amsterdam Ave. (btw. 83rd and 84th sts.)

Jacob's Pickles ★★ SOUTHERN   Pickles, pick-ups, and artisanal beers: Those are the holy trinity at this buzzy tavern. It's become THE place for the neighborhood's singles to scope one another out, and they do so over some of the finest comfort food in town. I'm talking fried chicken atop huge and satisfyingly flaky biscuits; creamy grits with head-on shrimp; and, yes, jars of artisanal pickled foods of all sorts (the beets, the dilly beans, and the eggs are particularly delish). As for the beer, some 20 taps gush out unusual brews from around the Northeast, with a particular emphasis on sour beers. One warning: The noise level in this brick-walled, railroad track of a restaurant is epic, so don't choose Jacob's if you're hoping for a quiet tête-à-tête.

509 Amsterdam Ave. (btw. 84th and 85th sts.). www.jacobspickles.com. © **212/470-5566.** Main courses $14–$21. Mon–Thurs 10am–2am; Fri 10am–4am; Sat 9am–4am; Sun 9am–2am. Subway: 1, B, C to 86th St.

Kefi ★ GREEK   Kefi almost didn't make it into the book this year. Redesigned after a recent water-main break, it's now a much louder, more frenetic place to dine, and the service is decidedly slower (I suspect they crammed more tables in). But since there are few places in the city where you can get food of this quality for such a reasonable price (most mains run less than $20), it squeaked by. So let's talk about that food, which is, in short, primo. Not only does Kefi do the classics well—creamy spreads on piping hot pita, perfectly grilled fish, tender souvlaki—it brings to NYC the more complex Greek dishes that aren't usually seen on this side of the Atlantic. These include a flat pasta dish with braised rabbit and a salty cheese, and lemon-chicken soup

FAMILY-friendly RESTAURANTS

While it's always smart to call ahead to make sure a restaurant has kids' menus and highchairs, you can count on the following to be especially accommodating. And what kid doesn't love pizza? See p. 96 for that.

Here are some other options for the entire family:

Brooklyn Crab ★★ (p. 111)   Before dinner (there's always a wait), parents can belly up to the bar while their kids play minigolf, shoot basketball, clamber around on the restaurant's playground, and generally have a ball. The food is seafood with some kid-friendly options (like mac 'n' cheese), and to get here from Manhattan you take a boat! What could be more fun?

Gyu Kaku ★ (p. 94)   At this Times Square–area Japanese BBQ joint, the food is simple enough for even the most picky kid to like. Better yet, the young 'uns get to cook it themselves, which

most love (though with hot grills set in the tables, this is only recommended for kids over the age of 6).

Norma's ★ (p. 94)   Half-a-dozen types of pancakes (many with ice cream) make breakfast the most fun meal of the day (it's served here for lunch, too).

Robataya ★★★ (p. 76)   My daughters' favorite restaurant: They love the ritual of watching a kneeling chef cook dinner, love the food, and love heading to the Japanese toilet here.

Serendipity 3 ★ (p. 107)   Kids adore this whimsical restaurant and ice-cream shop, which serves up a huge menu of American favorites, followed up by colossal ice-cream treats.

Shake Shack ★★ (p. 91)   Burgers and shakes, consumed outdoors (perhaps in the playground that shares this park)—what could be more tyke-pleasing?

that's studded with velvety rice and veal meatballs. Desserts are also unusual and delish. A warning: The house wine is just one step above cough syrup. Spend a dollar more for vino that won't numb your tongue.

505 Columbus Ave. (at 84th St.). www.kefirestaurant.com. ✆ **212/873-0200.** Main courses $15–$27. Mon–Thurs noon–2:30pm and 5–10pm; Fri noon–2:30pm and 5–11pm; Sat 11am–11pm, Sun 11am–10pm. Subway: B or C to 86th St.

Parm ★ ITALIAN   There's Italian food and then there's Italian-American food. And for decades the latter version was looked down upon as being, well, a bit déclassé. No more. This proudly old-fashioned red-sauce joint does such a superb job with the "canon" of Italian-American staples—chicken parmigiana, sausage and peppers, baked ziti—that you come away feeling like you've experienced something brand-new (and very satisfying). And all in a cute, checkered-tablecloth restaurant that will bring you back, in spirit, to 1950s NYC. This roomy, uptown outlet is sister to the original down in Little Italy.

235 Columbus Ave. (btw. 70th and 71st sts.). www.parmnyc.com. ✆ **212/993-7189.** Main dishes $15–$26. Sun–Thurs 11am–11pm; Fri–Sat 11am–midnight. Subway: 1, 2, 3, C, E to 72nd St.

UPPER EAST SIDE

A number of good downtown restaurants have opened outlets uptown, including **Boqueria** (see p. 74; 1460 Second Ave. between 76th and 77th sts.) and **Toloache** (see p. 95, 166 E. 82nd St. between Lexington and Third aves.).

Expensive

Daniel ★★★ FRENCH Restaurants, as we know, are more than just places to get fed. We use them to celebrate our lives' milestones. Though some may disagree, I can't think of a better place for this important type of meal than Daniel (I celebrated my first wedding anniversary here, so I'm partial). The look is right: a Versailles-opulent setting, with neoclassical architecture and towering vases with fresh flowers. So is the service, formal but unusually kindly; these waiters know that people are here for event eating and do their darndest to keep things festive and happy. And then there's the food, which is inventive yet classic. So a butter-poached abalone will come with a beurre blanc infused with sake; a trio of veal will include the cheek and the sweetbreads and be sided by caramelized artichoke. I've yet to taste anything here that wasn't exquisite.

20 E. 76th St. (btw. Madison and Fifth aves.). www.danielnyc.com. *C* **212/772-2600.** 4-course prix fixe $142, 7-course tasting menu $234. Tues–Sat noon–2:30pm (no lunch Sat July–Aug); daily 5:45–11pm. Subway: 6 to 77th St.

The Mark Restaurant ★★ CONTEMPORARY AMERICAN Some interesting sleights of hand are taking place at The Mark. It's huge and bustling . . . yet feels exclusive. And its menu is mostly what I'd call comfort food—pea soup, Caesar salad, pasta with tomato and basil, burgers, and pizza are all hallmarks—but the food tastes like haute cuisine. Chalk it up to the wizardry of chef/restaurateur Jean-Georges Vongerichten, one of Gotham's most acclaimed foodistos and a master at making meals feel like celebrations. To that end, he's hired an interior decorator who put creature comforts first: tables are set at a civilized distance from one another, guests sink half-an-inch into the ultra-plush chairs, and the lighting flatters. His waitstaff is uniformly gracious and informative. And meals are crafted from the highest quality ingredients, and often involve a surprise or two, which keeps them fresh (crab cakes garnished with grapefruit, say, or a pesto sauce given additional oomph thanks to ground pistachios). Though it is an elegant scene, kids love it and the waiters are good at keeping them entertained.

In the Mark Hotel, 25 E. 77th St. (at Madison Ave.). www.themarkrestaurantnyc.com. *C* **212/606-3030.** Main courses $21–$48. Daily 7am–11pm. Subway: 6 to 77th St.

The Simone ★★ FRENCH When the New York Times listed an Upper East Side eatery as one of the 10 best new restaurants in the city recently, you could just about hear the clanking of jaws hitting the floor. Why? This upper crusty neighborhood is inhabited by people who own two homes (or more!), so it empties out on weekends and in the warm weather months, making it

Uptown & Harlem Restaurants

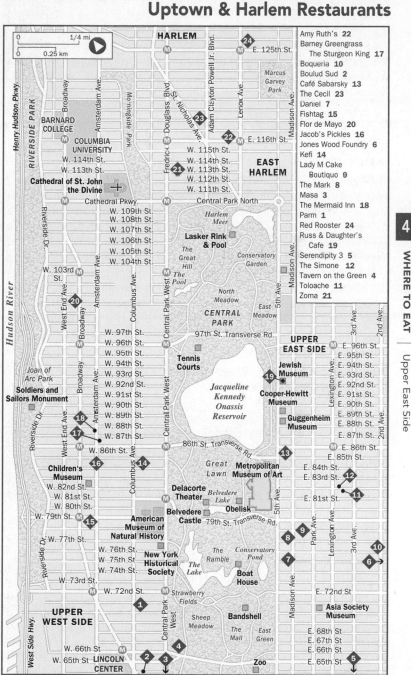

Amy Ruth's **22**
Barney Greengrass
 The Sturgeon King **17**
Boqueria **10**
Boulud Sud **2**
Café Sabarsky **13**
The Cecil **23**
Daniel **7**
Fishtag **15**
Flor de Mayo **20**
Jacob's Pickles **16**
Jones Wood Foundry **6**
Kefi **14**
Lady M Cake
 Boutiquo **9**
The Mark **8**
Masa **3**
The Mermaid Inn **18**
Parm **1**
Red Rooster **24**
Russ & Daughter's
 Cafe **19**
Serendipity 3 **5**
The Simone **12**
Tavern on the Green **4**
Toloache **11**
Zoma **21**

very hard for decent restaurants to stay afloat. Let's hope The Simone can buck the odds, because this tiny charmer has a staff who are expert in keeping the "masters of the universe" who dine here feeling like royalty, and a menu that's just as coddling. I'm talking perfectly cooked and very Gallic proteins, like rabbit brought to life by a peppy dijonnaise sauce or pan-seared flounder with fiddle-head ferns and a delicate citrus beurre blanc. Desserts (like the outrageous rhubarb tart) are so good, even the private fitness trainer set can't resist 'em.

181 82nd St. (btw. Lexington and Third Ave.). www.thesimonerestaurant.com. ℭ **212/772-8861.** Main courses $22–$42. Mon–Thurs 6–9:30pm; Fri-Sat 6–10:30pm. Subway: 4, 5, 6 to 86th St.

Moderate

Café Sbarsky ★ AUSTRIAN Right on Museum Mile and set in a wood-paneled mansion designed by Carrere and Hastings (architects of the New York Public Library at 42nd Street, see p. 144), there are few places as pleasant for breakfast, lunch, or tea in the city. The eatery is actually part of the Neue Galerie, a museum of Austrian and German art (p. 157), so this transplanted Viennese cafe serves all the heavy Teutonic specialties of that city, from bratwurst to creamy spaetzle, along with an assortment of lighter salads and sandwiches. These are all fine, but you really come here for the delicious pastries and Viennese coffee, so strong it will grow hair on your tongue.

Inside the Neue Museum, 1048 Fifth Ave. (at 86th St.). www.neuegalerie.org. ℭ **212/288-0665.** Main courses $6–$30. Thurs–Sun 9am–9pm; Mon and Wed 9am–6pm. Subway: 4, 5, 6 to 86th St.

Jones Wood Foundry ★★★ BRITISH If this restaurant were in my neighborhood, I'd eat here at least once a month, and I can't say that about any other Upper East Side joint. The Foundry reminds us that British food can be quite tasty and British people exceptionally cool (think David Bowie rather than Tony Blair). An extra-long bar greets diners as they enter, followed by a warren of little rooms filled with Brit-a-brac, and a sweet little garden. Sit at the bar so you can flirt with the David Beckham–handsome bartenders as you dine; they have a nice habit of complimenting those people who pick the most British of the selections (like the perfect steak and kidney pie, the crispy Scotch eggs, and kedgeree, a happy saffron rice dish with smoked haddock and a hard-boiled egg).

401 E. 76th St. (near First Ave.). www.joneswoodfoundry.com. ℭ **212/249-2700.** Main courses $11–$34. Daily 11am–4pm and 6–11pm. Subway: 6 to 77th St.

Russ & Daughters Café ★★ DELI After peddling smoked fish, caviar, and other "appetizings" for a full century out of their iconic Lower East Side shop (at 179 E. Houston Street), the family behind Russ & Daughters (yes, they're ancestors of the founders) decided to go into the restaurant biz. And though it seems odd to say this about a company this old: they were an overnight success! One so huge that within less than a year they had branched out from their downtown restaurant to create this winner in the elegant, gleaming

EAT & learn: COOKING CLASSES

Though ideally you should be interested in cooking to take a class, the **Institute of Culinary Education** ★★★ (225 Liberty St. at West St.; www.iceculinary.com; ℂ **212/847-0700**) has another trait that makes it fun for visitors: It's one of the easiest places to meet and actually get to know New Yorkers in the city. That's because since its inception, originally as the Peter Kump School in 1976, the emphasis here has been on "hands-on" classes. You won't be sitting in some dim lecture hall among a group of strangers. Instead, your class will be divided into small groups and for 3 to 4 hours, you'll cook or bake with your partners, poring over recipes, consulting with the teacher, and chatting away. Recreational classes, while serious (the school engages some of the most expert chefs in the city), are tremendously social. And the crowd is well mixed: There are young people in

their 20s; professional types in their 30s, 40s, and 50s; and a smattering of retirees. At night classes, the ratio of men to women is pretty close to 50:50 (in the daytime women predominate).

If you're serious about cooking, you won't find a better school in the city. The instruction here is highly practical, and it aims to teach as much about the principles of cooking as specific recipes. The classes in which I recently sat taught me the technique of putting my thumb and forefinger on the blade of a knife to stabilize it; when it's important to buy expensive ingredients and when it won't matter; and how to choose fresh herbs. I.C.E. offers over a thousand recreational classes a year, more than any other cooking school in the world. Class prices range from $75 to $135 for a good 4 hours of instruction, plus a feast at the end, including wine.

white basement of the Jewish Museum. I can think of few better places for a midday "reset" after a morning of high culture on Museum Mile, because the food here is restorative: bright pink borscht so flavorful it would make your bubbe kvell, the silkiest of smoked salmons lazily draped over a cream cheese-laden bialy, deviled eggs, pickled herring, beet salad, and to top it all off, sinful halvah-flavored ice cream.

1109 Fifth Ave. (at 92nd St.). www.thejewishmuseum.org. ℂ **212/423-3200.** Main dishes $12–$23. Fri and Mon–Wed 11am–5:45pm, Thurs 11am–9pm, Sun 9am–5:45pm. Subway: 4, 5, 6 to 86th St.; 6 to 96th St.

Inexpensive

Serendipity 3 ★ AMERICAN   A good ol'-fashioned ice cream parlor complete with Tiffany-style lamps and a toy shop that you have to pass to get in and out (quite a feat when you have sugar-crazed kids in tow). The dish to order here (one tureen of it will easily satisfy two or three) is the deservedly famous Frrrozen Hot Chocolate, a slushy, utterly satisfying chocolate soup. You can get an idea of the magical effects of that treat if you rent the treacly John Cusack comedy *Serendipity* (filmed here).

225 E. 60th St. (btw. Second and Third aves.). www.serendipity3.com. ℂ **212/838-3531.** Main courses $9–$23; sweets and sundaes $6–$20 (most under $10). Sun–Thurs 11:30am–midnight; Fri–Sat 11:30am–1am. Subway: N or R to Lexington Ave.; 4, 5, or 6 to 59th St.

HARLEM

Moderate

The Cecil ★★ AFRICAN/SOUTHERN   Red Rooster (see below) was the first restaurant since approximately the 1930s to draw diners from around the city, especially those seeking an upscale, gourmet experience. Now a second Harlem contender has come along, and, I'd argue, it's doing its predecessor one better. Founded by chef and opera singer Alexander Smalls, its menu, in his words, explores "the African diaspora." What that means is food from all the corners of the globe where African peoples were flung, either by slavery or other forces. Much of the food is fusion, like the wacky "Hands Only," a utensil-less tour of Trinidad, India, and West Africa on a plate combining roti with rabbit sausage, coconut rice, spicy black-eyed peas, and cinnamon-stewed cauliflower. Other dishes taste utterly authentic, like the superb *moqueca*, a salt cod stew from Brazil. And still other plates seem to have come directly from the chef's imagination, like the fab fried chicken fried rice (it's just what it sounds like). The dining room has a monumental quality to it, thanks to its size and the majestic, oversized portraits of African American women that grace the wood walls. The crowd, as at Red Rooster, is wonderfully diverse.

210 W. 118th St. (at St. Nicholas Ave.). www.thececilharlem.com. ✆ **212/866-1262.** Main courses $21–$35. Mon–Thurs 5pm–midnight; Fri 5pm–1am; Sat 11am–1am; Sun 11am–10pm. Subway: 2, 3, B, C to 116th St.

Red Rooster ★ SCANDINAVIAN/SOUTHERN   A destination restaurant, Red Rooster was, for its first 2 years in business, the only reason many well-heeled New Yorkers ever came to Harlem. Three words why: Chef Marcus Samuelsson (formerly of Aquavit, see p. 98, he won *Top Chef Masters* in 2012). So is it "all that"? I'm on the fence. Yes, it has a wonderful atmosphere (it's one of the few truly multiracial social scenes in the city), a hopping bar, live music in the basement, and a handsome decor. Most of the appetizers—which, like the rest of the menu, range from Southern classics to African fare to Scandinavian cuisine—are delish. But when it comes to the pricier main dishes I'm inevitably disappointed, especially in the signature yard bird (fried chicken, very dry), and Helga's meatballs (too heavy). Since I once lived in the neighborhood for 6 months, I ate there a dozen times, and eventually started making my meals entirely of appetizers. If you do the same, I think you'll enjoy it immensely.

310 Lenox Ave. (btw. 125th and 126th sts.). www.redroosterharlem.com. ✆ **212/792-9001.** Main courses $18–$33. Mon–Thurs 11:30am–3:30pm and 4:30–10:30pm; Fri 11:30–3:30pm and 4:30–11:30pm; Sat 10am–3pm and 4:30–11:30pm; Sun 10am–3pm and 4:30–10pm. Subway: 2, 3 to 125th St.

Inexpensive

Amy Ruth's ★ AMERICAN REGIONAL   Amy Ruth's was named for the grandmother of owner Carl Redding, and he'll readily admit that it's her recipes that he uses in the dining room. But part of what makes the food here so good is the freshness of the ingredients: very green veggies, perfect sweet potatoes, and honey (for the honey-fried chicken) that comes from beehives on the roof. You'll also enjoy dining here if you know anything about New York politics, as this is the unofficial clubhouse for Harlem's political elite, many of whom have dishes named for them. It's not unusual to see State Senator Bill Perkins when you're eating salmon with peach butter named for him, or Al Sharpton when you're munching on "his" chicken and waffles platter.

113 W. 116th St. www.amyruthsharlem.com. ℰ **212/280-8779.** Main courses $10–$20. Mon 11am–11pm, Tues–Thurs 8:30am–11pm, Fri 8:30am–5:30am, Sat 7:30am–5:30am, Sun 7:30am–11pm. Subway: 2, 3, B, C to 116th St.

Zoma ★★ ETHIOPIAN   For those who've never tried it, Ethiopian food is a true culinary adventure. Long-simmering stews of lamb or chicken, beef tartars (called *keftas*), and grilled beef dishes (*tibs*) are dusted with a slow-burning spice mix called *berbere*, giving many dishes an eye-opening wallop. Onion, ginger, and cinnamon, important supporting characters, lend sweetness and depth of flavor. And because the Orthodox Ethiopian religious calendar requires numerous days be set aside for meat-free fasts, lentils, collard greens, potatoes, and other vegetables are the focus of a number of dishes, making this an excellent cuisine for vegetarians. Most fun of all, Ethiopian cuisine banishes the fork. Instead, your dishes are served on a pizza-sized round of *injera*, a winningly sour, spongy bread, that diners use to scoop up their meals. Yup, you get to eat with your hands! Though some might disagree, I'd say that Zoma serves the best Ethiopian in NYC, in a spare but elegant room.

2084 Frederick Douglas Blvd. (at 113th St.). www.zomanyc.com. ℰ **212/662-0620.** Main courses $14–$24. Cash payments and American Express only. Mon–Fri 5–11pm, Sat–Sun noon–11pm. Subway: B, C to Cathedral Pkwy.

THE OUTER BOROUGHS
Brooklyn

Pizza is big in Brooklyn. Beyond Juliana's (see p. 131), the borough's other superstars are **Totonno's** at 1524 Neptune Ave. between West 15th and West 16th streets in Coney Island (ℰ **718/372-8606**), and **Roberta's,** a sprawling party pizzeria which uses a wood-burning stove, in Bushwick at 261 N. Moore St. (www.robertaspizza.com; ℰ **718/417-1118**).

EXPENSIVE

Chef's Table at Brooklyn Fare ★★★ GOURMET AMERICAN   An oddly glamorous culinary experience awaits those who get one of the few coveted reservations at the Chef's Table at Brooklyn Fare. Seating (for just 18) is in a gleaming steel kitchen at a D-shaped counter. The intensely focused chef Cesar Ramirez and his acolytes, er, sous chefs, perform their magic at the front of the room, moving like precisely choreographed Stepford cooks around the massive stove (really, they're an eerily focused group; in the course of the 2½-hour meal, not a plate clinked, a pot rattled, or, it seemed, a chef spoke a word). I can't tell you what I ate because it's forbidden to photograph the food or even take notes here (I got caught trying). I remember, however, hearing the names of fish I had never encountered before ("blue nosed"-this, and "shark grin"-that) during the 14-or-so-course extravaganza. We were also plied with caviar, gold leaf, foie gras, and many other pricey delicacies, which, I suppose, justified the $255 tasting menu cost (that price does not include alcohol). All in all, it was an unusual, only-in-New-York type of experience that I'd love to do again . . . especially if someone else foots the bill. **One warning:** Brooklyn Fare has a dress code, so don't show up in shorts and flip flops, as my husband did, or you'll find yourself having to run to the nearby Bloomingdales for a new outfit.

200 Schemerhorn St. (btw. Bond and Hoyt sts.), Downtown Brooklyn. www.brooklyn fare.com/pages/chefstable. ℂ **718/243-0050.** Call for a reservation at 10:30am sharp, 6 weeks to the day before you want to dine. Tasting menu $306 including gratuities. Subway: A, C, G to Hoyt–Schemerhorn.

Peter Luger Steakhouse ★★★ STEAK
Grumpy waiters? Check. Sawdust on the floor? But of course! Beef so tender you can use a butter knife on it? Well, that's why people are still coming to this iconic steakhouse set in a barren stretch of Williamsburg, Brooklyn. It's still hard to beat a meal here, and that goes for everything from the beef to the lamb chops to the legendary creamed spinach. Two important notes: Credit cards aren't accepted, so be sure to bring wads of cash. And you'll need to reserve well in advance to get a table.

178 Broadway (at Driggs Ave.), Williamsburg. www.peterluger.com. ℂ **718/387-7400.** Main courses (steaks) $49 and up. Mon–Thurs 11:45am–9:45pm; Fri–Sat 11:45am–10:45pm; Sun 12:45–9:45pm. Subway: J, M, or Z to Marcy Ave.

Semilla ★★★ GOURMET AMERICAN
An open kitchen with a long bar at which 18 diners sit, for a super-gourmet meal cooked as they watch—it's a formula that Chef's Table at Brooklyn Fare (see p. 109) pioneered. So it shouldn't come as any surprise that chef/owner Jose Ramirez-Ruiz was once an employee at that celebrated eatery. But other than these basics, the two restaurants couldn't be more dissimilar. The price here, while not cheap, is a third of what you'll pay at Brooklyn Fare; and the atmosphere is far more casual, with no dress code and perky salsa music thrumming in the background. The main difference, though, is that Ramirez-Ruiz is a vegetable whisperer, so greens take center stage. He can coax flavors from a carrot or an asparagus stalk that are nothing short of miraculous, especially when paired with the unusual items that he gets from foragers (knotweed, a sort of green rhubarb, and geranium oil were game changers at my last dinner). The menu changes based on seasonality, but if you're lucky you'll get a winter salad topped with cocoa nubs and warm crème fraîche that's as rich as any dessert; or the beet tart, its sweetness cut by a smoked trout. Desserts, based around fruits, are spectacular as well.

160 Havermeyer St. (at South Second St.), Williamsburg. www.semillabk.com. ℂ **718/782-3474.** Tasting menu $85. Tues–Sat, 2 seatings nightly (in the 6pm hour and btw. 8:30 and 9:15pm). Subway: L to Bedford Ave.

MODERATE

Brooklyn Crab ★ SEAFOOD   The delightful quirkiness of Brooklyn is in full flower at this three-story crab shack. On the ground level are several out-door bars surrounded by a minigolf course, carnival games, and a small play-ground. All the games are free, so groups of laid-back families come here, the parents enjoying a beer while their youngsters work off energy before dinner. Upstairs are two stories of open-sided dining with one fully open patio, all with glorious views of the Statue of Liberty. Diners are served all sorts of seafood from heaping piles of crabs (which one attacks with a mallet) to fish and chips and Maryland crab cakes. Just as much fun is how you get here from Manhat-tan: Diners head down to the South Street Seaport where they hop the free "IKEA NY Water Taxi" (the restaurant is not far from that behemoth store) and take a 15-minute boat ride, seeing all the sights of Lower Manhattan on the way. *One tip:* The hostess seating guests inevitably tells everyone there's a 2-hour wait. I've been told that each of the five times I've been here, and have never waited more than 50 minutes (in fact, my kids are usually in the middle of a game, and complain that we were called to dinner too quickly!).

24 Reed St., Red Hook. www.brooklyncrab.com. ✆ **718/643-CRAB** [2722]. Main courses average $15–$25, though some seafood dishes are market priced and can go higher. Sun–Thurs 11:30am–10pm; Fri–Sat 11:30am–midnight. Subway: G or F to Smith–9th St.

La Vara ★★ SPANISH   NYC has no dearth of terrific tapas joints but this one has an unusual focus: the recipes left in the Spanish canon from the days when Moors and Jews inhabited the Iberian peninsula. It's an intriguing con-cept, one that results in wonderfully appetizing dishes, like juicy lamb meat-balls atop mint yogurt; Persian cucumber and grain salad with tahini; and fried artichokes with garlic aioli (they reminded me of the famed Jewish-Italian artichoke preparation). Cocktails, too, are splendid here, as is the spirited atmosphere, thanks to the lovely staff and a very local crowd of regulars. An ideal place to head after an evening stroll in Brooklyn Bridge Park.

268 Clinton St. (at Verandah Pl.), Cobble Hill, Brooklyn. www.lavara.com. ✆ **718/422-0065**. Main courses $17–$28. Mon–Thurs 5–11pm, Fri 5pm–midnight, Sat 11:30am–3:30pm and 5pm–midnight, Sun 11:30am–3:30pm and 5–10pm. Subway: F, G to Bergen St., 2, 3, 4, 5 to Borough Hall.

Shalom Japan ★★★ FUSION   Chutzpah! That's what it takes to marry what is arguably the world's heaviest cuisine (so-called Jewish food) with the world's lightest (Japanese cuisine). The concept came about through a collab-oration of two young chefs—Sawako Okochi and Aaron Israel (and no, I'm not making those names up)—both of whom worked their way up the ladder in some of the most prestigious kitchens in NYC before starting this restaurant together. The food is, in a word, revelatory. After eating here, you'll realize that ramen soup should *always* have matzoh balls in it and lox is meant to be sided, not by bagels, but by sushi rice, pickled daikon, and seasoned seaweed. Other exquisite mashups on the menu include the "spring Jewish egg" (a soft-boiled egg, deep-fried inside of falafel and plated atop a gingery pea sauce); and Japanese pancakes with takoyaki sauce (it's a bit like a ketchupy Worcestershire), corned tongue, and sauerkraut. Next step for this little wonder restaurant: Create decor that's as quirky as the food (right now the brick-walled decor is a tad too generic for a concept this outrageous).

310 S. 4th St. (at Rodney St.), Williamsburg. www.shalomjapannyc.com. ℃ **718/388-4012.** Main courses $15–$32. Tues–Wed and Sun 5:30–10pm; Thurs–Sat 5:30–11pm. Subway: J, M, Z to Marcy Ave, L to Metropolitan, or G to Broadway.

Talde ★★ ASIAN FUSION   On first glance, Talde looks like so many other Brooklyn restaurants: pressed-tin ceiling, large marble bar at the front, decorative carved wooden trim everywhere. But when you look a bit closer, you realize that Buddha is carved into the wood, along with other Asian symbols. And the menu contains all sorts of unlikely marriages, like pretzel-crusted pork dumplings (spectacular!) and yuzu guacamole (which turns out to be avocado and yuzu mashed together and slathered, finger-food–style, over cakes of crispy rice). Other tongue thrillers include a creamy tom kha soup with lobster, a pad Thai with bacon and oysters, and the *halo halo* dessert—shaved ice with a changing mix of toppings (when we were there, it was fresh berries, Captain Crunch, and balls of tapioca, which sounds odd but tasted fabulous). My one complaint: The waiters push customers to order more than they need.

369 Seventh Ave. (at 11th. St.), Park Slope. www.taldebrooklyn.com. ℃ **347/916-0031.** Main courses $15–$27. Mon–Wed 5–11pm; Thurs–Fri 5pm–midnight; Sat 11am–3pm and 5pm–midnight; Sun 11am–3pm and 5–11pm. Subway: F to Seventh Ave.

INEXPENSIVE

Frankie's Spuntino 457 ★★ ITALIAN   "How do you like your meatballs?" the waitress innocently asked the guy sitting at the table next to me. "They're pissing me off," he growled. "They're better than my grandmother's." Then he stabbed his fork into one of the three tennis-ball–sized orbs in front of him, and silently ate on. I did the same, because, like most everyone who eats here, I had come specifically for the balls, doused in a richly tomatoey sauce with pine nuts, and so good, they don't need spaghetti. But meatballs are not the end-all of the menu, which does extremely well by other classic Italian-American dishes (like the sausage and peppers), as well as by the items that wouldn't be considered part of this cuisine (like a luscious kale crostini, with a generous helping of sriracha aioli). All is served up by a friendly staff, in a cozy, brick-walled, pressed-tin ceiling joint with few pretensions and even less elbow room. *Two notes:* Choose seats in the garden out back when the weather's nice; it has a much less crowded feeling than the interior of the restaurant. And if you're a light eater, know that they will serve a one-meatball portion, even though it's not on the menu.

457 Court St. (btw. 4th Place and Luquer St.), Carroll Gardens. www.frankiesspuntino. com. ℃ **718/403-0033.** No reservations. Main courses $14–$21. Sun–Thurs 11am–11pm; Fri–Sat 11am–midnight. Subway: F or G to Carroll St. Also at 570 Hudson St. (btw. Perry and W. 11th sts.), ℃ **212/924-0818;** Sun–Thurs 11am–11pm, Fri–Sat 11am–midnight; subway F or M to Delancey St.

THE real LITTLE ITALY

You'll notice there are no listings for Manhattan's "Little Italy" in this book. That's because this once vibrant neighborhood is a shadow of its onetime self, with few recommendable Italian restaurants. Smart foodies head instead to Arthur Avenue in the Bronx, an authentic Italian enclave that's been going strong since it was settled by Neapolitan immigrants in the late 1800s.

There are two ways to "do" Arthur Avenue. You can either "graze" it lightly or have a real sit-down feast. For a simple snack, there's a wondrous variety of options. You might start with a half-dozen bocconcini (creamy, salty, mozzarella balls, at **Casa Mozzarella,** 64 East 187th St., just off Arthur Ave.), and then gulp down some freshly opened oysters—either sweet west coasters or briny east coast varieties—from the ice-covered tables outside **Cosenza's Fish Market** (2354 Arthur Ave.). Or else you might grab a slice from **Full Moon Pizza** (600 East 187th St.), washed down with the local brew at the **Bronx Beer Hall** (in the Arthur Avenue Market at 2344 Arthur Ave., a covered market created by the legendary Mayor Fiorello LaGuardia). And then for dessert, nothing beats cannolis at **Madonna Bakery,** which has been filling the morning-baked shells fresh for each customer since 1916.

If you decide to go the full-scale restaurant route, you have a ton of options. I'm partial to **Roberto's** (603 Crescent Ave., just around the corner from Arthur Ave.; Mon–Thurs noon–2:30pm and 5–11pm, Fri–Sat noon–2:30pm and 4:30–10pm; ✆ 718/733-9503), because I'm wild for their house specialty: different types of pasta placed into tinfoil and then set over a grill, which gives the noodles a smoky and at points crispy taste. But pizzeria **Zero Otto Nove** (2357 Arthur Ave.; Tues–Thurs noon–2:30pm, Fri–Sat noon–2:30pm and 4:30–11pm, and Sun 1pm–9pm) is also beloved by many—its pies emerge from a beehive oven imported from "The Boot." For still another old-school red-sauce alternative, head to **Enzo's** (2339 Arthur Ave.; Mon–Sat noon–10pm, Sun noon–9pm), which features grandmotherly service and classic Italian-American cooking.

To reach Arthur Avenue, take the B, D or 4 subway to Fordham Road and walk from there (about 15 min.) or a Metro-North Train to Fordham (Metro-North leaves from Grand Central Station).

Juliana's ★★ PIZZA   The secret New Yorkers keep from the tourists is this: famous Grimaldi's Pizzaria is an imposter (it is tourists *only* in the huge line out front). If you want to eat the *real* pies of pizza impresario Patsy Grimaldi, you need to go to Juliana's next door. Patsy and Carol Grimaldi sold the original a decade ago, but when the new owners moved to a larger place up the block in 2012, they decided to reclaim the first space, with its superb coal oven. So try the real deal: Juliana's crusts are thin, with nicely charred edges; its sauce is just sweet enough; its cheese is always melting on the pies; and if you ask for delicate adds, like arugula, they'll put it on after the pizza is cooked, so that it doesn't lose its crisp. *One tip:* The lines here get loooong, too, so if you just want 'za (they also do excellent salads and pastas), skip the line and head inside to ask for pizza to go. Then picnic in Brooklyn Bridge Park.

19 Old Fulton St. (btw. Front St. and Elizabeth Place), DUMBO. www.julianaspizza.com. ✆ **718/596-2700.** Small pizza (big enough for 3 adults) from $17; full pies only. Subway: A, C to High St., 2, 3 to Clark St.

Tom's Restaurant ★★★ BREAKFAST   Pair a trip to the nearby Brooklyn Museum with a meal at the classic diner, Tom's. Just slide into one of the vinyl booths, marvel at how many American flags a place this small can hold (interspersed with all sorts of commemorative plates and other knick-knacks), and order up one of the best breakfasts in town. You can do so at breakfast time, or at lunch, because the overstuffed omelets, French toast, smoked sausage, and other morning fare are served all day long, as they should be (they're damn good). My favorite: the lemon ricotta pancakes, which taste like the best lemon poppy seed muffin you've ever had, but fluffier. This is also the place to try NYC's fast-disappearing staple: the egg cream soda. And service is the friendliest in the borough.

782 Washington Ave. (at Sterling Pl.), Prospect Heights. www.tomsbrooklyn.com. ℱ **718/636-9736.** No reservations (lines on weekends). Main courses $6–$15, most in the $6–$9 range. Daily 6am–4pm. Subway: 2, 3 to Grand Army Plaza.

Zizi Limona ★★ MIDDLE EASTERN   The food is just marvelous at Zizi Limone, drawn from the family recipes of chef Nir Mesika (of Moroccan heritage, he grew up in Israel) as well as, one gathers, from his fertile imagination. He takes such classic dishes as *shakshuka* (an Israeli tomato stew with a fried egg on top) and elevates it with strips of perfectly medium-rare skirt steak; or slowly roasts oxtail for 5 or 6 hours before encasing it in a filo dough shell and serving it with two delicious dipping sauces. Even such classics as a lamb kebab sandwich taste special here, as they're topped with a fabulous hummus and served in fresh-from-the-oven pita breads. Don't you dare skip dessert: Mesika's grandfather was a baker for the king of Morocco, and he turns out pastries that are as light as a dream. A final reason to head here? It gets you into the heart of artsy Willliamsburg, Brooklyn, a delightful place for a stroll.

129 Havemeyer St. (btw. 1st and Grand sts.), Williamsburg. www.zizilimona1.com. ℱ **347/763-1463.** Main courses $13–$23. Mon–Thurs 4–11pm, Fri noon–midnight, Sat 11am–midnight, Sun 11am–11pm. Subway: L to Bedford or J to Marcy Ave.

Queens

For a more sprawling—and some would say authentic—Chinatown experience than you'll find in Manhattan, you need to head to the very last stop of the 7 subway line and roam the streets of Flushing. Some of the finest eats here, all cheap, include the spicy wontons at **White Bear** (135-02 Roosevelt Ave. No. 5 at Prince St.); the scallion pancakes and soup dumplings at **NanXiang** (38-12 Prince St. near 39th Ave.); and anything with the red chili sauce at **Spicy & Tasty** (39-07 Prince St. near 39th Ave.).

MODERATE

Casa Enrique ★★ MEXICAN   For 8 hours each day, the spices, chocolate, plantains, almonds, raisins and sesame seeds that form the basis for Casa Enrique's *mole* bubble and blend on the stove, creating one of the most complex, rich, not-too-sweet iterations of this dish that Gotham has ever experienced. Not all get to try it, however, as the temptations here are many, from the guajillo-pepper marinated ribs, to *ceviche* crafted from fluke caught in nearby Montauk, to the creamy enchiladas that chef/owner Cosme Augilar recreates from his mother's favorite recipe. Originally from the state of Chiapas, Aguilar is bringing a sophisticated version of southern Mexican food to this near-to-Manhattan, gentrifying section of Queens (it's just one subway stop from Grand Central Station), His insistence that this type of food get respect is also apparent in the décor, which is minimalist in the extreme—white walls with no decorations, a stainless steel bar, and painted-white wood tables—all the better to set off the vivid colors of the food. *One warning:* I'm not the only one who knows about Casa Enrique, so it is imperative that you get advance reservations if you want to dine here (though there is some bar seating).

5 18 19th Ave. (near Vernon Blvd.). www.casaenrique.com. © **347/448-6040.** Main courses $10–$26. Mon–Fri 5pm–midnight, Sat–Sun 11am–4pm and 5pm–midnight. Subway: 7 to Vernon Blvd.

M. Wells Dinette ★★ AMERICAN   In 2011, M. Wells Dinette was the best-reviewed new restaurant in all of New York City. But that wasn't enough to keep it from losing its lease and abruptly closing. It has re-emerged as the in-house restaurant for the Museum of Modern Art's Queen's outpost, "P.S. 1," with all its moxie intact, though its hours (sadly) are cut to jibe with the museum's schedule (see below). Still, there are few finer lunch places in the city, especially if your tastes run to creatively elegant concoctions liked fluke crudo on a bed of smoked sour cream with gooseberries and jalapeno; or pillowy ricotta gnocchi with a cheese foam, a red sauce, and huge, juicy chunks of lobster. Those were just two of the dishes on offer when I last visited; Quebecois chef Hugue Dufour changes the menu daily (desserts are mighty fine, too). Taking its cue from the fact that the museum was a working public school until the mid-'60s, the restaurant is designed to look like a classroom, down to the little nooks in some of the "dining desks" that hold colored pens and pads of graph paper. Flipping through the notebook in my "desk" I came across a cartoon of a goggle-eyed diner with the words "Stop staring at me, weirdo, and keep eating." That's sage advice here. *One note:* While I recommend visiting the museum, you don't have to do so to dine here.

Inside P.S. 1, 22–25 Jackson Ave. (at 46th St.). www.momaps1.org/about/mwells. © **718/768-1800.** Main courses $12–$26. Thurs–Mon noon–6pm. Subway: E, M, 7 to Court Square or G to 21st St.

INEXPENSIVE

Sripraphai Thai Restaurant ★★★ THAI   Thai food the way it actually tastes in Thailand, so the baby corn actually has a flavor, ingredients like dried catfish (crispy, salty, and addictive) are common, and almost all the dishes perfectly balance sweet with sour, salty with spicy. On that last note: Take it seriously when they ask you how hot you want your meal. After my last visit I almost walked into a telephone pole, I was so lightheaded from the powerful spices I'd just eaten. Among the many recommended dishes are the green duck curry with pineapple, ground pork with lime and peanuts, and duck salad. Expect a wait, as the restaurant doesn't take reservations and it's always jammed. By the way, the name is pronounced *see-PRA-pie*.

64-13 39th Ave. (near 64th St.). www.sripraphairestaurant.com. © **718/899-9599.** No reservations; cash only. Main courses $8–$18, most in the $9–$10 range. Thurs–Tues 11:30am–9:30pm. Subway: R to 165th St. or 7 to Flushing/Main St.

Taverna Kyclades ★★ GREEK   Nobody will be smashing plates, but other than that, eating here is a Zorba-rific experience, thanks to the all-Greek waitstaff and the seafood, simply prepared, that tastes like it jumped out of the bluest of seas and right onto your plate. Start with a tasting of spreads (they're top-notch), make your way next to the grilled octopus (Taverna's signature dish), and end with some sort of fresh fish (your choice) sided by their famous lemon potatoes. The only downer here? The Taverna is the most popular restaurant in the Greek section of Queens and doesn't take reservations, so come early or be prepared to wait.

3307 Ditmars Blvd. (at 33rd St.). www.tavernakyclades.com. © **718/545-8666.** No reservations. Main courses $13–$25, more for larger, shareable whole fish. Mon–Thurs noon–11pm; Fri–Sat noon–11:30pm; Sun noon–10:30pm. Subway: N or Q to Astoria/Ditmars.

EXPLORING NEW YORK CITY

Ask New Yorkers about their feelings for their city, and they will often respond, "There's just one New York." By that they mean: one city so full—of museums (more than 40 major ones); historical sites; world-famous institutions; parks; zoos; universities; lectures; concerts and recitals; theaters for opera, musicals, drama, and dance; architectural highlights; presidents' homes; and kooky galleries—that its diversions are limitless, and you will never be bored. If you had the speed and stamina of a Usain Bolt, you would still be hard-pressed to cover all of the attractions in several months of touring.

Because your own time is more limited than that, I'm confining my coverage to two categories of sights in this chapter: First, the city's "iconic" attractions, by which I mean the places universally associated with Gotham—the headliners that make the city so massively popular. These include the major museums (the Metropolitan Museum of Art and the Whitney, just to name two); the great historical and architectural sites (including Grand Central Station and the Brooklyn Bridge); and, in a category all its own, New York's most sobering site: the 9/11 Memorial and Museum.

Second are the less famous attractions that, if they were magically transported to almost any other city in America, would instantly become that city's top cultural draw and bring it acclaim, prestige, and millions of dollars in tourist revenue (no, I do not exaggerate). These attractions—such as the Tenement Museum, the Museum of the Moving Image, The Frick Collection—while lesser known, can add immensely to a New York City visit. And therefore it's important occasionally to step off the tourist treadmill (Empire State, Times Square, Statue of Liberty) and try one of the so-called secondary sights. If you have the time, visit at least one of the places you might never have heard of before picking up this book.

How do you plan (and time) a satisfying itinerary? I've given you a slew of suggestions in chapter 2 of this book. This chapter contains individual sights which I've grouped by area. I do so because I truly believe you'll enjoy your visit more if you're not running yourself ragged, dashing to different parts of the city each day.

5

Instead, divide Manhattan into three sections (downtown, midtown and uptown) and create a daily plan that keeps you in one of those areas for a full day, or in one of our fabulous boroughs (again for the day). You'll see more that way, you'll have time to enjoy an unhurried meal, and you'll have the kinds of serendipitous sidewalk encounters that don't happen when you're stressed out by subway connections, hop-on bus pickup schedules, and attraction closing times.

NEW YORK CITY'S TOP SIGHTS

American Museum of Natural History (p. 158)
Brooklyn Bridge (p. 120)
The Bronx Zoo (p. 163)
The Brooklyn Museum (p. 165)
The Cathedral of St. John the Divine (p. 160)
Central Park (p. 172)
The Cloisters (p. 161)
The Cooper Hewitt Museum (p. 150)
Ellis Island National Museum of Immigration (p. 120)
Empire State Building (p. 140)
The Frick Collection (p. 150)
Grand Central Station (p. 141)
Guggenheim Museum (p. 155)

Intrepid Sea, Air, and Space Museum (p. 145)
Metropolitan Museum of Art (p. 155)
The Morgan Library (p. 143)
Museum of Modern Art (p. 146)
Museum of the Moving Image (p. 168)
New York Public Library (p. 144)
9/11 Memorial and Museum
One World Observatory (p. 125)
Rockefeller Center (p. 147)
Statue of Liberty (p. 127)
Times Square (p. 149)
The Tenement Museum (p. 132)
The United Nations (p. 145)
Wall Street and the New York Stock Exchange (p. 130)
The Whitney Museum (p. 134)

Downtown Financial District/New York Harbor

9/11 Memorial and Museum ★★★ HISTORIC SITE/MUSEUM   For well over two millennia, humans have been telling one another stories of the dangers of looking back at evil or death. Lot's wife turned to a pillar of salt because she dared glance over her shoulder into the maw of destruction. Orpheus lost his beloved forever for the same reason: He turned around before he'd reached the realm of light. And in a case of real life imitating iconic tales, on September 11, 2001, those people who were on the streets surrounding the Twin Towers when they fell had to run for their lives to escape the deadly debris cloud that pursued them with unrelenting fury. "Don't look back, just run" one bystander yells to another in one of the many moving videos at the 9/11 Memorial and Museum.

For over a decade it looked like the survivors, politicians, and others who had vowed to create this museum might not actually have the *ability* to look back at that world-changing September day. Bickering over every element of the design and contents of the museum caused endless delays and became newspaper fodder; controversies seemed to erupt daily over such issues as the high cost of entry to the museum, its portrayal of the Muslim religion, even the fact that it had a gift shop.

Yet despite all this, the 9/11 Museum has emerged as what may be one of the most important history museums in the United States. Out of all the chaos and well-publicized postponements comes an institution that seamlessly blends design and content, transporting visitors back, in a very visceral way, to the day in which four separate, airplane-fueled attacks killed close to 3,000 people (the museum relates the stories not just of the Twin Towers, but also of the Pentagon attack and Flight 93).

After a thorough security check (make sure you allot 15 minutes minimum for that and the entry line), visitors descend down, down, down, into this underground museum. It's a fitting metaphor not only for the escape route that the Twin Towers survivors had to take when fleeing by stair (a remnant of the famous "survivors stair" is to the right of the museum's staircase at one point) but also for the darkness the attacks plunged the United States into. At the bottom of the final staircase, to the left (oddly, as most visitors want to turn right), is the museum's beating heart: its history exhibition. A masterful mix of video, audio clips from survivors, wall text, and poignant artifacts—the burnt-edged papers that fluttered from the Towers, children's clothing recovered from Flight 93—the exhibit manages to bring to life the personal stories of those who lived or died that day, while also explaining some of the forces that led to the attacks. A thought-provoking section explores the rise of Al Qaeda (you even see a brick from Bin Laden's Abbottabad compound). The lingering health issues that survivors and first responders still struggle with is discussed, as is the issue of who, beyond the attackers, should be held accountable. Museumgoers also see the famous Ground Zero cross (metal beams of the structure that were broken off into this Christian symbol), a squashed fire truck, and the Memorial Room, which tells the story and shows the face of every person who died on 9/11.

I, for one, am glad that the founders of the museum were finally able to look back and to do so in such a clear-eyed, multifaceted way. I don't know if the museum has one over-arching point to make, but it offers revelations at every turn about our recent history and the men and women who shaped it. And everywhere are boxes of tissues (refilled every hour, according to the guard I spoke with), as the museum is ultimately quite an emotional experience.

Surrounding the museum is the 8-acre **Memorial Plaza,** which features two reflecting pools and waterfalls, located in the 1-acre footprints of the individual towers. Each reflecting pool is surrounded by a brass parapet where the names of the victims of both the 9/11 and February 1993 bombings are engraved and arranged in order according to where they worked, close to their co-workers or friends, or wherever their families thought they could best be located.

Entrances at intersections of Liberty & Greenwich sts., Liberty & West sts, or West & Fulton sts. www.911memorial.org. ℂ **212/266-5211.** Museum admission $24; $18 seniors, U.S. veterans, and students; $15 children 7–17; free for those 6 and under; free on Tuesdays 5–8pm. Additional costs for museum admission with guided tour. Memorial park open daily 7:30am–9pm; museum open Sun–Thurs 9am–8pm and Fri-Sat 9am–9pm; last entry 2 hrs before museum closes. Subway: A, C, J, Z, 2, 3, 4, or 5 to Fulton St. 2, 3 to Park Place, E to World Trade Center, R to Rector St.

Brooklyn Bridge ★★★ ICON/ARCHITECTURE New York has a grand Gothic cathedral in St. Patrick's, but for many New Yorkers, the city's true cathedral, the point at which earth and water join and thrust upwards toward the heavens, is the Brooklyn Bridge.

To fully appreciate its dazzle, you must **walk the bridge.** Start on the Manhattan side and walk first to one of the great Gothic towers that hold up the bridge's cables. It took 7 years and massive heartbreak to build these two structures. When architect and immigrant John A. Roebling was surveying the area in 1869 (just 2 weeks after the project had been approved), a ferry accidentally rammed into the place where he was standing, crushing his foot. He died of lockjaw 3 weeks later. His son Washington took over and created a method of sending pneumatic caissons—basically large pressurized pine boxes into which compressed air was pumped to keep the water out—down to the river bed. This allowed six workers at a time to descend and lay the foundation for these towers. Because they didn't have a good understanding of the effects of underwater pressure on the human body (known to scuba divers as "the bends"), many were killed or injured in the caissons, including Washington Roebling. In 1872 he had to be carried out of the chamber, partially paralyzed. He remained an invalid for the rest of his life, and his wife Martha took over directing the job, learning advanced mathematics in the process. Washington watched the progress of the bridge through binoculars from his apartment, and when the bridge was competed after 13 years, Grover Cleveland (then president), the governor, and the mayor all came to his home to personally thank him for his efforts.

Walk to the center of the bridge and take in the spectacular views of both Brooklyn and Manhattan. When the bridge was built, its span—1,595 feet—was the longest leap across an open space of any on Earth, and the first bridge to connect Manhattan with any of the lands that surrounded it. Take a look up at the cables; these, too, were an innovation, the first steel cables to be used on a bridge (before then cables were iron). It took 2 years to string the cables back and forth before work could begin building the suspension bridge. The cables each contain 5,434 wires and weigh 870 tons. Take a moment at the Brooklyn side to read the plaque on the construction of the bridge.

When you depart the bridge, consider taking a stroll in either Brooklyn Bridge Park (p. 178) or brownstone-heavy Brooklyn Heights, the first neighborhood in the city to be landmarked.

To start in Manhattan, 4, 5, 6 to Brooklyn Bridge–City Hall. To start in Brooklyn, 2, 3 train to Clark St or 2, 3, 4, 5, N, R to Court St.-Borough Hall.

Ellis Island National Museum of Immigration ★★★ HISTORIC SITE The epicenter of the largest migration in human history, Ellis Island was in near-continuous use from 1892 to 1954 as the point-of-entry processing center for the majority of immigrants (including my grandmother) who settled in the U.S. during those years. Over 12 million people passed through its halls, sometimes as many as 12,000 in a single day.

Downtown & Chelsea Attractions

CHELSEA

10th Ave. · Ninth Ave. · Eighth Ave. · W. 21st St. · E. 21st St
W. 20th St. · E. 20th St
W. 19th St. · E. 19th St
FLATIRON DISTRICT
W. 18th St. · E. 18th St
Seventh Ave. · W. 17th St. · E. 17th St
W. 16th St. · E. 16th St.
High Line Park · E. 15th St.
W. 14th St. · W. 14th St. · E. 13th St
W. 13th St. · E. 12th St.
Washington St. · Gansevoort St. · Greenwich Ave. · W. 12th St. · E. 11th St
Horatio St. · Jane St. · Sixth Ave. · W. 10th St. · Fifth Ave. · University Pl. · Broadway · Fourth Ave. · Third Ave. · E. 10th St. · Stuyvesant · E. 9th St. · **Tompkins Square Park**
W. 9th St. · E. 9th St. · St. Mark's Pl.
Eighth Ave. · W. 4th St. · Waverly Pl. · **GREENWICH VILLAGE** · E. 8th St. · St. Mark's Pl. · **EAST VILLAGE**
Washington Square · Astor Pl. · E. 7th St. · Lafayette · Ave. A
W. 4th St. · Washington Pl. · E. 5th St.
W. 3rd St. · Gt. · E. 4th St. · Avenue A
NOHO · Bond · Jones · E. 3rd St.
Bleecker · E. 2nd St.
E. Houston · E. 1st St.
W. Houston St. · **SOHO** · **NOLITA** · Suffolk · Stanton
King · Prince · Bowery · Elizabeth · Forsyth · Allen · Norfolk
Charlton · Varick St. · Spring · Mott · Mulberry · Chrystie · Rivington · Delancey
Vandam · Greene · Kenmare · **LITTLE ITALY** · Orchard · Essex
Dominick · Broome · Crosby · Broome
Watts · Canal · Mercer · Lafayette · Elizabeth · Grand · Allen · Ludlow
Desbrosses · Grand · Howard · Baxter · Hester · Canal
Vestry · Canal · Hubert · Lispenard · Walker · **CHINATOWN** · Pike
Laight · Beach · White · Franklin · Bayard · Henry · Madison · Cherry · Water
TRIBECA · N. Moore · Leonard · Centre · Bowery · Catherine · South
Hubert · Franklin · Worth · Division · **Manhattan Bridge**
Harrison · Jay · Thomas · Monroe
Greenwich St. · Duane · Reade · Henry
West Side Hwy. · Chambers · City Hall Park · Robert F. Wagner Pl.
Warren · Murray · Park Pl. · Park Row · Spruce · Frankfort · **Brooklyn Bridge**
Barclay · Beekman · Dover · Pearl · Water · Front · South
Vesey · Ann · John · Cliff
WORLD TRADE CENTER SITE · Fulton · Beekman · Fletcher
Liberty · Greenwich · John · Platt · Maiden · Maiden
Cedar · Trinity Pl. · Nassau · William · Liberty · Front
Albany · Broadway · Pine · Cedar · Water
Rector · Exchange · Pl. · Wall St. · Front · South
Bowling · Green · Beaver · Pearl
2nd Pl. · Stone · **FINANCIAL DISTRICT**
1st Pl. · Bridge · Whitehall · Broad · **Vietnam Veterans Plaza**
Battery Pl. · State · **Battery Park** · **East River**

9/11 Memorial and Museum **10**
African Burial Ground **16**
Brooklyn Bridge **14**
Center for Jewish History **26**
Ellis Island National Immigration Museum **2**
The Drawing Center **19**
Federal Reserve Bank **12**
Merchant's House **24**
Mmuseumm **17**
Museum at Eldridge St. **21**
The Museum at FIT **30**
Museum of the American Gangster **25**
Museum of Chinese in America **20**
Museum of Jewish Heritage **4**
Museum of Mathematics **27**
National Museum of the American Indian **6**
New Museum of Contemporary Art **23**
New York City Fire Museum **18**
One World Observatory **9**
Rubin Museum **28**
St. Paul's Chapel **11**
Skyscraper Museum **5**
South Street Seaport Museum **13**
Staten Island Ferry **3**
Statue of Liberty **1**
The Tenement Museum **22**
Trinity Church **8**
Wall Street & The NY Stock Exchange **7**
Whitney Museum of American Art **29**
Woolworth Building **15**

0 · 1/2 mi
NEW JERSEY · Hudson River · **NEW YORK**
Liberty State Park
Castle Clinton Nat'l Monument Ferry tickets
Ellis Island · **Ellis Island Immigration Museum** · Battery Park
Liberty Island · East River
Castle Clinton Natl. Mon. · Battery Park · **Staten Island Ferry Terminal**
South Gardens
Governors Island

To **1** **2** (see inset at left)

0 · 1/4 mi
0 · 0.25 km

colonial-era SACRED GROUND

African Burial Ground ★ Some 15,000 African slaves were buried in a Manhattan graveyard in the 17th and 18th centuries, but their final resting places were lost to memory until 1991 when construction workers stumbled upon human remains during renovations of a federal building. The site is now considered one of the most important archeological finds in the United States. In 2006, a handsome, symbol-laden National Monument (operated by the National Parks Service) was dedicated by poet Maya Angelou and Mayor Michael Bloomberg. A visit to the **African Burial Ground,** and the small museum that's attached, should take no more than half an hour, but it's a worthy pilgrimage, uncovering, as it does, a part of American history that is too often brushed to the side.

At the corner of Duane & Elk sts. www.nps.gov/afbg. ☎ **212/637-2019.** Free admission. Indoor exhibition center open Tues–Sat 10am–4pm; outdoor memorial open Tues–Sat 10am–5pm. Subway: 4, 5, 6, R to City Hall, J to Chambers St.

The stories of these immigrants—what they were escaping, what they found once here, and what they experienced in their short time in the purgatory that was Ellis Island—are at the core of the Ellis Island experience. But in 2015, Ellis Island decided to expand its mandate, widening its focus to embrace the *entire* history of immigration to America. This makes it a solid candidate for a repeat visit from those who've toured it before (more on that below). First time visitors, however, will want to concentrate on the original exhibits which remain the most emotionally resonant for the simple reason that they're about Ellis Island itself, and learning about this endlessly fascinating place while walking through its hallowed halls is a powerful experience.

Start in the second-floor **Grand Hall** (officially titled the **"Registry Hall"**), awe-inspiring with its massive white tile-vaulted ceiling (created by the same firm that did the ceiling in Grand Central Station's Oyster Bar) and, most likely, larger than any church or temple these immigrants would have attended in their home villages.

Behind the Grand Hall is a warren of small rooms where immigrants were tested for mental competency, literacy, and communicable diseases. How these tests were done—and the fear they inspired—is chronicled in historical photos, wall text, and most poignantly at listening stations (or over the free audio tour headphones) on which you hear actual immigrants share their memories of their time on the island.

The top floor chronicles the history of the processing facility itself. These exhibits can be skipped if you're short on time, but don't miss the **"Treasures from Home"** exhibit, also on this floor, which features 2,000 of the possessions that were brought through Ellis. Somehow seeing the china dolls, the precious wedding photos, the native costumes, and the letters home brings the immigrant experience more vividly to life than any other part of the museum.

For those coming on a repeat visit, on the ground floor there are four new exhibitions of note, two of which expand the story of immigration to America, to the era before Ellis Island opened (**Journeys: The Peopling of America**) and to the period after World War II through today (**The Journey: New Eras of Immigration**). Both are quite wall-text heavy, which may frustrate some visitors. If you have to choose between the two, I'd pick "New Eras of Immigration" as it features affecting videos profiling recent immigrants, both legal and illegal. It also tells a story that's rarely discussed in a balanced fashion: the myriad and surprising ways in which immigration is reshaping today's America. The highlight of the **American Stories** exhibit (new in 2015) is a set of interactive monitors that allow visitors to take an actual, current citizenship test (I'm proud to say I got a perfect score).

The final newish experience (it debuted in 2014) is the **Hard Hat Tour ★★,** which takes visitors through the haunting—and unrenovated—Ellis Island hospital. Some 10% of the Ellis Island immigrants spent some time here, often right before being shipped back to Europe, their only crime being ill. The facility was closed for 60 years and it's falling apart—hence the need for hard hats. The only new items are the oversized archival photos of hospital residents that French artist JR added onto the crumbling walls, broken windows, and metal lockers—a moving tribute.

There's also an on-site cafeteria, along with the **American Family History Center,** which was expanded by 32 million records in 2015 (immigration info from the years 1924 to 1957 was added). Trained genealogists are on site to help visitors navigate the computer search; a session costs $7.

I am one of the 40% of all Americans who had a relative come through Ellis Island, as I said at the start, and I find it difficult to tour this museum without tearing up at some point. I have no doubt that even those visitors without this direct a connection will find the journey through Ellis to be one of the most moving experiences of their New York visit.

In New York Harbor; ferry departs from Battery Park. www.nps.gov/elis/index.htm, www.ellisisland.org, or www.statuecruises.com. 📞 **212/363-3200** (general info) or 877/LADY-TIX (523-9849; ticket/ferry info). Free admission. Ferry ticket $18 adults, $14 seniors, $9 children 4–12. Hard Hat Tour, including ferry ticket: $53 adults, $49 seniors, ages 13 and up only. Daily 9am–5pm, last ferry to Ellis Island departs 3:30pm Sept–May, 5pm June–Aug. For subway and ferry details, see Statue of Liberty, p. 127 (ferry stops at both sights).

Federal Reserve Bank ★★

Although you won't see the currency being printed—that function was moved from this site to New Jersey in 1992—you will likely see more lucre than you ever will again in your lifetime when you descend 80 feet to the basement of this financial fortress, where a gold vault right out of *Mission Impossible* is housed. Down here, behind a door that's a good 5 feet thick, the Fed keeps $100,000 billion worth of gold bars, a full 25% of all the gold reserves in the world, and far more than is housed in Fort Knox. Ninety-five percent of the gold stored here belongs to foreign nations, who use this facility, embedded in the bedrock of Manhattan and guarded by a small army of marksmen (they have their own on-site firing range for practice), because it's considered the safest place in the world for this type of storage. I wish I could give you more details, but the security here is so span-dex-tight that my reporter's notebook was confiscated at the door.

The gold is supplemented by precious coins (one worth $7 million), in an exhibit in the lobby by the Numismatic Society in partnership with the Fed. Also featured are brief videotapes detailing the work of the Fed, and an interactive exhibit explaining what the massive, semi-governmental agency does (it's an interesting topic). The entire tour takes a bit less than an hour.

Entrance at 44 Maiden Lane. www.ny.frb.org. © **212/720-5000.** Free admission. Mon–Fri 1pm and 2pm; reservations required, book exactly 30 days in advance. Subway: 2, 3, 4, 5, A, C, J to Fulton St.

Museum of Jewish Heritage—A Living Memorial to the Holocaust ★ MUSEUM

It can be an emotionally draining experiences to visit the Museum of Jewish Heritage, which deals in explicit fashion with the Holocaust. To be fair, the museum is not in any way a showcase of horrors; its curators have been very careful to create a rounded picture of what life was like before, during, and after World War II. But be aware, before you decide to come, that you may need to skip other sightseeing after you leave here to recover a bit.

Your tour will begin in the older section of the museum—an elegant six-sided building by architect Kevin Roche, meant to evoke both the Star of David and the six million Jews who were murdered during the Holocaust. The first floor covers life before the war with a sensitively constructed exhibit detailing the various aspects of daily existence. The second floor is dedicated to the war years, and as might be expected, many of the images shown are quite graphic and disturbing. (People with children under 12 would be well advised to skip this floor by taking the elevator directly from the first floor up to the third.) In addition to photos, objects, and text, the museum is a repository for videos from Steven Spielberg's Shoah Foundation's Visual History project, and these vivid accounts of life in the camps and ghettos are the highlight of the museum.

The final floor discusses the *Diaspora*, with exhibitions on Jewish life in the United States, Israel, and Europe. There are also changing exhibits, and programs of lectures and music. For those looking for a very in-depth experience, there is a self-guided headphone tour (an additional $5) narrated by Meryl Streep and Itzhak Perlman. On-site, too: a kosher cafe.

36 Battery Place (at 1st Place), Battery Park City. www.mjhnyc.org. © **646/437-4200.** Admission $12 adults, $10 seniors, $7 students, free for children 12 and under; free admission Wed 4–8pm. Sun–Tues and Thurs 10am–5:45pm; Wed 10am–8pm; Fri and eves of Jewish holidays 10am–3pm (10am–5pm Fri during daylight saving time). Subway: 4, 5 to Bowling Green.

National Museum of the American Indian, George Gustav Heye Center ★ MUSEUM

A branch of the Smithsonian Institution, this museum is notable primarily for the touring exhibits it hosts (and to be truthful, while some have been impressive others have been duds). Housed in the

CityPass is New York's best sightseeing deal. Pay one price ($116, or $92 for kids 6–17) for admission to six major attractions:

o   The American Museum of Natural History (including the Space Show or an IMAX film)

o   The Guggenheim Museum *or* Top of the Rock

o   The Empire State Building Experience

o   The 9/11 Memorial & Museum *or* The Intrepid Sea, Air and Space Museum

o   The Metropolitan Museum of Art

o   The Statue of Liberty and Ellis Island, *or* a 2-hour Circle Line harbor cruise.

Individual tickets would cost 40% more, though I should point out that the "Met" (Metropolitan Museum of Art) and Museum of Natural History charge only "suggested" admission fees, meaning you could get in legally for a dollar, or less, at each.

More important, CityPass is not a coupon book. It contains actual tickets, so you can bypass lengthy lines. This can save you hours, as sights such as the Empire State Building often have ticket lines of an hour or more.

CityPass is good for 9 days from the first time you use it. It's sold at all participating attractions and online at **www.citypass.com/city/ny**. You can download and self-print the pass or you may buy the pass at your first attraction (start at an attraction that's likely to have the shortest admission line, such as the Guggenheim). However, if you begin your sightseeing on a weekend or during holidays, when lines are longest, online purchase is the smarter way to go.

magnificent Customs House, designed by architect Cass Gilbert (for more on the edifice, see p. 210), the museum offers a robust program of performances, lectures, and courses on Native American topics.

1 Bowling Green (btw. State and Whitehall sts.). www.nmai.si.edu. ℮ **212/514-3700.** Free admission. 10am–5pm (Thurs until 8pm). Closed on Christmas. Subway: 4, 5 to Bowling Green; R to Whitehall; 1 to South Ferry.

One World Observatory ★★ VIEW   I'm going to say what no polite travel writer does: a big part of the allure of seeing the view from atop the western hemisphere's tallest building (at 1,776 ft.) is the knowledge that you may be tempting fate by doing so. The skyscraper was built as a nose thumb to the terrorists who had *twice* attacked the World Trade Center on this same acre of ground. That has meant that the building's office space is still only 66% rented. But the observation deck should be a big hit because, along with the tremendous views, visitors can show their patriotism by choosing this eagle's-eye perch over the **Empire State Building** (see p. 140) or the **Top of the Rock** (see p. 148). That point is brought home by the introductory video, which details the pride that the men and women who built the building took in their work (touchingly, one of the construction workers did the same job on the Freedom Tower that his father had on the Twin Towers). The other side of the coin (whether the place is safe) is addressed when you head into the final part of the lobby: a tunnel the developers dug into the bedrock, and kept purposefully rough-hewn, filling it with signs (in lights) about the durability of the rock foundations and the fact that the building contains 5.4 million cubic feet of concrete "making this the strongest building ever constructed." Is this meant to reassure patrons or hype up the excitement? I'll leave that to the cynics among you to decide.

The Observatory also lures customers with some pretty whiz-bang features, like elevators that not only shoot passenger up 102 stories in an ear-popping 47 seconds (making these among the fastest elevators in the world), but have walls that turn into video "windows," through which riders see a computer-generated visual history of the city, from meadowlands through the skyscrapers of today. (Be sure to look right so that you can see the Twin Towers, which are just a brief blip in this 500-year timeline). At the top are more videos of the city and "ambassadors" who use what's called the "Citypulse," a wheel of video screens (the guide operates them via armband), to discuss the culture and life of the city. On the wheel are colorful photos, interactive maps, and live twitter feeds (it's not as compelling as it sounds, unfortunately). And I think the designers here made an error in taking guests to the top level for the introductory video, and then having them go *down* two stories for the actual observatory, with its 360-degree views. We've all paid to see the view from the highest point in the Americas, so why are we being told to descend to see it?

As for the marquee attraction, the view: on a clear day, one can see 50 miles in all directions through the 30-foot-tall windows here. That being said, as a matter of personal taste, I prefer the view from the Empire State Building, as you have Manhattan all around you, making it more of a buzzing, visceral experience. (At the ESB and at Top of the Rock, guests also can go outside, and there's something thrilling about feeling the whoosh of the winds that high up).

Some notes: On site are three eateries (take-out, grill, and fine dining), and a souvenir store. As at the Top of the Rock (but not at the Empire State Building) tickets are timed, which should mean minimal waits. Do get your tickets well in advance of your visit, though, as many dates sell out.

1 World Trade (entrance on Vesey St. at West St.). http://oneworldobservatory.com. ℂ **844/696-1776.** Basic admission $32 adults; $30 seniors, $26 children (priority pass $56, flexible pass $67). Early May–early Sept daily 9am–10pm, 9am–8pm rest of year. Subway: E to World Trade Center, A, C to Chambers St., N, R to Cortland St., 4, 5 to Fulton St.

Skyscraper Museum ★ MUSEUM Don't dismiss this small museum: It's far more interesting than one would expect. An architecturally innovative space in and of itself (notice how the shiny metals, ascending ramp, and mirrored surfaces gives the smallish room its own skyscraper aspect), the museum explores not only the structural feats behind these soaring structures, but also the economic forces that shaped them and their sociological impact.

39 Battery Place (Little West St. and 1st Place). www.skyscraper.org. ℂ **212/968-1961.** Admission $5 adults, $3 seniors and students. Wed–Sun noon–6pm. Subway: 4, 5 to Bowling Green.

South Street Seaport Museum ★ HISTORIC SITE Badly damaged during Hurricane Sandy, the South Street Seaport and its museum are still in the midst of a massive renovation as we go to press. I'd say the only reason to come down here in 2017 is for the daily tours of the humongous historic sailing vessels the museum has moored off Pier 16 (it owns six and many go for daily sails; ask). Other than that, the Museum has been reduced to a "ye olde printing shoppe," some walking tours, and an alcove with wall text on the area.

207-209 Water St., 12 Fulton St., and Pier 16. www.seany.org. © **212/748-8725** or 212/ SEA-PORT. Free admission, varied charges for tours. Daily 11am–5pm. Subway: 2, 3, 4, 5 to Fulton St. (walk east, or downslope, on Fulton St. to Water St.).

Staten Island Ferry ★★ ICON/TRANSPORTATION Most visitors—and even some New Yorkers—don't know that the **Staten Island Ferry** makes its own daily excursion within Polaroid distance of the Statue of Liberty, Ellis Island, and Governor's Island. And riders pay absolutely nothing for the great views. You simply board the ship (be sure to wait for one of the older orange-and-green boats, because the newer ones don't have decks for viewing). As with the Circle Line (p. 184), sit on the right side (stay at the back of the ferry for the best view of the Manhattan skyline). It's a joke here that this is the best "cheap date" in the city, so don't be shy about toting along a bottle of wine, some bread, and cheese. But be sure to dress warmly: In winter the outdoor decks can be frigid. One-way, the trip takes approximately a half-hour, after which you'll disembark and take the next ferry back.

Departs from Whitehall Ferry Terminal, 4 South St. (at Whitehall St.). http://home2.nyc. gov/html/dot/html/ferrybus/staten-island-ferry.shtml. © **718/727-2508.** Free of charge. 24 hr.; every 15–20 min during rush hour, every 30 min otherwise. Subway: N, R to Whitehall St.; 4, 5 to Bowling Green; 1 to South Ferry (ride in first 5 cars of train).

Statue of Liberty ★★★ ICON/MONUMENT The great harbor of New York and the grand lady who guards it are, after Ground Zero and the Empire State Building, the city's top must-visit attractions. You'll follow in the footsteps of the millions of immigrants and visitors who came here before you, their way lighted by the torch and the promise inscribed on the statue's base: that the "teeming masses yearning to breathe free" would find succor, freedom from persecution, and economic opportunity in this new land.

You will have a fine view of Lady Liberty from the shores of Battery Park, but planning ahead to take the ferry out to the island and visit the interior of the statue rewards the effort. Please do understand that if you *don't* make advance reservations, you'll likely only get to take a ranger tour of the grounds—a disappointment, and a common one these days thanks to NYC's booming tourist numbers. Some 3,000 visitors take the tour each day, but on many days, nearly 15,000 show up and have to be turned away. This and the 9/11 Museum and Memorial are the two major New York sites that you really do have to plan ahead for, as often capacity doesn't keep up with demand. So put down this book and make your reservation *now*. Most visitors who reserve ahead will be able to visit the statue's pedestal, which offers a splendid view

THE STATUE OF LIBERTY—in brief

The French connection: Dreamed up at a dinner party of French intellectuals in 1865, the statue was first proposed as a 100th-birthday present from France to the U.S. (and as a not-so-subtle jab at France's then-authoritarian Second Empire). Fundraising woes kept it from being completed in time for that anniversary, but in 1881, after over a decade of begging for money (a lottery finally did the trick), sculptor Auguste Bartholdi was able to finish the massive work.

The battle for the base: Though the statue was completed in 1881, it took another 2 years for the Americans to keep their half of the bargain and create a pedestal for it. Newspaperman Joseph Pulitzer finally stepped in, and in a series of angry editorials condemning the wealthy for not contributing, he convinced thousands of lower-income Americans to send in what they could to get the job done. Thanks to their dimes and nickels, the pedestal was finally built (designed by Richard Morris Hunt), and the statue was dedicated on October 28, 1886.

Crafting the Lady: *Repousse*, a technique of hammering and shaping thin strips of copper, was used to create Lady Liberty. Though the statue is massive at over 151 feet from base to torch, the "skin" of the piece is just ³⁄₃₂ of an inch thick. It is thought that the ancient Colossus of Rhodes was built using this method.

A key to the symbolism: Every piece of the statue has meaning. The seven rays in the crown represent the seven seas of the world, and the 25 windows there give a nod to the 25 gemstones found on Earth. On the tablet Liberty is holding are inscribed the Roman numerals for July 4, 1776. And though it's difficult to see, Liberty is breaking shackles with her right foot.

of New York City; a tour of the small, but nicely curated museum on the history of the statue; and photo ops in front of the original torch (it had to be replaced in the mid-1980s due to severe water damage). Very limited numbers of visitors conclude that tour with a thrilling, exhausting climb up a circular stairway, 146 steps up to the crown of the statue. On the way up, you'll view the intricate metal work that French engineer Gustave Eiffel (of the Eiffel Tower) created to anchor the statue; it acts like a spring, allowing the "skin" of the structure to adjust to different temperatures and sway up to 3 inches in 50-mph winds.

Those without tickets to the monument can take a ranger-led tour of the island, but the better option may be to simply stay on the ferry, which slows down as it approaches the statue, giving those onboard a good view of Lady Liberty in all of her surprisingly delicate beauty. Spend the time you'll save to go on to Ellis Island (see p. 120), Liberty's sister monument, with no entrance quotas. I think Ellis is ultimately the more rewarding of the two . . . unless you get to visit the crown of Lady Liberty (which is really, really fun).

Liberty Island, New York Harbor; ferry ticket booth at Castle Clinton fort in Battery Park. www.nps.gov/stli or www.statuecruises.com. ℂ **212/363-3200** (general info), or 877/523-9849 (ticket/ferry info). Free admission. Ferry ticket $18 adults ($21 with access to crown), $14 seniors, $9 children 4–12. Daily 9:30am–5pm (last ferry departs around 3:30pm Sept–May, 5pm June–July). Subway: 4, 5 to Bowling Green; 1 to South Ferry.

St. Paul's Chapel ★CHURCH/HISTORIC SITE Built in 1766, this is not only the oldest church in the city, it's the only public space to be in continuous use since the Colonial era. The design of the church, with its Ionic columns and huge pediment, was based on that of St. Martin-in-the-Fields in London, though I think the overall effect of this church is not nearly as graceful. Still St. Paul's is redolent with history: George Washington had a pew here (now marked by a plaque), and he came directly to the church after his inauguration to pray and give thanks. On 9/11, the church miraculously survived a rain of fiery metal when the Twin Towers collapsed. It served as a focal point for the volunteer effort that ensued as hundreds of people came from all over the world to search for survivors and then human remains. Many slept at St. Paul's and took meals here (an exhibit in the church details this history).

209 Broadway (btw. Fulton and Vesey sts.). www.trinitywallstreet.org. Free admission. Daily 10am–6pm. Subway: A, C, 2, 3, 4 and 5 to Fulton St.

Trinity Church ★ CHURCH/HISTORIC SITE   This is actually the third Trinity Church to stand on this site. The first version was destroyed in the fire set by fleeing colonists in 1776 to thwart British occupiers (the fire ended up razing one-third of the structures in Manhattan). The second church building was poorly constructed, and its roof collapsed in a heavy snowstorm. But the third was a keeper and is considered by many to be one of the best, if not *the* best, Gothic Revival buildings in the United States.

Designed by Richard Upjohn, the religious structure can be seen as the stone and mortar embodiment of a theological movement that was sweeping the Anglican Church at that time, one that attempted to invigorate the Church by harkening back to its Catholic roots. Specifically, it paid heed to the idea that the Church needed a strong hierarchy to survive. So instead of creating a boxy, continuous space, like so many churches of the period (and like St. Paul's further down Broadway), Upjohn used self-consciously medieval features to underscore the sacred nature of the clergy's space, including a chancel. Normally, in a Gothic cathedral, the chancel (which is the area behind the altar, reserved for the clergy and choir) is marked off by railings, but that idea was quite controversial in Democratic New York, so Upjohn created a subtle solution, raising this area a few feet above the ground to give the feeling of an exalted place, without prominent barriers in place. Other Gothic features include the towering 280-foot spire, which was the tallest structure in the city until the piers of the Brooklyn Bridge were built; the flying buttresses; and the lovely stained-glass windows. The doors were modeled after Ghiberti's famous bronze doors for the Baptistery of Florence and designed by noted American architect Richard Morris Hunt, though the sculptures on them were done by Austrian immigrant Karl Bitter. You can see the latter's self-portrait in the knoblike head sticking out of the lower right hand corner of the door; above him is Richard Upjohn and above that Richard Morris Hunt (who also designed the base of the Statue of Liberty).

Don't miss touring the graveyard, which holds the remains of many Revolutionary War–era New Yorkers. Among the notables are Captain James

Lawrence, who uttered the famous command, "Don't give up the ship" in the War of 1812; he's buried in the tomb that looks like a ship, on the southern side of the church, surrounded by a fence made from captured British cannons. Behind Lawrence and to the right a bit is the most famous tomb here, that of Alexander Hamilton; beside Hamilton is the grave of steamboat designer Robert Fulton.

Download the church's app if you'd like more info as you wander through; the church also gives free live tours (see below).

At Broadway and Wall St. www.trinitywallstreet.org. ✆ **212/602-0800.** Free admission. Daily 8am–6pm, free tours Mon–Fri at 2pm, Sun at 11:15pm. Subway: 4, 5 to Wall St.

Wall Street and the New York Stock Exchange ★ ICON

This is the most famous (some would say infamous) financial institution in the world, the New York Stock Exchange. The building's towering columns, crowded ornamental pediment, and huge flag trumpet louder than any opening bell that this is a place of incomparable might and prestige (interestingly, it's a much more imposing building than the government's plainer Federal Hall across the street). In front of the Stock Exchange is a scraggly buttonwood tree, meant to invoke the buttonwood that New York's first traders stood under in 1792 when they met to begin brokering the Revolutionary War debt—the first stock market in America.

One odd fact about the Stock Exchange: Though it's associated in the popular imagination with Wall Street, its facade actually fronts Broad Street, not Wall.

Unfortunately, the NYSE is no longer open to the public for tours, but you can grab a cup of coffee and "toast" the brokers in nearby Zuccotti Park, the place where the OWS (Occupy Wall Street) movement was founded.

For a walking tour of the Wall Street area, see p. 214.

11 Wall St. www.nyse.com. Subway: J, Z to Broad St.; 2, 3, 4, 5 to Wall St.

The Woolworth Building ★ ICON

This soaring "Cathedral of Commerce" cost Frank W. Woolworth $14 million worth of nickels and dimes in 1913. But no amount of money could get visitors into the famed interior of this private office building—until recently. The great-granddaughter of architect Cass Gilbert started offering tours in late 2014, and now anyone who makes an advance reservation can learn about this architectural wonder, the tallest edifice in the city until 1930, when it was surpassed by the Chrysler Building. (At its opening, President Woodrow Wilson pressed a button from the White House that illuminated the building's 80,000 electric light bulbs.) Called the "Mozart of skyscrapers" by architectural critic Paul Goldberger, the neo-Gothic architecture is festooned with spires, gargoyles, flying buttresses, vaulted ceilings, 16th-century-style stone-as-lace traceries, castlelike turrets, and a churchlike interior—all of which you'll examine in the company of knowledgeable, hand-picked guides (many noted architectural historians in their own rights).

233 Broadway (btw. Park Place and Barclay sts.). www.woolworthtours.com. See website for daily tour schedules. Half-hour tour $20, 1 hr. tour $30, 90-min. tour $45. Subway: 2, 3 to Park Pl, 4, 5, 6 to Brooklyn Bridge/City Hall, A, C to Chambers St.

Lower East Side & East Village

Museum at Eldridge Street ★★ SYNAGOGUE   An 1887 synagogue, the oldest house of worship in the city for Eastern European Jews, the Eldridge Street Project has the kind of grandeur that one normally associates with the cathedrals of Europe. There's a poignancy to the place as well, as the building was abandoned for 40 years before restoration began in the 1990s, and it's crumbling picturesquely away in places. An hourly "From Bottom to Top" tour covers the history of the synagogue and the issues involved in its restoration. Don't skip the superb videos, shown in a room next to the entrance, about all the work that went into the transformation of the synagogue.

12 Eldridge St. (btw. Canal and Division sts.). www.eldridgestreet.org. Admission $14 adults, $10 seniors and students, $8 children 5–18; free to all on Mon. Sun–Thurs 10am–5pm, Fri 10am–3pm; closed on all national and Jewish holidays. Tours every hour on the hour. Subway: B, D to Grand St.; F to W. Broadway.

The Museum of the American Gangster ★★ MUSEUM/HISTORIC SITE   A speakeasy once occupied the building that now houses this museum, and the many mysteries surrounding the end of that enterprise—and the possible end of the underworld kingpin who ran the joint—make visiting here surprisingly dramatic and fun. I don't want to give away the story, but I can tell you that to teach you about it, your guide will take you into the working theater and century-old pub below the museum, and then into the cellar, where you'll don a hardhat to clamber through the operation's former HQ (coincidentally, the foundation of a 17th-century fur trapper's cottage is down there too). In addition, you'll learn about the history of U.S. gangsters in general, with the help of such artifacts as the actual bullets that killed Bonnie and Clyde, an ice pick that Henry Hill himself donated, and more. **Two warnings**: To really get the full experience, you *must* take the 90-minute guided tour (included in the admission cost). Just seeing the permanent exhibitions, and not seeing the other parts of the building, won't be nearly as compelling. And this is not an attraction for children under 12. Too many gruesome tales are told.

80 St. Marks Place (just off First Ave.). www.museumoftheamericangangster.org. ✆ **212/228-5736.** Admission $20 adults, $12 students and seniors. Daily 1–6pm. Subway: 6 to Lafayette, N, R to 8th Street, L to First Ave.

New Museum of Contemporary Art ★ MUSEUM   Perhaps the greatest sign of New York City's ever-increasing prosperity is the fact that now, even the gritty, grimy Bowery (birthplace of the term "bowery bums" for the homeless people who used to swarm its cheap bars and bunk in its missions) now has a museum. And a bright and shiny one at that, a massive steel-and-glass tower. As with much of the art of the moment, the exhibits range from the sublime to the silly (I was stopped dead in my tracks at a recent exhibit by a cardboard box and a big plastic bag among all the sculptures—was it art, or the container the art came in? I knew the answer intellectually, but my heart kept crying out: Recycle that bag and box, and do something useful with them!). Wall text is hard to find, so buttonhole one of the gallery

AN art invasion ON THE LOWER EAST SIDE

In just the last 2 years, the Lower East Side has become a mecca for art galleries. Rising rents in Chelsea (see p. 138) pushed a number of them into this neighborhood, but the transformation of the area from immigrant enclave to haven for the hip also played a role. So which should you see? You never know what artists or types of artwork will be on display, but there's usually something intriguing to see at **291 Grand Street**, the neighborhood's first all-gallery building (it houses four; it's at the corner of Eldridge St., near the Grand St. subway stop, which gets the B and D lines). Other notable art dens include **Bridget Donohue** (99 Bowery, near Hester St.; www.bridgetdonohue.com); **Andrew Edlin** (212 Bowery St. btw. Prince and Spring sts.; www.edlingallery.com); **Pierogi** (155 Suffolk St. btw. Stanton and East Houston sts. www.pierogi2000.com); and **Mitchell Algus** (132 Delancey St. at Norfolk St.; www.mitchellalgusgallery.com).

guides wearing big "ask me" buttons; sometimes their explanations will be more interesting than the art itself.

235 Bowery (at Prince St.). www.newmuseum.org. ☎ **212/219-1222.** Admission $16 adults, $14 seniors, $10 students, free 18 and under; free Thurs 7–9pm. Wed–Sun 11am–6pm (Thurs until 9pm). Subway: 6 to Spring St; N, R to Prince St.

The Tenement Museum ★★★ MUSEUM   At first glance, this museum looks like just one of many brownstone building on this Lower East Side block . . . and that's exactly the point. The first-ever National Trust for Historic Preservation site that was *not* the home of someone rich or famous, it was preserved to tell the story of the immigrants who once lived in this building (97 Orchard St.) and in the surrounding buildings. Those stories are rich and varied: This five-story tenement housed some 10,000 people from 25 countries between 1863 and 1935. A visit here makes an excellent follow-up to Ellis Island (see p. 120).

Visits to the museum are by **hour-long guided tour only** (the Shop Life tour is 1½ hours). Visitors have a choice of five programs, each of which illuminates the lives of different sorts of tenants: from garment workers who did piecework in their apartment, to a family that survived not one but two depressions, to the German family that ran a saloon in their basement. Best for children is the weekend-only program, "Victoria Confino," which is less tour than interactive experience, as a costumed teenaged character instructs new "immigrants" (the people on the tour) in a candid, revealing, and totally improvised manner on how to get along in New York. (It sounds hokey, I know, but it's quite vivid.) Many of the other tours are only offered to those over the age of 12; check before booking. The museum also offers walking tours of the neighborhood, culinary experiences, and rotating exhibits. Tours are limited in number and sell out quickly, so it pays to buy tickets in advance.

108 Orchard St. (btw. Delancey and Broome sts.). www.tenement.org. ☎ **212/431-0233.** Tours $25 adults, $20 seniors and students. Tours daily 10am–5pm, until 6:30pm Thurs (schedule varies; check website or call). Subway: F to Delancey St.; J, M to Essex St.

Chinatown, Soho, Nolita & Noho

Merchant's House Museum ★ MUSEUM New York City has never been very good at preserving its past (perhaps we have too little room . . . or patience), but on East 4th Street this precious sliver of history has survived utterly intact. In fact, this is the *only* Victorian-era structure in New York City preserved both inside and out. A handsome Greek Revival town house, it was once the home of the Tredwell family, who furnished it in the highest style of the day, all mohair couches, crystal chandeliers, and deep red curtains. These furnishings, the clothing of the 10-person family, their cookware, and anything else you might want to see are all on display, thanks to the efforts in 1936 of a preservationist (before there really was such a thing) named George Chapman. A lovely garden and frequent ghost sightings add to the home's appeal.

29 E. 4th St. (btw. Lafayette and Bowery). www.merchantshouse.org. ℂ **212/777-1089.** Admission $13 adults, $8 seniors and students, children under 12 free. Fri–Mon noon–5pm, Thurs noon–8pm, guided tours 2pm (also 6:30pm Thurs). Subway: 6 to Astor Place; N, R to 8th St.; F, B to Broadway/Lafayette.

Mmuseumm ★★ MUSEUM Found objects in a found space—that in a nutshell is what makes this, yes, nutshell-sized gallery so beguiling. Set in a non-working, 60-square-foot freight elevator shaft off an alley, the museum was created by three indie filmmakers who found themselves drawn to objects that, in some way, illuminated the world around them. Pieces on the back and top three shelves are the fascinating permanent collection—a compass created for Muslims which points towards Mecca for prayer, a snowglobe from North Korea, a prison-issued fingertip toothbrush, and more. The changing exhibits tend to be either oddball—a collection of weirdly-shaped cornflakes, facsimiles of the currency Isis has said it wants to release—or poignant, such as a collection of "last text messages" (sent just before someone died, or cut off communication); objects abandoned by would-be migrants from Mexico and South America in the Arizona desert; or mortuary tools created to keep eyelids shut and mouths from gaping open. Exhibits change every 6 months or so.

4 Cortlandt Alley (near White St.). www.mmuseumm.com. Free admission (donation requested). Thurs–Fri 6–9pm, Sat–Sun noon–6pm; other times you can gaze through peepholes in the door.

Museum of Chinese in America ★ MUSEUM The story of the Chinese immigrant experience in the U.S. is wholly different from that of any other ethnic group that came here. Arguably, these Chinese-Americans, and the African Americans who came here as slaves, had it worst, and the tales of what they endured—thanks to the limited work they were allowed to do and the "Chinese Exclusion Act," a federal law barring further Chinese immigration (that separated countless families)—give this museum true power. For a preview, go to www.mocanyc.org/visit to look at Maya Lin's video tour of the museum (she's the museum's designer, as well as the creator of the Vietnam Veteran's Memorial in Washington, D.C.).

215 Centre St. www.mocanyc.org. ℂ **212/619-4785.** Admission $10 adults, $5 students and seniors, children 12 and under free. Tues–Sun 11am–6pm (Thurs until 9pm). Subway: 6, N, R, Q, J, M to Canal St.

The Drawing Center ★ MUSEUM It's all drawings, all the time at this little white box of a museum, and that can be enthralling…or deadly dull. One gets the feeling that the curators are so excited about being the only museum in the world dedicated to this medium that they pay less attention than they should to whether the works chosen deserve attention. Upcoming offerings include botanical drawings from the 19th century, visual works of poetry by Jackson MacLow, and a range of more traditional artworks (all drawn, of course).

35 Wooster St. (btw. Grand and Broome sts.). www.drawingcenter.org. ℂ **212/219-2166.** $5 adults, $3 students and seniors, children under 12 free. Wed–Sun noon–6pm (Thurs until 8pm). Subway: A, C, E, N, Q, R, 1, 6 to Canal St.

Meatpacking District

Whitney Museum of American Art ★★★ ART MUSEUM The canon of American art is celebrated, and, in some ways, was *created* by the Whitney Museum. It was Whitney curators, after all, and Whitney founder Gertrude Vanderbilt Whitney, who championed such now iconic artists as Edward Hopper, Georgia O'Keeffe, Alexander Calder and Jasper Johns at the start of their careers, collecting many of their most important works.

In most cities that would be enough, but the Whitney's current crew has greater ambitions, ambitions that have been turned into smooth concrete, steel, and glass in Manhattan's hippest neighborhood. In May of 2015, the new Renzo Piano-designed home for the Whitney opened right next to the High Line Park, and it is, in many ways, reshaping the idea of what this institution, and art museums in general, can and should be.

And what they should be is flexible. "We have no idea what artists will be doing in 2020, let alone later than that," Dana Miller, chief curator of the permanent collection, told me. "So we wanted spaces that could be reshaped in dozens of ways." What that means is a building that's not a looker (I think) but that allows artists to be as creative as they want: the floors can be drilled into, all of the interior walls are moveable, and every inch of the place is wired, which should make installing electronic art a snap. For visitors, this means they will have a wildly different museum experience each time they come: Not only will the art change, but the environment will cocoon them in different ways.

And I use the word "cocoon" quite deliberately, because this is one of the few museums that takes into account the comfort of its patrons. Many rooms are flooded with natural light and the floors are sprung on "sleepers," so there's no foot fatigue, even after hours of standing and looking at art. Two topnotch cafes, run by expert restaurateur Danny Meyer, provide sustenance. The hours are generous, allowing for nighttime museum-going. And there are few more fun neighborhoods to explore, before or after a visit, than the Meatpacking District.

Most importantly, the Whitney's new home is 60% larger than its old Upper East Side digs, meaning that the best-known pieces from its epochal permanent collection—Calder's "Circus" (along with a video of the artist moving all the little figures), bleak beauts by Hopper, blossoms by O'Keefe, and more—will always be on display on the fifth and sixth floors (so go there first if you have limited time). The museum will also have more room for its famed **Biennial,** a show that expertly displays the most important American art of the previous 2 years, and often shapes perceptions of what contemporary art should be.

99 Gansevoort St. www.whitney.org. ✆ **212/570-3600.** Admission $22 adults, $18 seniors, children 18 and under free; pay-what-you-wish Fri 7–10pm. Sun–Mon and Wed–Thurs 10:30am–6pm; Fri–Sat 10:30am–10pm. Free tours weekdays at 1pm, weekends 1 and 3pm. Subway: A, C, E to 14th St or L to Eighth Ave.

MIDTOWN

Center for Jewish History ★ CULTURAL CENTER/MUSEUM People interested in tracing their Jewish ancestry can visit the Center for Jewish History, which is the largest repository of Jewish records, artifacts, books, and letters in the world—100 million archived documents in all—and has a state-of-the-art genealogical library open to all. Three to four temporary exhibits, drawn usually from these vast archives, are housed in three large, on-site galleries.

15 W. 16th St. (btw. Fifth and Sixth aves.). www.cjh.org. ✆ **212/294-8301.** Admission to Yeshiva University Museum $8 adults, $6 seniors and students, free for children 4 and under; free to all Mon, Wed 5–8pm and Fri. Free admission to all other facilities. Gallery spaces: Tues and Thurs 9:30am–5pm; Sun 11am–5pm; Mon and Wed 9:30am–8pm; Yeshiva University Museum Mon 5–8pm; Sun, Tues, and Thurs 11am–5pm; Fri 11am–2.30pm. Subway: L, N, R, 4, 5, 6 to 14th St./Union Square; F, M to 14th St.

The Museum at FIT ★ MUSEUM You don't have to be a fashionista to appreciate NYC's premier design school's museum. Yes, you'll see a lot of clothing, but exhibits here tend to explore cultural history through the lens of fashion, looking at such topics as how denim went from factory wear to club gear; the history of uniforms; or how black designers reshaped stereotypes. A visit should take less than an hour.

Seventh Ave. at 27th St. www.fitnyc.edu/museum. ✆ **212/247-4558.** Free admission. Tues–Fri noon–8pm, Sat 10am–5pm. Subway: 1, N, R to 28th St. or A, C, E, F, M to 23rd St.

Rubin Museum of Art ★★ MUSEUM Travelers who need a break from the bustle and stresses of New York can escape to the Rubin, a serene, contemplative museum of art from the Himalayas. Secular in origin—the museum was founded by an American millionaire and his wife who fell in love with the art of this region—its effect is nonetheless tremendously spiritual, as the paintings, drawings, sculptures, and artifacts shown are all religious items, many used by traveling monks to teach Buddhism or to help worshippers deepen their meditation (that's why so many of the works are done on fabric—they're meant to be rolled up and carried). Many tell the stories of the various Buddhas, portraying meditating men with halos, snarling demons, teachers, and commoners in the deepest blues, ruby reds, emerald greens, and dazzling golds. For sheer beauty, the 1,500 works housed in this museum are hard to top.

Set on the site of the former Barney's Department Store (the Rubins chose it because the central circular stairway looked like a "mandala," a never-ending circle surrounded by a square, the Tantric Buddhist diagram of the cosmos), the museum also hosts an array of lectures, performances, film screenings, and more. Its children's and teen programs are particularly well done.

150 W. 17th St. www.rubinmuseum.org. ✆ **212/620-5000.** Admission $15 adults; $10 seniors and students, free for children 12 and under; free to all Fri 6–10pm. Mon and Thurs 11am–5pm; Wed 11am–9pm; Fri 11am–10pm; Sat–Sun 11am–6pm; closed Christmas and Thanksgiving. Subway: A, C, or E to 14th St.; 1 to 18th St.; 2, 3 to 14th St.

Flatiron District

Flatiron Building ★★ ARCHITECTURE You'll probably know the Flatiron Building even before you see it, thanks to the famous photos by Alfred Stieglitz, who snapped it numerous times, calling the Fuller Building (its original name) "a picture of new America still in the making." Many consider it the first skyscraper in New York; it certainly was one of the first to use a steel frame, the classic skyscraper structure. Its unusual triangular shape was architect Daniel Burnham's solution to a space problem: The building rests on the bow-tie intersection where Broadway and Fifth Avenue cross each other. In order to produce a decent amount of rentable space, he built it to a towering 375 feet on every sliver of land available to him. The apex is just 6 feet across at its narrowest point. When it was first erected in 1902, crowds used to gather in Madison Square Park across the street to wait for it to fall down! Later men were drawn here by the urban myth that the building's shape caused strange wind patterns that were effective in lifting up women's skirts. The cops who dispersed these groups of gaping men on 23rd Street would call out "23 skidoo!" and so a slang term was born. One of the most beloved buildings in the city, it has been compared to a mighty ship sailing up Fifth Avenue.

175 Fifth Ave. (at 23rd St.). Subway: N, R to 23rd St.

East Side

Chrysler Building ★★★ ARCHITECTURE In the Chrysler Building we see the roaring-twenties version of what Alan Greenspan called "irrational exuberance"—a last burst of corporate headquarter building before stocks succumbed to the thudding crash of 1929. Throughout the previous decade, real estate speculators had been throwing up building after building, adding almost 100 skyscrapers of 20 stories or more, and utterly transforming the

Midtown Attractions

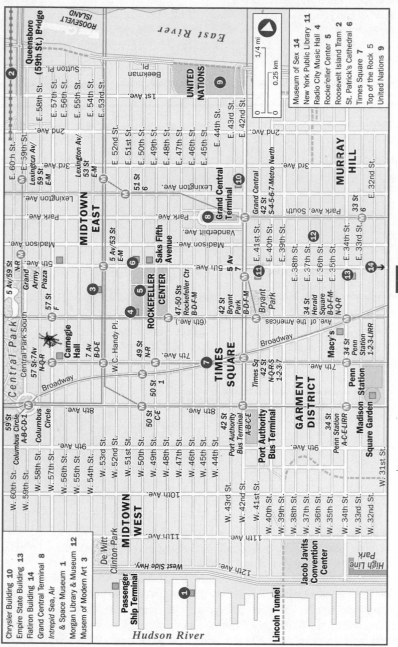

Chrysler Building **10**
Empire State Building **13**
Flatiron Building **14**
Grand Central Terminal **8**
Intrepid Sea, Air & Space Museum **1**
Morgan Library & Museum **12**
Musem of Modern Art **3**

Museum of Sex **14**
New York Public Library **11**
Radio City Music Hall **4**
Rocke'eller Center **5**
Roosevelt Island Tram **2**
St. Patrick's Cathedral **6**
Times Square **7**
Top of the Rock **5**
United Nations **9**

5

EXPLORING NEW YORK CITY | Midtown

CHELSEA CALLING: MEET NYC'S art district

More than 250 galleries are now on the blocks spanning 19th to 29th streets between Tenth and Eleventh avenues in West Chelsea, effectively making the Big Apple the planet's premiere marketplace for contemporary art. Gallery after gallery has taken over the former warehouse and industrial spaces of this dusty old 'hood, creating an eminently walkable arts district. You can have a perfectly lovely time simply getting lost in the area and wandering blindly from one space to the next, although you can hit a lot of clunky exhibitions (just as with any collection of new art, some are better than others)—but so what? If you want to take this course of action, start on 24th Street, which has the largest assortment of "name" galleries. A better tack might be to catch a tour of the area (see below) or to concentrate on the following eight galleries, which have made their reputations with consistently thought-provoking shows.

Note: The standard schedule for all Chelsea galleries is Tuesday to Saturday 10am to 6pm (June through August galleries are also closed on Saturdays). Your best subway option is either the C or E line to 23rd St.

Another Note: Because of rising rents in Chelsea, a number of excellent galleries have moved in the last few years to the Lower East Side—see p. 138.

303 Gallery   555 W. 21st St. (www.303gallery.com; ✆ **212/255-1121**). The Whitney biennial has this gallery on speed dial, having picked up works by several of the young to mid-career, cutting-edge photographers and painters who present here.

Andrea Rosen   525 and 544 W. 24th St. (www.andrearosengallery.com; ✆ **212/627-6000**). The Rosen gallery is a terrific place to see emerging artists, especially those who are "installation happy" and like to create entire environments for their viewers. It seems that each time I come here I'm stepping into some new type of utopia (or dystopia); the experience can be chilling and exciting.

Barbara Gladstone Gallery   515 W. 24th St. and 530 W. 21st St. (www.gladstonegallery.com; ✆ **212/206-9300** or 212/206-7605). Come here to see the artists who have emerged as honchos in the last decade or so, such as Matthew Barney and Richard Prince. Gladstone features conceptual, often highly political art—most prominently photography and videos, but also sculpture and paintings.

David Zwirner   525 and 533 W. 19th St. and 437 W. 20th St. (www.davidzwirner.com; ✆ **212/727-7020**). This is not the place for people with delicate sensibilities, but if you don't mind seeing art that's really on the edge, you'll often find

skyline of the city. Automaker Walter P. Chrysler commissioned architect William Van Alen to top them all, instructing him that he wanted a building "higher than the Eiffel Tower," the tallest in the world at that time. What Chrysler would soon learn was that the gentlemen behind the Bank of America had the same ambition, and they had hired Van Alen's former partner (and sworn enemy) H. Craig Severance to build them the tallest building on the planet down on Wall Street. Soon the race was on as each architect returned continually to the drafting board, adding 10 more stories of penthouses here, a lantern or a 50-foot flagpole there. In the fall of 1929, Severance was sure something here that will get your adrenaline pumping. Zwirner was profiled in the *New York Times* in March 2013, which praised his "idiosyncratic roster, with great oddballs like R. Crumb and Raymond Pettibon alongside institutional darlings like Stan Douglas and Francis Alÿs."

Gagosian 555 W. 24th St. and 521 W. 21st St. (www.gagosian.com; **℗ 212/741-1111**). A massive, important family of galleries (three uptown, two in California, one in Hong Kong, several in Europe), it presents blockbuster shows of such major 20th- and 21st-century figures as Julian Schnabel, Nan Goldin, and Cindy Sherman.

Pace Gallery 534 and 510 W. 25th St., 537 W. 24th St. (www.pacegallery.com; **℗ 212/929-7000**). Another "Blue Chip" gallery, with three outposts in Chelsea, as well as one in Midtown (32 E. 57th St.), one in London, one in California and two in China, Pace has been a powerhouse since the 1960s. Shows in 2016 featured the works of such biggies as David Hockney, Robert Rauschenberg, and James Turrell.

Paula Cooper 534 W. 21st St. (www.paulacoopergallery.com; **℗ 212/255-1105**). Cooper used to be one of the biggest names in art, the dealer that everyone wanted. Though she's slipped in the last decade and lost some of her big-name clients, she still has the exquisite taste she's always had, and exhibits a number of prominent artists, including Mark di Suvero, Claes Oldenburg, Sol LeWitt, and Donald Judd.

Yossi Milo 245 Tenth Ave. (www.yossimilogallery.com; **℗ 212/404-0370**). One of my personal favorites, Milo works almost exclusively with photographers and has a terrific eye for the next big thing. He also runs a very friendly gallery, and he and his staff are always happy to talk with interested patrons. Because he represents photographers, some of them selling multiple editions of their work, you just may be able to afford to buy something here.

A gallery tour: Allowing an expert to lead you through this ever-shifting maze of art is a good idea. And New York's foremost expert in the Chelsea Gallery scene—he visits 50 to 70 shows a week just to keep current—is Raphael Risemburg of **NY Gallery Tours** ★ (www.nygallerytours.com; **℗ 212/946-1548**). Risemburg, a former professor at Keane College in New Jersey, has a droll, friendly manner and leads his tours in Socratic fashion: He'll tell you what he thinks of the art at the four to five galleries you cover on your tour, and then ask your opinion on the unanswered questions it poses. His open tours are offered almost every Saturday ($25), and he also leads private tours for $195–$300 (varying by the number in the group).

he had won, so he completed the Bank of America building at 927 feet. Van Alen then unveiled the *coup de grâce* that he had been hiding in an elevator shaft—a silver spike to crown his building, making it, at 1,046 feet, an unbeatable 117 feet higher than his rival's.

Not only taller, the Chrysler was the more striking of the two buildings, its scalloped spire set like a jaunty jester's cap atop a sleek tower. Take a look at the sharp stainless-steel eagles that jut out just below the roof; the "gargoyles" below those on the 61st floor are actually modeled after the hood ornament of the 1929 Chrysler Plymouth.

The Chrysler remains one of the most impressive Art Deco buildings ever constructed, but it wasn't the tallest for long. Less than a year after it was completed, the Empire State Building assumed that mantle and held it until the World Trade Center came along.

405 Lexington Ave. (at 42nd St.). Subway: S, 4, 5, 6, 7 to 42nd St./Grand Central.

Empire State Building ★★★ ARCHITECTURE There's no better introduction to New York than a visit to the Empire State Building. An apex of the New York skyline, both literally (at 102 stories and 1,454 ft.) and figuratively, the view from its Observation Deck is at once instructive and exhilarating. From your bird's-eye perch, you orient yourself geographically and see, with a clarity not possible on the ground, the miracle of Manhattan, that runt of an island that couldn't get much wider or longer, and so did what no other city before it had done and expanded to the skies, becoming a dense, pulsating city of boxy towers set on a painfully narrow strip of land.

Look first to the **south,** where the Financial District's powerful skyscrapers loom over the field of lower, mostly residential housing that stands between it and Midtown. Beyond the Financial District, in the harbor, are the Statue of Liberty to the right and the Brooklyn Bridge to the left (the most graceful of the three bridges you'll see in this direction). **Right below** you will be the triangular Flatiron building, one of the most thrillingly odd in Manhattan (it was Frank Lloyd Wright's favorite building). Just to the side of it are the glittering gold roof of the Metropolitan Life Tower and the World Life Insurance Towers, once centers of New York's high society and now just part of the landscape. Drift to the **north side** of the building and you will be among a riot of skyscrapers, thrown up in a manner that seems wildly chaotic from this vantage point. This strip of Midtown contains more office space per acre than any other area in the world. Peer through the curtain of buildings to catch a glimpse of Central Park, looking like a modest lawn from this great height. To your right, take a good look at the shiny, scalloped spire of the Chrysler building (many have said it was designed to look like the grillwork of 1930s–era Chrysler cars).

The Empire State Building keeps longer hours than any other tourist attraction in the city, opening at 8am and closing at 2am to accommodate the four-million-plus visitors who troop through yearly. The attraction has been able to make the entry process much more efficient in recent years, but there still will be some waits for entry. Some ways to "game the line" include:

- Arrive promptly at 8am, during the dinner hour, or after midnight, which are relatively uncrowded times.
- Plan to visit on a Tuesday or Wednesday, the least popular days of the week. You'll encounter the biggest crowds on Saturday and Sunday, followed closely by Monday and Friday. July and August are the busiest months here.
- Purchase and print out a ticket from the Empire State Building website, which will allow you to skip the ticket line (though *not* the lines for security or the elevators). Purchase of the **CityPass** (p. 125) brings the same perks.

- It opened in 1931 after just 14 months of construction (total cost: $25 million).
- Tallest building in the world from 1931 to 1970, when the World Trade Center took the title. It is now the 32nd tallest building on the planet.
- The oddly shaped spire at the top was meant to be a landing port for blimps, but high winds kept dirigibles from ever being able to anchor here.
- In 1945, a plane accidentally crashed into the building, killing 17 people.
- Every Valentine's Day, 14 couples are married for free on the Observation Deck.

The **New York Pass** is not quite as good a deal, because you'll have to wait in the ticket line to change your voucher into a ticket. But all three passes will allow you to ignore the mad scrum of salesmen outside the building, harassing would-be visitors to buy from them.

- **Download the free Empire State Building app.** It will give you, as does the ESB website, a real-time look at how long the wait is to get to the top (the info is refreshed every 2 minutes). Know, however, that the fun starts well before "the top". As you make your way through the building, you'll see exhibitions on the building's move towards energy efficiency and its history, along with delicious views from the (slightly) lower floors. The app also has a terrific tour embedded in it, also free, which delivers commentary, historic photos and videos about the construction of the famed tower; and helps visitors identify the important buildings and parks they'll see from the observation deck (along with some background on them).

There is no snack bar on the observation deck but there is a souvenir shop as you exit (coolest gift: Empire State Building zipper pulls).

350 Fifth Ave. (at 34th St.). www.esbnyc.com. (C) **212/736-3100.** 86th Floor Observatory admission $32 adults, $29 seniors, $26 children 6–12, free for children 5 and under. Main Deck Express pass $55 (all ages). 86th and 102nd floor combination pass $52 adults, $49 seniors, $46 children 6–12. Express pass to Main and Top decks $75 (all ages). Daily 8am–2am (last elevator 1:15am). Subway: B, D, F, N, Q, R, M to 34th St.; 6 to 33rd St.

Grand Central Station ★★ ARCHITECTURE In ancient Roman times, the entrances to great cities were framed with monumental arches, meant to awe all who passed through. When Grand Central Terminal was being built at the turn of the last century, it was recognized that our railroad terminals were our grand gateways, the first view a traveler would have of the metropolis. So the architects of both Grand Central and the late great Pennsylvania Station (the original, torn down in the 1960s) conspired to create as much pomp and stateliness as possible, filling these spaces with the symbols and architecture of imperial Rome. On Grand Central's facade, 10 colossal Doric fluted pillars tower over Park Avenue; above them a massive statue of

A PARK & a ride

On October 24, 2012, a small miracle occurred: **Franklin D. Roosevelt Four Freedoms Park** on Roosevelt Island finally opened. An austerely beautiful tribute to the four-term president, it was designed by star architect Louis Kahn shortly before his death in 1974. It took the intervening 38 years for the project to finally come to fruition (mostly due to the efforts of Kahn's son, who created a documentary about his father's vision that helped raise the millions necessary to build the monument). The park offers wonderful views of the Manhattan skyline, as well as a serene break from the bustle of NYC. But perhaps one of its greatest lures is the amusement park–like ride one takes to the island aboard the **Roosevelt Island Tram (ℂ 212/832-4555;** www.rioc.com/transportation.htm). This is the aerial vehicle you have probably seen in countless movies, most notably *Spider-Man*. It originates at 59th Street and Second Avenue, costs $2.75 each way, and takes about 5 minutes to traverse the East River to Roosevelt Island, where there are a series of apartment complexes (part of the fun is peering into the apartments as you swoop by). The tram operates daily from 6am until 2am and until 3:30am on weekends.

Mercury, the god of travel, spreads his arms in welcome as Hercules and Minerva, gods of strength and wisdom, lounge at his feet. (The face of the clock below the sculpture is the largest piece of Tiffany glass in the world.)

The station's interior is no less impressive, its concourse soaring the equivalent of nine stories to a vaulted ceiling on which the signs of the zodiac are created from 59 fiber-optic lights and 2,500 painted stars. The side walls feature massive windows that throw shafts of light onto the acre-long Indiana marble floor. Not that the station needed them: One of its innovations was the use of electric lights, so you'll see bare bulbs sprinkled throughout the station and on the massive chandeliers that overhang the concourse. Two hundred buildings were demolished to make way for the station, which opened on February 2, 1913, bearing a price tag of $80 million.

As you walk through, take in all of the trendy shops and food markets housed in the arteries of the main concourse; another dining concourse below, with the famed **Oyster Bar** at its heart (p. 99); a huge Apple Store on one balcony; and the **Campbell Apartment,** former office of a finance tycoon and now a fab bar (p. 248). If you're traveling with children, take them to the "whispering gallery" right outside the Oyster Bar. Stand on one side of the arch there and have your child stand on the other, and then whisper to each other back and forth; a trick of acoustics allows sound to travel from one side of the vault to the other.

Walking tours of the station are offered two ways: via audio tour (go to www.grandcentralterminal.com/info/tours.com to download the tour at a cost of $4.99, or rent headphones and a player at the specially marked window in the central terminal, for $9); or with a docent from the Municipal Arts Society, daily at 12:30pm for a 75-minute tour ($25 adults, $20 students, seniors and children under 10, meet at the ticket window marked GCT Tours in the main concourse).

42nd St. at Park Ave. www.grandcentralterminal.com. ✆ **212/532-4900.** Subway: S, 4, 5, 6, or 7 to 42nd St./Grand Central.

The Morgan Library & Museum ★★ LIBRARY/MUSEUM   Famed Canadian scientist George Mercer Dawson once wrote that a great library contained "the diary of the human race." With that definition, very few libraries come as close to greatness as the Morgan, which contains examples of the written word from the beginning of recorded time—from pictorial Mesopotamian cylinder seals (4th millennium B.C., a precursor to writing); to papyrus rolls from ancient Egypt, Greece, and Rome; to brilliantly colorful medieval illuminated manuscripts. Its crowning jewels are three editions of the Gutenberg Bible, the first book to be created using movable type. (This is the only collection in the world to boast three editions; scholars come from across the globe to study them, as each is unique). Also in the collection today are manuscripts by Mark Twain, Jane Austen, Charles Dickens, the Brontë sisters, Galileo, Bob Dylan, Alexander Calder, and James Joyce. One of the 25 known surviving copies of the Declaration of Independence is another highlight, along with a First Folio of Shakespeare. (The fragility of these treasures means that they cannot be constantly on display, but you'll usually see one of the Gutenbergs when you visit, along with other exquisite books.)

The Morgan in the name of the library was 19th-century billionaire J. Pierpont Morgan (1837–1913), and he collected more than just books. But many of his greatest artistic acquisitions were donated to the Wadsworth Atheneum (in Hartford) and the Metropolitan Museum after Morgan's death.

When you visit, be sure to set aside at least an hour and a half to take in the ever-rotating special exhibitions, along with the exquisite architecture. In 2017, these will include an homage to Emily Dickinson (with displays of original manuscripts, photographs, and other visual materials); and masterworks from the National Museum of Sweden, including works by Rembrandt, Raphael, and Peter Paul Rubens.

The original library, a marble villa in High Renaissance style, was designed by Charles Follen McKim (of the famous firm of McKim, Meade, and White). An expansion by lauded architect Renzo Piano, completed in 2006, added massive steel and glass pavilions, doubling the size of the facilities without diluting their Italianate flair. Along with a gift store, a good cafe and restaurant were added (so you may want to combine your visit with lunch).

225 Madison Ave. (btw. 36th and 37th sts.). www.themorgan.org. ✆ **212/685-0008.** Admission $20 adults, $13 seniors and students, free for children 12 and under; free for all Fri 7–9pm. Tues–Thurs 10:30am–5pm; Fri 10:30am–9pm; Sat 10am–6pm; Sun 11am–6pm. Subway: 6 to 33rd St.

Museum of Sex ★ MUSEUM   Though it tries hard to avoid a carnival atmosphere, with voluminous and often soporific wall text, this museum still has a major "wink, wink, giggle, giggle" quotient. If you're interested in the subject from an anthropological perspective, you may be disappointed. For the rest of us, including all of the folks who seemed to be out on dates (or perhaps they met there?), the museum is good, dirty fun. *Warning:* Due to the graphic nature of its exhibits, this museum is not for everyone.

233 Fifth Ave. (at 27th St.). www.museumofsex.com. © **212/689-6337.** Admission adults $18.50, seniors and students $16.50 (online discounts often available); no one under 18 admitted. Sun–Thurs 10am–8pm; Fri–Sat 10am–9pm. Subway: N, R, 6 to 28th St.

New York Public Library ★★ LIBRARY/LANDMARK Many art historians consider this to be the finest Beaux Arts building in the United States. It certainly is one of the grandest, completed in 1911 at a cost of over $9 million and built by the famous firm of Carrere and Hastings. The exterior takes its inspiration from the twin palaces on the north side of the Place de la Concorde in Paris and is done in the same French Renaissance style, a perfect harmony of columns, pediments, and statuary. Famous stone lions guard the entrance and are said to roar whenever a virgin passes by. Want to use the library? Well, you will be "reading between the lions" (sorry, I couldn't resist).

The library itself holds thousands of volumes, many of which are housed underground below what is now Bryant Park. A "non-browsing" facility, it uses an ancient dumbwaiter system for retrieval of books in which tomes are stacked into a small elevator and sent up when requests are made. Along with books, **Gottesman Exhibition Hall** (first floor) often houses world-class exhibits on topics as varied as the history of children's literature, New York literary figures, innovations in photography, and more. Don't skip the Lionel Pincus and Princess Firyal room, which houses one of the most extensive collections of maps in the world (and is magnificent after a $5 million renovation).

Entrance is always free, and the palatial interior, with its expanses of marble and carved oak ceilings, is worth a look-see. For a more formal tour, time your visit to occur at 11am or 2pm Monday through Saturday.

Fifth Ave. at 42nd St. www.nypl.org. © **917/275-6975** (exhibits and events) or 212/930-0800 (general number). Free admission to all exhibitions. Mon and Thurs–Sat 10am–6pm; Tues–Wed 10am–8pm; Sun 1–5pm. Subway: 1, 2, 3 to 42nd St./Broadway; B, D, F, M to 42nd St./6th Ave.; S, 4, 5, 6 to Grand Central/42nd St.; 7 to Fifth Ave.

St. Patrick's Cathedral ★ CATHEDRAL The largest Roman Catholic cathedral in the United States, St. Pat's is also the seat of the Archdiocese of New York. Designed by James Renwick, begun in 1859, and consecrated in 1879, St. Patrick's wasn't completed until 1906. Strangely, Irish Catholics picked one of the city's WASPiest neighborhoods for St. Patrick's. The vast cathedral seats a congregation of 2,200; if you don't want to attend Mass, pop in between services to get a look at the impressive interior. The St. Michael and St. Louis altar came from Tiffany & Co. (also located here on Fifth Ave.). A free app, available on the website, provides an erudite tour of the premises; there are also live, free tours most days of the week at 10am.

Fifth Ave. (btw. 50th and 51st sts.). www.saintpatrickscathedral.org. © **212/753-2261.** Free admission. Daily 6:30am–8:45pm. For mass times, check the website. Subway: B, D, F, M to 47th–50th sts./Rockefeller Center.

United Nations ★★ ARCHITECTURE/HISTORIC SITE It's this seven-block stretch of international territory that makes New York City the capital of the world. No, really. It's become fashionable of late in some political circles to denigrate the U.N. Though some reform is obviously necessary, a tour here will remind you of just how much the United Nations has done since its inception. It was founded, after all, with the express purpose of ensuring that there would never be another world war, and it has accomplished that, no small task. Perhaps more importantly, a visit here will remind you of how much potential the U.N. still has for effecting meaningful progress in numerous fields, from the elimination of disease and poverty to the resolution of ethnic conflicts.

Those who take the hour-long tour will visit not only the **General Assembly** (where Khrushchev once famously pounded his shoe in anger) and the **Security Council,** but also the less well-known **Economic and Social Council Room** that oversees the work of UNICEF, the World Health Organization (WHO), and 28 other U.N. programs of development. (Little-known fact: It's thanks to recommendations by the WHO that most countries have expiration dates stamped on milk.) It's in this room that officials are working to create standardized tests for avian flu, vaccinate the world's children against polio, and promote the cause of world literacy. The Nobel Peace Prize won by the U.N. Peacekeeping forces in 2001 is displayed just outside the council room, along with an enlightening exhibit on the important work these troops are still doing throughout the world.

Along with the interior rooms, visitors view the lobby of the General Assembly building, with its free, changing exhibits (photojournalism mostly), meditation room, and the memorial stained-glass window Marc Chagall created for former Secretary General Dag Hammarskjöld in 1964 (to the right of the entrance). An international gift shop, with trinkets from across the globe, and the U.N. post office are in the basement.

Important note: Due to increased security measures, the U.N. no longer allows on-the-spot ticket purchases for the tour. Only those who have purchased a ticket in advance online will be admitted into the building Mondays through Fridays (on weekends, visitors can see the visitor center without a ticket but there are no tours). Many days sell out entirely, so buy tickets as far in advance as possible.

At First Ave. and 47th St. http://visit.un.org. ℂ **212/963-8687.** Guided tours $22 adults, $15 seniors and students, $13 children 5–12. Children 4 and under not permitted. Weekday tours 9am–4:30pm; weekends Visitor Center access only, 10am–4:30pm. Guided tours may be canceled when heads of state are speaking and tend not to take place in Sept and Oct when the General Assembly is in session. Subway: S, 4, 5, 6, 7 to 42nd St./Grand Central.

Times Square/West Side

Intrepid Sea, Air, and Space Museum ★★ MUSEUM/HISTORIC SITE How's this for an all-star lineup? Not only does the Intrepid Sea, Air & Space Museum now display the Space Shuttle *Intrepid,* it's got the world's only tourable nuclear submarine, the famed **Concorde** jet, nearly two dozen grounded jets, a Revolutionary War–era submarine, and is itself a World War II–era aircraft carrier. Whew! Even those who profess no interest in aviation or military history will find themselves wowed by the breadth and depth of this collection. You'll likely have to devote a good 3 hours or more to get your fill here, so arrive early if you can.

You'll want to begin your visit at the **USS *Growler*** submarine, built in 1958 and so narrow that only small groups can enter at a time (which keeps the lines here long). You'll be taken on a brief, thrillingly claustrophobic tour introduced by a short video. Children under the age of 6 are not admitted.

Next, make your way to the Concorde, the oversized luxury lawn dart that, after flying half-empty for a number of years, was finally taken out of commission in 2003. (The jet isn't in the classic bent-nosed pose; that was only used for take-offs and landings.) This ultra-deluxe flying bus carried a mere 100 passengers at a time, most of them paying $6,000 each way for the privilege of crossing the Atlantic faster than the speed of sound (it went from 0 to 165mph in just 2½ seconds). Take a close look at places A and B, the seats reserved for Queen Elizabeth II and Prince Philip of England.

Visiting the pavilion of the **space shuttle *Enterprise*** costs an extra $7, but most will find it worth the outlay. A terrific new exhibit in this area explores what day-to-day life on a space shuttle is like.

Then turn your attention to the **Fighting I,** the main focus of your visit, a 40,000-ton aircraft carrier that had one of the greatest survival stories of World War II. Though it was hit by five kamikaze planes (two of them in a single day) during its tours of duty, it continued to serve (the Japanese called it "The Ghost Ship" because it couldn't be sunk). Go directly to the Information Center on the hangar deck to inquire if there's a tour starting anytime soon. You can wander through the ship on your own, but you'll get more out of the experience with the hour-long guided tour, led by highly informed docents, most with military backgrounds.

Pier 86 (W. 46th St. at Twelfth Ave.). www.intrepidmuseum.org. (℡ **877/957-7447** or 212/245-0072. Admission $26 adults; $24 seniors and students; $19 children 5–12; free for active or retired military and children 4 and under. Various combo tickets add extras like space shuttle or simulator rides. Daily 10am–5pm, summer weekends 10am–6pm. Closed Christmas and Thanksgiving. Subway: A, C, E to 42nd St./Port Authority. Bus: M42 Crosstown.

Museum of Modern Art ★★ ART MUSEUM MoMA, as it's nicknamed, doesn't want for masterpieces. This is where you'll find seminal works by Picasso, van Gogh, Brancusi, Dalí, and Matisse, among others. Its riches, however, aren't apparent on first glance. Oddly, the museum hides most of its masterworks waaaay up on the fifth floor—a ploy, I think, to get patrons to first look at the more contemporary, and often less celebrated, pieces that are housed in the lower galleries. Foil the curators by heading upstairs first and seeing the museum in "reverse order" to ensure that you have enough time to meander in front of the works that make the museum great

MOMA'S mona lisas

Though there are many masterworks in the museum, be sure you give yourself enough time for the following highlights:

o Vincent van Gogh's **Starry Night,** which has an even more vivid impact when viewed in person, the thickness of the brush strokes making it as much sculpture as painting. Created a year before his suicide, when van Gogh was in an insane asylum, the painting is filled with premonitions of what was to come, the foreground taken up with a soaring cypress tree, symbol of death.

o Pablo Picasso's **Desmoiselles d'Avignon,** a massive brothel scene in which Picasso experimented with a number of art styles—look closely and you'll see that one of the women's heads looks like an African mask, another profile is taken from Egyptian art, the woman in the middle assumes a classical Venus-like pose, and a leg of one of the figures devolves into cubist abstraction. Reportedly, Picasso painted the work when he was suffering from syphilis, which may be why the women appear so threatening.

o Salvador Dali's **Persistence of Memory,** in which watches melt and a long-nosed figure (some say it was a self-portrait of Dali, others think it represents an unborn baby) lies prostrate on the ground. You may be surprised at how small this seminal work is.

o Soaring sculptures by Brancusi, Andrew Wyeth's **Christina's World,** vibrantly colorful masterpieces by Matisse, Jackson Pollock's splatter art, and painted metaphors by Magritte are among the other wonders of the museum's collection, the most important in the world for art of this era.

(important in a museum with 125,000-square-feet of gallery space). Pick up and study the museum's gallery map; while the architecture of MoMA is justly renowned, it can be sometimes tricky to navigate from one area to the next. And don't just spend your time indoors. The **Abby Aldrich Rockefeller Sculpture Garden,** which was enlarged during a 2004 renovation, is one of the most delightful spots to linger in the city.

Note: MoMA has installed a museum-wide Wi-Fi network so that visitors can access audio tours and commentary on their wireless devices; this includes specialized versions for children, teens, and the visually impaired.

11 W. 53rd St. (btw. Fifth and Sixth aves.). www.moma.org. ✆ **212/708-9400.** Admission $25 adults, $18 seniors, $14 students, children 16 and under free if accompanied by adult. Free admission Fri 4–8pm. Sun–Thurs 10:30am–5:30pm; Fri 10:30am–8pm. Subway: E, M to Fifth Ave.; B, D, F to 47th–50th sts./Rockefeller Center.

Rockefeller Center ★★ ARCHITECTURE Gotham's splendid "city within a city" was built in the 1930s at the height of the Depression. Thanks to the jobs it gave construction workers, it was the second-largest employer in the city at the time, surpassed only by the federal Works Progress Association (WPA). And it remains a marvel of elegance and aspiration, a several-blocks-wide collection of 19 buildings that, despite their mass, create a space that is airy and light, a welcoming haven for both tourists and residents. No matter how many times I come here, I still get goose bumps on the walk from Fifth Avenue through the gardened central path—called "The Channel," as it runs between the French and the British buildings.

Follow this channel-like route down to the **ice-skating rink** (the first commercial one in the world), and the golden statue of *Prometheus,* or "Leaping Louie," as wits have called him over the years, his prone position under the soaring vertical of the RCA building making him look like he just jumped. The rink is open October to early April, Monday through Thursday 9am to 10:30pm, Friday and Saturday 8:30am to midnight, Sunday 8:30am to 10pm.

There's much to see at the Rock. Directly behind the statue is where the yearly 70-plus-foot Christmas tree is set on November 20 each year, a plaque marking the space. Take a left and walk toward 49th Street to the small side street with the glassed-in TV studio on the corner. This is where NBC's *Today Show* is taped, the small street the area where sign-waving crowds gather every weekday morning, as early as 4:00am, to attempt to get their faces on TV. (When the show has musical performances, people line up days before and guests play on a stage in this narrow alley. It looks much bigger on TV, doesn't it?)

Stroll over to Fifth Avenue between 50th and 51st streets, where *Prometheus*'s brother, mighty *Atlas,* the finest piece of art in the complex (by artist Lee Lawrie), hoists a giant globe on his shoulders, muscles rippling. From the back, *Atlas* looks a bit like a Christ figure, especially superimposed on St. Patrick's Cathedral across the street. Go into the lobby directly behind the *Atlas* statue for a peek at one of the most magnificent public spaces in the city, the walls bedecked with a rare, swirling Greek marble, the gold "curtains" at the side creating an ever-changing dance of shadows on the ceiling.

Although I don't recommend the Rockefeller City tour (it doesn't go anywhere you can't go yourself, and the guides are a dull lot), the **Tour at NBC Studios** ★★ (www.thetouratnbcstudios.com; ✆ **212/664-7174;** $33 adults, $29 seniors and children 6–12; daily 8:30am–5pm; subway B, D, F to Rockefeller Center) has been revamped (after a 2-year hiatus) and is now an engrossing experience. It recounts the history of TV and radio through videos and visits to NBC's major studios, including the set for Saturday Night Live and the NBC Nightly News with Lester Holt. Best time to go is Saturday morning, so you can see the sets for Saturday Night Live being constructed, the theater where The Tonight Show with Jimmy Fallon takes place (it's off limits when Fallon is taping during the week) and watch live as the Today Show is being engineered (visitors get to peer into the glassed-in control rooms),

Equally exciting is the 70th-floor observation deck at Rockefeller Center, **Top of the Rock** ★★ (30 Rockefeller Plaza; www.topoftherocknyc.com; ✆ **212/698-2000;** basic tickets $30 adults, $28 seniors, $20 ages 6–12, see website for other combo packages; daily 8am–midnight; subway B, D, F to Rockefeller Center). While not as high as the one in the Empire State Building or One World Observatory, it gives them a run for the money with its own striking views (you have a much better vista of Central Park from here, a grand bumpy green blanket laid at your feet) and its use of timed tickets, which eliminate the painful waits that can sour the experience at the Empire State Building. The Rock re-creates very closely the cruise-ship-themed look of the deck from the 1930s, when it was first constructed.

Finally, there's **Radio City Music Hall** (1260 Avenue of the Americas at 50th St.; www.radiocity.com; © 212/247-4777; $50–$300 show tickets, tour daily 11am–3pm $27 adults, $19 seniors and children 12 and under, discount for on-line pre-order; subway B, D, F to Rockefeller Center), which remains the kitschy, thrilling delight it's always been: The Christmas Show is a marvel of excess, with hundreds of people and hooved animals on stage at one time; orchestras magically rising from the pit; and best of all, the Rockettes chorus line, that superhuman all-leg dancing machine. Those who don't want to shell out for a show, or who visit when the theater is dark, can take the tour, which is well worth it to see the exquisite Art Deco features of this sensational pleasure hall and get a picture taken with a Rockette.

Btw. 48th and 50th sts. from Fifth to Sixth aves. www.radiocity.com. © **212/247-4777** (tour info). Subway: B, D, F, M to 47th–50th sts./Rockefeller Center.

Times Square ★ ICON   Adam Gopnik wrote about Times Square in *The New Yorker*, "No other part of New York has had such a melodramatic sensitivity to the changes in the city's history, with an image for every decade." Think for a moment and those visions of Times Square should start flooding your mind: snazzy clubs and peroxide blonde chorus girls in the 1920s and '30s, sailors kissing girls at the end of World War II, the wisecracking small-time hoods of *Guys and Dolls* in the '50s, and, of course, the bleak urban decay of the '60s and '70s when, as Gopnik put it, "everything fell apart and Hell wafted up through the manhole covers."

Times Square is back on the upswing now, the porn shops banished and crime held (mostly) at bay. To get the full effect of today's Square, it's imperative you visit at night. It's then that the rainbow glitter of the flashing lights from the dozens of billboards, giant TV screens, electronic news crawls, and headlights of cars whizzing by wash over the Square, sweeping all of the litter and crowds into the background. The effect is like watching fireworks. (This tradition of massive "spectaculars" is codified into law—in the 1980s, ordinances were passed requiring that new buildings abutting the Square have 16,000 square feet of light shows on their facades, with "moving elements" that are sufficiently bright.) One of the best views is from the massive stairs atop the TKTS booth at 46th Street.

Beyond this theater of the streets is the legitimate theater, and Times Square still has more playhouses per acre than any other area in North America. For dawn theater, peer into the sidewalk-level television studios of *Good Morning America* (44th and Broadway). *Warning:* If you take a photo with any of the costumed characters or "painted ladies" roaming Times Square you'll be expected to tip them.

Subway: 1, 2, 3, 7, N, Q, R, S to Times Square; A, C, E to 42nd St./Port Authority.

UPTOWN

Upper East Side

Cooper Hewitt National Design Museum ★★★ MUSEUM   After a 2-year closure for renovations, the Cooper Hewitt Museum transformed itself in 2015 into the museum equivalent of Steve Jobs. The museum, which is the design division of the Smithsonian, has always been a forward-thinking institution since its founding in 1897. But today, it's taken its mission to explore the "impact of design on everyday life" to another level with its use of technology, turning the museum-goer from simple viewer into on-the-spot designer.

Let me explain: when a visitor enters this handsome museum (set in a mansion built by tycoon Andrew Carnegie in 1902), he or she is loaned a whiz-bang, first-of-its-kind, electronic stylus/pen to use throughout the visit. With this in hand, visitors can press the "X"-marked end of the tool to the wall text to save what they're seeing to a customized website, so they can learn more about these objects and design at home (no need to worry about privacy: your ticket comes with a personal URL, meaning you don't have to give up your email address or any other personal info). It sounds gimmicky, I know, but I for one delighted in revisiting my favorites once at my personal computer. The other side of the gadget works as a pen, which visitors use at large electronic drafting tables throughout the museum. In a wallpaper room, for example, what you design at the table (sometimes with the help of the historic samples stored in the table's computer) can be projected onto the walls all around you. It's great fun for kids, though I must say I saw as many adults scribbling away at the tables as youngsters.

They had much to inspire them. Thanks to the renovation, the museum now has 60% more exhibition space, which it fills with wondrous objects from its collection, everything from a psychedelic Bob Dylan poster, to a contemporary shoulder implant that looks like a crocheted snowflake (it moves inside the body with the flexibility of a sweater), to a 1.2 million-year-old scraping tool. The exhibitions are themed and always changing, so hit the website to see what'll be there when you arrive.

2 E. 91st St. (at Fifth Ave.). www.cooperhewitt.org. © **212/849-8400.** Admission $18 adults, $12 seniors, $9 students, free 18 and under; $2 discount if you buy online; free Sat 6–9pm. Daily 10am–6pm (Sat until 9pm). Closed Thanksgiving and Christmas. Subway: 6 to 86th St. or 4, 5 to 96th St.

The Frick Collection ★★★ MUSEUM/HISTORIC HOME   Arguably the best small museum in the nation, the Frick provides a deeply satisfying experience on a number of levels. There's the highbrow fun of seeing some of the world's greatest masterpieces; the lowbrow kick of getting a firsthand peek at the home of one of the super-rich and famous; and the somewhat macabre thrill, akin to a séance, of communing with someone long dead through his choices in art. In the end, the Frick Collection is as much about Henry Clay Frick and the world he created as it is about the art itself.

And that's a good thing, as Frick (1849–1919) was a fascinating figure, an entrepreneur in the steel and coke industries with only 3 years of formal schooling, who became a self-made millionaire by the time he was 30. On his death, he bequeathed his enormous art collection and the colonnaded neoclassical mansion that housed it (built by Carrere and Hastings, architects of the N.Y. Public Library) to the formation of a public museum for the purpose of "encouraging and developing the study of the fine arts" in the United States.

It's not a large museum, but in each of the 16 galleries there are wonders to behold, paintings and sculptures from nearly every great artist in the Western Canon. Because Frick wanted viewers to have their own experiences of the art, there is very little wall text posted, nor is the art arranged in any "instructive" manner—different periods of art are mixed together, as are artists of various nationalities. Unlike the Barnes Collection in Philadelphia, Frick gave his trustees the right to change the arrangement of the works, and acquire new ones; a full third of what you'll see was purchased after Frick passed away.

But most of the great pieces are from Frick's era and they are a testament to his astute taste as a collector. This is a man who not only collected Rembrandts (a trifecta of them!), but chose none but the most intriguing works, such as the painter's portrait of fur merchant Nicholas Ruts, Rembrandt's first commissioned portrait and the one that launched his career.

Masterpieces by Vermeer (three of the meager 36 that still exist today), Renoir, Degas, Velazquez, El Greco (his *St. Jerome,* of which the Metropolitan Museum's version is a copy), and more are also on view. The most famous painting in the collection, Holbein's portrait of Sir Thomas More, hangs next to the mantel in the Living Hall, though in an ironic move, Frick also hung Holbein's portrait of Thomas Cromwell—More's longtime political rival, who was also executed by Henry VIII—on the other side of that mantel, so that the two can stare each other down through eternity.

An erudite **audio tour,** free with admission, serves as a pleasant companion for a walk through the museum. Every hour on the half-hour, a short but interesting **movie** on the life of Frick is screened. And if you have the foresight, visit the Frick website to learn if a classical music concert will be taking place during your time in New York—the collection has a history of hosting some of the best up-and-coming talents.

1 E. 70th St. (at Fifth Ave.). www.frick.org. © **212/288-0700.** Admission $20 adults, $15 seniors, $10 students; pay-what-you-wish Sun 11am–1pm. Children 9 and under not admitted. Tues–Sat 10am–6pm; Sun 11am–5pm. Closed all major holidays. Subway: 6 to 68th St./Hunter College.

The Jewish Museum ★★ MUSEUM   The "modest" goal of this intriguing museum is to explore 4,000 years of Jewish culture through art. Surprisingly, it succeeds much of the time. Its two-story permanent exhibition (which starts on the fourth floor) gently guides viewers from the biblical era, and the many clashes over such issues as animal sacrifice and the role of the Temple (Jesus wasn't the only one up in arms over that), through the Diaspora, when the Israelites, forced out of their home by successive conquerors, became

Uptown Attractions

American Folk Art Museum **2**
American Museum of Natural History **6**
Cathedral of St. John the Divine **17**
Children's Museum of Manhattan **7**
The Cloisters **19**
Cooper Hewitt National Design
    Museum **12**
El Museo del Barrio **15**
The Frick Collection **3**
Gracie Mansion **11**
Hamilton Grange National Memorial **18**
Solomon R. Guggenheim Museum **10**

Hudson River

Harlem

To Cathedral of
St. John the Divine
and Hamilton
Grange National
Memorial
(see inset at left)

THE CITY
COLLEGE OF
NEW YORK

Hamilton
Grange
National
Memorial

RIVERSIDE PARK

UPPER WEST
SIDE

81 St-
Museum of
Natural History
B-C

MORNINGSIDE PARK

COLUMBIA
UNIVERSITY

The
Lake

Sheep
Meadow

LINCOLN
CENTER

Lincoln Center

Cathedral
of St. John the Divine

CENTRAL
PARK

Columbus
Circle
A-B-C-D-1

0   200 y

The Jewish Museum **13**
The Met Breuer **4**
Metropolitan Museum of Art **8**
Museum of Arts and Design **1**
Museum of the City of New York **14**
Neue Gallery of New York **9**
New-York Historical Society **5**
Studio Museum in Harlem **16**

0   1/4 mi
0   0.25 km

Ⓜ Subway stop

East River

E. 104th St.
E. 103rd St.
103 St 6
E. 102nd St.
E. 101st St.
E. 100th St.
Mt. Sinai Hospital
E. 99th St.
E. 98th St.
E. 97th St.
96 St 6
E. 96th St.
E. 95th St.
E. 94th St.
Jewish Museum **13**
E. 93rd St.
E. 92nd St.
Cooper Hewitt Museum **12**
E. 91st St.
E. 90th St.
Guggenheim Museum **10**
E. 89th St.
E. 88th St.
E. 87th St.
9
E. 86th St.
86 St 4-5-6
E. 85th St.
UPPER EAST SIDE
E. 84th St.
E. 83rd St.
E. 82nd St.
8
E. 81st St.
Metropolitan Museum of Art
E. 80th St.
E. 79th St.
77 St 6
E. 78th St.
E. 77th St.
E. 76th St.
E. 75th St.
E. 74th St.
E. 73rd St.
4
E. 72nd St.
E. 71st St.
3
E. 70th St.
E. 69th St.
68 St/ Hunter College 6
E. 68th St.
E. 67th St.
E. 66th St.
E. 65th St.
Lexington Av/ 63 St F
E. 64th St.
E. 63rd St.
E. 62nd St.
E. 61st St.
5 Av/ 59 St N-R
E. 60th St.
Lexington Av/ 59 St N-R
59 St 4-5-6
Roosevelt Island Tram
Queensboro (59th St.) Bridge
E. 59th St.

Jacqueline Kennedy Onassis Reservoir

Transverse

The Great Lawn

Transverse

CENTRAL PARK

Transverse

Central Park Zoo

Wollman Rink

Central Park South

Fifth Ave.
Madison Ave.
Park Ave.
Lexington Ave.
Third Ave.
Second Ave.
First Ave.
York Ave.
East End Ave.
FDR Dr.

Carl Schurz Park
11

MUSEUM MILE

Upper Manhattan

Uptown

Midtown

Downtown

MAYOR ATTRACTION gracie mansion

New York City has been at the center of United States history since well before the country itself was founded. So it makes sense that a tour of the mayor's house—built in 1799 and one of only three dedicated mayors' homes in the United States—will be compelling even for those who know nothing of Gotham's history.

We can partially thank current Mayor Bill de Blasio, and his family, for that. When they took residence they decided to fill the house with artifacts and works of art that speak to the diversity of the city and country. So as you wander through you'll see portraits of Colonial-era Jewish merchants, pre-Civil War abolitionists, and 19th-century home-factory workers, plus the combo tomahawk/peace pipe that was used for the last New York treaty with the Seneca people

(if things hadn't gone well, the sharp side might have been used!) and handbills distributed to stop discrimination against early Irish immigrants. This is alongside all the telling artifacts of the home itself, from panes of glass etched with the names of various mayors' children, to the fireplace mantel beside which Alexander Hamilton took his last breath after his famous duel (it was added to Gracie Mansion after the home it was in was pulled down). All of this, and more, is explained by the enthusiastic, highly knowledgeable docents who lead the tours.

Located in Carl Schurz Park (entrance at 88th St. and East End Ave.), the mansion can be toured free of charge; go to www.nyc.gov. (© **212/676-3060**) to sign up for tours, which are conducted on Tuesdays at 10am, 11am, 2pm, and 3pm.

"wandering Jews," spreading to every part of the known world. The modern section brings the exhibition up to today, with only the briefest mention of the Holocaust (if that's what interests you, you'll be better served by the Museum of Jewish Heritage downtown; p. 124). The story is told through a mixed marriage, so to speak, of nearly 800 exquisite artifacts and works of art, and by a variety of story-telling devices, including a free audio tour, interactive computer programs, videos, television clips, and wall texts. What finally emerges is a portrait of a people who have not only managed to survive against the steepest odds, but have become magnificently diverse in the process. In fact, the second half of the exhibit could be seen as a survey of world art styles as seen through Jewish eyes, making the museum of interest to a wide audience.

The fourth floor also houses a nifty playroom for kids. On the first and second floors are galleries for changing exhibits, which in the past have housed blockbuster shows on children's book author William Steig, artist Marc Chagall, and fashion designer Isaac Mizrahi. There are also two handsome gift shops and the terrific **Russ & Daughters** restaurant (see p. 106).

1109 Fifth Ave. (at 92nd St.). www.thejewishmuseum.org. © **212/423-3200.** Admission $15 adults, $12 seniors, $8 students, free for kids 18 and under; free for all Sat. Sun–Tues and Sat 11am–5:45pm; Thurs 11am–8pm. Subway: 4, 5, 6 to 86th St.; 6 to 96th St.

Metropolitan Museum of Art ★★★ ART MUSEUM The giant among New York museums both figuratively and literally: At 1.6 million square feet, it's not just the biggest museum in the city, it's the largest one in this hemisphere. And I'd argue it competes in stature with the Louvre in Paris, the Prado in Madrid, the Uffizi in Florence, and the British Museum in London.

On view are masterworks from nearly all the world's cultures—from Egyptian mummies to ancient Greek statuary to Islamic carvings to Renaissance paintings to Native American masks to 20th-century decorative arts. Obviously, there's no way to see it all in one, two, or even five visits. So you must choose carefully among the 18 curatorial departments and decide what interests you most.

One way to do so is by taking one of the hour-long scholarly **"Highlight" tours**—free with admission and offered five times a day—led by volunteer docents. These enthusiastic art lovers are a treasure in and of themselves, highly trained and well-spoken. They'll run you all over the museum, pointing out and expounding upon the various gems of the collection, offering a quick taste of the museum's highlights so that you can come back yourself and feast upon what really interests you.

If I had to pick the top five highlights, I'd select:

o **The European paintings collection** on the second floor (expanded in 2013 from 450 works to 700) with such jewels as Velazquez's truer-than-life portrait of Juan de Pareja (the slave whom the painter respected enough—you can see it in the painting—to set free); El Greco's brooding landscape of Toledo; 20 Rembrandts; five light-kissed Vermeers; a roomful of van Goghs; and works by Manet, Monet, de Goya, Breughel, Van Eyck, and every other master you read about in your college art-history course.

o **The period rooms,** which re-create dozens of important chambers, including Louis XIV's state bedroom in Versailles; and the stunning Cubiculum from Boscoreale, a perfectly preserved, brilliantly colorful room from a villa a mile from Pompeii that was buried by the eruption of Mount Vesuvius in A.D. 79. Whenever I visit these rooms I'm always reminded of the terrific children's novel *From the Mixed-Up Files of Mrs. Basil E. Frankweiler,* in which the protagonists slept each night in a historic bed. Share it with your tweens and they'll be dying to come here.

o **The American Collection,** the most comprehensive in the world, featuring masterworks by Sargent, Homer, Tiffany, Leutze (his sentimental but rippingly fun *Washington Crossing the Delaware*), and many more.

o **The Egyptian Collection** includes some pieces discovered by the Met's own teams of archaeologists, such as the miniature figures found in a tomb in Thebes that show in intricate detail what daily life for a wealthy Egyptian was like. There's also elaborate statuary; mummy cases; jewelry; wall paintings; and the Temple of Dendur, an actual temple to the goddess Isis (ca. 15 B.C.) that was saved from the rising waters of the Nile after the construction of the Aswan Dam.

o The hidden **Hall of Art from Japan,** with its famed Iris Screens (reproduced on many Metropolitan Museum products), as well as architectural-looking suits of armor, delicate woodcuts, and dazzling kimonos. To my mind, this one of the most ravishingly beautiful sections of the museum.

Along with all the art, the Met has half a dozen cafes and restaurants, fab gift shops and bookstores, and tremendously engaging art and culture programs for children of all ages (mostly on the weekends; visit the website for info).

Note: The Met's modern and contemporary art collection is at the **Met Breuer** (see below) until 2022 . . . or thereabouts. The "mother ship" is undergoing a $600-million renovation of its modern wing, which is expected to take 7 to 8 years.

Fifth Ave. at 82nd St. www.metmuseum.org. © **212/535-7710.** Suggested admission (meaning you can pay what you wish): $25 adults, $17 seniors, $12 students, free for children 11 and under. Sun–Thurs 10am–5:30pm; Fri–Sat 10am–9pm. Subway: 4, 5, 6 to 86th St.

The Met Breuer ★ MUSEUM   It's hard to gauge, at this early date, just how successfully the Metropolitan Museum will draw in the public with its take on modern and contemporary art. In 2016, it took over the Whitney Museum's iconic Marcel Breuer building (abandoned when the Whitney moved to the Meatpacking District, see p. 134), to house its ever-growing 20th- and 21st-century collection, while its own modern wing is being renovated. And the Met buffed that fortresslike edifice to a fine shine with a multi-million-dollar renovation. But its opening salvo in the new space was a mixed bag. Called "Unfinished," the show featured sculptures and paintings that never made it over the finish line, either because the artist died, moved on, or decided (in the more recent works) that the work looked better with its raw canvas, or unpolished stone, showing. The exhibit was brilliant when showcasing the works of DaVinci, Van Eyck, Rembrandt, and other classic masters, but a yawn when it came to newer works of art (two other smaller shows of contemporary art were also numbingly dull). Their first efforts suggest that the Met may not be so hot at moving beyond its traditional comfort zone. But it may be too soon to make that judgment. My advice: make your decision based on the exhibit calendar.

945 Madison Ave. (btw. 74th and 75th sts). www.metmuseum.org/visit/met-breuer. © **212/731-1675.** Suggested admission $25 adults, $17 seniors, $12 students. Tues–Wed and Sat–Sun 10am–5:30pm, Thurs–Fri 10am–9pm.

Museum of the City of New York ★ MUSEUM   Just what it sounds like, this museum chronicles the life of the Big Apple. Its heartbeat is a masterful 25-minute video, narrated by Stanley Tucci, which recounts the tale of the city's growth from tiny Dutch colony to world capital. Along with a sumptuous collection of Gilded Age jewelry and housewares, and a provocative retrospective on activism in the city (including engrossing video portraits of current activists), the museum mounts temporary exhibits, like its fall 2016 show about cartoonist Roz

Chast. If you're choosing between this one and the New-York Historical Society (see p. 161), however, go with the latter—it has more to offer.

1220 Fifth Ave. (at 103rd St.). www.mcny.org. ℂ **212/534-1672.** Suggested admission $14 adults, $10 seniors and students, free for children 18 and under. Tues–Sun 10am–6pm. Closed Thanksgiving, Christmas, and New Year's Day. Subway: 6 to 103rd St.

Neue Galerie New York ★ ART MUSEUM/ARCHITECTURE   Most notable for its jewel-toned paintings by Gustave Klimt (including the famed "Woman in Gold"), its "Didn't I sit on that in the '70s?" Bauhaus furniture, and its collection of drawings by such Teutonic masters as Dix, Schiele, and Breuer, the Neue Galerie offers a swift but effective overview of German and Austrian arts and design. Because some of these drawings are a bit racy, children under the age of 12 are not admitted, and those 16 and younger must be accompanied by an adult. Also on site: a transporting Viennese cafe (see p. 106 for a full review), a theater for lectures and films, and a pricey gift shop.

1048 Fifth Ave. (at 86th St.). www.neuegalerie.org. ℂ **212/628-6200.** Admission $20 adults, $10 seniors and students. Children under 12 not admitted, children 12–16 must be accompanied by adult. Thurs–Mon 11am–6pm. Free admission 6–8pm 1st Friday of month. Subway: 4, 5, 6 to 86th St.

Solomon R. Guggenheim Museum ★★ ART MUSEUM/ARCHITECTURE   New York is the city of the rectangle, of the sharp right angle. Our streets form a severe grid, our buildings are boxy and regular. Until you get to the Guggenheim, that is. Frank Lloyd Wright's delirious spiral of a museum sits among the towers of Fifth Avenue like a steroidal peacock among guinea hens. Architectural critic Herbert Muschamp described the look best when he wrote, "What else but a building brought back from a dream would be windowless, have walls and floors that tilt and twist, begin on the top floor, and spiral in towards the center like an enigma?"

Visiting this 1959 masterpiece and trudging up the ramps of curving halls transforms the standard museum experience into a profound journey (and sometimes a battle against vertigo), no matter what artworks are on display. Early critics dismissed the museum (*Newsweek*'s insipid review was headlined "Museum or cupcake?"), but I think today even the most jaded visitor will feel the power of the place, the symbolic weight of infinite circle upon circle upon circle.

Cocktails & Art: Evenings at the Met

On Friday and Saturday evenings, the Met remains open late not only for art viewing but also for cocktails on the roof and in the Great Hall Balcony Bar (4–8:30pm). Indoors, classical music from a string ensemble accompanies the tippling. A slate of after-hours programs (gallery talks, walking tours, family programs) changes by the week; call for the current schedule. The restaurant at Petrie Court Café and Wine Bar stays open until 10:30pm (last reservation at 8:30pm), and dinner is usually accompanied by piano music.

Beyond the architecture, the museum is popular, thanks to its curators' abilities to formulate blockbuster retrospectives on top contemporary artists (like On Kowara) and topics that combine art with history and in some cases sociology—shows on contemporary Middle Eastern and North African art, Aztec culture, and motorcycles, to mention just a few that created headlines in past years. And in a long-overdue move, in late 2015, the museum opened larger permanent gallery space devoted to the stars of the Guggenheim's core collection, towering figures such as Chagall, Brancusi, Mondrian, Miró, and Kandinsky, among other modernists.

And to answer the question that nobody ever voices aloud: No, there haven't been any suicide jumps from over the low-slung rails, nor has anyone ever accidentally fallen to their death.

1071 Fifth Ave. (at 89th St.). www.guggenheim.org. ✆ **212/423-3500.** Admission $25 adults, $18 seniors and students, free for kids 11 and under; pay-what-you-wish Sat 5:45–7:45pm. Sun–Wed and Fri 10am–5:45pm; Sat 10am–7:45pm. Subway: 4, 5, 6 to 86th St.

Upper West Side

American Folk Art Museum ★ ART MUSEUM   Self-taught artists are the focus of this small museum, and their stories (told in wonderful detail by the wall text) illuminate the art in invigorating ways. You'll see works from the 18th century to the present, and the breadth and variety of the art can be quite stunning. Most popular objects are likely the quilts, though I prefer the sculptures. The book-and-gift shop is terrific, filled with one-of-a-kind pieces.

2 Lincoln Square (Columbus Ave. at 66th St.). www.folkartmuseum.org. ✆ **212/595-9533.** Free admission. Tues–Sat noon–7:30pm; Sun noon–6pm. Subway: 1 to 66th St.

American Museum of Natural History ★★★ MUSEUM/PLANE-TARIUM   Since 1869, this institution has served as both the country's pre-eminent private scientific research facility and its top museum for paleontology, zoology, anthropology, and, in recent years, astronomy. It's this constant flow of energy and insight between the research side and the curatorial side that has kept the museum fiercely vital, fresh, and unique. Just a few years ago, for example, scientists concluded that dinosaurs had not dragged their tails as had long been thought but waved them in the air as they walked. The curators responded, painstakingly dismantling the Museum's famed dino skeletons and reassembling them with tails erect. Then, in a brilliant stroke, they placed one skeleton atop a section of a Texas riverbed where they had found fossilized dino footprints (sans tail-dragging marks), giving museumgoers a peephole into how scientific theories emerge.

This double spotlight on the science itself and on how science is "made" is one of the pleasures of a visit here, with many of the exhibits focusing on the current "educated guesses" and the scientists who are making them. An extraordinarily interactive museum, it challenges visitors to figure out which theories make the most sense via computer stations, wall text, videos, soundscapes, and, of course, the artifacts themselves.

Timing your visit: Because the museum is so popular with school groups, it can get crowded, particularly midmorning. Also, since so many families head here, attendance is often in inverse proportion to the weather: When it's lovely outside, the crowds will be sparse within. When it's blustery or rainy . . . watch out. Weekdays tend to be less crowded than weekends.

An overview tour: First-time visitors should consider taking one of the guided introductory tours that begin at 15 minutes past the hour until 4:15pm.

Led by highly knowledgeable and well-spoken volunteer guides (they take classes for 6 months), tours vary by guide and will hit different highlights of the museum.

Especially for kids: Families with children will want to visit the **Discovery Room,** an educational center where kids can pretend to dig up dinosaur bones, do a scavenger hunt, peer through microscopes, and more. Timed free tickets are given for admission here, so be sure to grab one early in the day before they run out.

Start your visit by exploring the dinosaur rooms on the **fourth floor,** as these get most crowded later in the day. The museum has the largest such collection in the world, and the hot questions surrounding dinosaurs—How did they die out? Did they care for their young? Did they live in organized herds? Are birds their ancestors?—are fully explored.

Floors 2 and 3 are diorama-driven, with half the floors devoted to the anthropological study of the various peoples of the world; the other half to African and North American mammals. If you're short on time, take the mammal route, which features the poetic work of taxidermist/zoologist/sculptor Carl Akeley, who eventually died in Africa while collecting animals to stuff and display. Akeley pioneered a new technique of sculpting papier maché, which he would then cover with actual animal skins, antlers, and hoofs, often using the animal's bones for structure as well. The results are remarkably lifelike. The exhibit also fulfills his mission to conserve these animals and their environment for future generations—many of the wilderness areas depicted have changed beyond recognition in the past 50 years.

Other highlights include the dazzling **Hall of Minerals,** with its Fabergé-carved gems and the largest star sapphire in the world; the **Hall of Ocean Life,** with its famed 10-ton blue whale replica hanging from the ceiling; and the **Spitzer Hall of Human Origins,** an extraordinarily persuasive argument for the theory of evolution. You'll also want to carve out time for the **Rose Center for Earth and Space ★★★,** a monumental 120-foot-high glass box enveloping a colossal sphere, which is the virtual reality theater, the Hayden Planetarium. The Planetarium's stellar (sorry, I couldn't resist) space show is narrated by astrophysicist Neil deGrasse Tyson, former host of PBS's *Cosmos* and the director of the Planetarium.

When you first enter the museum, be sure to get a timed ticket to a planetarium show—they're terrific.

Central Park W. (btw. 77th and 81st sts.). www.amnh.org. **212/769-5100.** Suggested admission (meaning you can pay what you wish) $22 adults, $17 seniors and students, $12.50 ages 2–12. Space Show admission goes up to $27 adults, $22 seniors and students, $16 ages 2–12. Additional charges for IMAX movies and some special exhibitions. Daily 10am–5:45pm. Closed Thanksgiving and Christmas. Subway: B, C to 81st St.; 1 to 79th St.

Cathedral of St. John the Divine ★★ CATHEDRAL/ARCHITECTURE

Little-known fact: The largest cathedral in the world is *not* St. Peter's in Rome (which is technically not a cathedral but a basilica), it's St. John the Divine in upper Manhattan. Odder fact: Despite the popish name, it isn't Catholic, it's Episcopalian. Oddest fact: Though construction began on the cathedral in 1892, the building is yet to be completed, and many estimate that it will take another 100 years for that to happen.

All of which makes this a fascinating building to visit, as you'll see a bit of how the ancient cathedrals of Europe might have been built. The 121,000-square-foot structure, a blend of Romanesque and Gothic elements (thanks to the varying tastes of the architects who worked on it over the past century), is being built without steel, in the classic Gothic manner. (To that end, in 1979 a master stonecutter was brought from England to train Harlem youths in the art of traditional stonecutting.) There's still much work to be done (including a lot of fundraising!) but what is in place—and there's a lot—is quite beautiful, especially the Rose Window in the apse, the largest in North America.

Services here tend to be among the most musical and progressive in the city. I particularly recommend the New Year's Eve service, featuring original work from some of the best composers in town; the Halloween concert; and the Blessing of the Animals (on the feast day of St. Francis of Assisi, usually early October), a ceremony in which New Yorkers bring their pets—ranging from puppies to pythons to thoroughbred horses—to be blessed.

You can explore the cathedral on your own or on the **Public Tour,** offered Mondays at 11am and 2pm and Tuesdays through Saturdays at 11am and 1pm; also inquire about the **Vertical Tour** (offered on Wednesday and Friday at noon and Saturday at noon and 2pm), which takes you on a hike up the 11-flight circular staircase to the top, for spectacular views.

1047 Amsterdam Ave. (at 112th St.). www.stjohndivine.org. **212/316-7490.** Public tour $12 adults, $10 seniors and students; Vertical Tour $20 adults, $18 seniors and students. Daily 7:30am–6pm. Subway: B, C, 1 to Cathedral Pkwy.

Museum of Arts and Design ★ MUSEUM

It's not easy to get a New Yorker's attention, but this museum has done that consistently, and is one of the few museums in town where you'll see more locals than visitors. It draws them in with creative, sometimes wacky, exhibitions on design. One, for example, highlighted the pins worn by former Secretary of State Madeleine Albright, another used visitors' sense of smell to delve into how perfumes are created. On the top floor, artists in residence work at their crafts—furniture, textiles, you name it—making the static exhibits below feel that much more vital. It also has one of the best gift stores in the city and a lovely restaurant on the top floor.

2 Columbus Circle. www.madmuseum.org. © **212/299-7777.** Admission $16 adults, $14 seniors, $12 students, free for ages 18 and under; pay-what-you-wish Thurs 6–9pm. Tues–Sun 10am–6pm; Fri–Sat 10am–9pm. Subway: 1, 2, 3, A, B, C, D to 59th St./Columbus Circle.

New-York Historical Society ★★ MUSEUM NYC's oldest museum (founded in 1804) feels like one of its freshest, thanks to a recent $70-million renovation. Now when you enter, there are nifty features wherever you look, from an actual Keith Haring ceiling piece over the front desk, to important artifacts embedded in the floor (including a desk clock rescued from the 9/11 site, its hands frozen to the moment the plane hit).

Head first to the superb 18-minute film narrated by Liev Schreiber that dramatizes the history of the city in such a compelling fashion, you'll truly feel as if you're at the center of the known universe (which you are, of course). The bulk of the museum is made up of expertly curated temporary exhibits on the intersection of the city's history and world history (recent ones have dealt with Abraham Lincoln's time in NYC, the place of Chinese immigrants in New York City over the centuries, and presidential campaigns over the decades). As we went to press, the superb fourth floor, with its open storage units (this was one of the first institutions to create those) was undergoing a massive renovation. Though curators hadn't yet settled on all the details, they had decided to create a permanent exhibit space for their Tiffany lamps and glass collection (one of the largest collections in the world and a dazzling sight). In addition, the museum is planning to create a permanent area for women's history, which should be a treat.

170 Central Park W. (at 77th St.). www.nyhistory.org. © **212/873-3400.** Admission $19 adults; $15 seniors, military, and educators; $12 students; $6 children 7–13; free for ages 6 and under; pay-what-you-wish Fri 6–8pm. Tues–Sat 10am–6pm (Fri until 8pm); Sun 11am–5pm. Subway: B, C to 81st St.; 1 to 79th St.

Harlem and Upper Manhattan

The Cloisters ★★ ART MUSEUM/ARCHITECTURE An offshoot of the **Metropolitan Museum** (see p. 155), the Cloisters is the only museum in the United States devoted wholly to medieval art. And it shows its masterworks in a setting that appears to have been airlifted, utterly intact, from some remote corner of the Pyrenees, or from a castle-lined town in Bavaria.

Opened in 1934, the museum was, in fact, constructed in the United States, but 30% of the architectural elements—columns, pedestals, naves, door frames, exquisite stained-glass windows—were salvaged from medieval European structures. It's a stunning mirage—even the land across the river was bought by patron John D. Rockefeller to thwart development and ensure that the Cloisters' views would forever have a medieval face. At its heart are four cloisters, ancient garden areas centered with a fountain and surrounded by covered walkways of the type that appear in every monastery and abbey in Europe. Off these tranquil gardens are galleries devoted to different periods of art and architecture—a peak-ceilinged Gothic chapel here; a squat, square Romanesque-era hall there—each housing the treasures of that time period.

Though you can see the entire museum in an hour or so, pay special attention to the **Unicorn Tapestries,** one of only two full sets with a unicorn theme in the world (the other's in Paris). These richly detailed tapestries can be enjoyed on a number of levels: Many scholars see the unicorn as a symbol of Christ, and the hunt to slay it as evocative of the Passion. Others write that the work is a metaphor for courtly love, with the hunt itself courtship, and the last tapestry of the unicorn trapped inside a wedding-ring-like fence symbolizing marriage (despite this captivity, the unicorn does look happy). Whatever you decide, they are strikingly beautiful, an evocative slice of the past.

I highly recommend timing your tour to coincide with one of the curator-led gallery talks or garden walks (usually held midday).

North end of Fort Tryon Park. www.metmuseum.org/cloisters. ℭ **212/923-3700.** Suggested admission (includes same-day entrance to Metropolitan Museum) $25 adults, $17 seniors, $12 students, free ages 11 and under. Mar–Oct daily 10am–5:15pm; Nov–Feb daily 10am–4:45pm. Open Fri until 7:30pm late May–early Sept. Subway: A to 190th St., then a 10-min. walk north along Margaret Corbin Dr. Bus: M4 Madison Ave. (Fort Tryon Park/the Cloisters).

El Museo del Barrio ★ MUSEUM This showplace for the art of Latin America and the Caribbean owns hundreds of pre-Columbian pieces, contemporary and modern paintings and sculptures, and, most significantly, 500 Santos de Palo, mostly from Puerto Rico. These hand-carved, wooden saints are very beautiful and well worth a visit to see. The museum also throws fun parties for every Latin and Caribbean holiday and hosts changing exhibits.

1230 Fifth Ave. (at 104th St.). www.elmuseo.org. ℭ **212/831-7272.** Suggested donation $9 adults, $5 seniors and students, free for children under 12. Tues–Sat 11am–6pm, Sun noon–5pm. Subway 6 to 103rd St.

Hamilton Grange National Memorial ★ HISTORIC HOME What was for many years an obscure under-visited attraction now sells out many days a week, thanks to the popularity of a certain musical. I wish I could tell you that seeing the house is a worthy alternative to scoring a precious ticket to the show. It isn't. While the house itself is original (and moved three times—the highlight of a visit is the video about the engineering efforts behind getting the house to where it sits now), very little of the furniture belonged to founding father Alexander Hamilton's family: it's either reproductions or similar pieces from the era. And visitors only see four rooms; the servants quarters are now the museum part of the memorial, and the bedrooms aren't open to the public.

414 W. 141st St. (at Hamilton Terrace). www.nps.gov. ℭ **646/548-2310.** Free admission. Wed–Sun 9am–5pm. Subway: A, B, C, D to 145th St.

Studio Museum in Harlem ★ ART MUSEUM Though it's not a large museum, the Studio Museum is one of the most respected in Gotham, known for presenting challenging, intricate shows of African-American and

ENJOYING THE gospel OF HARLEM

There are over 400 churches in Harlem. Some are large and ornate, while others are small, one-room churches housed on ground floors of brownstones. And many of those churches, large or small, feature fiery sermons and magnificent gospel services every Sunday. Gospel tours (see p. 186) of these churches have become big business. Mainly frequented by foreign visitors who line up on Sunday mornings and pay handsomely, there's something uncomfortably voyeuristic about the scene. But the pastors and the churches that are drawing in the crowds—and their donations—are certainly not complaining. If you want to skip the guided tour and go to services on your own, here are several that are worth visiting:

○ **Abyssinian Baptist Church,** 132 Odell Clark Pl. (138th St.); www.abyssinian.org; ℮ **212/862-7474.**

○ **Canaan Baptist Church,** 132 W. 116th St.; www.cbccnyc.org; ℮ **212/866-0301**

○ **First Corinthian Baptist Church,** 1912 Adam Clayton Powell Jr. Blvd. at 116th St.; www.fcbcser mons.com; ℮ **212/864-5976.**

○ **Greater Refuge Temple,** 2081 Adam Clayton Powell Jr. Blvd.; www.greaterrefugetemple.org; ℮ **212/280-5268.**

Most services begin promptly at 11am; seating for non-members is on a first-come, first-serve basis. Make sure you arrive in plenty of time; there will most likely be a line. At some churches, tour groups get preference over "walk ups"; call in advance to find out that particular church's policy. Service lengths vary, but expect at least 2 hours and up to 3. Most tours leave after the gospel choir and before the sermon—you'd think that would be disrespectful, yet because this is a profitable venture for the churches, there are no complaints from the faithful.

Caribbean-American art (contemporary and from the 19th and 20th centuries). In addition to two floors of galleries that host changing exhibitions, there's a space right off the lobby for the semi-permanent "Harlem Postcards" wall, on which famous artists share their own memories of the neighborhood through text, photography, paintings, and drawings.

144 W. 125th St. (btw. Lenox Ave. and Adam Clayton Powell Jr. Blvd.). www.studio museum.org. ℮ **212/864-4500.** Suggested admission $7 adults, $3 seniors and students, free for children 11 and under; Sun admission free. Thurs–Fri noon–9pm; Sat 10am–6pm; Sun noon–6pm. Subway: 2, 3 to 125th St.

THE OUTER BOROUGHS

The Bronx

Note: See p. 113 about exploring Arthur Avenue, a much more authentic Italian American enclave than Manhattan's Little Italy.

Bronx Zoo ★★★ ZOO   If you count number of animals as well as acreage, the Bronx Zoo is the largest zoo in the United States, an innovative, unbeatably entertaining place to spend the day. But with over 4,000 animals and 24 exhibits, it requires strategy to see what you want without meltdowns from the younger set. When I visit with my girls, I most often make a direct path to the **Congo Forest** first, a remarkable exhibit of silverback gorillas that begins with a short film. Once the film is over, curtains dramatically part to reveal floor-to-ceiling windows, with cavorting gorillas galore (unlike other animals at the zoo, the gorillas are always awake if you visit in the daytime; along with the adults there always seem to be half-a-dozen baby gorillas in sight as well). From here we hop over to the nearby "bug carousel" or the butterfly exhibit (a tent with thousands of beautiful butterflies fluttering about your head), or to lunch at nearby Flamingo Park. Then we blow off steam at the children's zoo—with all the usual farm animals, plus a spider-web jungle gym and a prairie dog park where children crawl into tunnels and pop their heads up right next to the critters. Dozens of other animals, a fun monorail ride, feeding shows, and more keep you entertained.

Tip: To beat the crowds, try to visit on a weekday or on a nice winter's day. In summer, come early, before the heat of the day sends the animals back into their enclosures. Expect to spend an entire day here—you'll need it.

Getting there: The BxM11 express bus, which makes stops on Madison Avenue, will take you directly to the zoo. By subway, take the no. 2 train to Pelham Parkway and then walk west to the Bronxdale entrance. For info on both, go to **www.bronxzoo.com/plan-your-trip/directions.aspx**.

Fordham Rd. and Bronx River Pkwy. www.bronxzoo.com. ✆ **718/367-1010.** Admission $34 adults, $29 seniors, $24 ages 3–12; pay-what-you-wish Wed year-round. Paying in advance online shaves 10% off the rate. Apr–Oct Mon–Fri 10am–5pm, Sat–Sun and holidays 10am–5:30pm; Nov–Mar daily 10am–4:30pm. Transportation: See "Getting There," above.

New York Botanical Garden ★ GARDEN

An equal to the Brooklyn Botanic Garden (see p. 165) in both scope and interest, the New York Botanical Garden boasts the world's largest Victorian greenhouse; a "home gardening" section with classes and demonstrations for all the green thumbs out there; a children's garden and play center; and a 50-acre native forest. If there's any difference between the two gardens—they're both wonderful, and both world-class—the wealth of hands-on programming just may give this place to edge. Other than that, if you're interested in visiting just one of these world-class gardens, you have a difficult choice.

Getting there: Take Metro-North (www.mta.info/mnr; ✆ **212/532-4900**) from Grand Central Terminal to the New York Botanical Garden station; the ride takes about 20 minutes. By subway, take the D or 4 train to Bedford Park, then take bus Bx26 or walk southeast on Bedford Park Boulevard for eight long blocks.

200th St. and Kazimiroff Blvd. www.nybg.org. ✆ **718/817-8700.** Admission $20 weekdays, $25 weekends for adults, $18/$22 seniors and students, $8/$10 ages 2–12. NYC residents grounds-only pass $13 adults, $6 seniors and students, ages 2–12 $3. Tues–Sun 10am–6pm (Jan–Feb until 5pm). Transportation: See "Getting There," above.

Brooklyn

Brooklyn Botanic Garden ★ GARDEN Right down the street from the Brooklyn Museum, the Brooklyn Botanic Garden is not only one of those necessary green safety valves, it's also quite an innovative garden in many ways. It was the first in the world to have a "children's garden," allowing local kids to develop green thumbs (it's still here, along with a fun play area for youngsters). There's also a "fragrance garden" for sight-impaired visitors, where everyone is encouraged to sniff and touch the plants; and an authentic Japanese garden, complete with a large pond, pagodas, and plants from that area of the world. The best time of year to visit is spring, when the gardens' many cherry trees are in bloom, though there are seasonal displays, both out-doors and in the on-site greenhouses, year-round.

900 Washington Ave. (at Eastern Pkwy.). www.bbg.org. © **718/623-7200.** Admission $12 adults, $6 seniors and students (free for seniors Fri), free for children 11 and under. Combo tickets available with the Brooklyn Museum (see below). Mar–Oct Tues–Fri 8am–6pm, Sat–Sun 10am–6pm; Nov–Feb closes 4:30pm. Subway: Q to Prospect Park; 2, 3 to Eastern Pkwy./Brooklyn Museum.

Brooklyn Museum ★★ ART MUSEUM Though not as big as the Met-ropolitan Museum (what is?), this "mini Met"—it covers almost all eras of history in its holdings—is a superb museum on its own terms. Its Egyptian Collection, while not as extensive as the Met's, arguably has more master-pieces. In fact, when an ancient Egyptian piece comes up at auction, dealers often ask, "Is it Brooklyn quality?"—the Brooklyn Museum's collection being the benchmark for this sort of artifact. Among the collection's many wonders are a tiny 5,000-year-old, pre-dynastic terra-cotta sculpture of a woman, which curators have nicknamed "Birdwoman" for her beaklike face, one of the very few intact sculptures from this long-ago era. The Cartonnage of Nespanetjerenpere is another highlight, a mummy case that looks like it was swiped from the set of *Revenge of the Mummy,* its colors electrically bright and unfaded. I highly recommend renting the audio tour for this gallery, as it will explain how these works were created, what the symbolism means, and what they reveal about life in ancient Egypt.

Second most popular among the museum's offerings are the Decorative Arts Galleries (fourth floor), which re-create important rooms from different eras of American history, including John D. Rockefeller's "Moorish Smoking Room," an over-the-top Victorian version of the Middle East, every single bit of space lavishly carved, gilded, inlaid, or embroidered. Also worth a look: the Museum's American Collection (works by such masters as Albert Bierstadt, Thomas Eakins, Winslow Homer, and Georgia O'Keeffe); the Elizabeth A. Sackler Center for Feminist Art (permanent and rotating exhibitions of art made by women, including Judy Chicago's famous "The Dinner Party"); and whatever special exhibitions are taking place (they're often stellar).

One final thing the Brooklyn does better than the Met: party. The first Sat-urday of each month, the museum throws open its doors, hires deejays and performers of all sorts, and throws a "First Saturday" fiesta free to the public from 5 to 11pm.

200 Eastern Pkwy. (at Washington Ave.). www.brooklynmuseum.org. ✆ **718/638-5000.** Suggested admission $16 adults, $10 seniors and students, free for children 11 and under; free to all first Sat of the month. Wed and Fri–Sun 11am–6pm; Thurs 11am–10pm. Subway: 2, 3 to Eastern Pkwy./Brooklyn Museum.

Coney Island ★ ICON/BEACH/AMUSEMENT PARK Honky-tonk paradise, Coney Island has been rescued from extinction a few times (first from developers and most recently from severe Hurricane Sandy damage). Parts of it are given over to brand-new amusement parks and rides, but it's still possible to try some of the classic attractions from times past, including the **Cyclone** (a huge wooden roller coaster, one of the scariest you'll ever ride because you'll do so with the knowledge that nearly a dozen people have been killed on it over the years), and the **Wonder Wheel** (a Ferris wheel with gliding compartments). If you visit in summer, don't skip the Coney Island Circus Side Show (formerly known as The Freak Show), which features a "human pincushion," a snake charmer, a man who hammers nails up his nose, and other odd performers. It's one of the last shows of its kind in the U.S., and though it sounds unsavory, it's G-rated. You also have the beach itself, a motley swatch of sand where gaggles of Brooklynites gather in summer to pitch umbrellas, practice kung fu, blast music, picnic, and swim. It's a social scene, with many different ethnic groups represented, and fascinating in its own way. **Note:** In 2016, this swatch of Brooklyn became a major concert venue, thanks to the opening of the Coney Island Amphitheater (see p. 237).

www.coneyisland.com. Subway: D, F, N, Q to Coney Island–Stillwell Ave.

Green-Wood Cemetery ★★ HISTORIC SITE As you wander through New York City, you'll come upon a number of street names named for the important Gothamites you'll also encounter at Green-Wood. The "first families" of the city were all interred here, as were such notables as DeWitt Clinton (a Presidential candidate who was the mastermind behind the Erie Canal), Leonard Bernstein (composer of Broadway's *West Side Story*) and artists Louis Comfort Tiffany and Jean Michel Basquiat. Heck, even pets were buried here…until the funeral of a devoted horse convinced the cemetery's staff to stop the practice in 1870 (the cemetery itself was founded in 1837). It's not hard to understand why New Yorkers would pick Green-Wood for their eternal rest: Set on the highest point of Brooklyn, it's a stunning place, considered an arboretum as well as a cemetery for the 7000 trees that grow here. The monuments are equally beautiful, hand-carved in dozens of different styles, ranging from Tiffany-glass-adorned mausoleums to bronze and marble statuary. A final lure: one of the most important battles of the Revolutionary War took place on this hill; you'll learn about it on the excellent trolley tour.

Main entrance Fifth Ave. at 25th St., Sunset Park. www.green-wood.com. ✆ **718/210-3080.** Admission free. Daily 8am–6pm. Trolley tours Weds and Sun 1pm (advance reservations required).

The Museum of Morbid Anatomy ★ MUSEUM Tim Burton would feel right at home in this tiny gallery devoted to the darker side of existence. Previous exhibits explored the "art of mourning," displaying such items as elaborate picture frames made with the hair of the dead (did you know hair can last for centuries?), exquisite painted Jewish death certificates, renderings of dead babies in all mediums, and other painful mementos. In 2016, *Castum's Panoptica*, a collection of curiosities rendered in wax in early 20th century Germany, was the focus; it included gruesome models of food in the digestive tract, death masks, busts of leprosy sufferers, and more. Seeing the museum takes 40 minutes at most, though it does have a crowded program of lectures and special events. Recommended only for those who are in the area or who have a special interest in, well, death.

424 Third Ave. (at 7th St.), Gowanus. www.morbidanatomymuseum.org. ℂ **347/799-1017.** Admission $8 adults, $6 seniors, free for children 12 and under. Wed–Mon noon–6pm.

New York Aquarium ★ AQUARIUM The effects of Hurricane Sandy continue to be felt at the Aquarium, which is still only able to welcome visitors to 40% of its facilities (renovations are expected to end in 2018). If you're planning on visiting Coney Island anyway, stop by to see the California sea lions perform, as well as the huge Amazonian river fish, black-footed penguins, seals, and sea otters. But I wouldn't make a special trip.

502 Surf Ave. (at W. 8th St.), Coney Island. www.nyaquarium.com. ℂ **718/265-FISH** [3474]. Admission $12, $10.75 pre-booked online. Memorial Day–Labor Day 10am–6pm; rest of year 10am–4:30pm. Subway: F, Q to West 8th St.

New York Transit Museum ★ MUSEUM Best for kids and train nuts, this underground museum (yes, it's in a former subway station) covers the storied history of the NYC subway system. The museum houses a number of handsome vintage subway cars, turnstiles, and mosaics that used to adorn the stations.

Boerum Place and Schermerhorn St. http://web.mta.info/mta/museum. ℂ **718/694-1600.** Admission $7 adults, $5 seniors and children 2–17 (free for seniors Wed). Tues–Fri 10am–4pm; Sat–Sun 11am–5pm. Subway: A, C to Hoyt St.; F to Jay St.; M, R to Court St.; 2, 3, 4, 5 to Borough Hall.

Queens

Isamu Noguchi Garden Museum ★ ART MUSEUM Utterly unique, it's the only museum in the nation to be founded by an artist in his lifetime, dedicated to his work and curated by him. As Noguchi (1904–88) was a genius in a number of fields—sculpture, architecture, ceramics, furniture design—he was more than up to the task, and created a space that is at once balanced and (often) rapturously beautiful. On site are also a small cafe/bookstore and an updated Zen sculpture garden (one of the most serene spots in the city). Gallery talks, held at 2pm each day, are helpful for those not familiar with Noguchi's work, as they illuminate the complex engineering issues and intentions behind his large, sometimes slablike, non-representational works.

9-01 33rd Rd. (at Vernon Blvd.), Long Island City. www.noguchi.org. ℂ **718/204-7088.** Admission $10 adults, $5 seniors and students. Wed–Fri 10am–5pm; Sat–Sun 11am–6pm. Subway: N to Broadway. Walk west (toward Manhattan) on Broadway to Vernon Blvd.; turn left on Vernon and go 2 blocks.

Louis Armstrong House Museum ★★ HISTORIC HOME/ MUSEUM The visitor experience here is as gracious, warm, and intriguing as the man himself, thanks to the marvelous guides (all ex-musicians and jazz historians) who lead visitors through the home every hour on the hour. The only house that this traveling musician ever owned, it was perfectly preserved after the death of his wife Lucille in 1983 (Armstrong himself passed away in 1971), and opened to the public in 2003. The sense that someone still lives here is so eerie that you may find yourself expecting Satchmo to emerge from the kitchen, turn on the stereo, and tell a joke. In the course of your tour, you'll hear about Louis's rags-to-riches history (son of a prostitute, learned to play trumpet in the juvenile detention center, made his name in mobster-owned clubs) and see the fairly modest two-story home that he and his wife lavished with every luxury, from custom-made 24-karat bathroom fixtures to Baccarat chandeliers and a state-of-the-art audio system. The highlight: recordings of everyday life that Armstrong made on his tape recorder—your guide will play them as you wander through, allowing you to hear the family and visiting musicians talking, laughing, and jamming together.

34-56 107th St., Corona. www.louisarmstronghouse.org. ℂ **718/478-8274.** Admission $10 adults; $7 seniors, students, and children; ages 3 and under free. Tues–Fri 10am–5pm; Sat–Sun noon–5pm; last tour 4pm. Subway: 7 to 103rd St./Corona Plaza. Walk north on 103rd St., turn right on 37th Ave., turn left on 107th St.; the house is a half-block north of 37th Ave.

Museum of the Moving Image ★★★ MUSEUM For sheer unadulterated fun, there's no museum in town that can beat this one. The first museum anywhere to look at TV, film, and video games together (a heretical concept when the museum opened in 1988), it's not simply an archive of past shows. Instead, it explores the craft and technology behind these arts with startlingly imaginative interactive exhibits, commissioned art works, video sequences, and, of course, artifacts. Just how much fun is all this? Well, City-search ranked it the best place in the city for a family outing, while *Time Out* magazine called it the number-one place to go when you're "baked"—if that doesn't hit all the bases, I don't know what does.

Start your visit with the museum's core exhibit, **Behind the Screen,** which explores the many technical issues behind moving images, from explanations of how the eye is tricked into seeing movement in rapidly repeating images, to the intricacies of sound and film editing. You'll have a chance to dub your own voice into such classics as *My Fair Lady,* create original computer animation, transmute the musical score of a famous film scene, and more.

Several times a day, working editors, animators, and educators give demonstrations of how these techniques are used on actual productions.

Next, the focus shifts from technical issues to design issues, with exhibits devoted to the make-up, costumes, sets, and publicity stills that help create the image the director (or studio) is looking for. If you've been harboring a secret yen to play *Galactica* just one more time, you'll have your chance in the playable video games exhibit. Likely you'll want to take in whatever blockbuster special exhibit is on; recent ones have covered the TV show *Mad Men* and the artistry of cartoon voiceover icon Mel Blanc. In 2016, a permanent exhibit on the oeuvre of Jim Henson (creator of the Muppets) opened.

On the first floor is the museum's full-sized movie theater, which offers included screenings of feature films from around the world, often followed by discussions with the artists involved, including such big names as Glenn Close, Tim Burton, David Cronenberg, and Jennifer Connelly.

The 98,000-square-foot museum is built on the site of Astoria Studio, and this part of Queens was where many of the early American films were made. The overall experience is to see how far we've come in so brief a span of time, and just how powerful is the human imagination.

35th Ave. at 37th St., Astoria. www.movingimage.us. ✆ **718/777-6800.** Admission $15, $11 seniors and students, $7 children 5–18, free ages 5 and under; free Fri 4pm–8pm. Wed–Thurs 10:30am–5pm, Fri 10:30am–8pm, Sat–Sun 11:30am–7pm. Subway: R, M to Steinway St.; N to 36th Ave.

P.S. 1 Contemporary Art Center ★★ ART MUSEUM   A proving ground for young artists, the work you're going to see here will be challenging, right of the moment, and sometimes downright wacky. "P.S. 1 is mythological," says former assistant director Brett Littman. "Wherever I go, people know that there's this crazy building in Long Island City where you see crazy art. They come here to put a notch on their culture belt."

That "crazy building" was once a public school (hence the name), and its somewhat decrepit charm is part of the experience. Because it's not a fancy white box of a space (like its sister institution the Museum of Modern Art), P.S. 1 allows artists to create full-blown, sometimes invasive, installations in the space. (One summer several years ago, an artist blasted holes in the brick wall of a gallery.) It uses all kinds of unusual spaces to house art, such as the basement boiler room.

The bulk of the work you'll see here will be in changing exhibits, as the museum does not collect art. Instead, visitors are usually greeted with as many as 14 different shows in all parts of the building. As I've said, some can be quite, well, bizarre. In its retrospective of New York City art several years back, one framed sculpture turned out to be the actual hand of the artist who was sitting on the other side of the wall, personifying her art. Now if that's not worth $10, I don't know what is.

22-25 Jackson Ave. (at 46th Ave.), Long Island City. www.ps1.org. ✆ **718/784-2084.** Suggested admission $10 adults, $5 seniors and students. Thurs–Mon noon–6pm. Subway: E, M to 23rd St./Ely Ave. (walk 2 blocks S on Jackson Ave.); 7 to 45th Rd./Court House Square (walk 1 block S on Jackson Ave.).

Queens Museum ★ MUSEUM   Long before there was Google Earth, there was the Panorama of the City of New York. A diorama of 9,335 square feet, it was created for the 1964–65 World's Fair with the help of photographers who swooped in helicopters over the city, taking over 7,000 photos to capture every building in the five boroughs. The Panorama is still a wonder today, and the heart of the Queens Museum. It was fully updated in 1992, and subsequently, building owners can pay to have their newer edifices added, which makes for some odd anomalies (Trump Tower was added but the Twin Towers have yet to be replaced by the Freedom Tower.) I highly recommend taking the museum's free guided tour (offered several times a day) as the docent does a masterful job of making the geography come alive, with discussions of the city's history and what on the map is wrong and right. Other exhibits cover the museum building's storied history: It was erected for the 1939 World's Fair and served as the site of the United Nations during its first 5 years. There's also a lovely exhibit of Tiffany lamps (a nod to the fact that the Tiffany factory was in Corona, Queens) and changing art exhibits.

Flushing Meadows Corona Park, Queens. www.queensmuseum.org. ✆ **718/592-9700.** Suggested admission $8. Wed–Sun noon–6pm. Subway: 7 to Mets–Willets Point.

ESPECIALLY FOR KIDS

Museums

In addition to the museums specifically for kids detailed below, consider the **American Museum of Natural History** ★★★ (p. 158), whose dinosaur displays are guaranteed to wow both you and your children; the **Museum of the Moving Image** ★★★ (p. 168), where you and the kids can learn how movies are actually made (and play vintage video games); the **Tenement Museum ★★★** (p. 132), whose weekend living-history program intrigues school-age kids; and the **New York Transit Museum** (p. 167), where young 'uns can explore vintage subway cars and other hands-on exhibits. Another good distraction: the **Children's Museum of the Arts,** 103 Charlton Ave. (www.cmany.org; ℂ **212/274-0986**), a visual arts–based institution. "Game" places for slightly older kids can be good for blowing off steam, like **Modern Pinball,** 362 Third Ave. at 26th St (ℂ **646/415-8440**; daily 11am–midnight), a squeaky clean, bar-free pinball parlor; and **Escape the Room** (several locations; www.escapetheroomnyc.com) a "challenge course" in which groups are locked into a room and have 1 hour to solve riddles and find clues which will allow them to get out. It's tons of fun.

The Brooklyn Children's Museum ★ MUSEUM

The very first museum of its type in the nation, the Brooklyn Children's Museum isn't easy to get to from Manhattan, but it rewards those who make the trek (there's a shuttle from the nearest subway stop many days of the week; check the museum's website). Inspired by the idea that children love to play at working, the museum gives them a number of places in which to "toil": a garden where they can plant things and learn about botany, a pretend restaurant and grocery store where they can "feed" their parents, a "building brainstorm" area that teaches the basics of architecture and engineering with blocks and other building toys, and more. And for those who end up spending the entire day here (it happens!), there's an on-site cafe.

145 Brooklyn Ave. (at St. Marks Ave.). www.brooklynkids.org. ℂ **718/735-4400.** Admission: $11, free for children under 1; free Thurs 2–6pm. Tues–Sun 10am–5pm (Thurs until 6pm). Subway: 3 to Kingston Ave., A to Nostrand Ave., C to Kingston/Throop Ave.

Children's Museum of Manhattan ★ MUSEUM

A glitzy affair of changing exhibits that highlight the kiddie zeitgeist of the moment: Red Grooms, Maurice Sendak, and William Wegman's dog art were just a few of the recent exhibit themes. Those with toddlers should go directly to the Child Development Center on the fourth floor, where kids can fingerpaint to their hearts' delight, play with little stoves, and send rubber balls rocketing down a twisted tube from a loft to the floor (there were days when I never got past this room). Older children will want to take part in the classes and special exhibits, and since these fill up fast, it's important that you stop by the sign-up desk right when you enter.

212 W. 83rd St. (btw. Broadway and Amsterdam Ave.). www.cmom.org. ℂ **212/721-1234.** Admission $12, $8 seniors, children 1 and under free; free for all 1st Fri of month 5–8pm. Tues–Sun 10am–5pm (Sat until 7pm). Subway: 1 to 86th St.

The Museum of Mathematics ★ MUSEUM

When this museum first debuted in 2012, I warned my children that if they didn't behave, I'd take them there. It was no punishment, however, when we finally went. Creatively designed to bring math concepts to life, this little museum (it takes about an hour to see it) has two floors of interactive displays that will have your kids riding bikes with square wheels, re-creating Galileo's experiments, and doing all sorts of fun numbers games. It's a great new addition for the under-11 set.

11 E. 20th St. (near Fifth Ave.). www.momath.org. © **212/542-0566.** Admission $15 adults, $9 seniors and children 2–12. Daily 10am–5pm. Subway: R to 23rd St.

New York City Fire Museum ★ MUSEUM   What kid can resist a big red fire engine roaring by, or a room full of swooping red fire hats? You'll see both in abundance at the New York City Fire Museum, which has one of the largest collections of firehouse memorabilia in the nation. It also has the good sense to hand out a free scavenger hunt map on arrival, which should keep even the most restless of youngsters amused.

278 Spring St. (btw. Varick and Hudson sts.). www.nycfiremuseum.org. © **212/691-1303.** Admission $8 adults, $5 seniors, students, and children. Daily 10am–5pm. Closed Easter, New Year's Day, Christmas, and Thanksgiving. Subway: C, E to Spring St.; 1 to Houston St.

New York Hall of Science ★ MUSEUM   Set in one of the few remaining buildings from the 1964 World's Fair, this museum is a big hit with science-attuned youngsters, as most of the exhibits here are hands-on and interactive. For those who just want to blow off steam, there's a mini-golf park in good weather and an excellent, science-themed playground. The only negative for most visitors—and it's a serious one—is how remote it is from Manhattan (it can take a good hour on the subway each way). Still, if you've been to NYC with your kids a few times and want to try something new, this is definitely a good option.

47-01 111th St., Corona, Queens. www.nysci.org. © **718/699-0005.** Admission $15 adults, $12 seniors and children 2–17. Mon–Fri 9:30am–5pm; Sat–Sun 10am–6pm. Subway: 7 to 111th St.

OUTDOOR ACTIVITIES

Central Park ★★★

Manhattan's 843-acre green oasis is the yin to the city's neon, concrete, and office tower yang. It serves as the city's backyard, its concert hall, its daytime pick-up bar, and, in the summer, when dozens don bathing suits to soak up the rays, its green beach. The marvel of the park, besides its size (a full 6% of the total area of Manhattan), is its ability to provide just the right sort of experience for the myriad of very different personalities who think of it as their own. I think it's that chameleon-like quality that makes it such an interesting place for visitors to tour. Seeing it from an outsider's perspective, it's much easier to recognize that the park is a great mirage and paradox.

Because, let's face it, very little here is natural. Every tree, every shrub, every lake, and most of the rolling hills were designed, planted, or blasted into existence by landscape architects Frederick Law Olmsted and Calvert Vaux back in the 1850s, and their efforts still shape our experiences today. These two geniuses took a 2½-mile tract of swampland, farms, and suburban towns

Central Park

and created an Arcadia that had no resemblance whatever to what had come before. Below the park, 95 miles of drainage pipes were installed, many to both fill and periodically empty the four lakes that were created; at ground level the site was transformed using six million bricks, 65,000 cubic tons of gravel, 26,000 trees, and 250,000 shrubs. Even the dirt was imported; the natural topsoil was so poor that 500,000 cubic feet of topsoil was shipped in from New Jersey. As Olmsted once wrote, "Every foot of the park, every tree and bush, every arch, roadway and walk, has been fixed where it is with a purpose."

And what was that purpose? No less than the health of the city. Those who rallied for its creation felt that it was crucial to create a place where New Yorkers could blow off steam and get away from the stresses of urban life. Moreover, Olmsted wanted to create a park that would be a bridge between classes. "There need to be places and time for re-unions," Olmsted wrote, "[where] the rich and the poor, the cultivated and the self-made, shall be attracted together and encouraged to assimilate." Though that didn't happen when the park was first finished—it was too far from the homes of poor New Yorkers for them to visit it—that ideal was realized when the city itself began to wrap around the park, making it finally a true *central* park.

In your own strolls around the park, you'll encounter three different types of landscapes: **pastoral vistas** such as the Sheep Meadow, which are meant to invoke a cultivated countryside; **primitive portions** where dense forestation shuts out any view of the city; and the **promenade zones,** which were once used by the city's aristocracy as an extension of their parlors, a place to strut and be seen. An ideal visit here will include all three. I've created a relatively brief list of highlights, along with the activities you can engage in once in the park, that should allow you to do just that. Feel free to ignore the following list altogether and just wander the curving paths of the park, exploring its hidden nooks, surprise vistas, ball fields, and dog runs. There's no right way to see or do this park.

ORIENTATION & GETTING THERE The park runs from 59th Street (also known as Central Park South) at the south end to 110th Street at the north end, and from Fifth Avenue on the east side to Central Park West (the equivalent of Eighth Avenue) on the west side. A 6-mile rolling road, Central Park Drive, circles the park, and has a lane set aside for bikers, joggers, and in-line skaters. A number of transverse (crosstown) roads cross the park at major points—at 65th, 79th, 86th, and 97th streets—but they're built down a level, largely out of view, to minimize intrusion.

A number of subway stops and lines serve the park; which one you take depends on where you want to go. To reach the southernmost entrance on the west side, take an A, B, C, D, or 1 to 59th Street/Columbus Circle. To reach the southeast corner entrance, take the N or R to Fifth Avenue.

There's now an app that will guide you around Central Park and comes complete with GPS should you get lost and need to find a nearby exit. Both Android- and iPhone-compatible, it's created by the Park Service and downloadable from the App Store.

Central Park Highlights

Belvedere Castle and the Delacorte Theater ★★ THEATER Olmsted and Vaux's "folly" (or fantasy building), this turreted castle sits atop the second-highest elevation in the park. Inside is a nature observatory with good rainy-day activities for children. In front of the castle is the **Delacorte Theater** ★★, where the famed **Shakespeare in the Park** (p. 235) is performed, a star-studded and free evening of theater staged in the summer months only. If you decide to take in a show, know that you could end up spending 4 or more hours standing in line to get tickets; they're passed out at 1pm in front of the theater, but depending on the popularity of the show, crowds have been known to show up hours before that, and even camp overnight at the gate to the park. From Belvedere, you'll also look down on the **Great Lawn,** which has gone through a number of incarnations, first as a reservoir and later in the 1930s as "Hooverville," the shantytown where hundreds of homeless families lived out the Depression. Today it's most famous as a concert space: Simon and Garfunkel reunited here in the 1980s in a widely televised concert.

Enter the park at either 72nd or 79th St. For info on Shakespeare in the Park: www.publictheater.org. ✆ **212/539-8500.** Free admission.

The Carousel ★ CAROUSEL A Victorian spinner, this is most children's favorite park stop (it certainly is my daughters'). Though it's not the original carousel (the first burned down in the 1950s), it's a beaut, built on Coney Island in 1908, and featuring some of the tallest merry-go-round horses in the U.S. It's also a much more humane carousel than the original, which was rotated by a blind mule and horse toiling in the basement.

At approximately 65th St., in the dead center of the park. www.centralpark.com. $3 per ride. Apr–Nov 10am–6pm; Dec–Mar 10am–dusk.

Central Park Zoo/Tisch Children's Zoo ★ ZOO Because of its small size, the zoo is at its best with its displays of smaller animals. The indoor multilevel **Tropic Zone** is a real highlight, its steamy rainforest home to everything from black-and-white colobus monkeys to Emerald tree boa constrictors to a leaf-cutter ant farm; look for the new dart-poison-frog exhibit, which is very cool. So is the large penguin enclosure in the **Polar Circle,** which is better than the one at San Diego's SeaWorld. Despite their pool and piles of ice, however, the polar bears still look sad.

The zoo is good for short attention spans; you can cover the entire thing in 1½ to 2 hours. It's also very kid-friendly, with lots of well-written and illustrated placards that older kids can understand. For the littlest ones, there's the $6-million **Tisch Children's Zoo** ★. With goats, llamas, potbellied pigs, and more, this petting zoo and playground is a real blast for the 5-and-under set.

830 Fifth Ave. (at 64th St., just inside Central Park). www.centralparkzoo.com. ✆ **212/439-6500.** Admission $18 adults, $15 seniors, $13 children 3–12, free for ages 2 and under; $6 less if you don't include the children's zoo or 4-D theater; 10% discount online. Mon–Fri 10am–5pm, Sat–Sun and holidays 10am–5:30pm. Last entrance 30 min. before closing. Subway: N, R to Fifth Ave; 6 to 68th St.

Cleopatra's Needle ★ MONUMENT This handsome obelisk was a gift to the United States from Egypt in 1881, in recognition of the help this country gave in the construction of the Suez Canal. Transporting the 200-ton pillar took 38 days from Alexandria to New York by ship, and then another 144 just to get it from the Hudson River to Central Park. It originally stood at the Temple of the Sun in Heliopolis, and is believed to have been erected in 1600 B.C. The Romans moved it in the 12th century to the front of a temple built by Cleopatra, hence the name. A plaque at the base translates the hieroglyphics.

Near the back of the Metropolitan Museum at roughly 83rd St.

Conservatory Gardens ★★★ GARDENS The park's only formal gardens are simply stunning, which may be why this is a favorite for wedding photographers. Walk around and you'll notice that each of the gardens' three sections has a different ambience; one is meant to mimic the gardens of France, another those of Italy, and the third pays tribute to Britain's blossoms.

Enter at Fifth Ave. and 105th St.

Conservatory Waters ★★ POND Here's the model boat pond where Stuart Little had his fabled race. You can rent a model boat to float around (via remote control), take a look at the Hans Christian Andersen statue (where storytelling takes place on weekends in summer), or visit the Alice in Wonderland statue, an artistic jungle gym for the city's youth.

Enter at 79th St. on Fifth Ave.; the pond is directly uptown of the entrance, down a hill.

The Dairy ★ ARCHITECTURE/TOURS Completed in 1871, this frou-frou–laden Gothic structure was an actual dairy set up to give city children access to fresh milk. Today it serves as the park's visitor center, so it's a good place to stop to pick up maps. Most of the Central Park Conservancy's free tours start from this point; see below for info on their scheduling.

At roughly 65th St., closer to Fifth Ave. (at 64th St., just inside Central Park). Go to www.centralparknyc.org/tours for tour info.

The Mall, Bethesda Terrace & the Loeb Boathouse ★★★ PARK LAND In their original plans for the park, Olmsted and Vaux called the area known today as the Mall "the Promenade," and intended for it to be an "open air hall of reception." Today when you visit you'll be greeted by a grand elm–lined walkway bedecked with statues. At its uptown end is an underused band shell, and west of that is one of the park's premier party places: an unofficial roller-blading rink where regulars dance-skate for hours each weekend to blasting disco music. It's quite a scene.

Bethesda Terrace is at the uptown end of the mall (just across the road) and is, without a doubt, the architectural heart of the park. You're likely to see a bride or two here, as many use this extraordinarily lovely area of the park as a backdrop for wedding photographs. If you approach it from the Mall, you'll

A word on playgrounds: With a few exceptions, most of Central Park's 22 playgrounds are located on the rim of the park near the entrances. They tend to pop up every 5 blocks or so, with some of the more elaborate playgrounds located on the south end of the park (conceived as the children's side of the park because it was nearer to where lower-income families lived at the time of the park's opening).

Horse-drawn carriage rides: Mayor DeBlasio hasn't outlawed them yet! At the entrance to the park at 59th Street and Central Park South, you'll see a line of horse-drawn carriages waiting to take passengers on a ride through the park or along certain of the city's streets. A ride is about $50 for 20 minutes (plus tip), but I suggest skipping it. Not only are the horses sad-looking, the "tour" you'll get is likely to be filled with misinformation.

An alternative to the horse-drawn carriages are the human-drawn ones. I'm speaking of pedicabs, which can be a fun way to get around midtown Manhattan or Central Park but will be pricey. **Manhattan Rickshaw Company** (www. manhattanrickshaw.com; ℂ **212/604-4729**) is the best of the companies; its fares range from $20 to $40 for a street hail ride; call to arrange a guided tour and make sure you get the rate agreed upon in writing.

Wildlife in the park: Birdwatchers from all over the city flock to the park for the variety of species it hosts, the most coveted sightings being of the endangered red-tailed hawks that make their nest on Woody Allen's Fifth Avenue building (at Fifth Ave. and 74th St.).

come to a ravishingly carved gate with symbols representing day and night (the side with the witch on a broom is "night"). Take a look as well at the carvings on the stairs down to the fountain area; they represent the four seasons, and no two are alike. Bethesda Fountain was erected to celebrate the opening of the Croton Aqueduct, which finally solved New York's water problems in 1842. Sculpted by Emma Stebbins, the first woman to receive this type of commission from the city, the statue represents the angel Bethesda. She blesses the water with one hand, carrying a lily—the symbol of purity—in the other.

Added to the park in 1874 is **Loeb Boathouse.** This is where you rent the boats that you see bobbing on the lake. It's also a fine place to eat, with a decent fast-food counter and a very good restaurant (get reservations). Carrie and Mr. Big, of *Sex and the City,* fell into the water together at the end of a disastrous date on the dock that pushes out from the cafe.

At approximately 74th St. off Park Dr. www.thecentralparkboathouse.com. ℂ **212/517-2233.** Boat rentals Apr–Nov $15 first hr., $4 every 15 min. thereafter. A gondola with singing oarsman is often available for $45 per half-hour.

Sheep Meadow ★ MEADOW The premier see-and-be-seen spot for New York's teenagers, who turn this expanse of grass into a sunbathing party come spring and summer. They're following a long tradition: This is where New York's hippie "be in," a day of non-political grooviness created by Abbie

Hoffman, took place in 1967. The meadow got its name in 1864 when park commissioners set sheep to graze here in an attempt to stop the First Division of the NY National Guard from using the meadow as a parade ground (it didn't work). In 1934 the sheep were exiled to Prospect Park in Brooklyn.

Between 64th and 68th sts., toward the West Side.

Strawberry Fields ★ MEMORIAL   A memorial to John Lennon, who was shot to death in front of the Dakota apartment house (1 W. 72nd St.) just across the street from here. A mosaic spells out "Imagine" on the ground; many come here to play music and leave flowers.

Enter at 72nd St. and Central Park W. and follow the crowds.

Wollman/Trump Rink ★ SKATING RINK/PARK   A wonderfully scenic place to skate, you may remember it from the movie *Love Story*. In the summer, the rink is transformed into a mini-amusement park called **Victorian Gardens.**

Enter at Central Park S., across from the Plaza Hotel. Open for skating late Oct–Apr. Skating Mon–Thurs $11.25 adults, $5 seniors, $6 children 11 and under; Fri–Sun $18 adults, $9 seniors, $6 children 11 and up. Mon–Tues 10am–2:30pm; Wed–Thurs 10am–10pm; Fri–Sat 10am–11pm; Sun 10am–9pm.

Though the places I list above are just a few of the wonders of the park, there are many others. And many may feel familiar if you're American. Central Park was and remains the most influential piece of landscape architecture in the United States; and many parks around the country were directly copied from this one.

Other Parks in New York City

Battery Park ★ PARK   At the southernmost tip of Manhattan, Battery Park has been growing kudzu-like for the past several decades and is now really a string of eclectic park spaces that hug the waterfront from just above the original Battery Park (where the ferry terminal for the Statue of Liberty is located) all the way up to Chambers Street (21 acres in all). At the downtownmost park are a number of stirring war monuments and the new **Seaglass Carousel** (daily 10am–10pm; $5/ride), which dips and swoops riders around on massive plexiglass fish. Walking uptown from the original battery, you'll encounter expansive lawns, a promenade along the river that runs the length of the park, terrific playgrounds, and a yacht marina. My favorite parts are the South Cove (on the Esplanade between First and Third places), an artfully varied collection of quays, bridges, and meandering walkways with great river views; and the **Irish Hunger Memorial,** a grassy outcropping direct from Ireland, complete with a real Irish stone fence.

From State St. to New York Harbor. www.thebattery.org. ℂ **212/344-3491.** Subway: R to Whitehall St.; 1 to South Ferry; 4, 5 to Bowling Green.

Brooklyn Bridge Park ★★ PARK   Many visitors who take the walk over the Brooklyn Bridge from Manhattan find they have the urge to linger in this handsome 85-acre waterfront park. A relatively recent addition to the city's green spaces (this once-industrial area officially opened as a park in 2008), it's home to a spectacular 1922 carousel (surrounded by a pavilion by contemporary star architect Jean Nouvel); **Smorgasburg** on summer weekends (see p. 89); the bouncy and architecturally significant **Squibb Park Bridge**; and several dozen play spaces including basketball, volleyball, handball, bocce, and shuffleboard courts as well as terrific playgrounds for the little ones. Free guided tours are periodically offered and events of all sorts make this an exciting place in the warm weather months (see website for more info). Do I need to mention that the views of Manhattan are killer from here?

On the waterfront from Manhattan Bridge to Brooklyn Bridge, in the Brooklyn neighborhoods of Dumbo and Brooklyn Heights. www.brooklynbridgepark.org. Subway: A,C to High St., F to York St., R to Court St., 2, 3, 4, 5 to Borough Hall

Bryant Park ★ PARK   Just behind the New York Public Library, this park is a welcome respite from the endless high-rises and crushing crowds of Midtown, a 4-acre lawn surrounded by benches, statuary, and London plane tree–shaded promenades (like the Tuileries Gardens in Paris). It's notable for its extensive programs of public concerts, movies, and even free language classes. From roughly May through October, the Sixth Avenue end of the park is set up as a stage, where Broadway performers are often invited to give concerts, free movies are shown in the summer (Monday nights), and other events are held. In winter a small "pond" is erected for free ice-skating. On the 40th Street side is the elegant little merry-go-round **Le Carrousel** ($3 per ride, June–Oct daily 11am–8pm; Nov–Jan 11am–9pm weekdays, until 10pm weekends; Feb 11am–8pm; Mar–May 11am–7pm). A good spot for a picnic, Bryant Park has a bunch of chain restos across the street, including salad nirvana **Chop't.** There are pricey, so-so restaurants on the north side of the park (go for drinks, not dinner).

Behind the New York Public Library, at Sixth Ave. (btw. 40th and 42nd sts.). www.bryantpark.org. ✆ **212/768-4242.** Subway: B, D, F, Q to 42nd St.; 7 to Fifth Ave.

Governors Island ★ PARK/HISTORIC SITE   Situated a half-mile south of Manhattan, the 172-acre Governors Island was for many years a Coast Guard installation. Before that, it was an army post for nearly 200 years and played a part in the Revolutionary War. In April 2010, New York City took over. Because it was a military base for so long, few New Yorkers, much less tourists, had visited Governors Island. But that has changed. Much of Governors Island is now a public park and 22 acres on the island are already a national monument, centered around two 1812-era fortresses. In 2016, new parkland crowned by four man-made hills opened, giving visitors even more stellar views of Manhattan. The island is open to visitors from the end of May to October. During that time, you can take a free ferry from the Battery Maritime Building adjacent to the Staten Island Ferry in lower Manhattan. (There is also a ferry from Pier 6 in Brooklyn Bridge Park.) On the island, you can walk or bicycle in a car-free environment and attend any number of activities from jazz concerts to pop-up museum exhibits.

www.govisland.com. ℂ **212/440-2200.** Free admission. Free ferries depart from Battery Maritime Building (large green building next to Staten Island Ferry terminal); in Brooklyn free ferries depart from Pier 6, at the foot of Atlantic Ave.; check website for schedules. Open Fri–Sun late May–Oct. Subway: 1 to South Ferry; 4, 5 to Bowling Green.

High Line Park ★★★ PARK   For years, a secret, untamed garden hovered above the cityscape of Chelsea and Hell's Kitchen. Formed from the wild grass, flower, and weed seeds that randomly blew onto the tracks of a 1½-mile abandoned elevated railway, it became a hidden-in-plain-sight oasis for those New Yorkers brave (and limber) enough to scale the trestles. When the city started planning to tear down the historic rail structure (constructed 1929–34), a movement was born to save it and create a "grand public promenade," with easy access from the street, and that has now happened. Beautifully landscaped (in many places with the "weeds" that once grew there naturally, replanted in areas where they wouldn't destroy the rest of the plants), with benches and gourmet food vendors galore, and a unique vantage for viewing surrounding buildings and the streets below, it's become THE place to head for a stroll on a balmy summer evening.

From Gansevoort St. to W. 34th St. (btw. 10th and 12th aves.). www.thehighline.org. ℂ **212/500-6035.** June–Sept 7am–11pm, Apr–May and Oct–Nov 7am–10pm Dec–Mar 7am–7pm. Subway: A, C, E, or L to 14th St. or 7 to Hudson Yards.

Hudson River Park ★★ PARK   Located at Pier 62 on the Hudson River next to Chelsea Piers, the carousel and skatepark are part of a 9-acre park (which includes the adjacent Pier 63) that is, without exaggerating, an urban miracle. With a Sheep Meadow–like expanse of grass, marvelous landscaping, and terrific views of the Hudson River, this is an ideal place to bring the kids for a sunny afternoon. Its pride and joy is a custom-designed 36-passenger **carousel** with all the hand-carved animals indigenous to the greater New York City area; the mini-golf course is also fun (open in warm weather only).

Enter at West 23rd St. and the river. www.hudsonriverpark.org. ℂ **212/627-2020.** Carousel $2 per ride. (Children under 42" tall must be accompanied by adult 18 or older.) Carousel Sat–Sun 11am–6pm weather permitting. Free skatepark. Skatepark 8am–dusk. Subway: C, E to 23rd St. *Note:* The M23 bus will take you almost directly to the entrance of Pier 62.

Prospect Park ★★ PARK   Designed by Frederick Law Olmsted and Calvert Vaux after their success with Central Park, this 562 acres of woodland, meadows, and ponds is considered by many to be their masterpiece and the *pièce de résistance* of Brooklyn.

The best approach is from **Grand Army Plaza,** presided over by the monumental **Soldiers' and Sailors' Memorial Arch** (1892) honoring Union veterans. For the best view of the lush landscape, follow the path to Meadowport Arch and proceed through to the Long Meadow, following the path that

THE ATTACK OF THE double-decker buses

If you were to climb aboard any public bus (cost $2.75), turn to the person next to you, and ask, "What building is that?" you'd probably get a response as informative, accurate, and interesting as what you'll find on the much pricier, hop-on, hop-off bus tours of New York City. I know, as I rode a slew of them doing research for this book, and I was appalled by the poor quality of the guides and audio guides. I think New York is best appreciated on foot, or on public buses and subways. Not only do you learn more about the city that way, you meet locals, rather than peering at the streets from afar, almost as if you were watching it all on TV. And you'll actually see more than you will if you waste time waiting . . . and waiting . . . and waiting for the next of these hop-ons to arrive, rather than just footing it to the next sight. If you insist, the top bus tour is **Big Bus** (http://eng. bigbustours.com; ℂ **800/669-0051**). Tours depart from various locations. Hop-on, hop-off bus tours start at $52 adults for an 8-hour Manhattan tour— more if you get a 48-hour pass, less if you book online.

loops around it (it's about an hour's walk). Other park highlights include the 1857 Italianate mansion **Litchfield Villa** on Prospect Park West; the **Friends' Cemetery** Quaker burial ground (where Montgomery Clift is eternally prone—sorry, it's fenced off to browsers); the wonderful 1906 Beaux Arts **boathouse;** the 1912 **carousel,** with white wooden horses salvaged from a famous Coney Island merry-go-round (Apr–Oct; rides $2); and **Lefferts Homestead Children's Historic House Museum** (ℂ **718/789-2822**), a 1783 Dutch farmhouse with a museum of period furniture and exhibits geared toward kids (hours vary by season; see website for details). There's a map at the park entrance that you can use to get your bearings.

On the east side is the **Prospect Park Zoo** (www.prospectparkzoo.com; ℂ **718/399-7339**), a modern children's zoo where kids can walk among wallabies, explore a prairie-dog town, and more. Admission is $8 adults, $6 seniors, $5 children 3 to 12. The zoo is open April through October daily 10am to 4:30pm, and November through March Monday to Friday 10am–5pm, Saturday to Sunday 10am to 5:30pm.

At Grand Army Plaza, bounded by Prospect Park W., Parkside Ave., and Flatbush Ave., Brooklyn. www.prospectpark.org. ℂ **718/965-8951** (general info). Subway: 2, 3 to Grand Army Plaza (walk down Plaza St. W. 3 blocks to Prospect Park W. and the entrance) or Eastern Pkwy/Brooklyn Museum.

Riverside Park ★ PARK   Another masterwork by landscapers Olmsted and Vaux (the visionaries behind Central Park and Prospect Park). As its name suggests, Riverside Park has always had one advantage over Central Park: glorious river views. Many of its garden-laced promenades make the most of these vistas, as does the lovely boat basin and rotunda area at 79th Street (a hopping bar enlivens evenings at the Boat Basin). As in Central Park, there is a smattering of playgrounds; there's also a skatepark with assorted ramps and half-pipes; and a handful of monuments, including **Grant's Tomb** (at 122nd

The Little Red Lighthouse

Also known as Jeffrey's Hook Lighthouse, this historic beaut located under the George Washington Bridge in Fort Washington Park on the Hudson River was the inspiration for the 1942 children's book classic, *The Little Red Lighthouse and The Great Gray Bridge,* by Hildegarde Swift and Lynd Ward. Built in New Jersey in 1880 and reconstructed and moved to its current spot in 1921, it was operational until 1947. The lighthouse was to be removed in 1951, but because of its popularity there was a public outcry and it was saved. It's now a New York City landmark and on the National Register of Historic Places. It's a fun place for the kids to explore and a scenic picnic spot in nice weather. It's sporadically open to the public, with guided tours (for more info go to www. historichousetrust.org) from spring through fall.

St., open daily 9am–5pm), the largest mausoleum in the United States at 8,100 square feet. (And the answer to who's buried in Grant's tomb is: No one. Ulysses S. Grant and his wife are not buried; their sarcophagi lie above ground.)

From 72nd to 158th St. along the Hudson River. www.nycgovparks.org/parks/riverside-park.

Tompkins Square Park ★ PARK   This would be my pick for the city's funkiest green space. It's seen its share of political protests—in 1988 a stand-off between the police and the homeless people living here culminated in 5 days of rioting and charges of police brutality—but today it's better known for the very free expression it gives home to. The yearly dance parade ends here with a smorgasbord of dancing of all sorts (go to www.danceparade.org for more on that); live music is also a fixture on weekends. Best is the daily sidewalk catwalk of pierced, tattooed, fashion-forward locals. Incorporated as a park in 1878, Tompkins Square has a number of meditative green spaces, playgrounds, a swimming pool, and a smattering of undistinguished monuments. It used to have a band shell where an early version of the Grateful Dead made their East Coast debut, but that has since been torn down.

Located btw. aves. A and B, between 7th and 10th sts. Subway: L to First Ave.

Union Square Park ★ PARK/MARKET   The spirit of the 1960s is still very much alive here, though Union Square Park's tradition of political activism goes back to the first Labor Day Parade in 1882, which ended in the park. Since that time, it has become soapbox central, a place where orators come on a daily basis to blast whatever current administration is in power, weighing in on all the big topics of the day. A statue of Gandhi, a gift of the Indian people, calmly watches over these proceedings, a fresh wreath of flowers always draped about his neck. Along with the political folk, Union Square hosts the finest **greenmarket** in the city (on the western side of the park) every Monday, Wednesday, Friday, and Saturday. Most days you'll find about 100 vendors hawking locally grown produce, organic wines, flowers, artisan cheeses, even honey from a rooftop in Brooklyn. It's a lot of fun to visit. Two playgrounds, a dog run, and a very fine equestrian statue of George Washington also on-site.

14th to 17th sts. btw. Park Ave. S and Broadway. www.nycgovparks.org/parks/union-square-park. Subway: 4, 5, 6, L, N, Q, R to 14th St./Union Square.

Washington Square Park ★★ PARK   This park is nothing if not tuneful, and has long been a place for amateur musicians to gather in groups, lugging along instruments for impromptu concerts each weekend (and many weeknights when the weather is nice). The round fountain in the center of the park serves as a stage for a dozen or so regular comedians, acrobats, and dancers who are good enough to draw crowds of 100 people or more. Entertaining as well are the intense chess matches played from noon to sundown on the southwest corner of the park (the regulars are real sharks). Children will enjoy the two playgrounds on the north side of the park.

For history buffs, there's much to mull over here. In 1797, the land was designated a potter's field; it was put to good use a year later when yellow fever swept through the city, killing 5% of the population, the poorest of whom were buried here in what was a drained swamp. Nearly 20,000 New Yorkers were laid to rest here before it became a military parade ground in 1826. Tales are still told today of soldiers doing their maneuvers on the fields, boots slipping through the crust of dirt and crunching down on shroud-covered skeletons. If all this weren't enough of an invitation for hauntings, the square was often used for public hangings, the condemned strung up on the massive elm that still stands on the northwest corner of the park.

The magnificent marble arch was designed by Stanford White; in front of it are two statues of President George Washington by Alexander Stirling Calder (father of the great modern artist Alexander Calder).

South end of Fifth Ave. (where it intersects Waverly Place, btw. MacDougal and Wooster sts.). Subway: A, C, E, F, M to W. 4th St. (use 3rd St. exit).

ORGANIZED SIGHTSEEING TOURS

Reservations are required for some of the tours listed below, but even if they're not, it's always best to call ahead to confirm prices, times, and meeting places.

Harbor Cruises

Note that some of the lines below may have limited schedules in winter, especially for evening cruises. Call ahead or check online for current offerings.

Bateaux New York ★   The most elegant and romantic of New York's evening dinner cruises, aboard a boat designed for 300 guests with two suites, one dance floor, two outdoor strolling decks, and windows galore. Dinner is a formal, three-course sit-down affair (though the food is just so-so). A live quartet entertains with jazz standards and pop vocal tunes.

Departs from Chelsea Piers, W. 23rd St. and Twelfth Ave. www.bateauxnewyork.com. © **866/817-3463.** 3-hr. dinner cruises around $135 per person. Subway: C, E to 23rd St.

Circle Line Sightseeing Cruises ★★ A New York institution, led by witty, informed guides (many are also actors), the Circle Line takes travelers round the harbor on 3-hour, 2-hour, and 75-minute cruises (the website fudges the amount of time each takes, subtracting half an hour from each of the options). The longest makes a complete circle of Manhattan, but I'd recommend the 2-hour "semi-circle" cruise instead. You'll miss Yankee Stadium and the view of the Palisades (the wooded cliffs of New Jersey) on that one, but all of the other highlights—the Statue of Liberty, the lower Manhattan skyline, the Empire State Building, the Chrysler Building—are included. Make sure to arrive at the dock early because you'll want to grab a good seat: on the right side of the boat, facing inward as you enter (that's the side that faces Manhattan; ask the staff if you're unclear). It can get very chilly on the water, so be sure to dress in layers, or take a seat inside.

In addition, a number of adults-only live music and DJ cruises sail regularly from the seaport from May through September ($20–$40 per person). Depending on the night of the week, you can groove to the sounds of jazz, Latin, gospel, dance tunes, or blues as you sail along viewing the skyline. The company also runs **The Beast,** a speedboat tour of the island that kids enjoy.

Departs from Pier 83, at W. 42nd St. and Twelfth Ave. www.circleline42.com. © **212/563-3200.** Check website or call for up-to-date schedule. 2-hr. cruises $42 adults, $40 seniors, $32 children 3–12, free for children 2 and under. Combo tickets with other attractions are available, and a good way to save. Subway to Pier 83: A, C, E to 42nd St.

Spirit Cruises ★ Spirit Cruises' modern ships are floating cabarets that combine sightseeing in New York Harbor with meals, musical revues, and dancing to live bands. The atmosphere is festive, fun, and relaxed. The buffet meals are nothing special, but you can't beat the views.

Departing from Chelsea Piers, W. 23rd St. and Twelfth Ave. www.spiritcruises.com. © **866/483-3866.** 2-hr. lunch cruises around $52; 3-hr. dinner cruises around $95 per person. Subway: C, E to 23rd St.

Take the M5: A City Bus that Hits the Highlights

If your feet are worn out from walking but you still want to see some sights: hop the **M5 bus.** Its route runs from Washington Heights down to the Staten Island Ferry terminal. If you board uptown, around 125th Street and Riverside Drive, and take it downtown, you'll pass landmarks such as Grant's Tomb, Riverside Church, Lincoln Center, Columbus Circle, St. Patrick's Cathedral, Rockefeller Center, the New York Public Library, the Empire State Building, the Flatiron Building, and Washington Square. And all you need is a MetroCard (or exact coin change) and this trusty guidebook. The bus will move slowly enough that you will be able to consult your book and find the corresponding landmarks.

OFFBEAT NEW YORK tours

Soundwalk (www.soundwalk.com; ℭ 212/674-7407): You don a pair of earbuds, and then walk into all sorts of oddball places in the Bronx, Chinatown, the Lower East Side, Times Square, DUMBO, and the Meatpacking District. You might find yourself on the roof of a private building admiring the views or peering into the window of an artist's basement studio, watching her work. For $1, download the app at Apple's iPhone store and you'll be taken into places where tourists never go.

Wildman Steve Brill ★ (www.wildmanstevebrill.com; ℭ 914/835-2153): If you ever get stranded in Central Park, a tour with Wildman Steve Brill might help you survive. Brill, with his raggedy beard, shorts, hiking boots, and pith helmet, heads off to the city's green spaces each weekend, teaching group members what flora and fauna they can forage. If you're lucky, maybe he'll regale you with the tale of his arrest by a park ranger for eating a dandelion. Reservations must be made in advance. Suggested donation is $20 ($15 for children 11 and under)—cash only, exact change.

Museum Hack ★ (www.museumhack.com; ℭ 212/604-1284): Geared towards the museum-phobic among us, Museum Hack leads an irreverent, and sometimes bawdy, sweep t... Metropolitan Museum and ... of Natural History. During yo... of one or the other, you'll see... oddities and some of the icon... ... collection (and whiz right by other masterpieces, so build in time to explore on your own afterwards), while playing silly games, learning about the museum's history, and taking lots of deliberately kooky photos. Teens love the tour, but it can be too off-color for younger kids (making it perfect for bachelor and bachelorette parties). Tours are $59 per person.

Big Apple Jazz Tours (www.bigapplejazz.com): These tours, hosted by New York jazz experts Gordon Polatnick and Amanda Hones, are the real deal for music buffs. If you're into bebop, book the Harlem tour; it hits Minton's Playhouse, the jazz club that was the supposed birthplace of bop. From there you'll head to other active Harlem clubs that embody Minton's bebop spirit. If you're into the 1960s bohemian Village scene, the Greenwich Village jaunt is what you want as it covers the joints popular during the golden era of Village jazz clubs (and today). The tour fee is $99 for 4 hours, plus the cost of entrance fees, drinks, transportation, and so forth.

Specialty Tours
CULTURAL ORGANIZATIONS

The **Municipal Art Society** ★ (www.mas.org; ℭ 212/935-3960) offers excellent historical and architectural walking tours. Each is led by a highly qualified guide; topics range from "Walt Whitman's New York" to "Upper East Side Arts." Tours cost $30 and do sell out (book early).

The **92nd Street Y** ★ (www.92y.org; ℭ 212/415-5500) has a wonderful variety of walking and bus tours, many featuring funky themes or behind-the-scenes visits. Subjects can range from "Carnegie Hall Tour and Tea" to "Jewish Harlem." Prices range from $35 to $100, but many include ferry rides, afternoon tea, dinner, or whatever suits the program. Guides are well-chosen experts. Advance registration is required for all tours.

PENDENT OPERATORS

g Onion Tours (www.bigonion.com; ✆ **888/806-WALK** [9255]) are led by local graduate students, most of them studying history, with a few sociologists and literature majors thrown in. The emphasis therefore is on the history of the area you may be visiting—Greenwich Village, Times Square, Central Park—and the lectures tend to be complex, illuminating portraits of those places. My only quibble with these tours is that the talk is often only tangentially related to the building or park you may be viewing at the time, so the walking tour can feel more like a classroom lecture than an afternoon's exploration. Adults pay $20, seniors and students $15 for these 2-hour tours.

Free Tours by Foot (www.freetoursbyfoot/new-york-tours) offers what I think are the most well-rounded, spirited historical tours of the city. No, they're not actually free; you're expected to tip at the end, about $20, and you really should because the guide has to hand over a percentage of the tips to the "boss" who runs the operation. But because the guides are dependent on tips (and so is the boss who picks the guides), only truly gifted raconteurs make the cut. Tours hit all the classic areas of the city—Harlem, Brooklyn Heights, Greenwich Village, Chinatown, Central Park—but also include some more unusual offerings, like street art tours of Bushwick, Brooklyn, and ghost tours of the High Line area and Greenwich Village. They also offer food tours at a much lower price than the competition, since you pay what you want for the tour, and then can pick and choose among the treats offered, paying for each as you go.

Harlem Spirituals (www.harlemspirituals.com; ✆ **800/660-2166** or 212/391-0900) specializes in gospel and jazz tours of Harlem that can be combined with a traditional soul-food meal. Prices start at $65 ($49 for children 5–11) for a "Harlem Gospel" tour, and go up from there based on length and activities/meals.

Urban Oyster (www.urbanoyster.com) tours mix history and food in both Brooklyn and Manhattan. Many concern craft beers, often those that are locally brewed. You'll pay between $69 and $105 for these outings, but we promise you'll be very full (or drunk) and happy at the end.

On Location Tours (www.sceneontv.com; ✆ **212/209-3370**) has the "as seen on screen" version of NYC, basing its tours on sites made famous by *Gossip Girl*, *Sex in the City*, *Real Housewives* and even *TMZ* (that tour's a gossip fest). Schedules and departure points vary depending on what tour you take, and tickets average $47 per tour. Reservations are required; most tours sell out in advance.

For shopping tours, see p. 187 and for art gallery tours, see p. 138.

SHOPPING

Why do the highest numbers of visitors to New York descend on the city in fall and early winter? They come here to shop. In the run-up to Christmas, Chanukah, Kwanzaa, and other big-spender holidays, avid shoppers storm the city because they know that if you can't find it in the Big Apple . . . well, it simply doesn't exist. In this chapter, I attempt to bring some order to the massive number of shopping options in the Big Apple, concentrating on the locally owned shops and shopping experiences that can only be had in NYC.

SHOPPING BY AREA

Often in Gotham, finding what you want has less to do with picking the right store than with choosing the right area in which to shop. Similar types of stores tend to cluster together, making it quite easy for shoppers to flit from one to the next, comparing merchandise and prices. Here, beginning at the bottom of Manhattan and working my way north and then to Brooklyn, is my list of the city's best shopping streets and their areas of specialty.

Downtown

TRIBECA
Duane Street between Greenwich and Hudson streets: A delightful block of antique and fine furniture stores with such unusual options as Brazilian collectibles and "pop" furniture options. *(Subway: 1, 2, 3 to Chambers St.)*

CHINATOWN
Canal Street between Mott and Lafayette: Best for super-cheap knockoff accessories: purses in the style of Kate Spade, watches of all types, beaded jewelry, sunglasses, and luggage. If you're planning to buy a T-shirt to commemorate your New York vacation, buy it here for half of what you'd spend in Times Square. *Tip:* Very few stores in this area use price tags. That's because bargaining is expected, so be prepared to walk away if the price seems too high—often the mere gesture of turning toward the door will halve the cost.

For browsing: The fish and herbal markets along **Canal, Mott, Mulberry,** and **Elizabeth streets** are fun for their bustle and exotica—as well as for the handful of Italian joints still hanging on from pre-Chinese days when this area was known as Little Italy. *(Subway: 1, 2, 4, 5, 6, N, Q, R to Canal St.)*

LOWER EAST SIDE

Orchard, Allen, Delancey and Ludlow Streets: A number of art galleries have been priced out of Chelsea (see p. 138) and have moved to the Lower East Side in just the last 2 years. They're joining a vibrant array of indie fashion stores and craft beer purveyors, making the LES tops for off-beat shopping. *(Subway: B, D to Grand St., F to Delancey St., J, M, Z to Essex St.)*

SOHO, NOHO & NOLITA

Broadway between West Houston and Canal: Club-kid central. If you're between the ages of 15 and 29, want affordable, flashy fashions (TopShop, Yellow Rat Bastard, H&M)—plus the usual chains (Old Navy, Zara)—this is where to shop. You'll find a similar crop of shops on **Lafayette Street between Houston and Spring,** though head farther uptown on Lafayette and you'll encounter a slew of fine furniture shops.

On the **smaller side streets** (Spring, Elizabeth, Mott, Mulberry) is an entirely different scene, with local designers and couture mavens next to high-fashion consignment stores and such stellar big names as the **Museum of Modern Art Design Store** (see p. 205). There also are several galleries along West Broadway and sprinkled throughout SoHo. A full list of shops and galleries is at www.artseensoho.com. *(Subway: R, Q to Prince St. or 6 to Spring St.)*

THE EAST VILLAGE

9th Street between Second Avenue and Avenue A: New, younger designers populate this street, so you'll find a terrific assortment of "only in New York" fashions, along with designers who have now become a bit more established (like the outlet store for **Eileen Fischer** at 314 E. 9th St.), vintage stores, and bridal boutiques. If you have the time, wander down to **St. Marks Place east of Second Avenue and 7th Street** for similar stores (though not in the same density). **St. Marks** (the continuation of 8th St.) **between Second and Third avenues** is a fun place for teens, filled with cheap sunglasses stands and T-shirt shops. *(Subway: 6 to Astor Place or L to First Ave.)*

GREENWICH VILLAGE

Bleecker Street between Seventh and Eighth avenues: Boutique heaven. If cutting-edge style is your thing and you have the pocketbook to support that appetite, the small stores along this stretch have all the latest fashions, with friendlier service than you'll find Uptown. And oddly, **Bleecker Street between Sixth and Seventh avenues** is foodie paradise, selling all the fine cheeses, gelatos, and other goodies that will prevent you from fitting into the fashions further west! *(Subway: A, E, C to 14th St.)*

CHELSEA/MEATPACKING DISTRICT

Far west Chelsea from 14th to 29th streets between Tenth and Eleventh avenues has been transformed into the **Chelsea Art District,** where more than 200 galleries have sprouted up. See p. 138 in chapter 5. *(Subway: A, C, L to Eighth Ave., 7 to Hudson Yards)*

UNION SQUARE/THE FLATIRON DISTRICT

Union Square is "big box heaven" with **Forever 21, Barnes & Noble, DSW (Designer Shoe Warehouse),** and the city's first **Nordstrom Rack,** along with other stores. It also is the site of the city's best open-air food market.

For more mall-type stores, **Fifth Avenue between 14th and 23rd streets** is a mecca, mixing home furnishings (Restoration Hardware) with brand name clothiers (Eileen Fisher, Armani, the Gap). At 23rd is the city's best food store/Italian food court **Eataly** (p. 199), as much tourist site as store. *(Subway: 4, 5, 6, N, Q, R, L to Union Square, N, R, 6 to 23rd St.)*

Midtown

HERALD SQUARE & THE GARMENT DISTRICT

Herald Square—where 34th Street, Sixth Avenue, and Broadway converge— is dominated by **Macy's,** the self-proclaimed "biggest department store in the world," but it's also host to a number of other retailers whose names you'll recognize. *(Subway: 1, 2, 3, B, D, F, M, N, Q, R to 34th St.)*

FIFTH AVENUE FROM 38TH ST. TO 57TH ST.

This is a window shoppers' paradise, with such grand old beauties as Saks Fifth Avenue, Tiffany's, and Bergdorf Goodman, along with flagship stores for Uniqlo, Louis Vuitton, LEGO, and others. For store lists and links to their websites, visit **www.fifthavenuebid.com**. *(Subway: E, M to Fifth Ave./53rd St.)*

Uptown

MADISON AVENUE FROM 57TH ST. TO 79TH ST.

This stretch is home to the most expensive retail real estate in the world, which means pricey baubles and garments for the 1% as far as the eye can see. Along with Barneys New York, you'll find flagships of Ralph Lauren, Chanel, Hermès, Vera Wang, and Prada. The ritziest boutique of all may well be **Five Story**, set in a magnificent town house of, yes, five stories that's a fascinating wander (18 E. 69th St. just off Madison). Visit **www.madisonavenuebid.org** for a shop list *(Subway: 6 to 59th, 66th, or 77th sts.)*

LEXINGTON AVENUE FROM 70TH ST. TO 80TH ST.

Ladylike apparel, and the types of home decor items that Upper East Side doyennes use to beautify their apartments, are sold on this 10-block stretch. Happily, prices tend to be about 25% less than you'd pay two avenues over, on Madison. *(Subway: 6 to 66th or 77th sts.)*

Brooklyn

WILLIAMSBURG

Get off at the Bedford Avenue stop of the L Train and just wander. Bedford Avenue, like the surrounding streets, is a treasure trove of hip boutiques, bookstores, galleries, vintage clothing stores (Beacon's Closet, see p. 199, for one), food fests (see **Smorgasburg**, p. 89), and the best flea market in the city, **Brooklyn Flea** (at 50 Kent Ave., Sundays only). *(Subway: L to Bedford St.)*

THE BIG DEPARTMENT STORES

Beyond the shops listed below are two Fifth Avenue department stores that you may want to wander into. **Henri Bendel** at 712 Fifth Ave. (between 55th and 56th St., www.henribendel.com, subway N, R to Fifth Ave.) specializes in accessories: candles, sleek handbags, and jewelry. Alas, they no longer sell clothing, and I find the goods they do have are more expensive than their quality seems to warrant. The other famed department store, **Bergdorf Goodman** at 754 Fifth Ave. (at 58th St., www.bergdorfgoodman.com; same subway as above), frankly scares me. The price tags here rarely have fewer than three digits on them—and often sport four!—the staff is snooty, and when I wander in, I always become very aware that my hair isn't nearly as well-coifed as that of the other shoppers. Still, if you want to see cutting-edge fashions, it's hard to beat Bergdorf.

ABC Carpet & Home ★★★ A museum. A temple. A sanctuary. I can't afford to buy a darn thing at ABC Carpet except for spiffy soaps, but I sure do love trawling the floors here, as the goods on offer are simply exquisite. You might find children's furniture and bedding fit for Kate and William's kids, throw pillows straight from a high-class harem, and all manner of delightful antique furnishings. Across the street is the multi-floor carpet store. The Bronx branch (1055 Bronx River Ave.) offers periodic sales. 881 and 888 Broadway (at 19th St.). www.abchome.com. ✆ **212/473-3000.** Subway: L, N, R, 4, 5, 6 to 14th St./Union Square.

Barneys New York ★★ One week it's on the runways in Paris, the next it's in the windows of Barneys. This is where well-heeled New Yorkers buy their heels . . . and suits and sweaters and other items of apparel, all at outrageous prices. Who knew a pair of shoes could serve as the down payment on a car? *Tip:* Barneys hosts a warehouse sale in Chelsea twice a year, usually at 110 W. 19th St., featuring discounts of 50% to 80% off original retail prices. These sales have better goods than you'll find at "Barney's Warehouse" outlets. Check the site for sale dates, and arrive early. 660 Madison Ave. (at 61st St.). www.barneys.com. ✆ **212/826-8900.** Subway: N, R to Fifth Ave. Also at 2151 Broadway (at 76th St.) and at 194 Atlantic Ave. (in Brooklyn, near Court St.).

Bloomingdale's ★★★ Classier than Macy's (see p. 191) and a bit more logical in terms of layout, Bloomingdale's is a shopping behemoth with enough excitement to keep shopaholics occupied for several hours. Founded in 1872 as a hoopskirt store, the vast emporium is still in the forefront of fashion, with four complete floors just for garments (basement for men's; second, third, and fourth floors for women's). It also sells housewares, furniture, kids clothing, luggage, kitchenware, accessories, cosmetics, and jewelry, but its strength is the clothes. 1000 Third Ave. (Lexington Ave. at 59th St.). www. bloomingdales.com. ✆ **212/705-2000.** Subway: 4, 5, 6 to 59th St. Also at 504 Broadway (at Broome St.), ✆ **212/729-5900.** Subway: N, R to Prince St.

Century 21 ★   Though it's near-heresy to say so, I count Century 21 as the most overrated store in the city. A four-floor discount department store diagonal from the 9/11 Memorial and Museum, it made its reputation by selling designer clothing, shoes, and housewares at steeply discounted prices. But though the clothing may say "Calvin Klein," "Mosconi," or "DKNY," I've found that in nine out of ten cases, the really inexpensive offerings look nothing like the goods you'd get from these designers at retail stores. Instead, the fabrics are the cheapest polyesters; the colors are gaudy, the fit is off, and even the labels themselves look different. I suspect this is where designers go to unload the terrible mistakes they've made, or perhaps to peddle lines of cheaper goods created explicitly for this store and others like it. I'm in the minority on this, as witness to the fact that a new outlet of the store opened in 2012 on the Upper West Side. 22 Cortlandt St. (btw. Broadway and Church St.). www. c21stores.com. ✆ **212/227-9092.** Subway: 2, 3, 4, 5, J, M to Fulton St.; A, C to Broadway/Nassau St.; E to Chambers St.; R, W to Cortlandt St. Also at 1972 Broadway (at 66th St.). ✆ **212/518-2121.** Subway: 1 to 66th St.

Dover Street Market ★   An all-couture department store, Dover specializes in clothing ($6,000 dresses, $500 T-shirts, $1,200 denim jackets) from such NY-based and international labels as Comme des Garcons, Smith and Smith, Rick Owens, and Alexander Wang. All of the goods are displayed as if this were an art installation, and the customers wander around uttering such only-in-Manhattan inanities as "When I bought my first pair of $400 shoes, people thought I was nuts. Now you can't GET a pair of shoes for less than $400!"—which makes the store interesting to visit from an anthropological perspective even if you can't afford anything here. 160 Lexington Ave. (at 30th St.). www.doverstreetmarket.com. ✆ **646/837-7750.** Subway: 6 to 28th St.

Lord & Taylor ★★   Flagship of a small chain of department stores, this is New York's overlooked gem. So when you come here, you won't be battling the crowds as you will at Bloomingdale's and Macy's. Still, you experience the best of those two stores: Bloomingdale's sense of high style at Macy's discounted rates (thanks to rolling discounts; check the Internet for coupons). A number of stylists I know head here when they have to find clothing for magazine fashion shoots, and TV shows, on a budget. 424 Fifth Ave. (btw. 38th and 39th sts.). www.lordandtaylor.com. ✆ **212/391-3344.** Subway: F, M to 42nd St.

Macy's ★   With approximately one million items for sale and a huge two-building space that stretches the very long block between Broadway and Seventh Avenue, this, the World's Largest Store, is also one of New York's top tourist attractions. It has some of the best prices of the major department stores, and in general, a higher quality of goods

> ### Additional Sources for Serious Shoppers
>
> If you're looking for specific items or sales, check the daily shopping listings at **http://ny.racked.com**, and **http:// nymag.com.**

sale SEASONS

Thanksgiving: "Black Friday," or the day after Thanksgiving, is the beginning of the holiday shopping season. Many stores inaugurate this high time with major sales.

Post-Christmas: With the Christmas returns and overstocked storerooms come the markdowns.

Whites: Usually in January, this is a sale of linens . . . which these days, are rarely white, but the name persists.

January Clearance: You'll find many boutiques advertising clearances around the third week of January.

Presidents' Day: This February long weekend brings great deals on winter inventory.

Memorial Day: Promotional sales sail in the last weekend in May.

Fourth of July: Blowouts on bathing suits and summer attire over the long weekend.

Midsummer Clearance: If there is anything summer-related left on the racks after the Fourth of July, you'll find it on clearance through about mid-August.

than Century 21, though the fashions here are definitely more middle-of-the-road. The basement is devoted to cookware, of which there's a dazzling variety; the house brand of pots and pans (called Tools of the Trade) may be the best buy, well-made and usually quite affordable. And the return policy here is one of the most generous in the city, so mistakes are not irrevocable.

Those are the reasons you should visit. But there are also reasons why you may want to pop a valium before you attempt it. The vast scale of Macy's and the huge crowds it attracts are its Achilles heel. There's never a salesperson around when you need one; on sale days the masses can be crushing; and even native New Yorkers get lost here. At Herald Square, W. 34th St., and Broadway. www.macys.com. © **212/695-4400** or 212/494-7300. Subway: B, D, F, N, Q, R, 1, 2, 3 to 34th St.

Saks Fifth Avenue ★★ Despite the fact that it's now a chain, there's still definite glamour to the original Saks. It's a classic, and unlike Macy's, its size is manageable. As for its prices . . . . They may not be within the realm for many people, but browsing here is a delight and the cosmetics and shoe departments include brands you won't find elsewhere in the U.S. 611 Fifth Ave. (btw. 49th and 50th sts.). www.saksfifthavenue.com. © **212/753-4000.** Subway: B, D, F, Q to 47th–50th sts./Rockefeller Center; E, F to Fifth Ave.

RECOMMENDED STORES
Antiques & Collectibles

New York has such a bounty of antique stores that you often do better visiting them in packs, to get a well-rounded look-see at what's available. Head, for example, to **10th street west of Broadway** and you'll find half a dozen stores that carry only the best of French and American Art Deco pieces,

Scandinavian heirlooms, and historic tapestries. Antiques hunters will also want to scout **East 59th, 60th,** and **61st streets** around Second Avenue, not far from the **Manhattan Art and Antiques Center ★,** at 1050 Second Ave. between 55th and 56th streets (www.the-maac.com; ✆ **212/355-4400**), which is one of the largest antique malls in the nation.

Individual stores to try include:

1st Dibs @ New York Design Center ★★   Though it's hidden on the 10th floor of an office building, this massive space—the first bricks-and-mortar iteration for the esteemed online design peddler—is open to the public. It showcases the holdings of 50 top antiques dealers, with an emphasis on Mid-Century Modern (you'll also find French Empire pieces, antique Murano glassware, and more). 200 Lexington Ave, 10th floor (btw. 32nd and 33rd sts.). www.1stdibs.com/nydc. Subway: 6 to 33rd St.

Dienst + Dotter Antikviteter ★★   Opened by Jill Dienst, a former curator from the Metropolitan Museum, this shop celebrates all that is old and Scandinavian, which means that many of the pieces look more contemporary than those that were created yesterday. You'll find everything from rococo inlaid tables to low-to-the-ground Danish Modern armchairs. 411 Lafayette St. (btw. Astor Pl. and E. 4th St.). www.dienstanddotter.com. ✆ **212/861-1200.** Subway: 6 to Astor Pl.

Mallett Antiques ★★★   The only outlet outside of the United Kingdom of this 150-plus-year-old furniture dealer, Mallett specializes in 18th-century English and French pieces, often of museum quality. 929 Madison Ave. (at 74th St.). www.mallettantiques.com. ✆ **212/2490-2783.** Subway: 6 to 77th St.

Todd Merrill ★★   Merrill is both a store owner and the co-author of a seminal design history book, *Modern Americana.* Well before *Mad Men* hit the airwaves, he was stoking the craze for Mid-Century Modern furnishings. Merrill now also makes custom contemporary furniture that's pretty darn snazzy. 64 Bleecker St. (btw. Broadway and Lafayette St.). www.toddmerrillstudio.com. ✆ **212/673-0531.** Subway: 6 to Bleecker St.

Beauty

C.O. Bigelow ★★★   The oldest apothecary shop in the nation (it was founded in 1838), Bigelow has become known for its huge range of beauty supplies, carrying European and Japanese products that aren't available anywhere else in the U.S. Some of the products are quite unusual (like "frownies," an 1800s stick 'em on cure for frown lines that claims to train the wrinkles to go in another direction as you sleep). Even if you don't need to buy anything, stop by to browse under the Victorian gas chandeliers (converted to electric, but still lovely). 414 Sixth Ave. (btw. 8th and 9th sts.). www.bigelowchemists.com. ✆ **212/533-2700.** Subway: A, C, E, F, M to W. 4th St.

Kiehl's ★   Founded in 1867 as an apothecary shop—its specialty back then was such magic potions as "Money Drawing Oil"—it switched to more modern snake oil, facial creams and cleansers, in the 1960s and has been wildly popular ever since. Head to the original of this now-massive chain for the historic decor (the original chandeliers are still in use) and the generous gift of numerous small samples. 109 Third Ave. (btw. 13th and 14th sts.). www.kiehls.com. © **212/677-3171.** Subway: L, N, R, 4, 5, 6 to 14th St./Union Square.

Ricky's ★   This punky, funky chain of cosmetics stores goes beyond the typical "Duane Reade" selection of beauty products into wigs, hair dyes for every shade of the rainbow, body glitters, and shampoos even your stylists never heard of. It's also tops for souvenirs and small gifts, as it has a number of silly toys and grooming products. All in all, there are 23 stores in all parts of the city. 728 Ninth Ave. (btw. 49th and 50th sts.). © **212/245-1265.** Subway: C, E to 50th St.

Books

In addition to the following, don't forget the giant **Scholastic Store** (557 Broadway, between Prince and Spring sts.; www.scholastic.com/sohostore; © **212/343-6166**) in SoHo for children's books and events.

Barnes & Noble ★★★   This famous chain—largest in the nation—was founded in NYC, and while the original store is now closed, the rest are a wonderland for bibliophiles, of which numerous branches are found throughout the city and its suburbs. 555 Fifth Ave. at 45th St. Consult www.bn.com for other locations. © **212/253-0810.** Subway: 4.5,6 and L to Grand Central/42nd St.

Books of Wonder ★★★   Do you remember the charming bookstore in the Meg Ryan rom-com *You've Got Mail?* It was inspired by Books of Wonder (Meg even worked here briefly to train for the role), and the real thing is just as magical (and jam-packed with great kiddie reads) as the cinematic store. 18 W. 18th St. (btw. Fifth and Sixth aves.). www.booksofwonder.com. © **212/989-3270.** Subway: L, N, R, 4, 5, 6 to 14th St./Union Square.

Drama Book Shop ★   As much clubhouse as bookstore, when it was damaged by a burst pipe in 2016, *Hamilton*'s own Lin Manuel Miranda led the campaign to save the shop (he used to sit among the stacks and write when he was less well-known). Not surprisingly, it's filled with scripts (including those of all the shows on Broadway, if you want that kind of souvenir), plus a myriad of books about the art and craft of theater. 250 W. 40th St. (btw. Eighth and Ninth aves.). www.dramabookshop.com. © **212/944-0595.** Subway: A, C, E to 42nd St.

Idlewild Books ★★★   This innovative travel bookstore makes perusing the shelves intuitive by mixing guidebooks with works of history, memoirs, and other titles about the destination in question. It also boasts one of the most knowledgeable, cheery staffs in the city. 12 W. 19th St. (off Fifth Ave.). www.idlewildbooks.com. © **212/414-8888.** Subway: N, R to 23rd St.

Kitchen Arts & Letters ★   A superb cookbook store. Along with titles from the standard celeb chefs are out-of-print, rare, and even foreign language books, all just brimming with recipes and advice. 1435 Lexington Ave. (btw. 93rd and 94th sts.). www.kitchenartsandletters.com. © **212/876-5550.** Subway: 6 to 96th St.

OPEN FOR business?

Hours can vary significantly from store to store—even different branches of the Gap can keep different schedules in this city!

Generally, stores open at 10 or 11am Monday through Saturday; 7pm is a common closing hour. Both closing and opening hours tend to get later as you move downtown, with some East Village stores keeping their gates down until 1pm, and staying open until 8pm or later. In the Financial District, some stores close for the entire weekend (this is the only part of the city, however, where that happens).

All of the big department stores are open 7 days a week, with many staying open until 9pm on Thursdays. Nervous you'll show up and nobody will be there to sell? Call ahead or go on the Internet to double-check hours.

McNally Jackson Books ★   Many bookstores post recommendations from their staff, but few are as right on as the ones here. A great place to find that book for the plane ride home, or take a break from the shopping madness of SoHo (there's a nice cafe on-site). 52 Prince St. (btw. Lafayette and Mulberry sts.). www.mcnallyjackson.com. ℗ **212/274-1160.** Subway: N, R to Prince St.; 6 to Spring St.

The Mysterious Bookshop ★   Another specialty book dealer; do you need a clue as to what's sold here? Didn't think so. The store has both antique and current mystery novels. 58 Warren St. (at W. Broadway). www.mysteriousbook shop.com. ℗ **212/587-1011.** Subway: 1, 2, 3, A, C, E to Chambers St.

Rizzoli ★★   Lovers of majestic olde New York groaned when news came that Rizzoli would be losing its spectacular long-time home on 57th Street. Amazingly, Rizzoli found a spot as palatial (high ceilings, fluted columns) and as appropriate to their wares: handsome coffee table books on fashion, interior design, architecture, and art (though you'll also find the usual fiction and non-fiction tomes here). A truly grand shopping experience! 1133 Broadway at (btw. 25th and 26th sts.). www.rizzolibookstore.com. ℗ **212/759-2424.** Subway: N, R to 23rd St.

The Strand ★★★   Grungy, maddeningly disorganized, stuffy, and crowded, the Strand is nonetheless one of New York's premier bookstores, a place that rivals the legendary "Library at Alexandria" in its scope and variety. Its motto is "Eight Miles of Books," and it certainly feels like it has that many when you visit; best of all, many of these are "front list" books that are ordered directly from the publisher at a substantial discount (sometimes as much as 50%). Those looking for rare books should look no farther: The Strand has the largest collection in the city. 828 Broadway (at 12th St.). www.strand books.com. ℗ **212/473-1452.** Subway: L, N, Q, R, 4, 5, 6 to 14th St./Union Square.

Clothing

3x1 ★   Right in the heart of this Soho store is a small, glassed-in factory with ten seamstresses behind whirring machines, knocking out two pairs of custom jeans a day. If you have a hard-to-fit physique (many athletes come here), it may be worth getting a pair (they cost upwards of $700 but are made from selvedge denim and so will last 7 years). For the rest of us 3x1 offers unusually well-fitting, ready-to-wear pairs (they use a stretchy denim that flatters everyone—really, it's like the sisterhood of the traveling pants), starting at $185/pair. 15 Mercer St. (btw. Canal and Grand St.). www.3x1.us. © **212/391-6969.** Subway: N, R, 6 to Canal St.

Brooks Brothers ★   Yes, it's a chain, but this is where it started and the store is a classic, all burnished woods, seas of ties, and salesladies in pearls. 346 Madison Ave. (at 44th St.). www.brooksbrothers.com. © **212/682-8800.** Subway: S, 4, 5, 6, 7 to 42nd St./Grand Central.

Christian Siriano ★★   If the name sounds familiar, that's because this shock-haired designer was the youngest person to ever win *Project Runway*. He learned some helpful lessons there, like the importance of creating fashions for a variety of silhouettes, and how to choose just the right fabrics. He's also grown since his time on the show, which means that his collection isn't all black, but comes in a peacock's array of lovely colors and patterns. But the most surprising thing about this shop is how affordable the clothing is (well, by NYC standards). You could very well walk out with a dress to wear to a wedding for $75 (and informal clothes for less). One other nice perk of coming here: The store carries many items unavailable at the department stores that carry the Siriano brand. 252 Elizabeth St. (btw. Prince St. and Houston). www.christiansiriano.com. © **212/775-8494.** Subway: 6 to Bleecker St.

Jeffrey New York ★   For its chic-er-than-thou clientele, it's either here or Barneys. As you might imagine, price is no object for this crowd. An outlet of the revered Atlanta mega-boutique, it offers shoes, accessories, and make-up along with the cutting-edge clothing. 449 W. 14th St. (near Tenth Ave.). www.jeffreynewyork.com. © **212/206-1272.** Subway: A, C, E, L to 14th St.

La Garçonne ★   The first physical store of the esteemed online women's clothing marketplace, it sells its usual mix of androgynous-looking basics, but here you can try them on. 465 Greenwich St. (at Watts St.). www.lagarconne.com. © **646/553-3303.** Subway: 1 to Canal St.

La Petit Coquette ★★   If you want new lingerie—flouncy, sexy, or everyday—there are few better places anywhere to get it. That's because the staff here is expert in sizing and will make your, er, "girls" look perkier than they have in years. Prices can be high, but these bras will last forever (especially if you follow the detailed washing instructions the staff will give you). 51 University Place (btw. 9th and 10th sts.). www.lapetitcoquette.com. © **212/473-2478.** Subway: 4, 5, 6, L, N, Q, R to Union Square.

Lee Anderson Couture ★   The trick to being able to afford any of the exquisite, hand-sewn clothing here (they look like updated versions of clothing Betty Draper from *Mad Men* would have worn in season 1 or 2) is to ring at the main store and ask to be taken to the second-floor outlet across the street. You see, this is a true couture outlet, which means that all of the goods are made to order and costs in the thousands. But samples (which are for sizes 8 and 10 usually) are taken across the street when a type of fabric no longer is available, which means that women can get a dress that would usually cost, oh, $6,500, for just $175 or so. 988 Lexington Ave (btw. 71st and 72nd sts.). www.leeandersoncouture.com. ℂ 212/722-2463. Subway: 6 to 77th St.

Liberty House ★   Softness is celebrated at this Upper West Side institution. The clothing here—for men, women and children—drapes languidly on the body, the colors and groovy patterns looking like they've been bleached just the right amount by summer sunlight, the fabrics so supple they feel as if they've already been in the washing machine 10 times. (Think outfits that Whoopi Goldberg or Jeff Goldblum would wear out to dinner.) Prices, alas, can be hard-edged, but Liberty House has frequent sales. 2878 Broadway (at 112th St.). www.libertyhousenyc.com. ℂ 212/932-1950. Subway: 1 to 110th St.

Meg ★★   You may not have heard of designer Meghan Kinney, but she's been a fixture in Manhattan for the past decade, thanks to this little boutique. Taking her inspiration from Martha Graham, her designs have a fluidity to them that is quite unique. I also like her use of kicky, unusual fabrics, her reasonable pricing, the way she's able to nip in the waist just so, and the fact that though the look is young, it doesn't look foolish on her middle-aged clients. Worth a visit. 312 E. 9th St. www.megshops.com. ℂ 212/260-6329. Subway: 6 to Astor Place.

Reformation ★★   Often when a designer touts how small his carbon footprint is, that means the visual impact of his clothes will likely be puny, too. Not so with Yael Aflalo, the founder of Reformation, who uses surprising silhouettes—a peekaboo panel here, a slung low shoulder strap there, just the right slit up a long skirt—to keep his 20- and 30-something customers looking on-trend and flirty. On the ecological side: almost all his wares are manufactured in the United States, all from sustainable fabrics. 23 Howard St. (btw. Lafayette and Crosby sts.). www.thereformation.com. ℂ 212/510-8455. Subway: 6, N, R to Canal St.

Saks Off Fifth ★   The outlet of the famous department store is also the location of the first bricks-and-mortar Gilt.com outlet, featuring the services of Gilt stylists. It's a basement store, so a bit grim looking, but the bargains are real, featuring such designers as Diane von Furstenberg, BCBGMaxAzaria, and Vince. (In fact, I found prices to be far better, often for the exact same merchandise, than what you'll find at the Neiman Marcus outlet in Brooklyn, which I don't list for that reason). 125 E. 57th St. (right off Lexington Ave.). www.saksofffifth.com. ℂ 212/634-0730. Subway: 4,5,6, N,Q, R to 59th St.

Searle ★★   Buy a winter coat here, and you'll never have to buy another. That isn't an exaggeration. High quality, beautifully cut, and wonderfully warm: these are good investments. Searle also has other clothes, but the women's outerwear is what makes this place such a find. 635 Madison Ave. (at 59th St.). www.searlenyc.com. ℂ 212/750-5153. Subway: 4, 5, 6, N, R to 59th St. Also at 1051 Third Ave. (at 62nd St.), ℂ 212/838-5990, subway 4, 5, 6, N, R to 59th St.; 1296 Third Ave. (at 74th St.), ℂ 212/717-5200, subway 6 to 77th St.; and 1124 Madison Ave. (at 84th St.), ℂ 212/988-7318, subway 4, 5, 6 to 86th St.

SHOP 'TIL YOU drop TOURS

It's an open secret in New York that you get the best bargains when you cut out the middleman and buy directly from the many designers who call Gotham home. But tracking down sample sales and getting into designer showrooms can be tricky, if not impossible, for outsiders.

The following tours contain the "keys" to the kingdom of fashion. They take would-be buyers into the "inner sanctums" of design: obscure offices in the garment district filled with "sample" clothing (goods that were created for runway shows or to show department stores). The savings can be ginormous! On one tour I took, I got a fabulous, real suede skirt for $20, a chic tweed dress for $40, two cashmere turtlenecks for $30 apiece, and about five lovely T-shirts for $15 total. I have no doubt that my savings more than paid for the cost of the tour.

There is, however, one major "gotcha" to these tours, and that's sizing. In general, the tours are not so hot for plus-sized customers. You'll find the most options if you're a size 0 to a size 6. Recommended tours include:

- **Shop Gotham** (www.shop gotham.com)
- **The Elegant Tightwad** (www. theeleganttightwad.com)
- **Style Room** (www.styleroom.com)

Uniqlo ★★★   How much do I love this Japanese chain (now on the East and West coasts of the United States but not yet in the middle)? I just looked down and realized that every item of clothing I'm wearing, as I type this, is from the store. That's because garments (and undergarments) here are among the least expensive in the city, and yet come in quality fabrics, in a wide range of styles from streamlined basics (T-shirts, good wool cardigans, dapper khakis and shorts) to clothes that ape items you'll see in the fashion magazines (smartly cut blazers, billowy skirts, patterned sweaters and more) but usually cost $100s more. Clothing for men, women and children. The Fifth Avenue outlet is the largest Uniqlo on the planet. 666 Fifth Ave (at 53rd St.). www.uniqlo. com. ✆ **877/486-4756.** Subway: F to 57th St., N, Q, R to Fifth Ave.

JUST KIDS

Ibiza Kids ★★   Fine leather footwear and modish sneakers, often from Europe, are the specialties here, though the store also stocks a range of adorable outfits, especially appealing to girls in the "princess phase." Best of all: There's a complete toy store on site, so the kiddos can play while you browse. 830 Broadway (at 12th. St.). www.ibizakidz.com. ✆ **212/228-7990.** Subway: 4, 5, 6, N, Q, R to Union Sq. Also at 340 First Ave (at 20th St.).

Greenstones ★★   Greenstones has a wide variety of trendy but tasteful clothing for newborns through tweens. For boys, that means everything from real suits to happy T's. On the girls' side, the clothing ranges from rompers to dresses to casual wear, all of it on-trend without looking like it should be worn to a dance club (a problem with lots of girls clothes these days). 454 Columbus Ave. (at 84th st.). www.greenstonesnyc.com. ✆ **212/580-4322.** Subway: B, C to 81st St.

Space Kiddets ★★★ Hip kids' wear—including dozens of patterned T-shirts and fancy jeans—sold by a friendly, helpful staff. Prices are on the high side, but they're tempered by frequent sales. 26 E. 22nd St. (btw. Broadway and Park Ave.). www.spacekiddets.com. © **212/420-9878.** Subway: N, R to 23rd St.

VINTAGE & CONSIGNMENT CLOTHING

Beacon's Closet ★★ Beacon's trades in both trendy and vintage clothes, brought in by the fashionistas of the city. Very few items cost more than $20 and the selection is huge. 10 W. 13th. St (nr Fifth Ave). www.beaconscloset.com. © **917/261-4863.** Subway: 4, 5, 6, N, Q, R, L to Union Square. Other outlets around city, see website for info.

Housing Works Thrift Shop ★ Do-gooder shopping: Not only will you find terrific buys on all of the top designers, but part of what you spend will go to help a homeless person living with HIV or AIDS. Along with designers such as Calvin Klein, Perry Ellis, and Diane Von Furstenberg, these stores carry wedding gowns and furniture. There are now 13 outlets around the city, but I always have the best luck at this one. 306 Columbus Ave. (btw. 74th and 75th sts.). www.housingworks.org. © **212/579-7566.** Subway: 1, 2, 3, B, C to 72nd. St.

Ina and Ina Men's ★★★ This is where the *Sex and the City* costume department resold its clothes once the series ended. Though those clothes are now long gone (they sold out in 2 hours flat), there's no other place in the city where you'll be able to achieve "Carrie's" look as affordably, replicating that character's haute but wacky sensibility. The men's part of the store has equivalently daring clothing for guys. There are now many outlets, but the one I list here has the best selection. 15 Bleecker St. (at Elizabeth St.). www.inanyc.com. © **212/228-8511.** Subway: 6 to Spring St. Other outlets around city, see website for info.

Michael's ★★ You'll find one-of-a-kind couture clothes (Gucci, Prada, Escada) at deep discounts here, including wedding gowns, all brought in by the doyennes of the Upper East Side. It also has the largest selection of hats and purses of any of the consignment houses. 1041 Madison Ave., 2nd Floor (btw. 79th and 80th sts.). www.michaelsconsignment.com. © **212/737-7273.** Subway: 6 to 77th St.

Edibles

Eataly ★★★ I LOVE Eataly. There, I said it. Sure, it's overcrowded, pretentious, and is fast becoming a chain. But Mario Batali's Italian food hall, which is split between half-a-dozen restaurants and shops selling all sorts of comestibles, was a game changer. Not only has it raised the level of what locals expect when they shop (there's a vegetable butcher who will prep your greens for free, and row upon row of imported dried pastas in every shape imaginable!), but it has also introduced the city to a broader range of Italian food. One restaurant is all vegetarian, for example, and the rooftop is an Italian beer garden. Come to eat, come to shop, but just come. I guarantee you'll enjoy the bustle and foodie frenzy. 200 Fifth Ave. (at Broadway). www.eataly.com. © **212/229-2560.** Subway: N, R to 23rd St.

NYC IS chocolate city

With this many chocolate makers in town, the Big Apple could be renamed the Big Bonbon. Many sweet shops now turn out homemade chocolates that are so good, the stores, like four-star restaurants, are bona fide destinations.

What I like best about **Jacques Torres Chocolates ★★★**—besides the fact that Jacques Torres is a dashingly handsome Frenchman who likes to cook (making him every woman's dream guy)—is its owner's willingness to blend common ingredients with splendid chocolates. He does this, for example, with two breakfast cereals—plain bran flakes and Cheerios—and the results are exquisite. You'll also want to pick up a can of his rich hot chocolate ($16 for an 18-oz. tin; the "Wicked" version is slightly spicy), which puts Hershey's to shame. The chain has 9 locations, including one in Grand Central Terminal. The 66 Water Street shop in DUMBO, Brooklyn, lets you watch chocolate being made—just don't neglect his nearby **Ice Cream Store** at no. 62. (www.mrchocolate.com; ✆ **718/875-1269**).

Just east of the Metropolitan Museum of Art is the Madison Avenue incarnation of the Paris import **La Maison du Chocolat ★**, 1018 Madison Ave., at 78th Street (www.lamaisonduchocolat.com; ✆ **212/744-7117**). This boutique takes its handiwork very seriously, and avoids any bitterness in its chocolate by using nothing stronger than 65% cocoa. If you're downtown, stop by their shop at 63 Wall St. (✆ **212/952-1123**), or duck into the two Midtown branches, the first at 30 Rockefeller Center (✆ **212/265-9404**) and the other in the Time Warner Center on Columbus Circle (✆ **917/891-3823**).

One of the oldest chocolate shops in the city is the 1923-established **Li-Lac Chocolates ★★**, 40 Eighth Ave. at Jane Street (www.li-lacchocolates.com; ✆ **212/924-2280**), home to new batches of handmade fudge daily. (You'll now also see them in the Grand Central Station food market, Chelsea Market, and several other locations). Nearby is Allison Nelson's sublime **Chocolate Bar ★**, 19 Eighth Ave. at West 12th Street (www.chocolatebarnyc.com; ✆ **212/366-1541**). Try the superdark 72%—so rich you might speak in tongues after a few bites.

Bond Street Chocolate ★, 63 E. 4th Street (www.bondstchocolate.com; ✆ **212/677-5103**) offers chocolate in innovative forms—like miniature skulls and the "divine collection" of Virgin Mary, Jesus, and Ganesh chocolate statues. Bond has lots of darks on the menu, as well as unusual flavors like tequila, elderflower, and absinthe.

Brooklyn's most famous chocolatier is **Mast Brothers ★**, 111 N. 3rd Street (in Williamsburg; www.mastbrothers.com) run by two bearded bros who have been embroiled in scandal since 2015, when a number of reports surfaced claiming their goods weren't "bean to bar" but instead remelted French chocolate, mixed with their ingredients. I can't say whether the allegations are true or not, but does it matter? Their goods are really tasty, their packaging is gift-worthy, and they hold fun factory tours ($10) daily, every half-hour on the hour from 11am to 5pm.

Kalustyan's ★★ This 72-year-old international market just keeps growing and growing and growing. At the close of 2015, it added 6,500 square feet upstairs and down, so the shop now encompasses three buildings. But the aisles still feel cramped because they're so crammed with goodies from all corners of the globe: Korean chili paste, candied violets, Tunisian harissa,

Sicilian pistachios, 100 different types of salt, za'atar spice mix from 17 corners of the globe, and every type of spice known to man. Best of all, the store doesn't let any herb or spice sit on the shelves for more than 3 months. For home cooks, Kalustyan's is mecca. 123 Lexington Ave. (btw. 28th and 29th St.). www.kalustyans.com. ✆ **212/685-3451.** Subway: 6 to 28th St.

Murray's Cheese's ★★★ Cheese is the new wine, attracting obsessive devotees who, like oenophiles, can spend hours tasting, musing, comparing. And Murray's is at the epicenter of this movement. A cavernous emporium with over 250 varieties of cheese from all over the world and multiple tasting stations, Murray's has a fanatical following (in fact, the *New York Times* once ran a story about a lawyer who takes off every Thursday just to work behind the counter there for fun). Murray's also has an attached restaurant, every dish featuring cheese. 254 Bleecker St. (btw. Sixth and Seventh aves.). www.murrays cheeses.com. ✆ **212/243-3289.** Subway: A, B, C, D, E, F, M to West 4th St.

Zabar's ★ Featured in films by Woody Allen, this is New York's most famous grocery/deli, an iconic New York emporium. It has some unique edibles, but frankly, I come here for the competitively priced housewares and cookware on the second floor, of which there are a jaw-dropping range and variety. 2245 Broadway (at 80th St.). www.zabars.com. ✆ **212/787-2000.** Subway: 1 to 79th St.

SWEETS

Dylan's Candy Bar ★ Dylan Lauren (the daughter of designer Ralph Lauren) created this Wonka-esque sugar palace, and it's turned into a bona fide tourist attraction over the years. I won't deny a visit to this shiny, sherbet-colored emporium is fun—heck, just seeing that many different varieties of gummy bears in one place is enough to keep my daughters grinning for days—but I always leave feeling a bit queasy. 1011 Third Ave. (at 60th St.). www.dylanscandybar.com. ✆ **646/735-0078.** Subway: 4, 5, 6, N, R to 59th St. Also at Union Square and in Turnstyle at Columbus Circle.

Economy Candy Store ★★ A better candy experience, I think, can be had at the old-fashioned Economy Candy. Founded in 1937 and little changed since, it's the place to go for all of those penny candies you can't find anywhere else, plus classic treats like bubble gum cigars (remember those?) and wax lips. The halvah and house-dipped chocolates are swell. A trip down a very sweet memory lane. 108 Rivington St. (btw. Delancey and Norfolk sts.). www.economycandy.com. ✆ **212/254-1531.** Subway: F to Delancey St.

Electronics

The Apple Store ★ The huge glass cube across from the Plaza Hotel is actually the biggest Apple Store in the world (at 18,000 square feet). It opened in early 2006, and only closed when Hurricane Sandy shuttered the entire city (it's open 24/7). Apple has opened several other branches, including one in Grand Central Terminal. 767 Fifth Ave. (at 59th St.). www.apple.com. ✆ **212/336-1440.** Subway N, R to Fifth Ave.

B&H Photo & Video ★★★   I know people who visit New York City *just* to shop at B&H. Not only is it the largest camera store in the United States, it also boasts the best prices in the country (and that's a rarity for NYC). But you'd be mistaken if you think the store is just for shutterbugs; it's also tops for most everything electronic, from computers to mixing boards to chargers. Best of all: the staff is extremely knowledgeable and, since so many customers shop at their online store now, these tech gurus have time to walk would-be buyers through all the options. (*Note:* B&H is closed Saturdays.) 420 Ninth Ave. (at 34th St.). www.bhphotovideo.com. ☏ **800/606-6969** or 212/444-6615. Subway: A, C, E to 34th St.

Gifts

Evolution Nature Store ★   Who knew that there'd be a market for freeze-dried mice, stuffed piranhas, and pendants made from butterfly wings? Apparently the mad scientists behind Evolution did, and in 1993 they opened this mesmerizing store-*cum*-museum, where you can spend an engrossing hour staring at perfectly preserved skeletons (all types of animals), pristine fossils, stuffed creatures, and bugs encased in plastic. A great place to take the kids. 120 Spring St. (at Greene St.). www.theevolutionstore.com. ☏ **212/952-3195.** Subway: N, R to Spring St.

Forbidden Planet ★★   Know anyone who lives in a fantasy world? This is where you should buy their gift. Forbidden Planet specializes in all of the "geek" obsessions: sci-fi, horror, Japanese anime, comic books, and fantasy games. That includes figurines from such cult classics as *Buffy the Vampire Slayer* and *Star Wars,* gaming implements, and more such ephemera. 832 Broadway (btw. 12th and 13th sts.). www.fpnyc.com. ☏ **212/473-1576.** Subway: L, N, R, 4, 5, 6 to 14th St./Union Sq.

Magpie ★★   Guilt-free whimsy is for sale at this cheery little store—all of the goods are either fair trade items from abroad, or crafted here in the good ole U.S. of A. So what will you find? If it's cute, and gift-worthy, it will likely be on sale, everything from baby's bibs with witty sayings, to attractive scarves and jewelry, to bath and body products to tech gadgets, again with funny sayings affixed. Need a card? You can get that here, too. 488 Amsterdam Ave. (btw 83rd and 84th St.). www.magpienewyork.com. ☏ **646/998-3002.** Subway: 1 to 86th St.

More and More ★★★   An apt name for this living cabinet of wonders, this tiny shop is jam-packed with delightful knick-knacks, toys, and housewares. It's the best store in the city for Christmas ornaments, but also has some wonderful things to put under the tree: candleholders dripping with crystals, antique jewel-toned cut-glass sherry glasses, painted porcelain eggs, frog-shaped scotch-tape holders, you name it. 378 Amsterdam Ave. (at 78th St.). www.moreandmoreantiquesnyc.com. ☏ **212/580-8404.** Subway: B, C to 81st St.

Story ★★★   The mother of all concept stores, Story reinvents itself every 4 to 8 weeks. The powers-that-be pick a theme ("Feminism," "Creativity," and

"Emojis" have been recent ones) and then stock the 2000-square-foot store with goods that artfully illustrate said theme. When I was last there, "Have Fun" was the exhortation on the wall, so that meant umbrellas that change color based on how hard it rains; an oversized mug/kit that allows users to shake up a fresh batch of ice cream; and the most darling walking shoes, each with a witty print by an American artists. I have NO idea what will be in the store when you visit—and that's totally the point. 144 Tenth Ave. (at 19th St.). www.thisisstory.com. ℂ **212/242-4853.** Subway: A, C, E, L to Eighth Ave./14th St.

Zee Dog ★★   Dude up your pooch at this Brazilian store, the first of its kind in the U.S., where the chew toys are shaped like coy Martians, collars have hip shark or cactus patterns (and detachable bow ties), and leashes have a smart spring built in as a shock absorber, protecting your wrists and your dog's throat if he pulls too hard as you walk. 442 Broome St. (btw. Broadway and Mercer St.). www.zee-dog.com. ℂ **646/666-0672.** Subway: N, R to Prince, 6 to Spring St.

Home Design & Housewares

Fish's Eddy ★   Want to bring home a set of dishes with the NY skyline on them? You'll find those here, along with a slew of equally peppy, original plateware. Those who like vintage styles for modern tableware—like soda fountain and pint glasses—will find them here. 889 Broadway (at 19th St.). www.fishseddy.com. ℂ **877/347-4733.** Subway: L, N, R, Q, 4, 5, 6 to 14th St./Union Square.

Gracious Home ★★   My family nicknamed Gracious Home the "everything store" because if it's something you're going to need for your house, they'll likely have it. Swanky sheets? They carry 16 brands, including a very nice house brand. Coasters? Can openers? Lawn chairs? Vases? Trays? Pizza knives? They have them all, and in a variety that's staggering. Even if you don't want to buy anything, it's fun to browse this cornucopia of domesticity. 1922 Broadway (at 67th St.). www.gracioushome.com. ℂ **212/231-7800.** Subway: 1, 2, 3 to 72nd St.

Jewelry & Accessories

Doyle & Doyle ★   Run by certified gemologist Elizabeth Doyle and her sister Irene (a veteran of the diamond trade), Doyle & Doyle specializes in Georgian, Edwardian, and Art Deco–era jewelry, which are shown to beautiful effect in display cases mounted on the wall (like fine paintings). Even if you're not buying, this is a fun store to visit. 412 W. 13th St. (btw. Ninth Ave. and Washington St.). www.doyledoyle.com. ℂ **212/677-9991.** Subway: A, C, E, L to 14th St./Eighth Ave.

Jill Platner ★   Ultra-modern designs mixed with unusual materials (many pieces are strung on a Gore-Tex–like thread called Tenara) make Jill Platner the go-to place for people who like to make a statement with their accessories. All the pieces are made in NYC, and happily, many sell for well under $100. 113 Crosby St. (btw. Houston and Prince sts.). www.jillplatner.com. ℂ **212/324-1298.** Subway: N, R to Prince St.

West 47th Street between Fifth and Sixth avenues is the city's famous Diamond District. They say more than 90% of the diamonds sold in the United States come through this neighborhood first, so there are some great deals to be had if you're in the market for a nice rock. The street is lined with showrooms and you'll be wheeling and dealing with the largely Hasidic dealers, who are friendly but can be tough negotiators. For a complete intro to the district, including buying tips, go to **www.dia monddistrict.org**. Stores open Monday through Friday only here.

Lunessa ★★ This tiny SoHo store, with its gem bar and wondrously friendly staff, make jewelry shopping a heckuva lot of fun. First off, using that gem bar, they'll help you design your own piece. Or you can choose one of the elegant, delicate creations by owner Elise Perelman. 100 Thompson St. (near Prince St.). www.lunessacom. © **917/305-0510.** Subway: N, R to Prince St.

Tiffany & Co. ★★ This is the original, and whether or not you decide to pose in front of it nibbling a Danish, you'll enjoy visiting the elegant, multilevel store. Its goods range well beyond jewelry, by the way; many brides register here for fabulous tableware and stemware. As tradition dictates everything you buy comes wrapped in the store's iconic robin's-egg-blue box. 727 Fifth Ave. (at 57th St.). www.tiffany.com. © **212/755-8000.** Subway: N, R to Fifth Ave. Also at 37 Wall St. (btw. William and Broad sts.), © **212/480-4587,** subway 2, 3 to Wall St.

Leather Goods & Shoes

Kathryn Amberleigh ★★ This is the flagship store of NYC–based, high-fashion cobbler Kathryn Amberleigh. Her designs are playful, color-rich (though she does have basic colors, too), and sexy. While these shoes don't come cheap, it's unlikely you'll find anyone else wearing them in your hometown. 13 Gansevoort St. (btw. Hudson and West 4th sts.). www.kathrynamberleigh.com. © **212/842-2134.** Subway: A, C, E to 14th St.

m0851 ★★ The only U.S. outlet of this Montreal-based company, m0851 sells handbags, jackets, backpacks, and other leather goods that have accomplished the neat trick of looking both contemporary and timeless. Prices can be steep, but the goods are so well made they last for a decade or more. 415 West Broadway (btw. Spring and Prince sts.). www.m0851.com. © **212/431-3069.** Subway: C, E to Spring St. or N, R to Prince St.

Mooshoes ★ Mooshoes, as you might guess from the name, sells "cruelty free" products—handbags, boots, pumps, men's dress shoes—all of which are crafted from plant-based fabric, but look like the finest suede and other forms of leather. Prices are good, too. 78 Orchard St. (btw. Grand and Broome sts.). www.mooshoes.com. © **212/254-6512.** Subway: F to Delancey, B, D to Grand St.

Peter Hermann ★★   The owners of this swank SoHo shop search the world over for artisans who create unique and stylish bags, wallets, and scarves. Many of the pieces come from small producers in Europe and can't be found anywhere else in the U.S. In 2016, these included ladylike but vibrantly colorful three-pocket purses, scarves with vivacious Indonesian patterns, and big, slouchy leather bags that just screamed "shabby chic." 118 Thompson St. (at Prince St.). www.peterhermannsoho.com. ℂ **212/966-9050.** Subway: C, E to Spring St. or N, R to Prince St.

Tip Top Shoes ★   Here's where you come when your feet start complaining about all the walking you've been doing in NYC. Tip Top specializes in shoes that are comfortable, but don't look nerdy. And prices aren't bad at all. A full selection for both men and women. 155 W. 72nd St. (btw. Broadway and Columbus). www.tiptopshoes.com. ℂ **212/787-4960.** Subway 1, 2, 3 to 72nd St.

Museum Stores

Metropolitan Museum of Art Store ★★★   Like something you've seen at the museum? It's likely you'll be able to bring it home . . . in the form of a mug, or a piece of jewelry, or a print for your wall. The Met is expert at turning the stars of its vast collection into lovely items for daily life. Also notable is the extraordinary collection of art books and posters for sale. 1000 Fifth Ave. (at 82nd St.). www.store.metmuseum.org. ℂ **212/570-3894.** Subway: 4, 5, 6 to 86th St. Also at Rockefeller Center, 15 W. 49th St., ℂ **212/332-1360,** subway B, D, F, M to 47th–50th sts./Rockefeller Center.

MoMA Design Store ★★★   Many of the iconic furniture items displayed at the Museum of Modern Art are sold here, in licensed reproductions, meaning you could take home an Eames recliner or Frank Lloyd Wright chair. The shop also has more affordable items, from nifty kids' toys to contemporary jewelry to swank cutlery. Also in SoHo. 44 W. 53rd St. (btw. Fifth and Sixth aves.). www.momastore.org. ℂ **212/767-1050.** Subway: E, F to Fifth Ave. or B, D, F, Q to 47th–50th sts./Rockefeller Center. Also at 81 Spring St. (at Crosby St.), ℂ **646/613-1367,** subway 6 to Spring St.

The Museum of Art and Design Store ★★   As you'd expect from a museum devoted to cutting-edge design, the items here are pretty special, ranging from ultra-chic jewelry to home goods of all sorts to the most fetching umbrellas you've ever seen. The store is a small one, but it's packed to the gills with unique items, many of which are made just for this gift shop (in tandem with exhibits) and can't be found elsewhere. 2 Columbus Circle (at 59th St.). www.madmuseum.org. ℂ **212/299-7777.** Subway: 1, A, B, C, D to Columbus Circle.

Toys

American Girl Place ★   Sigh. Will you be able to avoid this place if you're traveling with a girl under the age of 8? Probably not, though many people find the place underwhelming and overcrowded (despite the fact that this is a 43,000-square-foot store). To "do" the whole experience, you'll want to eat at the cafe, get a doll makeover at the salon, and head to the on-site theater. 609 Fifth Ave. (at 49th St.). www.americangirl.com. ☏ **800/247-5223.** Subway: B, D, F, M to 47th–50th sts./Rockefeller Center.

Kidding Around ★★★   This store stays away from all of those annoying beeping, buzzing, and flashing toys. Instead, the focus is on playthings that children manipulate themselves, hopefully learning something in the process. Prices are fair, and the shop has a number of unusual toys such as rubber horseshoes (hey, you can play in the living room), soap-making kits, musical instruments and all kinds of dazzling costumes. 60 W. 15th St. (btw. Fifth and Sixth aves.). www.kiddingaroundnyc.com. ☏ 212/645-6337. Subway: F to 14th St.

The Lego Store ★★★   A creative toy, Lego has spawned creative stores where patrons can not only buy Lego sets of all sorts (Star Wars, dollhouses, Spiderman, and more) but play to their heart's content. Along with boxed sets are huge bins of different Legos, which shoppers can scoop into buckets to create their own custom sets. But I think most people wander in just to build stuff and look at the masterpieces (including a recreation of Midtown Manhattan) that others before them have constructed. Within Rockefeller Center (near Fifth Ave. and 51st St.) www.lego.com. ☏ 212/245-5973. Subway: B, D, F, M to Rockefeller Ctr. Also at 200 Fifth Ave. (at 23rd St.), ☏ **212/255-2317,** subway N, R to 23rd St.

Toy Tokyo ★★   Be careful! People walk into this store and end up buying far more than they expected, from tiny "jewels" in the shape of anime figures to adorn smartphones (they are plugged into the hole atop), to Miss Kitty and/ or Star Wars and/or Godzilla—well, everything. The store is catnip for those who love collectibles from the '80s and '90s, and it also has an unusually wide selection of blind boxes (a package from a line of toys that hides its contents, so you don't know what you're getting until you open it). With hundreds of fist-sized or smaller toys, it's primo for stocking stuffers. And yes, there are a ton of Japanese toys here (as the name suggests). 91 Second Ave. (btw. 5th and 6th sts.). www.toytokyo.com. ☏ **212/673-5424.** Subway: 6 to Astor Place.

WALKING TOURS

I n the pages ahead, you supply the feet and the eyes, and
I supply the commentary. I've picked two neighborhood
walks that will envelop you in the sweep of the city's history,
architecture . . . and gossip. The first of them, a tour of Lower
Manhattan, the oldest area of New York City, obviously has
the most historical resonance. But the second, a Harlem tour,
touches on Revolutionary War history, along with 20th-cen-
tury issues. I'm willing to bet that one of these itineraries will
be the highlight of your visit. And if you happen to be a resident, a walking tour of one of these special areas of Manhattan is a fine exercise for natives, too.

WALKING TOUR 1: HISTORIC LOWER MANHATTAN

GETTING THERE:	**Take subway 4 or 5 to Battery Park, walk from there into Battery Park and toward the river.**
START:	**Battery Park, stand at a spot where you can see the river.**
FINISH:	**The 9/11 Memorial**
TIME:	**1½ to 2 hours**
BEST TIMES:	**Weekdays during the daytime, so that you can take in the hustle and bustle of the area.**

Not only is this the most historic part of the city—New York
reached no further than Wall Street for its first 100 years of existence—it also affords the best overview of architectural styles in the
city. Buildings range from jazzy Art Deco structures, to pseu-
do-Greek temples, to the soaring glass rectangles of the "International Style" heyday, one rubbing up against the other like guests at
a fantastic costume party where Martha Washington cha-chas
uninhibitedly with Donald Trump. All the sites inhabit a compact,
eminently walkable area.

More importantly, Lower Manhattan is the area of the city that has
seen the most tragedy, having endured not one but four terrorist
attacks over the years (I describe them below), terrible fires, and a
cruel occupation by the British during the Revolutionary War that

left the city in rubble. The scars of these events, the weight of the tears shed, and the lives lost give this area a resonance and presence unlike those found in most other areas of the United States.

1 Battery Park

Look out at the river. It's the reason this great city was built. When Henry Hudson and his crew of 16 sailed up it in 1609, mistakenly thinking they'd find Asia at its mouth, little did they know they were setting into motion a chain of events that would still be shaping lives over 400 years later. It was Hudson's reports about the trading possibilities of the area (particularly for valuable animal pelts), plus his amazement at the great natural harbor here, that spurred the Dutch to create settlements in the area. They guessed, rightly it turned out, that the harbor of New York would be the linchpin that would connect Europe (via the Atlantic Ocean) with the interior of this vast and wealthy continent (via the Hudson River). Later, after the building of the Erie Canal, which connected the Hudson with the Great Lakes, NYC became the most powerful city in the nation.

Walk toward the circular stone building known as:

2 Castle Clinton

Though it doesn't look like much now, this circular structure (it was taller in some earlier incarnations) has, over the years, been at the center of New York life. In 1807, the "West Battery," as it was then called, was built as a fort on a landfill island in the water off Manhattan to ward off British invasions; it never saw action—the Brits attacked Washington, D.C. instead, during the War of 1812. In 1823, the federal government ceded the site (renamed Castle Clinton in 1817, in honor of the city's mayor, De Witt Clinton) to the city, and it became an extremely popular entertainment center called Castle Gardens (the "Swedish Nightingale," Jenny Lind, was a headliner here in 1850) until 1855, when the space was transformed once more into the city's first immigrant processing center. Over eight million new arrivals, a full two-thirds of those who came to the United States at this time, spent their first hours in the United States here registering their names with the government, exchanging money, and getting information on jobs, medical care, and lodgings. In 1890, the vast number of immigrants—and the growing problem of outsiders scamming them—necessitated a move to a larger and more easily patrolled space, Ellis Island. The famed architectural team of McKim, Mead, and White then stepped in and transformed the site into the nation's first aquarium, visited by about 90 million people until it was moved in 1941 to Coney Island. After the site stood empty for many years, the National Parks Service took it over and restored the Castle Clinton of the original fort.

Walking Tour 1: Historic Lower Manhattan

1. Look at the River
2. Castle Clinton
3. Large Flagpole
4. National Museum of the American Indian
5. Bowling Green Park
6. Fraunces Tavern
7. Goldman Sachs Building
8. Stone Street
9. Mill Lane
10. Hanover Square
11. Wall Street
12. 40 Wall Street
13. Federal Hall
14. The NY Stock Exchange
15. 1 Wall Street
16. Trinity Church
17. Canyon of Heroes
18. 9/11 Memorial and Museum

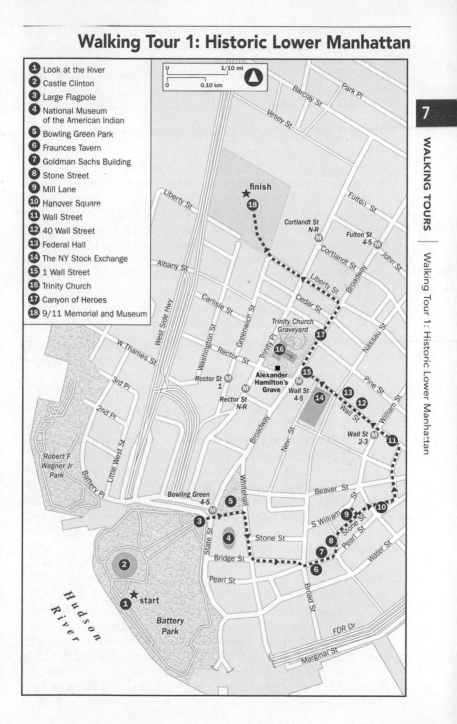

Walk around Castle Clinton, past the ferry terminal, and head inland (northeast) towards the tall buildings. Soon you'll come upon:

3 The Large Flagpole

At its base is a bas relief sculpture depicting the historic scene of Dutch official Peter Minuet "buying" Manhattan from Native American residents in order to consolidate the Dutch colony in one easily defended spot.

Just how the "sale" of the island went down is still a matter of controversy. It happened in 1626, and most likely the "sellers" were the Canarsie tribe who, according to a letter by Dutch merchant Pieter Schage, let the island go for 60 guilders (the equivalent of $24). But did the Indians know they were selling the island, or did they think that they were simply accepting shiny trinkets as part of a welcome ceremony? And were the Canarsie even in a position to sell it, as it had long been a communal hunting ground used by a number of tribes? We'll never know the truth of the matter or even if it happened on this spot, but this is the one place in Manhattan where the most infamous real estate deal in history is memorialized.

As for Peter Minuit, he was recalled from his post in Manhattan in 1631 (much to his dismay), but returned on behalf of the Swedish government in 1638 to set up a rival "New Sweden" colony on the Delaware River.

Walk further inland to the plaza in front of the:

4 National Museum of the American Indian

The original Dutch fort stood in just this place. But what you see in front of you is a building of just as much significance. Designed by Cass Gilbert, this was one of the most important structures in the city when it was built—the Alexander Hamilton U.S. Customs House. Before 1913, when the federal government instituted the personal income tax, the federal government's revenue came almost entirely from customs on goods imported into the States. And a full 75% of this revenue came from the Port of New York, where it was processed in this appropriately grand Beaux Arts colossus, completed in 1907 and comprising over 450,000 square feet of interior space.

It's a wedding cake of an edifice, with dozens of bright white sculptures adorning the gray granite facade. Daniel Chester French was the sculptor—he also did the moving sculpture of Lincoln at the Lincoln Memorial—and his choice of symbols could be used as a treatise on the prejudices of Victorian America. The four women seated at the front represent the four "great" continents of the world. From left to right as you look at them, they are Asia; the Americas (South America, barely present, is tellingly represented by the Aztec-like structure that North America has her foot on); Europe; and Africa. America and Europe look full of vigor and purpose, but Asia has her eyes closed (perhaps in meditation?), and Africa—in a metaphor for her lack of vision and power?—is in a deep slumber. America is sheltering a new immigrant who crouches to her left, and the immigrant is pushing forward a wheel with wings on it, those of the Roman god Mercury, the divine overseer of commerce (a comment, some think, on the essential role immigrants were playing in the expanding economy).

At the top of the building are 12 more figures, this time meant to represent the great trading nations of history: Greece, Rome, Phoenicia, Genoa, Venice, Spain, Holland, Portugal, Denmark, England, France, and Belgium. Why Belgium, you ask? The official story is that during World War I, "vandals" carved BELGIUM across the shield of the figure that had originally been "Germany." No explanation has ever been given on how vandals could surreptitiously make such a big change to one of the most visible and heavily guarded buildings in the city.

If you have the time, go inside the building for a peek at the marvelous WPA murals in the rotunda (depicting the great conquistadors, ironic as the building now houses the National Museum of the American Indian); the staircase on the right as you enter (meant to evoke the look of the inside of a nautilus shell); and in what is now the study center of the museum, the elaborate, imposing rows of teller windows where merchants would pay their Customs taxes.

Turn around and walk into:

5 Bowling Green Park

This was the city's first official park (est. 1733). Had you been a soldier during the British Colonial era, you would have been stationed at the fort that once stood here, Fort George, and likely you'd have passed your leisure time lawn bowling where the park now stands (hence the name Bowling Green Park).

On July 9, 1776, the Declaration of Independence was read aloud (near City Hall) and a small battalion of agitated colonists marched here to behead the statue of King George that stood in the center of the park. It had been erected just 5 years previously by many of these same men, in gratitude for the king's part in repealing the odious Stamp Act (the one that provoked the "no taxation without representation" movement). Though it can't be proven, legend has it that the lead statue was then melted down and used for cannon balls and bullets in the war against the British. The fence that rings the park is the original, one of the few Colonial structures of any sort left in Manhattan (when it was first erected, its spokes had royal crowns at their tips; these, too, were destroyed by the colonists).

Look north to the great skyscrapers that now shadow the park. On your left, the building with the Egyptian motif (5 Broadway) was the headquarters of the White Star shipping line. It is here that distraught relatives came to learn the fate of their loved ones after the sinking of the *Titanic*.

(There's a famous photo of a stricken Jacob Astor exiting the building after learning that his son had perished.) Across the street, to your right, is the former headquarters of Standard Oil, the company that made John D. Rockefeller his millions. Look up to see the elaborate oil lamp at the top.

Walk to the uptown end of the park to view Charging Bull. In 1989, a recession inspired artist Arturo di Modica to create the sculpture as a symbol of bull markets to come. The city hadn't asked for this work of boosterism, though: di Modica trucked it over to Wall Street in the dead of night, and dumped it below a giant Christmas tree in front of the N.Y. Stock Exchange. The 7000-pound statue proved so popular the city decided to let the "gift" stay, though not in its original spot.

Walk out of the park, going toward the museum and then walking on the side of the museum on Whitehall Street until you reach Bridge Street. Turn onto it and walk to Broad Street. Take a right, and in front of you will be:

6 Fraunces Tavern

The bad news first: This is not what Fraunces Tavern actually looked like, but a hopeful reconstruction completed in 1904 and based on the architectural styles of the period (about 40% of the building is original). Nonetheless, it was here that the Sons of Liberty met on dozens of occasions to discuss plans for evicting the British. Once the Revolutionary War was over, Fraunces Tavern was the place where George Washington delivered his famous "Farewell to the Troops" and where Alexander Hamilton set up his first Office of the Treasury.

On a more sobering note, in 1975 Fraunces Tavern was bombed by the Armed Forces Puerto Rican National Liberation Front. Four people were killed and dozens injured. The choice of this site for the bombing had dual reasons: Not only is it a symbol of American ideals, it is one of the few important historic buildings in New York that has a Caribbean connection, as Samuel Fraunces was an immigrant from the West Indies.

Look behind you to see the:

7 Goldman Sachs Building

Directly across the street from the tavern is the headquarters of Goldman Sachs, the massive glass-and-brownstone skyscraper that cuts Stone Street in two. When it was being constructed, crews found the foundations of old **Governor Lovelace's Tavern,** another Colonial-era watering hole, and briefly seat of the Colonial government. In a compromise with local archaeologists, part of the site was left open with a glass viewing pane atop it. If you walk around the perimeter of the skyscraper in the same direction that you've been going, you should be able to see these excavations through glass panels in the sidewalk (they're at the end of the rows of benches, one under the colonnade, one in the open air). Take a moment to read the plaques and gaze down.

Continue to walk northeast, curving around the Goldman Sachs building until you spot:

8 Stone Street

Here you'll have a remarkably accurate snapshot of what the city looked like in about 1837. This narrow winding street (it's the next street from Pearl Street) was the first to be paved in New Amsterdam and the only street that is thought to still be where the Dutch colonists originally placed it. All of the buildings were constructed in the period immediately following the great fire of 1835, which devastated the city, wiping out 20 square city blocks. Many blamed the volunteer firefighters of the time who, working in rival squads for cash payment, spent more time fighting one another than fighting the flames (Martin Scorsese's 2002 film, *Gangs of New York*, dramatically re-creates a similar firefighter battle).

The buildings we see today are classic Greek Revival structures of straight up-and-down brick with granite bases. They were built as counting houses and warehouses for local merchants. **57 Stone St.,** you'll notice, has a very Dutch steplike gable, added in 1908 by architect C. P. H. Gilbert as a nostalgic nod to New Amsterdam.

Continue to the middle of the street and then step to the left onto:

9 Mill Lane

Mill Lane has the distinction of being the shortest street on Manhattan (and yes, there was once a mill here). Folk tradition had it that it was here that Peter Stuyvesant, the Dutch Director-General of New Amsterdam, signed a treaty of surrender when the British invaded. Thanks to recently uncovered documents, we know that historic act actually happened at Stuyvesant's farm, which was in what is today the East Village. Stuyvesant surrendered unwillingly, having torn to pieces the first letter sent by the British warship commander. City leaders then pieced the letter painstakingly back together. Upon seeing the favorable terms it presented the colonists (they would be allowed to keep their land and businesses), 93 leading citizens—including Stuyvesant's 17-year-old son, a traitorous young fogey—demanded that Stuyvesant surrender the colony to the British. Stuyvesant did so, but mourned the loss of the colony for the rest of his life.

Take a Break ☕

Grab some lunch or a pint at **Ulysses** ★ (95 Stone St.; 11am–4am). There are both indoor and outdoor tables, and a carvery at lunchtime.

At the end of Stone Street lies:

10 Hanover Square

One of the only places in New York City to retain its "royalist" title after the American Revolution, it was named for the House of Hanover, from which the era's British monarchy was descended. Once the center of the social and political life of the city, this was where the colony's first newspaper was published. The cotton exchange dominated one corner. When he was still considered a respectable citizen, notorious pirate Captain Kidd lived here in bourgeois splendor with his wife (they were known for their grand dinner parties). India House, on the west side of the square, is a perfectly preserved example of a brownstone banking house from the 1850s.

Continue walking to the uptown point of the triangle that is Hanover Square and hook a left onto Hanover Street. Walk until you come to:

11 Wall Street

You are now standing at what was the boundary of the city during Dutch Colonial times. If you had been alive then, you'd be staring at a 9-foot-high wooden wall erected to keep out British invaders, who, it was thought (wrongly) would be more likely to invade by land than by sea. To your right, when you face north, would have been the largest slave market in the United States (approximately at the corner of Pearl and White sts.), a bastion of inhumanity that held more auctions than any other in the U.S. in the 18th century. Slavery was not fully outlawed in New York until 1827, making it one of the last two northern states to do so.

Take a left and walk to:

12 40 Wall Street

Here is New York's greatest monument to thwarted ambitions. Architect H. Craig Severance had a dream: He wanted to build the tallest building in the world, taller than the Woolworth Building (which held the record from 1917 to 1930). Problem was, his former partner and archrival William Van Alen had the same aspirations, and in the summer of 1929, at the height of the bubble that preceded Black Tuesday (the great stock market crash), they began a "race to the top," Severance at 40 Wall St., and Van Alen at the Chrysler Building (see p. 136). In a record 11 months, Severance completed 40 Wall St., then the Bank of Manhattan building, certain that the Chrysler Building was completed and his structure would be the tallest. But once Severance finished construction, Van Alen administered the *coup de grâce* that he'd been hiding in the elevator shaft of his building: the Chrysler Building's iconic Art Deco spire, which added an unbeatable 125 feet onto the building. I can only imagine that Severance felt some small measure of satisfaction when the Chrysler's title was snatched from it 1 short year later by the Empire State Building. Take a moment to gaze up at 40 Wall; it's still an impressive achievement and a beautiful building, with all of the ziggurat-like step-backs (cascading layers) of the prototypical late '20s skyscraper.

Keep walking in the same direction until you get to the corner of Wall Street and Broad Street. Our next stop is:

13 Federal Hall

The most historically significant piece of land in the city, Federal Hall is a quintessential Greek Revival edifice, a modified version of the Parthenon (can't get much more Greek than that!), completed in 1842. Note the statue of George Washington; it was here, perhaps on the very spot where the statue now stands, that George Washington took the oath of office to become president (though not in this actual building, but in an earlier one located on this spot).

That momentous occasion would be enough to secure its place in history, but matters just begin there: The Bill of Rights was drawn up in this former British City Hall (transformed into "Federal Hall" when the Brits quit the city); the famous Zenger Trial (which helped secure freedom of the press) took place in a court in the hall; and before the Revolutionary War, the Stamp Act Congress met here and railed against "taxation without representation." Head inside to see the magnificent rotunda, one of the loveliest public spaces in the city.

Note the austere, somewhat anonymous-looking building across the street from the hall; it was the headquarters of banker J. P. Morgan (the window of his former office is above the flagpole). If you look closely at the side of the building that faces Federal Hall, you'll notice that it is pocked with small indentations. These are the scars of the Financial District's first terrorist attack, which occurred in 1920. One bright and sunny morning (isn't it odd that these events always seem to occur on beautiful days?), a horse and carriage loaded with explosives parked here. Moments later a huge explosion shook the street, killing 31 people and wounding scores more. The blast was so powerful that all that was ever found of the horse was a horseshoe, and the police used this piece of evidence to trace the blacksmith who made it. He had vague recollections of shoeing the horse of an Italian man, and on this scanty piece of evidence the police (and press) decided that the blast must have been the work of Italian anarchists. No one was ever charged with the crime.

Next walk toward:

14 The New York Stock Exchange

You are now gazing at the most famous (some would say infamous) financial institution in the world. The building's towering columns, crowded ornamental pediment, and huge flag trumpet louder than any opening bell that this is a place of incomparable might and prestige (interestingly, it's a much more imposing building than the government's plainer Federal Hall across the street). In front of the Stock Exchange is a scraggly buttonwood tree, meant to invoke the buttonwood that New York's first traders stood under in 1792 when they met to begin brokering the Revolutionary War debt—the first stock market in America.

Continue crosstown on Wall Street toward Broadway until you arrive at:

15 1 Wall Street

Take a moment to gaze at this absolutely stunning Art Deco building, once one of the priciest addresses in the city. The beautifully fluted, curtainlike limestone of the facade; the spiderweb pattern of the cathedral window above the entry; and the sumptuous, soaring lobby remind us of a time when such excess and exquisite workmanship were the norm for places of business (which were, literally, in the heady times before the Stock Exchange crash, conceived as temples of commerce).

Cross the street to:

16 Trinity Church

For a full description of the history and architecture of Trinity Church, go to p. 129. Do wander the graveyard here, in addition to going inside the church; it has the remains of Alexander Hamilton and other notables.

Exit the graveyard and look uptown on Broadway as you are now in the:

17 Canyon of Heroes

Look down as you amble along at the brass plates with names and dates listing the ticker tape parades that have been held along this swatch of Broadway. Had you been here on one of those occasions in the 1930s or '40s, the crowds around you would have been shoulder to shoulder, and above your head, hundreds would have been standing at the windows, showering the street with the long paper ribbons of stock market quotations that spewed from their machines, marking the dance of the stock market. Read the plates. The catalogue of names is an interesting retread of American history and political alliances; along with athletes, astronauts, and presidents, you'll find parades for the American hostages released from Iran (1982), pianist Van Cliburn (1958), and the controversial President Sukarno of Indonesia (1956).

Walk uptown on Broadway, turn left on Liberty Street, and follow the signs to the:

18 9/11 Memorial and Museum

Be sure to reserve advance tickets online so that you can skip some of the lines at this sobering museum. For more information, see p. 118.

WALKING TOUR 2: **HARLEM**

GETTING THERE:	**Take the 2 or 3 subway to 125th Street.**
START:	**Walk downtown to 120th Street and Malcolm X Boulevard (also known as Lenox Avenue).**
FINISH:	**The Apollo Theater, 253 W. 125th St.**
TIME:	**1 hour**
BEST TIMES:	**Daylight hours**

More than in any other place in the city, you need to have a strong imagination and social sense to really enjoy touring Harlem. The tragic fact is that much of what made this area unique, lively, and . . . well, Harlem, during the fabled Jazz Era (aka the Harlem Renaissance), crumbled beneath the wrecking ball decades ago. What you now see here—the wide avenues, the rows of brownstones, the elegant apartment buildings—are somewhat an accident of history, the physical face of an area that housed a people, but wasn't necessarily "of" that people (I'll explain below). But despite all this, Harlem remains the African-American capital of the United States (sometimes called the "capital for Africans throughout the world"), a one-of-a-kind area with much to recommend it. Architect Zevilla Jackson Preston best sums up the appeal of the area in the book *HarlemWorld,* in which she writes, "Ultimately it is the energy on the street, the beat on the street—all of the beautiful black people on the streets—that make the experience unique."

Harlem was settled by a number of different groups over the years—Dutch farmers first, followed by their British counterparts, then poor Irish and Italian immigrants. But development of the area only took off in the years just prior to 1904, when the city's first subway line opened, a 9½-mile snaking tunnel connecting Lower Manhattan with points as far north as 145th Street. In anticipation of this event, an unprecedented housing boom hit the neighborhood, with developers slapping up Victorian row house after row house for the crowds of upwardly mobile immigrants—middle-class Jews and Germans, primarily—they were certain would soon flood this newly commutable neighborhood. What they didn't anticipate were recessions and panics in 1893, 1907, and 1910, which deflated the housing market and badly affected the development of large numbers of homes on the Upper West Side.

Because of these miscalculations, property owners were left with hundreds of unrentable homes and soon began doing what nobody else had done in the history of the United States: renting or selling brand-new, often beautifully appointed buildings to the race that had, until that point, always made do with the tumble-down, ghetto housing no other group would accept. In 1905, a pioneering real estate agent named Philip Payton persuaded a white landlord to rent him 31 W. 133rd St. so that he could re-lease it to African Americans. The landlord accepted the offer because Payton promised to pay far more than the going rate, a substantial $5 more per tenant per month (a lot of money in those days). Several other white landlords panicked and bought the buildings in order to evict the black tenants, but by then it was too late. Payton had the funding to buy several other buildings, and black migration into the area began in earnest.

So what you'll see in Harlem today are homes and businesses that were not created by or for African Americans. These lovely buildings, however, did allow for a standard of living and security, primarily in the 1920s, '30s, and '40s, that was unprecedented for African Americans in the United States.

Another thing you won't see in Harlem today are the Jazz Era nightclubs and theaters for which the area was famed. Tragically, those historic sites were torn down. But we will visit places where the great figures of Harlem, men and women such as Langston Hughes, Malcolm X, Mother Hale, and Adam Clayton Powell, Jr., lived, worked, and made history.

A note about this tour: Harlem is by far the largest neighborhood in Manhattan, stretching from approximately 116th Street all the way up to the river. There's no way to see it all in one walk, so I've devised a tour that gives you a taste of the area's history from different eras. I'd urge you to go back and see such historic gems as Striver's Row, Sugar Hill, and the home of Alexander Hamilton (see p. 162).

1 Mt. Olivet Baptist Church

Stand across the street (120th Street and Malcolm X Boulevard, aka Lenox Avenue) so that you can get a better look at this prominent Harlem Church (over the years, Presidential candidate Howard Dean and former Venezuelan President Hugo Chavez have addressed the congregation). If you look closely, you'll notice something that one doesn't usually see on the facade of a church: several Stars of David. This church epitomizes the neighborhood's transformation over the years; it was built (in 1907) to be the neighborhood's first synagogue. The architect, the first Jewish architect licensed in New York State, based its design on that of the Second Temple in Jerusalem, which had just been excavated, making worldwide headlines. Remember the name Louis Blumstein, a prominent member of this congregation, as he'll reappear later in this walking tour.

Walk uptown on Malcolm X Boulevard, turn left on 122nd Street, and walk to 152 W. 122nd St., which is:

2 Hale House

We jump forward now a century to 1969 when an act of kindness changed the lives of thousands of children. A young woman named Lorraine Hale was driving on 146th Street when she saw a drugged-out mother nodding off on the street, her 2-month-old baby almost slipping from her arms. Ms. Hale got out of the car and told the mother she needed to get treatment and that she could leave the baby with her own mother—Clara McBride Hale—while she got sober. The next day the drug-addicted mother did just that, and soon hundreds of babies were being left with "Mother Hale," who pioneered methods of treating babies born with addictions (and also took in a lot of HIV-positive babies).

This all happened during the 1960s, '70s, and '80s, a period of steep decline for Harlem, a time when many landlords stopped maintaining and even abandoned the buildings in the neighborhood (in 1960, a census showed only 50% of the housing in Harlem to be deemed sound, as opposed to 85% elsewhere in the city). Harlem became synonymous with urban decay, and Hale House, though a controversial institution later, was one of its few rays of hope. You can read more about the house and its mission on the plaque at the door.

Walking Tour 2: Harlem

1 Mt. Olivet Baptist Church
2 Hale House
3 4-16 West 122nd Street
4 Mount Morris Park
5 55 West 125th Street
6 The Former Home of Poet Langston Hughes
7 Collyer Park
8 The Corner of Adam Clayton Powell Jr. Boulevard and 125th Street
9 Blumstein's Department Store
10 The Apollo Theater

Walk back to Malcolm X Boulevard, cross the street, and walk east on 122nd Street until you get to:

3 4-16 West 122nd Street

This is not a famous building, but a very beautiful one and a good example of the kind of talent that was enlisted to build Harlem's brownstones when the neighborhood was first being developed. This one is by architect William Tuthill, who went on to design Carnegie Hall later in his career. Like many Gotham brownstones, the main entrance is on the second, not the ground, floor. Why? It's a tradition left over from when the Dutch settled Manhattan. A people from a sea-level land, prone to flooding, it was their tradition to place the more important rooms above ground level, locating the kitchen and servants quarters below.

Look toward the park at the east end of the street. It used to be called:

4 Mount Morris Park

Named for General Roger Morris, this park was created in honor of the very first American victory in the Revolutionary War. It was in the vicinity of where you're standing now, on September 16, 1776, that George Washington engaged in what he called a "brisk little skirmish" with the Redcoats. Just 1 month earlier, the largest British expeditionary fleet in history had sailed into New York Harbor, bringing with it 21,000 troops, a full 40% of all the men engaged by the Royal Navy at that time. In quick order, these trained soldiers slaughtered approximately 2,800 American militiamen at the Battle of Brooklyn, forcing Washington to escape Brooklyn under cover of night and hightail it to the northern reaches of Manhattan. At the small battle on this site, called the Battle of Washington Heights, enemy buglers taunted the colonists by playing the call that traditionally ended a foxhunt. Enraged, Washington called for reinforcements and drove the Redcoats back to what is now the Upper West Side. It was the first time his soldiers had won an engagement and did much to boost morale. Today, the park is known as Marcus Garvey Park, in honor of the founder of the Universal Negro Improvement Association.

Walk back to Malcolm X Boulevard and walk uptown to:

5 55 West 125th Street

Former President Bill Clinton had his first office, after he left the presidency, on the top floor of this high-rise building. You may remember that he decided to move to Harlem after a public outcry over the taxpayer-supported rent on his proposed Carnegie Hill office space (a whopping $850,000 per year, more than all of the other presidential offices combined). Alas, he's no longer headquartered here, but it was an appropriate choice: Harlem is one of the Business Empowerment Zones his administration created, and you'll see all around you signs of the prosperity that policy engendered.

Walk east to Fifth Avenue, turn uptown, and walk to 127th St. Turn east and walk to 20 E. 127th St.:

6 The Former Home of Poet Langston Hughes

Hughes bought this brownstone in 1947, likely with the royalties he received for writing the libretto to the Broadway musical "Street Scene." His was an open house, with other writers, musicians, and friends from the neighborhood dropping by at all hours. He was particularly known for his kindness to the children of the neighborhood; he called the garden in front of his house "The Children's Garden" and let the little ones plant whatever they wanted to there. It was in this house that he wrote his famous book-length poem, *Montage for a Dream Deferred*. Some decades after his death in 1967, the house was turned into a poetry center, but unfortunately, it was forced to close in 2007 due to lack of funding.

Walk back to Fifth Avenue and continue uptown to the corner of 128th Street. Here you'll see:

7 Collyer Park

Are you a fan of the TV show *Hoarders?* Here lived the most famous hoarders of the pre-television age, a pair of reclusive brothers who occupied this home from the 1880s until their deaths in 1947. Though rumors swirled about their compulsive behavior, nobody knew the extent of their hoarding until both were found dead in their home, surrounded by 140 tons of stuff, including books, musical instruments, towering stacks of newspapers, baby carriages, guns, furniture, and all manner of junk. All were set with booby traps to ward off outsiders. It took over a year to clear out the house, which was eventually razed as it was rotting on its foundations. If you need a rest, you can sit in the pretty pocket park where the house once stood for a moment before moving on.

Walk back to Malcolm X Boulevard and walk downtown to 125th Street. Turn right (west) and if you have time, stop at the Studio Museum (p. 162) to see the art. If not, proceed on to:

8 The Corner of Adam Clayton Powell Jr. Boulevard and 125th Street

Abuzz with history, this intersection is one of the most important in Harlem. Look over first at the windswept northwest corner, where the statue of Adam Clayton Powell, Jr., Harlem's first African American congressman, stands. This is also the spot where Malcolm X spent many long hours lecturing to Harlem residents on behalf of the Nation of Islam. His message—"We are blacks first and everything else second"—was such a powerful one, and he was such an effective orator, that before he left the NOI that organization had nearly half a million members (it dwindled rapidly after his resignation). His message, which rejected non-violence and condemned integration as cultural suicide, was a controversial one that went directly against the goals of the NAACP, the largest civil rights organization of the time.

Now, look across the street at the tall white building with geometric patterns climbing up its facade, the former Hotel Theresa. If your olfactory glands have any imagination, you may detect a hint of Cuban cigar smoke in the air. In 1960, a young Fidel Castro was scheduled to speak at the United Nations, but no hotel in town would take him and his contingent. After he threatened to set up camp on the lawn of the United Nations, the government ordered the city hotels to accommodate him, but Castro got into an argument with the hotel he had picked, the Shelburne.

So, after a conversation with Malcolm X, he moved up here to the Hotel Theresa. It was a dramatic gesture, and one he hoped would show his solidarity with Black Americans (and perhaps encourage a few to register with the Communist Party). Repeated clashes between the pro- and anti-Castro forces outside the hotel kept the 258-police contingent assigned to Castro busy. On his second day at the Theresa, Nikita Khrushchev came to visit, and his police contingent plus Castro's created the greatest show of force Harlem had ever witnessed (to this day it hasn't been matched).

Four years later, when Malcolm X broke with the Nation of Islam to found his own Organization of Afro-American Unity (open to people of all religions), he held his press conference at the Theresa and soon afterward moved his offices here. When he was assassinated in 1965, just 1 year later, this is where crowds gathered to mourn, until they were dispersed by the police.

Walk further west until you get to 230 W. 125th St., the former:

9 Blumstein's Department Store

When it opened its doors in 1900, this was the neighborhood's largest and most exclusive store, built at a cost of $1 million (notice the beautifully worked copper ornamentation on the facade, a mix of Art Deco and Spanish Renaissance in its patterning). And yes, it was owned by Louis Blumstein, whom we discussed at the beginning of this tour.

In 1934, the Urban League began a campaign, spearheaded by Reverends John H. Johnson and Adam Clayton Powell, Jr., to boycott and picket the store until it changed its hiring practices. Up until that point, though the vast majority of its clientele was African American, Blumstein's refused to hire any black store clerks (a particularly maddening policy as this was the Great Depression and jobs were scarce). The action lasted 2 months, with picketers carrying signs with the simple but effective request DON'T BUY WHERE YOU CAN'T WORK. Blumstein's finally relented, hiring 34 African-American women as clerks. Dr. Martin Luther King, Jr. often spoke of this strike in his speeches as an example of the power of non-violent protest.

In 1958, Dr. King himself was at the center of history at Blumstein's. He was seated at a table signing copies of his book *Strides Towards Freedom* when an African-American woman named Izola Ware Curry got to the front of the line. After asking, "Are you Martin Luther King?" she pulled a letter opener out of the book she was carrying. Shouting "You Communist, you Communist!" she stabbed him in the chest. Dr. King was rushed to Harlem Hospital with the blade still in (had it been removed he would have bled to death) and underwent surgery. The next morning, the *New York Times* reported that had King sneezed, he would have died, as the blade was touching his aorta. From his hospital bed, King issued a letter of forgiveness to Wade, who was committed to an insane asylum for the act (she had had a long history of mental instability).

Cross the street and you'll see the marquee of:

10 The Apollo Theater

For years 125th Street was known as the "Great Black Way," in comparison to Broadway's "Great White Way." This was the theater district of Harlem. Only a few of these great show palaces still exist, but right in front of us is the most famous and influential: the Apollo Theater (253 W. 125th St.). A whites-only burlesque house until 1934, it changed its policy and its lineup, becoming a music hall in January of that year and introducing the legendary "Amateur Night" a few months later. Among the many big names who jump-started their careers at Amateur Night: Sarah Vaughn, Lauryn Hill, James Brown, and most famously Ella Fitzgerald, who was planning to dance but fortuitously changed her mind backstage right before she went onstage. Amateur night continues here every Wednesday at 7:30pm, and it's as raucous as ever, with wild cheers for the performers the audience enjoys and painfully cruel shouts and boos for those who get the axe. If they're offering tours, do take one (see p. 234 for more information on that).

ENTERTAINMENT & NIGHTLIFE

8

I t isn't a boast but a plain fact: From opera to jazz, from nightclubs to bars, from concert recitals to theater and dance, New York offers the greatest variety and sheer quantity of evening entertainment in America.

It's a dizzying but important subject because most visitors enjoy New York's nightlife to the same extent they enjoy its daytime sightseeing. And in New York, unlike most other American cities, the sidewalks aren't "rolled up" when darkness descends. In the Big Apple (one of the only cities in the country that operates its public transportation throughout the night), the bright lights stay on until 4am and you owe it to yourself to take in all the after-dark excitement.

To make them easy to peruse, I've grouped the nighttime opportunities in this chapter by entertainment category.

THE NYC THEATER SCENE

You can traipse the entire Metropolitan Museum of Art, attend a Yankees game, and ascend to the top of the Empire State Building, but you can't really say you've *done* New York until you spend an evening at the theater. It's an essential element in a NYC vacation, like going to the beach in Hawaii or slurping pasta in Italy. And though every 3 years or so some major critic issues an obituary declaring New York theater is dead, somehow the corpse continues to rise from its glittering grave, producing Pulitzer Prize–winning plays, fine new musicals, and theatrical events of all sorts that just may, when done well, shift your perspective an iota, give you a peephole into another culture, or perhaps illuminate, for 2 fleeting hours, the human condition.

Ticket Tactics

Let's start with a trade secret that no one in the theater industry wants you to know: Only suckers and out-of-towners pay full price for most Broadway and Off-Broadway shows (see the box below for an explanation of the difference between the types of theater). I'd say that, on average, only five or six shows *per year* get away with charging full price for their seats eight shows per week. For the other 60-or-so productions, discounts *are the norm,* not the exception. Don't believe anyone who tells you otherwise.

THEATER basics

There are three types of theaters in NYC: Broadway, Off-Broadway, and Off-Off-Broadway:

Broadway shows: Tend to be performed in the Times Square area (the one exception being the shows at Lincoln Center). They cost, without a discount, between $99 for a balcony seat (as little as $65 at some plays), to $179 for an orchestra seat, all the way up to $350 for a so-called "premium" seat at certain musicals.

Off-Broadway shows: Are performed in venues all over town, with a good many now clustered in the Union Square area. Top prices for Off-Broadway musicals rarely go above $100, with plays topping out (usually) at $90. Off-Broadway theaters are much smaller than those on Broadway, pay less to cast and crew, and are thus able to present more controversial, less commercial plays and musicals. Many of the recent Pulitzer Prize drama winners (including *Hamilton*) began as Off-Broadway shows.

Off-Off-Broadway shows: Are staged in very small theaters, often featuring experimental works or actors' showcases. Some of the best-known venues are La Mama, and Here Arts Center. Although you'll rarely see these shows advertised or even reviewed in the *New York Times*, they will be listed in the *Village Voice* and *Time Out New York* magazine.

Schedule: Broadway and most Off-Broadway shows perform eight times a week, most commonly Tuesday through Sunday, though some do play on Monday (instead of Tuesday or Sunday). Matinee (daytime) performances are usually presented at 2pm on Wednesday and Saturday, and 3pm on Sunday. Evening performances take place 8pm Wednesday through Saturday, 7pm on Tuesday night—though increasingly, evening performances are taking place at 7pm on other nights of the week as well.

BUYING TICKETS ONLINE

Booking tickets before you arrive in New York City is the most time-effective strategy. You're able to schedule your time in advance, get early dinner reservations, and not waste any of your previous vacation hours standing in line at box offices or ticket brokers. To do so at a discount, try **Theatermania.com**, **BroadwayBox.com**, or the app **TodayTix.** In general, discounts will range from 35% to 50% off, though a handling fee will be tacked onto the cost of your ticket, varying by venue (it can come to as much as $10). With the first two companies you buy your tickets through Ticketmaster, but with a discount code that saves you money. Then the theater tickets are either mailed to you or held at the box office. With TodayTix (which does offer advance tickets, despite the name) you meet a "ticket concierge" who will be standing somewhere in the vicinity of your theater 30 minutes before the performance starts.

For the big hits, shows like *Book of Mormon* or *Hamilton,* you can use the sites above (though they won't be able to provide you with a discount), or you can deal directly with **Telecharge** (www.telecharge.com; ✆ **212/239-6200**) or **Ticketmaster** (www.ticketmaster.com; ✆ **212/307-4100**), both of which handle Broadway and Off-Broadway shows and most concerts. I don't recommend going through a broker not listed in this book, as their ticket prices can

8

ENTERTAINMENT & NIGHTLIFE

The NYC Theater Scene

be outrageous. Usually, if you plan far enough ahead, it's possible to get tickets to even the most popular shows through the sources listed here.

GETTING YOUR TICKETS ONCE YOU'RE IN NYC

Tickets are sold directly at **theater box offices,** and by using them, you don't have to pay the service charge (though you rarely get a discount this way, unless you have a code from one of the websites above). However, by going to the box office, you may be able to score better seats. Often, on the day of performance, the "house seats" that are reserved for the use of the cast and crew (who pass them along to family members, friends, and investors), are sold to the general public. And these are primo seats, in the center and near the stage. I should note that partial view seats for *Hamilton* are *only* sold through the box office, and at a normal, not inflated rate, so if you want a chance at seeing that show, stopping by is your best option, other than joining the online lottery, which you'll find at **www.lottery.broadwaydirect.com**. *Hamilton* lottery tickets are $10 each, but other shows (such as *Wicked* and *The Lion King*) charge between $30 and $40 per seat. Check the website to see which shows currently have lotteries.

Last but certainly far from least is the discount-ticket **TKTS Booth.** Its main branch is located on 46th Street, between Broadway and Seventh Avenue (Monday and Wednesday–Saturday 3–8pm, Tuesday 2–7pm, and, for matinees only, Wednesday and Saturday 10am–2pm, Sunday 11am–2pm). It also has a Brooklyn outlet (1 MetroTech Center, at the corner of Jay Street and Myrtle Avenue Promenade; Tuesday–Saturday 11am–6pm), and one at the South Street Seaport in Manhattan (corner of Front and John streets; Monday–Saturday 11am–6pm, Sunday 11am–4pm). TKTS often presents a greater breadth of shows than do the online discounters, but you pay for that choice with your time (during busy periods the wait in line can be up to an hour). Those who do brave the line are often rewarded with $45 seats to Off-Broadway plays and $75 seats at big Broadway musicals.

But there are ways to **"game" the TKTS line,** including:

o **Go to the TKTS in Brooklyn or at the South Street Seaport.** You'll rarely wait longer than 20 minutes at either outlet, and at both you can purchase matinee tickets the day before a show (at the Times Square booth, ticket purchases are day-of-show only). The only downside at these two outlets: No day-of-matinee tickets are sold.

o **Keep your ticket stubs if you go to more than one show in a week.** The staff at TKTS will let you jump to the front of the line if you can show a ticket stub purchased within 7 days from TKTS.

o **Don't go early.** Tickets are released from the theaters to the booths throughout the day, so you don't necessarily increase your chances of getting the show you want by going early in the day, or waiting in line before the booth opens. Instead, go when it's most convenient for you.

o **Go to the theater on a Monday or Tuesday night,** the slowest nights of the week. You'll encounter almost no line and will have a much bigger selection than usual (at least on Tuesday; on Monday many shows are dark.)

○ **Pick a play instead of a musical.** TKTS has one dedicated window for plays only, and its line is always shorter.

Warning: Do not buy from the **scalpers** who roam up and down the line at TKTS. A few may be legitimate—say, a couple from the 'burbs whose companions couldn't make it for the evening—but they could be swindlers passing off fakes for big money. It's not a risk worth taking.

Here are a few additional methods of garnering discounts or getting into sold-out shows:

Rush tickets: A number of Broadway and Off-Broadway theaters have taken to offering "rush tickets" for the first row of seats on the day of a show. The average price is $30 to $40 for these neck-benders (it's preferable to be a couple of rows back—the sightlines are better and there's less danger of being spit on by performers). Sometimes these seats are only available to students, while in other cases any member of the public can get them (call the theater in advance to ask). In the past, these seats were given out on a first-come, first-served basis, but recently a number of the theaters have adopted a more humane lottery (see p. 226).

Standing room: Some sold-out shows offer "standing room" tickets on the day of the show only, to about 10 people per show (depending on the size of the theater). They are sold at 10am when the box office opens; for the really popular shows a line will form an hour earlier for these "standing spots" at the back of the house. The cost of these non-seats are $27 to $30.

Student and youth discounts: Although Broadway theaters won't care how old you are or what you do, a number of the Off-Broadway houses do sell specially priced seats (sometimes for as little as $25) to students and those under 30. While some do this on the day of show only, others allow these theatergoers to purchase in advance with the correct identification. Among the theaters that usually discount in this way are the New York Theater Workshop, the Pearl Theater Company, and The Roundabout Theater Company. You'll also occasionally find $5 tickets to Off-Broadway shows and the NY City Ballet for teenagers (and their chaperones) at **High Five** (www.high5tix.org).

CHOOSING THE RIGHT SHOW TO SEE

I'll admit it: I'm a walker. If I accidentally pick an awful show, I leave at intermission rather than fork out extra money to the babysitter so that I can sit through something dull. It doesn't happen that often because over the years, I've formulated the following rules to help me choose which shows to see.

Skip the long-running Broadway musicals: There should be an expiration date on Broadway musicals, just as there is on milk. After about 2 years, they turn sour. Here's why: The first cast usually leaves around the 1-year mark, and then a second cast is announced to much fanfare. When it comes to the third go-round, big-name actors aren't willing to take over the roles, so they get lesser-known pros in the parts. These second-tier actors aren't any less talented, but because they have no clout they never get to rehearse with the

The NYC Theater Scene

KIDS TAKE THE STAGE: family-friendly THEATER

Broadway theaters do not allow children under the age of 5 to attend, nor do they give discounts to kids (with the exception of the **Kids Night On Broadway** discount program, go to www.kidsnightonbroadway.com; discounts are usually only offered in February). But beyond Broadway is affordable, often mesmerizing theater that's aimed squarely at the pre-puberty crowd. The following organizations, in particular, present a roster of consistently challenging and entertaining family shows.

The **New Victory Theater,** 209 W. 42nd St., between Seventh and Eighth avenues (www.newvictory.org; ℂ **646/223-3010**), books shows from around the U.S. and abroad that are inventive and smart enough for the entire family to enjoy. One musical that made its debut here even moved to Broadway (now how about that for a kiddie show?). Past offerings have included quality puppet shows, acrobatic and circus troupes, "new vaudeville" acts, and theater pieces.

The **Swedish Cottage Marionette Theatre** (www.cityparksfoundation.org/arts/swedish-cottage-marionette-theatre; ℂ **212/988-9093**) puts on marionette shows for kids at its 19th-century Central Park theater throughout the year. Reservations are a must.

Every summer, the marvelous touring theater company **Theaterworks USA** (www.theaterworksusa.com) presents a summer of free theater for kids at the Lucille Lortel Theater (121 Christopher St. near Hudson St.). Musicals written and performed by up-and-coming Broadway talents, they are among the most delightful shows in town for people of all ages.

Look for Young People's Concerts and Kidzone Live!, in which kids get to interact with orchestra members prior to curtain time, at the **New York Philharmonic** (www.nyphil.org/education; see p. 233). Also check to see what's on for the entire family at **Carnegie Hall** (www.carnegiehall.org; see p. 233), which offers family concerts at prices as low as $6; plus the CarnegieKids program, which introduces kids ages 3 to 6 to basic musical concepts through a 45-minute music-and-storytelling performance. And don't forget Jazz for Young People, Wynton Marsalis's stellar family concert series and curriculum at **Jazz at Lincoln Center** (www.jalc.org/educ; see box on p. 239).

director and put their own mark on the role. Instead, they are "put in" by a stage manager, and are expected to re-create what the previous actor did; that can lead to wooden performances. The chorus, which usually stays with the show for a few years, simply becomes bored and starts sleepwalking through their performances. That's why you'll often see a better show if you go to a newer one.

You can find out how long a show has been on by calling the theater; asking the folks at the TKTS booth; looking at Telecharge.com (which lists when shows opened); or checking *The New Yorker* magazine, which lists "long-running" shows separately in its theater section.

Beware the "un-nominated" Broadway shows: It doesn't matter which shows win a Tony Award—that's pretty much a crapshoot. But the nominating committee, which is made up of distinguished theater professionals—actors, writers, producers, and the like—is savvy about theater and usually does a good job rewarding the most interesting shows with nominations in late May. If a new play, musical, or revival can't manage to get a nod (and in some years there's very little competition), take it as a sign that your theater dollars may be better spent elsewhere. Each show that gets nominations will trumpet that fact in their ads (but don't punish the Off-Broadway shows, as only Broadway shows are eligible for the Tonys). A good source for this type of information is the Telecharge.com site, which lists nominations and awards for each show.

Do some research before you buy: The web is a treasure trove of information, including past reviews of shows. Instead of going blindly to the TKTS line (see above), surf **www.nytimes.com**, **www.timeout.com/newyork**, or **www.nymag.com** before you get to New York and pick a show that's garnered a fair number of good reviews. While the reviewers aren't always right (and lately, I think the *New York Times* critics have been really off in their recommendations), at least by reading up you'll have a better idea of what the shows are about.

Avoid "jukebox" musicals: *Mamma Mia* set off a frenzy of shows that simply take the catalogue of some famous pop composer and then string songs together with a silly, inorganic story. In most cases you'll hear better renditions of these songs at your local theme park—don't go!

CONSIDER SEEING AN OFF-BROADWAY SHOW

Because of the huge financial pressures on Broadway producers, they usually (but not always) stick with tried-and-true formulas, revivals, or shows with a clear marketing hook. For anything slightly edgy or intellectual, you often need to go to the smaller Off-Broadway theaters (see "Theater Basics" on p. 225). These theaters also tend to charge less for tickets.

Although I can't guarantee that you'll always see a great show, the following Off-Broadway theater companies consistently produce exciting, award-winning works:

o **New York Theatre Workshop** (79 E. 4th St., between Second Ave. and the Bowery; www.nytw.org; © **212/460-5475;** subway 6 to Astor Place). This is an intellectually heady and sometimes avant-garde company. **Biggest hits include:** *Once* (Tony Award), *Rent* (Pulitzer Prize), *Quills,* and *Mad Forest.*

o **Playwrights Horizons** (416 W. 42nd St., between Seventh and Eighth aves.; www.playwrightshorizons.org; © **212/564-1235;** subway 1, 2, 3, N, R, S to Times Square or A, E, C to 42nd St.). Dedicated to nurturing the art of the writer (lyricists and librettists as well as playwrights), Playwrights has always had a great eye for talent, producing the works of Stephen Sondheim, Christopher Durang, A. R. Gurney, and Wendy Wasserstein. **Biggest hits include:** *Clybourne Park* (Tony Award), *Driving Miss Daisy* (Pulitzer Prize), *Sunday in the Park with George* (Pulitzer Prize).

- **The Public Theater** (425 Lafayette St., off Astor Place; www.publicthe ater.org; 𝒞 **212/564-1235;** subway 6 to Astor Place). A strong emphasis on American playwrights, especially Asian-, Latin-, and African-American writers, has kept this theater relevant and popular since 1967. In all, Public Theater productions have been awarded 40 Tonys (for shows that moved to Broadway) and 138 Off-Broadway or "Obie" awards. **Biggest hits include:** *Hamilton* (Pulitzer Prize), *A Chorus Line* (Pulitzer Prize), *Hair* (Tony Award), and *Fun Home* (Tony Award).

- **The Vineyard Theatre** (108 E. 15th St., off Union Square; www.vine yardtheatre.org; 𝒞 **212/353-0303;** subway 4, 5, 6, N, R to Union Square). The Vineyard may well be the biggest risk-taker of the major Off-Broadway theaters, presenting out-and-out performance art alongside less far-out plays and musicals. When they're good, they're great; and when their shows miss the mark, they're still usually intellectually intriguing. **Biggest hits include:** *Avenue Q* (Tony Award), *Three Tall Women* (Pulitzer Prize), and *How I Learned to Drive* (Pulitzer Prize).

CLASSICAL MUSIC, OPERA & DANCE

New York has grown into one of the world's major opera, music, and dance centers. The season generally runs September through May, but there's usually something going on at any time of year.

Opera

City Opera ★★ You know that moment in Wagner's Ring Cycle when Brunhilde is awakened by Siegfried after being banished by the king of the gods to sleep forever in a ring of fire until a hero overcomes a lot of obstacles to rescue her? City Opera's recent history is something like that. After going bankrupt in 2013, and losing its home, a team of heroes came to the rescue (including famed Broadway director and producer Hal Prince) and brought it back to life. Though City Opera no longer has a "ring of fire" to call its own— the company will be producing works in a number of NYC venues in 2017—it will once again be fulfilling its mission to be "the people's opera," as it was when it was founded in 1943. That means it will continue to champion American singers (this is the company that gave Beverly Sills her start), it will produce contemporary works (primarily), and most importantly, it will charge less than the Met does for its productions—though prices will vary widely by venue. The trick will be being in town at the right time to see their productions, as there will be (sadly) fewer performances than in the heyday of this great company. www.nycopera.com. 𝒞 **646/981-1888.**

Metropolitan Opera ★★★ Everything about attending an opera here is grand—from the entrance you'll make, past monumental Chagall murals, to the world-class singers you'll hear (such as Renee Fleming and Deborah

LINCOLN CENTER: A one-stop shop FOR CULTURE

Lincoln Center (a complex of giant theaters on the west side of Manhattan, flanking Columbus Avenue between 62nd and 65th streets) hosts everything from major symphonic premieres to the Big Apple Circus. It's most famous for its presentation of classic works of music, dance, opera, film, and theater, and toward that end houses a number of permanent companies, as well as playing host to the world's leading performing arts organizations.

Resident companies include The **Chamber Music Society of Lincoln Center** (www.chambermusicsociety.org; © 212/875-5788); the **Film Society of Lincoln Center** (www.filmlinc.com; © 212/875-5601); and **Lincoln Center Theater** (www.lct.org; © 212/362-7600), the latter of which houses both a well-respected Broadway and Off-Broadway theater.

For details on the **Metropolitan Opera,** the **New York City Ballet, the Juilliard School,** the phenomenal **New York Philharmonic,** and the **American Ballet Theatre,** see "Classical Music, Opera & Dance" in this chapter.

Most of the companies' **major seasons** run from about September or October to April, May, or June. Summer brings outdoor/indoor events like **Midsummer Night's Swing,** with partner dancing, lessons, and music on the plaza in July; August's **Mostly Mozart** fest; and **Lincoln Center Festival,** which invites top troupes from across the globe to perform, both indoors and outdoors.

Tickets for performances at Avery Fisher and Alice Tully halls can be purchased through **CenterCharge** (© 212/721-6500) or online at **www.lincoln center.org**. Tickets for all Lincoln Center Theater performances can be purchased thorough **Telecharge** (www.telecharge. com; © 212/239-6200).

Terrific daily **guided tours** of Lincoln Center will take you into the bowels of the complex and sometimes even into rehearsals. Tours start at 10:30am and 4:30pm at the David Rubinstein Atrium on Broadway (between 62nd and 63rd streets), and cost $20. Info can be found at www.lincolncenter.org/show/lincoln-center-tours-1.

Voigt) to the pomp and glitz of the productions themselves. Though recent productions have received mixed reviews (clunky scenery that's louder than the singers when moving has been one culprit), you can't miss if you see *La Bohème* or one of the other of the Met's classic productions. And the lovely little secret about this house is that the cheap seats get the best sounds. Sit in the theater's ground floor section and you may have trouble making out the words, but buy a "family circle" seat, and the voices will float up to you in all their crystalline clarity. The Met makes $25 rush tickets available for all shows, at noon for evening performances and 4 hours before matinees. The seats can only be obtained online, and an individual can only win 2 seats every 7 days. See the Met website for more. *Warning:* Don't show up late unless you want to watch the first act on a video screen in the basement; the Met does not seat latecomers. Metropolitan Opera House, Lincoln Center, Broadway and 64th St. www.metopera.org. © **212/362-6000.** Subway: 1 to 66th St.

ATTEND A tv taping

Though it may seem odd to take time out of your vacation to do what you do at home—watch TV—it's the behind-the-scenes elements that make the experience here: the scurrying grips and cameramen, the "warm-up act" before the show, and seeing what the host does when the camera isn't on.

Attending tapings is a very popular activity, so it's important that you request tickets *far* in advance. In fact, 6 months ahead of time is not too early. If you can't plan that far ahead, or are rejected for an advance seat, all hope is not lost—stand-by seats are distributed for most shows. To snag one of these, you'll need to get up early and do a lot of waiting around, but many people on the stand-by list do get in. **One warning:** Stand-by tickets are given out by person, not by couple, so if you're traveling with someone else, both of you have to brave the line to attend the show.

As for timing: many of the late night shows actually tape in the afternoons, so don't assume that you'll have to stay up past your bedtime to see a taping.

Note: The better you dress, the more likely you are to get on camera (if that's important to you). And some shows will turn you away if you're wearing loud patterns or clothing that's too revealing, so read the rules carefully on all the sites below.

Some shows to try and see (with info on how to do so):

- *Good Morning America:* http://abcnews.go.com/GMA
- *Last Week Tonight with John Oliver:* www.lastweektickets.com (the ticket lottery here takes place 2–4 weeks in advance of tapings)
- *Late Night with Seth Myers:* Call ℂ **212/664-3056** Monday through Friday, 9am–5pm 1 month in advance
- *Live with Kelly:* http://dadt.com/live/get-tickets.html
- *Rachael Ray:* www.rachaelray-show.com/show-info/be_in_the_audience (Tues, Weds & Thurs tapings)
- *Saturday Night Live:* send e-mail in August *only* to snltickets@nbcuni.com
- *The Chew:* www.abc.go.com/shows/the-chew (tickets often available week of taping)
- *The Daily Show with Trevor Noah:* www.showclix.com
- *The Dr. Oz Show:* www.doctoroz.com/get-show-tickets (show on hiatus June–July)
- *The Late Show with Stephen Colbert:* www.lateshowstephen colbert.com
- *The Nightly Show with Larry Wilmore:* www.showclix.com
- *The Tonight Show with Jimmy Fallon:* www.tonightshowtix.com
- *The Nightly Show with Larry Wilmore:* www.showclix.com/event/TheNightlyShowwithLarryWilmore
- *The View:* www.abc.go.com/shows/the-view/tickets

To see the **Today Show,** simply get up at dawn and head over to Rockefeller Center. You'll see where the crowds are that day.

Classical Music

Bargemusic ★ This small theater (125 seats), set on an actual barge moored near the Brooklyn Bridge, has big views of the Manhattan skyline and acoustics to die for. Pianissimos are more piano here and fortissimos molto-loud, even when played by a solo piano or string quartet. This is one of the few truly intimate stages in the city, and the prices are intimate, too, starting at just $35 a pop ($30 seniors, $15 kids and students). At Fulton Ferry Landing (just S of the Brooklyn Bridge), Brooklyn. www.bargemusic.org. © **718/624-2083** or 718/624-4061. Subway: 2 or 3 to Clark St.; A to High St.; F to York St.

Carnegie Hall ★★ More than 100 years ago, Tchaikovsky himself presided over the opening performance of Carnegie Hall, just one of a legion of great musicians who have graced this famous stage. Today, you may see such stars as Anne Sophie-Mutter, Elvis Costello, the Berliner Philharmoniker, or more—all drawn by the unsurpassed acoustics and the honor of playing this magnificent hall (you can tour it from October through the end of June in the daytime; info on the web). Unfortunately, the hall is as often rented out by school groups, so it's no longer a guarantee that there will be a great concert going on when you're in town. Ticket prices ricochet up and down, depending on the day of the week, the act, and, of course, the area in which you choose to sit. 154 W. 57th St. at Seventh Ave. www.carnegiehall.org. © **212/247-7800.** Subway: N, Q, R to 57th St.

New York Philharmonic ★★★ Constantly reinventing itself, the nation's oldest orchestra hired one of the youngest musical directors working today, native New Yorker Alan Gilbert (he was hired at the age of 42). He shook things up, creating several "semi-staged" performances (with noted actors alongside the orchestra), championing new music, and instituting both a composer-in-residence program and an artist-in-residence program. And concerts had serious star power, often: Emanuel Ax, Joshua Bell, and Renee Fleming were on the bill in recent performances. Alas, though concertgoers tended to love Gilbert's innovations, the orchestra, rumor has it, did not (and his parents are both players in the orchestra; they must have had some Thanksgivings!). The 2016 season was Gilbert's last. No word as we go to press who will replace the maestro. Philharmonic tickets range from about $42 to $164, with $16 rush tickets available to students (with ID at pickup, purchased online up to 10 days in advance) and seniors (63 and older, available only at the box office on the day of performance). A number of concerts feature pre-show talks and meet-the-artist events, and tend to quite intimate and informative. There are also kids' concerts and free concerts in NYC parks over the summer. Avery Fisher Hall, 10 Lincoln Center Plaza, Broadway at 65th St. www.nyphil.org. © **212/875-5656.** Subway: 1 to 66th St.

Dance

American Ballet Theatre ★★ ABT features more of an emphasis on story ballets than the New York City Ballet—*Coppelia, Swan Lake, Sleeping Beauty*—and tends to produce more bravura stars than NYCB (where the emphasis is on ensemble work). Currently, ABT has a raft of Latino leapers who are thrilling audiences with the artistry and sheer physical prowess of their dancing. Metropolitan Opera House (in Lincoln Center). www.abt.org. © **212/477-3030.** Subway: 1 to 66th St.

City Center ★★ Alvin Ailey, the American Ballet Theatre, and Paul Taylor perform here, along with other major dance companies. You'll understand why, once you've attended a show in this splendid Moorish-revival space (formerly a temple). In the basement are the stages of the excellent off-Broadway **Manhattan Theatre Club** (www.manhattantheatreclub.com). 131 W. 55th St. (btw. Sixth and Seventh aves.). www.nyccitycenter.org. ✆ **212/247-0430** or 212/581-1212. Subway: F, N, Q, or R to 57th St.; B, D, or E to Seventh Ave.

Joyce Theater ★★ The blockbuster modern dance shows tend to play the Joyce, and it's not hard to see why: It's simply the best space in the city to see dance—there's not a bad seat in the house. In this renovated, Art Deco–era movie theater, the audience sits slightly above the dancers, meaning that you won't be seeing just the feet or just the bodies—you'll get the whole picture. In past years, this is where Pilobolus has played, as well as the Twyla Tharp Company, Wendy Whelan, and Savion Glover. 175 Eighth Ave. (at 19th St.). www.joyce.org. ✆ **212/242-0800** for tickets, or 212/691-9740 for theater. Subway: A, C, or E to 14th St.; 1 to 18th St. Joyce SoHo at 155 Mercer St. (btw. Houston and Prince sts.), ✆ **212/431-9233,** subway R to Prince St., 6 to Bleecker, B, D, F, or M to Broadway/Lafayette.

New York City Ballet ★★★ NYCB was founded by Lincoln Kirstein and the 20th-century's greatest ballet choreographer, George Balanchine. And it is for Balanchine's work that you still attend performances at the New York City Ballet; his choreography is the staple here and remains as diamond-sharp, elegant, and moving as when it was first performed as many as 50 years ago. Balanchine's version of *The Nutcracker* is a holiday classic and one of the most difficult tickets to get each Christmas season. David H. Koch Theater, 20 Lincoln Center Plaza, Broadway at 64th St. www.nycballet.com. ✆ **212/870-5570**. Subway: 1 to 66th St.

LANDMARK MULTIUSE VENUES

In addition to the theaters listed below, the new-in-2016 **National Sawdust** ★ (80 North 6th St., Brooklyn; http://nationalsawdust.com), an artists' collective, began programming eclectic evenings of music (jazz, classical, and otherwise) and talk. Let's hope the theater is able to find its audience and thrive.

Apollo Theater ★★ Is there a more resonant place in all of Manhattan to listen to music than the legendary Apollo Theater? To me, it's a thrill just to walk past the collage of all of the greats who've played here and then take a seat in this lovely, surprisingly intimate theater (built in 1914, it looks much bigger on TV). Perhaps most famous for launching the careers of Ella Fitzgerald, Aretha Franklin, and Duke Ellington, it doesn't schedule as many concerts as it did in its heyday. But Amateur Night on Wednesday remains the headline attraction, a gladiatorial music demonstration where the winners may emerge stars and the losers are skewered with the unkindest of boos and shouted insults. 253 W. 125th St. (btw. Adam Clayton Powell and Frederick Douglass blvds.). www.apollotheater.com. ✆ **212/531-5300** or 5301. Subway: B or D to 125th St.

park it! SHAKESPEARE, MUSIC & OTHER FRESH-AIR FUN

As the weather warms, NYC culture goes outside to play. Here are some top picks:

o **Shakespeare in the Park,** an offering of the Public Theater (see p. 230), casts big stars (Meryl Streep, John Lithgow) in elaborate outdoor productions at the outdoor Delacorte Theater in Central Park (near 79th Street in the center of the park). Tickets are free, but hard to come by. Either sign up for the daily online lottery (at **www.public theater.org**) or get on line in the park. Tickets there are distributed at the theater free on a first-come, first-served basis (two per person) at 1pm on the day of the performance. Would-be theatergoers usually line up 3 to 4 hours in advance of the show, but for big hits, people have been known to camp overnight in the park!

o **New York Philharmonic**: Free concerts are held beneath the stars on Central Park's Great Lawn and in parks throughout the five boroughs. For schedules, go to **www.nyphil.org**.

o **SummerStage,** at several stages around the city (see website), presents music, comedy, and dance. In 2016, they featured Barenaked Ladies, the Indigo Girls, and an evening of stand-up with Trevor Noah. The season usually runs mid-June through August. For info, visit **www.cityparksfounda tion.org/summerstage**.

Beacon Theatre ★★ They really knew how to build theaters back in the 1920s: Every seat at this Art Deco landmark has a good view, and the acoustics are remarkable. Which may be why this is such a favorite of the touring bands who make this their New York home. While you won't get the mega-names, you will see talented stars either on the way up or down, names such as Tedeschi Trucks Band, Cyndi Lauper, comedian Jerry Seinfeld, and Alice in Chains. Prices vary widely by show and seat. 2124 Broadway (at 74th St.). www.beacontheatre.com. © **212/465-6500.** Subway: 1, 2, or 3 to 72nd St.

Brooklyn Academy of Music ★★★ Outside of Manhattan, BAM is the finest of the multiuse facilities. In fact, it may well be the best place in the United States for challenging, inventive, and acclaimed international productions of music, dance, performance art, and theater. It's at BAM where you'll see the latest theater opus from Brit director Peter Brooks or Phillip Glass's newest symphony.

Along with the large **BAM Opera House** and the smaller **BAM Harvey Theater,** the organization has a dedicated movie theater (the **BAM Rose Cinema**) for art films, and a cafe space where up-and-coming talent perform. I've never been disappointed by anything I've seen here, though occasionally I've had difficulty getting a seat. *For penny pinchers:* Discounts are sometimes offered to students and seniors, so inquire when purchasing a ticket. 30 Lafayette Ave. (off Flatbush Ave.), Brooklyn. www.bam.org. © **718/636-4100.** Subway: 2, 3, 4, 5, M, N, Q, or R to Pacific St./Atlantic Ave.

Tickets for events at all larger theaters as well as at Hammerstein Ballroom, Irving Plaza, and S.O.B.'s can be purchased through **Ticketmaster** (www. ticketmaster.com; ✆ **212/307-7171**).

Advance tickets for an increasing number of shows at smaller venues—including Bowery Ballroom, Caroline's Comedy Club, Highline Ballroom, Mercury Lounge, Jazz Standard, and others—can be purchased through **Ticketweb** (www.ticketweb.com; ✆ **866/468-7619**). Do note, however, that Ticketweb can sell out in advance of actual ticket availability. Just because Ticketweb doesn't have tickets left for

an event doesn't mean it's completely sold out, so check with the venue directly. You can also visit **www.livena tion.com** for tickets to many concerts.

Even a sold-out show doesn't mean you're out of luck. There are usually a number of people hanging around at show time, trying to get rid of extra tickets for friends who didn't show, and they're usually happy to pass them off for face value. You'll encounter pushy professional scalpers, too, who peddle forgeries for exorbitant prices and are best avoided (you'll probably know who the professionals are when you see them). Be aware that all forms of resale on-site are illegal.

Joe's Pub ★★★   It's hard to classify just what Joe's Pub is, beyond a very handsome space in a landmark building that hosts performances and serves strong cocktails and pub food. Its show roster is all over the map—it's hosted spoken-word artists, rising singer/songwriters, jazz bands, pop stars, you name it. All I can tell you is the quality of the talent, whatever it may be, is always high, and the room is wonderfully festive. Too vague? Here's a list of past performers to give you a taste of what you might be in for: Leonard Cohen, Kiki & Herb, fashion designer Isaac Mizrahi, monologist Mike Daisy, Alicia Keys, Patti Lupone, and Wynton Marsalis. Confusing, right? But in a good way. 425 Lafayette St. (btw. Astor Place and 4th St.). www.joespub.org. ✆ **212/539-8778** or 212/967-7555 for advance tickets. Subway: 6 to Astor Place.

Symphony Space ★★   For many years this has been where the National Public Radio Show **Selected Shorts** taped. But that's just the beginning of the offerings at this always-busy theater. It also hosts yearly readings of James Joyce's *Ulysses,* dance performances, world music concerts, and a wonderful series called **New Voices**, which features new musical works from Broadway composers (and would-be Broadway composers). The theater has two stages and a small cafe for cabaret performances and open-mic nights. 2537 Broadway (at 95th St.). www.symphonyspace.org. ✆ **212/864-1414.** Subway: 1, 2, or 3 to 96th St.

ROCK, JAZZ, BLUES & MORE

If you're in town to see one of the mega-concerts, you probably already know to go to **Radio City Music Hall** (www.radiocity.com), **Barclays Center** (www. barclayscenter.com), **Madison Square Garden** (www.madisonsquarden.com), or nearby **Jones Beach** (www.jonesbeach.com). Added to that list in 2016, the

Coney Island Amphitheater (www.coneyislandlive.com) is a 5000-seat state-of-the-art outdoor (but covered) venue that's steps off the boardwalk. For slightly smaller, but still rewarding, concerts with artists like Veruca Salt, The Strokes, or The Killers, your best strategy is to see what's on the roster at the following well-respected venues:

- **Bowery Ballroom,** 6 Delancey St. (at the Bowery). www.boweryballroom.com. ℂ **212/533-2111.** Subway: F to Delancey St.; J, M, or Z to Bowery.
- **Highline Ballroom,** 431 W. 16th St. (btw. Ninth and Tenth aves.). www.highline ballroom.com. ℂ **212/414-5994.** Subway: A, C, E, or L to 14th St.
- **Irving Plaza,** 17 Irving Place (1 block west of Third Ave. at 15th St.). www.irving plaza.com. ℂ **212/777-1224** or 212/777-6800. Subway: L, N, Q, R, 4, 5, or 6 to 14th St./Union Square.
- **Knitting Factory,** 361 Metropolitan Ave., Williamsburg, Brooklyn (at Havemeyer St.). www.knittingfactory.com. ℂ **347/529-6696.** Subway: L to Bedford Ave.; G to Metropolitan-Grand.
- **Music Hall of Williamsburg,** 66 N. Sixth St., Williamsburg, Brooklyn (btw. Kent and Wythe aves.). www.musichallofwilliamsburg.com. ℂ **212/260-4700.** Subway: L to Bedford Ave.
- **Terminal 5,** 610 W. 56th St. (btw. Eleventh and Twelfth aves.). www.terminal5nyc. com. ℂ **212/260-4700.** Subway: A, B, C, D, or 1 to 59th St./Columbus Circle.

Local Rock Clubs

Give one of the following neighborhood clubs a whirl, as they usually book solid, emerging talent:

Arlene's Grocery ★   The longest-running music club on the Lower East Side—the Strokes were discovered here—Arlene's Grocery looks like a typical neighborhood *bodega* from the outside (hence the name). Inside, there's a spacious bar with cozy seating nooks toward the back, and a lower-level club, with a big seatless pit for the audience, sided by a few tables and chairs. Grungy, loud, and dark, it's the epitome of a rock club, and rock is what you'll get here, usually five or six acts per night for a flat cover charge (usually $10). 95 Stanton St. (btw. Ludlow and Orchard sts.). www.arlenesgrocery.net. ℂ **212/995-1652.** Subway: F to Second Ave.

Baby's All Right ★★   The rare live-music venue with more-than-decent food and a space that doesn't seem too grungy to eat it in, Baby's All Right is the epitome of the Williamsburg scene: maybe a little too cool for school, but overall on-trend and friendly. Plus the booker has real talent for bringing in new talent. 146 Broadway (btw. Driggs Ave and 6th St.). www.babysallright.com. ℂ **718/599-5800.** Subway: J, M, Z to Marcy Ave.

Bitter End ★   Bob Dylan, Linda Ronstadt, Arlo Guthrie . . . all of the big names of the '60s and '70s played the Bitter End, and the club still has the posters to prove it—so old they can't really be called "yellowing," they're now a permanent deep woodsy brown. This is no nostalgia club, though: The Bitter End continues to act as a tryout house for new singer-songwriter types (primarily), many of whom are quite talented. $10 cover charge and 2 drink minimum most nights. 147 Bleecker St. (btw. Thompson St. and LaGuardia Place). www.bitterend.com. ☎ **212/673-7030.** Subway: A, B, C, D, E, F to W. 4th St.

Mercury Lounge ★★ You visit Mercury Lounge because of the talent of its booker: If there's a band playing in and around New York City that's on the edge of hitting it big, you're going to hear them here. It's just a shame that the room they have to play in isn't more comfortable. With very few seating options, it's not a great place to hang out. Still, if the music is your main priority, this is the place to hit. 217 E. Houston St. (at Essex St./Ave. A). www.mercury loungenyc.com. ☎ **212/260-4700.** Subway: F to Second Ave.

Rough Trade ★★ Like its "mothership," a London institution since the punk era, Rough Trade is an actual record store (yes, vinyl!) that doubles as a concert venue. Its performance space is intimate (with room for just 300), which all but guarantees good sightlines; the sound system is primo, and the club often gets acts that usually play bigger venues (like Television and Astronautalis). 64 N. 9th St. (btw Wythe and Kent aves., Brooklyn. www.roughtradenyc.com. ☎ **212/477-4145.** Subway: L to Bedford.

Jazz, Blues, Latin & World Music

Big-name jazz clubs can be really fun in New York, and likewise, expensive. Music charges and bar-tab/drink minimums vary dramatically, depending on who's playing; beware especially of a dinner requirement at some, even for a late show. Reservations are almost always essential at top spots.

Bill's Place ★ This tiny club was started in 2005 in the same historic Harlem brownstone where Billie Holiday was discovered (singing in a previous club there at the age of 17). It's a wee place, so reservations are required and costs are low (a $20 donation is requested, no alcohol allowed). Performances are on Friday and Saturday nights only, but by some great old-timers who know how to bend a note. 148 W. 133rd St. (btw. Lenox and Seventh aves.). www.billsplaceharlem.com. ☎ **212/281-0777.** Admission $20. Subway: 3 to 135th St.

Birdland ★★ Though this is not the original Birdland where Coltrane played, it still presents top acts. In fact, if your idea of jazz is a small battalion of men blowing horns, this is where to come, as the large space (4,000 square ft.) is able to accommodate big bands that other venues simply can't fit. My favorite night is Monday, when Jim Caruso's Cast Party takes place, and Broadway stars from nearby theaters stop by to sing standards and trade wisecracks. 315 W. 44th St. (btw. Eighth and Ninth aves.). www.birdlandjazz.com. ☎ **212/581-3080.** Subway: A, C, or E to 42nd St.

Blue Note ★ The Blue Note has the most corporate feel of all the clubs (perhaps because it's now a chain, with clubs in Europe and Asia). Tables are jammed together, the bar area is even more crowded, and the second floor is given over to a huge souvenir stand. But it still attracts some genuine talent so it can't be overlooked. Ticket prices vary widely and can go as high as $55 plus drinks; it's cheaper at the bar (though I'd recommend avoiding the bar at

JAZZ AT LINCOLN CENTER: not actually at LINCOLN CENTER

You've heard of food courts? This is the "jazz court," a massive, three-theater facility with an on-site mini-museum that has been wedged into the uptown corner of the city's premier mall, the Time Warner Center. Its centerpiece is the **Rose Hall,** a concert hall in the round (usually, though it can also be configured as a standard proscenium theater), with remarkable acoustics and a splendidly be-bop look created by huge boxes of light that change color throughout the night—from subtle creams to striking autumn-leaf colors—forming a glowing crown around the performance space. Some seats are actually behind the musicians, giving real aficionados a chance to check out the fingering as the musicians perform. This is where Wynton Marsalis, the center's director, struts his stuff in concert with the Lincoln Center Jazz orchestra. Programs are primarily focused on swing and New Orleans–style jazz. Though the hall can be intimidating, Marsalis does his best to keep the informal jazz vibe, encouraging the audience to clap along and call out; usually by the end of the evening, they're doing just that.

The **Appel Room,** the center's second-largest space, has a configuration that can be switched to accommodate a dance floor, a seven-tier amphitheater, or cocktail-table seating. Whatever the look, it's a splendidly beautiful room with a wall of glass behind the performing space, lending to the music a Central Park backdrop. **Dizzy's Club Coca Cola** is the most traditional of the theaters, a smaller cocktail and dinner jazz club (again with that transcendent view of Columbus Circle and the park), and the only one of the three facilities to operate year-round, serving as a showcase for some of the younger talents in jazz (called the "upstarts").

It's all in the Time Warner Center (at Broadway and 60th St.), www.jalc.org, ℂ **212/258-9800;** subway 1, A, E, C to 59th St.

all costs; you're too far from the music here and the atmosphere is like Grand Central Station at rush hour). 131 W. 3rd St. (at Sixth Ave.). www.bluenote.net. ℂ **212/475-8592.** Subway: A, B, C, D, E, or F to 4th St.

S.O.B.'s ★ A large club decorated with fake palm trees and giant parrots, S.O.B.'s specializes in the music you'd find in the places where, well, you'd find parrots and palm trees: the Dominican Republic, Trinidad, Cuba, Puerto Rico, Jamaica, and Brazil. Admission ranges from $12 to $25. 204 Varick St. (at Houston St.). www.sobs.com. ℂ **212/243-4940.** Subway: 1 to Houston St.

The Village Vanguard ★★★ Though it will turn 82 in 2017, The Village Vanguard still has the youngest spirit of any of the jazz clubs in town, consistently featuring the best of the new talents and cutting-edge jazz. It also looks the most like a jazz club *should* look, to my mind. You enter a red door and descend a steep staircase to a battered, triangular room, cluttered with posters and pictures of all the greats who played and recorded albums here (Mingus, Davis, Monk, Marsalis). The club has also showcased singers such as Pete Seeger and Harry Belafonte over the years, but today it's strictly jazz and its prices are among the most reasonable: a $30 cover, plus one drink. *One* *warning:* Sightlines can be problematic, so reserve ahead online to nab a front table. 178 Seventh Ave. S. (just below 11th St.). www.villagevanguard.com. *©* **212/255-4037.** Subway: 1, 2, or 3 to 14th St.

CABARET

Sadly, most of New York's famed cabaret rooms have closed in recent years. For consistently good cabaret nowadays, you have exactly two choices:

Café Carlyle ★★ You come here for the big stars of the cabaret world: Chita Rivera, Betty Buckley, Megan Hilty, and the like. So the shows are terrific, the setting elegant, but being in this rarified atmosphere will be pricey: Admission ranges from $90 to $140, plus a drink minimum. Value-minded cabaret fans can save by reserving standing room (which usually results in a spot at the bar) for $55–$80. On most Mondays, Woody Allen joins the Eddy Davis New Orleans Jazz Band on clarinet to swing Dixie-style ($165 cover). Carlyle Hotel, 35 E. 76th St. (at Madison Ave.). www.thecarlyle.com. *©* **212/744-1600.** Closed July–Aug. Subway: 6 to 77th St.

Feinstein's/54 Below ★★ This is Broadway's cabaret. What that means is the vast majority of performers are playing hooky from their real jobs at the big Broadway houses nearby. They're often trying out new material, giving the shows a joyously loose feel, but because the talent is so stellar—in recent years *Glee*'s Matthew Morrison and Jane Lynch, Tony winner Norbert Leo Butz, and composers Lynn Ahrens and Stephen Flaherty (of *Ragtime* and *Once On This Island*—it never feels like a rehearsal. And the club itself is charming, with a 1930s speakeasy decor, much better food than necessary, and great sightlines. A winner! 254 W. 54th St. (btw. Eighth Ave. and Broadway). www.54below.com. *©* **646/476-3551.** Subway: C, E to 50th St.

STAND-UP COMEDY

Here's a dirty little secret about most comedy clubs in New York City: In order for comics to make a living, they need to play at more than one comedy club in an evening. So you'll often see a very similar show from club to club, one that can feel stale, simply because the guy performing is doing his set for the third time that night after negotiating two long subway rides. That isn't *modus comincandi* at the clubs below (which is why these clubs were chosen; I think they give more, and fresher, laughs for the buck). *Note:* Most clubs charge a cover and a two-drink minimum. Reservations are recommended.

Caroline's ★★ Caroline's builds its shows around headliners, folks you might see on a sitcom or in a film. Among owner Caroline Hirsch's regulars are Dave Chappelle, Colin Quinn, Kathy Griffin, Gilbert Gottfried, and a lot of *Saturday Night Live* alums. 1626 Broadway (btw 49th and 50th sts.) www.carolines.com. *©* **212/757-4100.** Subway: N or R to 49th St.; 1 to 50th St.

Comedy Cellar ★ When Jerry Seinfeld, Robin Williams, Ray Romano, and other equally famous New York–based comedians decide to "try out" material in front of an audience, they usually drop into this basement room in the Village. In fact, Louis C.K. filmed almost all the stand-up routines he did on his show *Louie* here. On nights when these "biggies" don't make an appearance (and their sets are never advertised in advance), newer headliners take the stage. In general, the comedy is more "blue" (read: vulgar) than at Caroline's. 117 MacDougal St. (btw. Bleecker and W. 3rd sts.). www.comedycellar.com. ℂ **212/254-3480.** Subway: A, B, C, D, E, F, or M to W. 4th St. (use 3rd St. exit). 2nd location around the corner at 130 W. 3rd St.

Union Hall ★★ Though it's a multi-use venue (with concerts, too), Brooklyn's Union Hall has become renowned for its comedy nights, especially *2 Dope Queens*, which is co-hosted, and programmed, by the Daily Show's Jessica Williams. You'll often see accomplished comics do full-hour shows here, like Daily Show alum Wyatt Cynac (he filmed his comedy special *Brooklyn* here). 702 Union St. (at Fifth St). www.unionhallny.com. ℂ **718/638-4400.** Subway: R to Union St.

Upright Citizens Brigade Theatre ★★★ In 1996, four "missionaries" of improv comedy came to New York from Chicago and founded this theater. Dedicated to the art of "long-form improvisation," in which performers riff on one or two subjects for up to half an hour, the troupe's appreciation for the absurd, along with their smart, fearless performing style, quickly made them a hit among jaded young New Yorkers. So much so that Comedy Central created an *Upright Citizens Brigade* TV show. Alumni of UCB include Tina Fey, Seth Myers, and Amy Poehler, and sometimes they come back to perform. With tickets that range from free to about $12, a show here will always be less expensive than at the more standard comedy clubs in town. 307 W. 26th St. (btw. Eighth and Ninth aves.). www.ucbtheatre.com. ℂ **212/366-9176.** Subway: 1 to 23rd St. Second theater: UCBeast: 153 E. 3rd St. (btw. Aves. A and B). http.//east.ucb theatre.com. ℂ **212/366-9231.** Subway: F to Second Ave.

BARS, COCKTAIL LOUNGES & DANCE CLUBS

Of the many thousands of bars in Gotham, I've chosen two dozen or so either because they'll (likely) be utterly different from those you'd find in your own hometown, or because they're the kinds of places where you can easily meet and mingle with locals. Obviously, this is just a small selection, so if you see a watering hole that intrigues you, head in and belly up to the bar!

Financial District & Lower East Side

On warm summer nights, the outdoor party on **Stone Street** (see p. 213), in the Financial District, can be tons of fun. The pedestrian-only street becomes a sea of tables, serviced by the bars along the street (one's a German beer garden); it's a scene unlike anywhere else in the city. Go beyond Stone Street and the area is dead at night (with the exception of the Dead Rabbit, see below).

AUTHOR! AUTHOR! WHERE TO hear THE SPOKEN WORD

As the home base of the American news media, New York is matched only by London in the number of free or inexpensive lectures and readings that take place each evening, year-round. The folks in charge of creating buzz for a new book, product, or even a policy decision know that by getting it in front of the opinion-makers here, they have a better chance of getting their message out to the rest of the world. You become their witting audience, not just by attending a lecture but by becoming part of the opinion-making machine (for all the good and the bad that implies).

By the way, readings can be some of the most inexpensive and entertaining events in New York. Many readings are free; most others charge only a small cover.

Thorough weekly listings can be found at www.timeout.com/newyork/books. There's almost always a major author in town reading at one of the local Barnes & Noble stores (www.bn.com). In addition to the choice below, you can stop by Brooklyn bar Pete's Candy Store (p. 251) for its Tuesday "ProseBowl" and Thursday readings.

o **The 92nd St. Y** ★★ at Lexington Avenue (www.92y.org; ℂ 212/415-5740; subway 4, 5, or 6 to 96th St.). The top venue in the city for lectures and "conversations" of all types, the 92nd Street Y (originally called the Young Men's Hebrew Association) has been a fixture of the Jewish community since 1845. And though a number of programs are devoted to Jewish topics, the vast range of talks (open to all) in a Monday, Tuesday, and (sometimes) Thursday lecture series are more far-reaching, covering issues of health, politics, gastronomy, ecology, and the arts. Some of the distinguished

You won't be short of choices when it comes to LES (Lower East Side) bars, especially in the vicinity of Rivington, Orchard, and Allen streets.

Bar Goto ★★ Named for owner Kenta Goto, formerly of the iconic Pegu Club (see p. 245), this sophisticated drinkery puts a Japanese spin on its décor, cocktails, and snacks. That means liquors mixed with green tea powder, miso, a topping of marshmallow, or a shochu and sake, served in a woodsy, square room that wouldn't be out of place in Kyoto. I have to admit, I considered putting this in the restaurant section, because the pub grub here may well be the tastiest in the city, particularly the cabbage pancakes (*okonomiyaki*). 245 Eldridge St. (near E. Houston). www.bargoto.com. ℂ **212/475-4411.** Subway: F to Second Ave.

The Box ★★ New York nightlife at its raunchiest, the Box is a Belle Epoque–styled bar/theater, with a Gen Y mentality. Guests arrive around midnight for drinking, dancing, and mingling; a burlesque show starts at 1am, always featuring topless dancers and usually some kind of oddball magician, acrobat, transsexual performer, or comedian. It can be a lot of fun, though it's definitely R-rated. 189 Chrystie St. (btw. Stanton and Rivington sts.). www.theboxnyc.com. ℂ **212/982-9301.** Subway: F to Second Ave.

guests who have spoken here include Nobel Laureate Elie Wiesel, author Joyce Carol Oates, actress Sarah Jessica Parker, domestic diva Martha Stewart, and comedian Steve Martin.

o **Nuyorican Poets Café ★**, 236 E. 3rd Street between Avenues B and C (www.nuyorican.org; ✆ **212/505-8183**; subway F to Second Ave.). Since 1989, the Nuyorican has presented poetry, drama, music, and film. The raucous, energetic **Poetry Slams** (the café fields a championship Slam Team) "perform" poetry as a sport: Aspiring stars show up and throw down their work in front of a mixed crowd and three teams of audience judges, who score them on the poetry and presentation. The Friday slams begin around 10pm (cover charge $13–$25) and feature an invited slam poet. Slam Opens are held most Wednesdays ($10 cover). The storefront bar gets crowded quickly, so get there early.

o **KGB ★**, 85 E. 4th St. between Second and Third avenues (www. kgbbar.com; ✆ **212/505-3360**; subway F to Second Ave., 6 to Astor Place). This second-floor bar (sadly not wheelchair-accessible) in an East Village brownstone was once a Ukrainian social club and is decorated with vintage Communist memorabilia. There's never a cover, so it's affordable to refresh your drink often for the near nightly readings (7pm for most events). It's a tiny bar, holding perhaps 40 to 50 comfortably, and double that for a hot reader, with theme nights curated by individual writers for poetry, mystery tales, science fiction, and other genres.

Dead Rabbit ★★★   Just the type of bar you'd hope to find in the historic Financial District, Dead Rabbit is housed in an 1884 building and handsomely cluttered with relics of bygone eras: numerous black-and-white photos on the beams, gay '90s knick-knacks, even trinkets from the set of the movie *Gangs of New York*. Except for the building, though, the age of the place is an illusion: It opened in 2013. No matter! Dead Rabbit has old-fashioned hospitality down pat, and old-timey tipples, to boot. The punches here are scrumptious, as are the 72 "historically accurate cocktails" and craft beer selection. Upstairs is The Parlor for nibbles and mixed drinks, downstairs is the Tap Room. 30 Water St. (near Broad St.). www.deadrabbitnyc.com. ✆ **646/422-7906.** Subway: 1 to South Ferry, N, R to Whitehall, 4, 5 to Bowling Green

The Ten Bells ★★★   You become 10 times cooler just by walking into this sexy, very European bar that seems entirely candlelit (though it's not) and has an extraordinary selection of wines and sherries by the glass from small producers across Europe and the U.S. The seemingly all-French waitstaff will help you select the right vino, and since this is a place you'll want to linger, you may also go for one of the tapas or cheese plates. As for the clientele:

BREEZES & booze: THE BEST OUTDOOR BARS

When the weather turns nice, New Yorkers like to take their tippling out-of-doors. Here are some lovely places to imbibe under the night sky:

Birreria ★★ Part of Eataly, see p. 199 for a full review.

Bohemian Hall Beer Garden ★★★ For over 100 years, this has been the go-to party place for residents of the borough of Queens in summer. Oom-pah music (and, on some nights, pop) is the soundtrack, 16 varieties of craft beers are on tap, and the food is authentically Czech. (29-19 24th Ave., Astoria; www.bohemianhall.com. Subway: N or Q to Astoria Blvd.)

The Frying Pan ★★ A historic floating lighthouse turned bar, the Frying Pan is permanently docked at Pier 66, which can be accessed at 26th Street off the West Side highway. It's an atmospherically grungy dive and not a place for people who get seasick, as you'll bob up and down as you drink. But the views of the other boats on the river can't be beat, especially at sundown. Burgers and snacks are served on the pier to which the boat is moored. (Open May 1–Oct 1; http://fryingpan.com. Subway: A, E, or C to 23rd St.)

Rooftop Bar at the Standard High Line ★★ From the roof of the hotel that's set square in the middle of the elevated High Line park, you'll have spectacular views of midtown, the river, and all of the action on the stretch of park below you. Reservations required, so call ahead. The Standard also has a rollicking outdoor biergarten. (848 Washington St. btw. Little West 12th and 13th sts., www.standardhotels.com/highline; ℭ 212/645-4545. Subway: A, C, L to Eighth Ave/14th St.).

The Roof at the Viceroy New York ★ With the sweep of Central Park at your feet and a chilled cocktail in your mitt, there are few places as tantalizing on a summer evening than this intimate, 45-seat rooftop lounge. (At the top of the Viceroy Hotel, 124 W. 57th St.; www.viceroyhotelsandresorts.com. Subway: F, N, Q, R to 57th St.).

They're an unusually stylish group of folks of all ages, which is unusual for a NYC bar. I think the European jazz soundtrack, kept at a conversation-enhancing level, may be why Ten Bells is popular across generations. 247 Broome St. (btw. Ludlow and Orchard sts.). www.thetenbells.com. ℭ 212/228-4450. Subway: F, J, M, or Z to Delancey/Essex St.

SoHo & NoLiTa

Ear Inn ★★★ The Ear Inn is set in one of the oldest buildings on the isle of Manhattan: a gable-roofed, two-story Federal townhouse built by African American Revolutionary War hero James Brown in 1817. It got its current name when the "B" on the neon sign outside went on the fritz. Today, this mini-museum of a bar (there's historical ephemera everywhere) is popular with a wide range of New Yorkers, from the city's motorcycle enthusiasts to its gallery owners. You're assured an interesting conversation if you belly up to the bar. 326 Spring St. (near Greenwich St.). www.earinn.com. ℭ 212/226-9020. Subway: 1 to Canal St., C, E to Spring St.

Mother's Ruin ★   A premiere pick-up joint, with sneaky cocktails that taste less potent than they are (especially those made with the slushy machine), a genetically blessed crowd, and wonderfully tasty bar snacks—that's Mother's Ruin in a nutshell. If you want to hang with the beautiful people, head here (the look of the place is clean and pretty, too, with large windows and a classic pressed-tin ceiling). 18 Spring St. (btw. Mott and Elizabeth sts.). www.mothersruinnyc.com. ☏ **212/219-0942.** Subway: 6 to Spring St.

Pegu Club ★★★   A refreshingly adult place to start or end an evening, Pegu has an elegant decor meant to evoke the 19th-century officer's club in Burma for which it's named. The sophisticated cocktails, many of which are made with house-infused liqueurs and bitters, are designed by owner and famed mixologist Audrey Saunders, formerly of Bemelman's Bar in the Carlyle Hotel. 77 W. Houston St., 2nd Floor (at W. Broadway). www.peguclub.com. ☏ **212/473-PEGU** [7348]. Subway: A, B, C, D, E, F, or M to W. 4th St.

Pravda ★★   Vodka is czar at this Russian-themed basement lounge, which serves 21 different brands from all parts of the potato-distilling world (cheers, Moldova!). You sling them back in a curved-ceiling cellar alongside cyrillic signs posted on the walls, surrounded by chic SoHo types lounging in armchairs and plush circular leather booths. 281 Lafayette St. (just south of Houston St.). www.pravdany.com. ☏ **212/226-4944.** Subway: F, B, or D to Broadway/Lafayette St.; R to Prince St.; 6 to Bleecker St.

The East Village

In addition to the bars recommended below, I highly recommend three mixologically-themed bars run by booze impresario Ravi Derossi, who also owns Death and Company (see below). They are **Mayahuel ★★**, a bar dedicated to agave-based liquors (mescal and tequila); **Amor y Amargo ★★**, which focuses on bitters; and **Mother of Pearl ★**, a chic Tiki bar, if you can imagine such a thing. All three are on East 6th street (hey, a walking tour, or a staggering tour, depending on how much you imbibe). The first is at #304, the second at 443, and the last at 95 Avenue A (at 6th St.).

Death & Company ★★★   The cocktails here are as colorfully named as the bar itself—like the "Scallywag," which mixes five different types of rum (including a 75-year-old one) with two types of bitters, vanilla syrup, and demarara syrup; or the perfectly balanced "Mortal Enemy," which blends Dorothy Parker gin with crème de cacao, black currant cordial, absinthe, and fresh lime juice. They're liquid art and can be enjoyed in a civilized fashion, as the bouncer at the door stops letting people in when all the seats are taken. The music is more likely to be tango or Dixieland jazz than pop. 433 E. 6th St. (btw. First Ave. and Ave. A). www.deathandcompany.com. ☏ **212/388-0882.** Subway: 6 to Astor Place.

Decibel ★★   A gritty, underground sake bar, Decibel is a center of social life for many of the ex-pat Japanese living in NYC. In fact, most of the clientele are Japanese, the soundtrack is Japanese rock, and the bar food can be exotic (dried squid, anyone?). But all are welcome, and if you feel a bit out of place when you enter this Tokyo transplant, you'll relax once you tuck into any of the 30-odd sakes on offer here each evening. A real experience. 240 E 9th St. (btw. Second and Third aves.). www.sakebardecibel.com. ✆ **212/979-2733.** Subway: 6 to Astor Place.

Kavasutra ★   Proof positive that you can find *anything* in New York City, this narrow, bar-counter-only space serves kava and kratum, liquids (not liquors) with psychotropic properties, derived from the roots of Polynesian trees. Kava has a more "body-centric" high, giving users a deep sense of physical relaxation; kratum, when drunk in the right quantities, imparts a sense of euphoria. "Nobody comes here for the taste of the stuff," laughed the bartender as I grimaced while sipping my bowl, my mouth numbing. But in a moment . . . the taste didn't seem to matter all that much. 261 E. 10th St. (btw. First Ave. and Ave A). www.kavasutra.com. ✆ **646/649-4214.** Subway: L to First Ave.

Mace ★★★   No, this isn't the type of place where you'll need to have pepper spray handy. The "mace" in the name refers to the spice; all of the superb cocktails here are built around either a spice or a grain. The concept might sound odd, but the results are some of the tastiest, most unusual libations in the city (my fave: the "barley seed," which mixes barley tea-infused tequila with salted caramel mescal). Also pleasing: the spare but classy décor, lit with lamps that give everything a golden hue; and the sophisticated soundtrack, which is low enough for conversation, but still will have you bopping on your bar stool. 649 E. 9th St. (near Avenue C). www.macenewyork.com. No phone. Subway: L to First Ave.

McSorley's Old Ale House ★   If you're a man's man (which I'm obviously not), you'll like New York's oldest continuously operating pub (est. 1854), and one that famously kept out women until a lawsuit in 1970 ended the bigotry (it was a landmark case that ultimately outlawed discrimination in all public places in the city). With sawdust on the rough wooden floor, yellowing photos, newspaper clips chronicling all of the famous people who got smashed here (Abraham Lincoln was one of them), and a jumble of relics in every nook and cranny (the handcuffs hanging from the ceiling once belonged to Houdini), it's an evocative place to hang out . . . if you're smart enough to visit before 4pm in the afternoon. After that point it gets ugly—kind of like the frat parties I pretended to like in college—with out-of-towners jammed together tighter than on a rush-hour train, shouting over the din. 15 E. 7th St. (btw. Bowery and Second Ave.). www.mcsorleysoldalehouse.nyc. ✆ **212/473-9318.** Subway: 6 to Astor Place.

PDT ★★★   The name stands for "Please Don't Tell" and is meant to speak to the exclusivity of this bar, which hides in the back of a hot dog stand (you enter through a hidden door in the old-fashioned phone booth—no, really!); and requires a reservation. The owners say it's because they don't want an overcrowded bar, so once the seats and stools are spoken for (the reservations line opens at 3pm), they turn would-be patrons away. It's a lot of rigmarole to get a drink, I admit, but the cocktails here are so unusual and tasty (many created on-site from liquor that's been specially doctored in-house) and the scene so urbane that once you're in, well, it's worth it. And the bar snacks—high-quality hot dogs and tater tots—hit the spot. 113 St. Marks Place. (btw. Ave. A and First Ave.). www.pdtnyc.com. ℂ **212/614-0586.** Subway: L to First Ave.

Greenwich Village & Chelsea

Employees Only ★★★   The place to come if you take your cocktails seriously. A crack staff of veteran bartenders man the joint, squeezing their own juices daily and infusing liquors with interesting additions, such as lavender (in the gin) and herbes de Provence (in the vermouth), which they then mix into some of the most bizarre but delicious drinks in town. Upping the festivity factor is a psychic who does readings in the front, and a cute garden out back for those sultry summer nights. 510 Hudson St. (btw. Christopher and W. 10th sts.). www.employeesonlynyc.com. ℂ **212/242-3021.** Subway: 1 to Christopher St.

The Half King ★★   Owned by journalist Sebastian Junger (author of *The Perfect Storm*), this classic British-style pub draws a lot of literary types and occasionally hosts readings. Low-key and cozy, it's the perfect place to down a pint after exploring the nearby galleries. 505 W. 23rd St. (at Tenth Ave.). www.thehalfking.com. ℂ **212/462-4300.** Subway: C or E to 23rd St.

Wallflower ★★★   I've nicknamed this place "Hole in the Wallflower" for reasons that will be clear once you squeeze into the bar area. But you get the real Manhattan experience here, which I'd say boils down to "living large in small, small spaces." Wallflower's two rooms are tony despite being tiny, the drinks (mixed by the owner and former head bartender from Per Se) are superb, as is the food. 235 W. 12th St. (off Greenwich Ave.). www.wallflowernyc.com. Subway: 1, 2, or 3 to 14th St.

The Flatiron District & Union Square

Birreria ★★   Meet the Italian beer garden, a sweeping space on the 14th floor of the building that houses the food court **Eataly** (see p. 199; it's part of that eating group). When the weather is nice, the retractable ceiling is pulled back to reveal the sky, a rarity in New York nightlife. Home-brewed, unfiltered, naturally carbonated cask ales (you'll see the massive vats as you enter) are part of the appeal, though you can also try unusual Italian wines, which are stored in large wooden barrels behind the bar. Along with a buzzing bar scene are long, communal tables for diners. 200 Fifth Ave. (at 23rd St.). www.eataly. com. ℂ **212/229-2560.** Subway: N, R to 23rd St.

Old Town Bar ★   People have been tippling here since 1892 and that includes during Prohibition; if you check under the seats in the high-backed booths, you'll see the hiding spaces for bottles. The appeal of Old Town is easy to see: with its 14-foot-ceilings, its memorabilia-laden walls, and its Belle Epoque decor, there are few places as quintessentially "olde New York." Sit near the dumbwaiter so you can watch the staff hand-crank the food and dishes up and down like they did a century ago. 45 E. 18th St. (off Broadway). www. oldtownbar.com. ℂ **212/529-6732.** Subway: 4, 5, 6, L, N, Q, R to Union Square.

Times Square & Midtown West

Aldo Sohm Wine Bar ★ Don't gasp aloud, as I did, when you see the $90 glass of wine on the menu (welcome to Manhattan, kiddies!). Scan down and you'll see that there are also $11 glasses on offer, and the staff are too genteel here to look down their decanters at you if you go for the cheaper option. Whatever you drink, you'll feel like Midas, tippling away in a room that's literally glittering—from the 20-foot-high ceilings are hung dozens of twinkling light bulbs, and, around them, fine works of contemporary art. Grab a spot on one of the plush couches and pretend you're one of the "masters of the universe" who sip wine here regularly. 151 W. 51st St (btw. Sixth and Seventh aves., entrance on uptown side of small plaza. www.aldosohmwinebar.com. ℂ **212/554-1133.** Subway: 1, 2, 3, N, R, Q, S to Times Sq.

Morrell Wine Bar & Café ★ Morell offers over 2,000 types of wine, with a good 100 available by the glass. Although it can get crowded—it's in the heart of Rockefeller Center, after all—the scene never feels overly touristy, and the people-watching, especially from the sidewalk tables (open in good weather), can't be beat. 1 Rockefeller Plaza (at 49th St.). www.morrellwinebar.com. ℂ **212/262-7700.** Subway: B, D, or F to 47th–50th sts./Rockefeller Center.

The Rum House ★★ You don't expect to find a place that's both this hip and this unpretentious right in the heart of Times Square, but here it is. Set in the Edison Hotel, this classic, old-time watering hole serves up a mean cocktail and decent bar food. On some nights, a live pianist adds to the ambience, softly playing hits from the days of Gershwin and Irving Berlin. 228 W. 47th St. (btw. Broadway and Eighth Ave.). www.edisonrumhouse.com. ℂ **646/490-6924.** Subway: A, C, or E to 42nd St., N, Q, R to 49th St.

Russian Samovar ★ Infused vodkas are the draw here (my favorite is the dill), which you sample carefully, as they serve them straight. I'm also a big fan of the borscht; it somehow makes a lovely side to the tipples (or a pre-theater meal). Many nights, a live pianist will be accompanying your drinking. 256 W. 52nd St. (btw. Eighth Ave. and Broadway). www.russiansamovar.com. ℂ **212/757-0168.** Subway: 1 to 50th St.

Swing 46 ★★ Gotham's active swing dance community supports this wonderful supper club (though you can come to dance without eating), which means there's live music here 6 nights a week (on Mondays a DJ takes over), as locals Lindy Hop, jitterbug, waltz, and freestyle well into the wee hours. Don't know how to swing dance? Lessons are offered early in the evening most nights. "Nice casual" is the dress code (so no sneakers or jeans); music charges are $15. 349 W. 46th St. (btw. Eighth and Ninth aves.). www.swing46.com. ℂ **212/262-9554.** Subway: C or E to 50th St.

Midtown East

The Campbell Apartment ★★★ For an F. Scott Fitzgerald experience, head here and drink the types of cocktails that Zelda over-imbibed: tall fruity drinks in oddly shaped glasses with such names as "Flappers Delight" and "Prohibition Punch." The "apartment" was once the office of tycoon John W. Campbell, who turned this 60-foot-long room into a replica of a Florentine palazzo, inlaying the ceiling and adding an ornate balcony. Visit on a weekend, early afternoon, or late evening when the commuting hordes will have already sloshed onto Metro-North trains to the suburbs, leaving you free to enjoy this elegant space in peace. Proper attire is required—no athletic gear, shorts, or torn jeans. In Grand Central Terminal, 15 Vanderbilt Ave. www.hospitality holdings.com. ✆ **212/953-0409.** Subway: S, 4, 5, 6, or 7 to 42nd St./Grand Central.

Hudson Malone ★★★ Revenge is a well-mixed martini served chilled, to a crowd that will follow you anywhere. When charismatic bartender Doug Quinn was fired from his job of over a decade at the iconic midtown saloon P. J. Clarke's, he didn't slink away, he opened his own tavern just two blocks away. Today, Hudson Malone is what Clarke's *used* to be: a real New York "joint" (tin ceilings, brass rail at the bar, photos of famous customers on the walls) that may well be the friendliest pub in town. That's because Quinn is dazzling not just at retaining the loyalty of his old customers (each is greeted by name and with a "I'm great now that you're here" or "I saw you coming in, babe, so your drinks are already mixed") but in making newcomers feel part of the "club." 218 E. 53rd St. (off Third Ave.). www.hudsonmalone.com. ✆ **212/355-6607.** Subway: E, M to 53rd St. or 6 to 51st.

Upper West Side

Dublin House ★ NYC doesn't have many of this kind of old-fashioned, plain-as-porridge Irish pubs anymore. Started as an illegal speakeasy in 1921 (have the same bartenders been here all that time? It seems like a possibility), this is a welcoming neighborhood bar where shots of whiskey are about as complicated as the mixology gets. And that's just fine. 229 W. 79th St (near Broadway). www.dublinhousenyc.com. Subway: 1 to 79th St.

Stone Rose Lounge ★ For moguls and the models they squire, this is a "see and be seen" bar. Owned by a bar mogul (Randy Gerber) and his model wife (Cindy Crawford), Stone Rose is an elegant, noisy, huge (5,000-sq.-ft.) bar with floor-to-ceiling windows. Try to nab a seat near them for one of the loveliest views in New York: Columbus Circle at night, lit up, with fountains spraying and Central Park slumbering in the background. In the Time Warner Center, 10 Columbus Circle, 4th floor. www.stoneroseny.com. ✆ **212/823-9970.** Subway: 1, A, B, C, D to Columbus Circle.

Upper East Side

Bemelman's Bar ★★★ Put on the ritz at this iconic bar, decorated with murals by Ludwig Bemelman, the illustrator behind the famous *Madeline* children's books. How plush is it? The ceiling is covered by 24-karat gold leaf, and the bar is made of a rare black granite. Live jazz plays as you tipple, to account for a $15 cover charge on top of the already pricey drinks here. 35 E. 76th St. (on Madison Ave.). www.rosewoodhotels.com/en/the-carlyle-new-york/dining/bemelmans-bar. ✆ **212/744-1600.** Subway: 6 to 77th St.

Lexington Bar and Books ★ It takes a moment to register, and then you suddenly realize why the atmosphere at Lexington Bar and Books is at once decidedly strange and deeply familiar: People are smoking (!) and no one is turning them in to the cops. That's because Lexington Bar and Books is one of the few "cigar bars" in the city with a special license allowing cigar smoking—and cigarettes by extension. For cocktails with a cig you'll have to dress up, though: This is a highly patrician joint, with a crowd in their later 30s and 40s, and a dress code requiring jackets in winter and collared shirts year-round. 1020 Lexington Ave. (at 73rd St.). www.barandbooks.cz. © **212/727-3902.** Subway: 6 to 77th St.

Seamstress ★★ The front bar looks like a scene out of a Dickens novel, with deep brown walls, elaborately framed mirrors (hung gallery-style), and serious, bearded bartenders. Out back, it's a bit more contemporary, with low tables made from tree trunks and a full, and very good, food menu. Drinks are from master mixologist Pamela Wiznitzer (she's not bearded) and they are dangerously delicious (you'll be tempted to order one too many). Lowdown: this place is waaaay too cool for the usually stodgy Upper East Side. 339 E. 75th St. (near First Ave.). www.seamstressny.com. © **212/288-8033.** Subway: 6 to 77th St.

Harlem

67 Orange Street ★★ Named for the address of the first black-owned bar in the city (it's confusing, I know, as this isn't on "Orange Street"), this tiny, super-hip cocktail haven serves up creative libations, often made with home-infused liquors (I had an excellent Manhattan made with cigar-smoke-infused bourbon), and bearing such tongue-in-cheek names as "The Color Purple" and "Cleopatra's Lust." The bar can be hard to find, as the windows are totally covered with drapes, so look for the address. 2082 Frederick Douglass Blvd. (at 113th St.). www.67orangestreet.com. © **212/662-2030.** Subway: B, C to Cathedral Pkwy./110th St.

Bier International ★ Take the word "International" seriously. On my last visit, this buzzing nightspot had 10 German beers; 2 from Belgium; 1 each from France, the Czech Republic, and Great Britain; and 2 from NYC. And those were just the beers on tap. The bottle list is far more extensive. It's all served in an airy, industrial-chic space with breeze-catching tables on the sidewalk outside. 2099 Frederick Douglass Blvd. (btw. 113th and 114th sts.). www.bierinternational.com. © **212/876-8838.** Subway: B, C to Cathedral Pkwy./110th St.

Brooklyn & Queens

It would take an entire book to list all of the spectacular outer-borough haunts, but here's a small, subway-friendly sampling of the can't-miss variety.

Brooklyn Bowl ★★ Yes, it's a bowling alley, but you don't have to hit the pins to have a delightful night out here. A massive Williamsburg space with an updated carny decor, and a wide selection of beers, cocktails, and food, this is a great place just to come and hang out. Live DJs spin catchy music on the nights that bands aren't playing. 61 Wythe Ave (btw. N. 11th and N.

12th sts.), Williamsburg, Brooklyn. www.brooklynbowl.com. © **718/963-3369.** Subway: L to Bedford Ave.; G to Nassau St.

Dutch Kills ★★★   Venturing beyond the Manhattan and Brooklyn nightlife scene gets you two rewards: lower booze prices and far more room to spread out. That's particularly true at Dutch Kills out in Queens, where the masterful bartending is better than you'll find at most of the city's boîtes (just tell a staffer what flavors you like, and they'll create the perfect cocktail for you on the spot), and the high-ceilinged space has more than enough room at the bar, plus comfy British-style wooden snugs (booths), easily big enough for a party of six. Bar snacks are by M. Wells (see p. 115), another major plus. Dutch Kills is within walking distance of several of the Queens hotels recommended in this book. 27 24 Jackson Ave. (at Dutch Kills St.), Long Island City, Queens. www.dutchkillsbar.com. © **718/383-2724.** Subway: E, M, R to Queens Plaza or N, Q, 7 to Queensboro Plaza.

Maison Premiere ★★★   Channeling the spirit of New Orleans—Garden District, *not* Bourbon Street—this oyster and cocktail bar in Williamsburg is a wonderfully atmospheric place to while away an evening. And while you don't have to pay homage to the "green fairy" to hang here, it is interesting to take a gander at the working replica absinthe fountain, based on the one that once graced Crescent City's Olde Absinthe House. The Casablanca cocktail, made with both absinthe and yogurt, is absolutely scrumptious. In 2016, Maison Premier won a coveted James Beard award for having the best bar program in the United States. 298 Bedford St. (near First St.), Williamsburg, Brooklyn. www.maisonpremiere.com. © **347/335-0446.** Subway: L to Bedford St.

Pete's Candy Store ★★   It seems appropriate that grown-up games should be the focus of a bar in a former candy store. You come here if you love pub quizzes, spelling bees, and other contests of the beer-buzzed brain. Pete's also hosts lectures and live music, making this little neighborhood joint in Willliamsburg a primo place not just for a frosty mug, but for serious entertainment (see the website for a current schedule). 709 Lorimer St. (btw. Richardson and Frost sts.), Williamsburg, Brooklyn. www.petescandystore.com. © **718/302-3770.** Subway: L to Lorimer St.

The Shanty ★★★   New York City's first distillery since Prohibition is attached to this convivial Williamsburg bar, and through one large glass wall, drinkers can see the giant vats where the owners are creating both gin and whiskey. Alan Katz is one of those co-owners, and he was, for many years, the host of "The Cocktail Hour" on Martha Stewart radio, so you know the mixology here is world-class (the drink menu changes with the seasons, but always includes liquors created on the property). Ask nicely, and they'll take you on a tour of the distillery. 79 Richardson St. (at Leonard St.), Williamsburg, Brooklyn. www.nydistilling.com. © **718/878-3579.** Subway: L to Lorimer St.

Tatiana ★★   Acrobats! Showgirls! Crooners! Tatiana is a Las Vegas-meets-Vladivostok experience, a Russian supper club on the Brighton Beach boardwalk where the meal is an endless feast (of Russian and

GETTING beyond THE VELVET ROPE

There's nothing that will transport you back to the worst day of high school quicker than facing the gatekeeper at the door of a New York dance club. It's a humbling, depressing experience (especially if you don't get in), but there are ways to increase your odds of spending more time in the club than on the sidewalk.

1. **Choose your companions carefully.** Large groups of men have little chance of getting into a club together, so if you're traveling in a pack of guys, split up until you get inside. Women have a better chance of getting in, as do couples.

2. **Dress the part.** Look at the celebrity magazines and see what they're wearing when they sashay past the ropes. Usually it's an upscale casual look, but that will change season to season. Avoid suits at all costs, the same for "business casual," and if you plan to wear sneakers, make sure they're clean.

3. **Make nice.** The "chooser" at the door has been entrusted by the owner to create a cool "mix" of people inside the club, so though you may not get in right away, you could be picked in 15 minutes, especially at a larger club, when they need more redheads, or tall women, or perhaps when the moon goes into

Jupiter (I don't think even the gatekeepers have a clear idea of what they're looking for). You'll blow your chances, however, if you give the all-powerful guy at the door any argument or attitude.

4. **Call in advance for a reservation.** Some dance clubs have restaurants attached, and those who dine get automatic entry, later in the evening. You can also reserve a table at a club in advance for you and your guests, but be careful: Those who get a table are required to take "bottle service," which means you buy a bottle of liquor for you and your companions that can easily cost upward of $400. And be aware that some clubs add a 20% to 25% gratuity to bar tabs. Ask.

5. **Never admit to being a tourist.** Clubs are where the worst New York snobbery comes to the fore. It's sad but true: They really don't want tourists. That doesn't mean you shouldn't go; just don't attempt to get in by telling them it's your "last night before you go back to Alabama."

6. **Say you're there to meet the deejay.** This is my sneakiest tip, but it actually works. Go to the club's website in advance, find out who the deejay will be that night, and say that you're meeting him or her inside.

Continental foods), the vodka flows freely, and ex-pat Russians of all ages boogie until dawn. It's not cheap, but going here may well be your most memorable, if weird, night in Gotham. 3152 Brighton 6th St. (at the boardwalk), Brighton Beach, Brooklyn. www.tatianarestaurant.com. ✆ **718/891-5151.** Subway: B, Q to Brighton Beach.

Yours Sincerely ★★ "We serve craft cocktails at a dive-bar price," the bartender told me, when I marveled at how (relatively) cheap the potables were here at this Bushwick bar (just $8 for a cocktail!). Here's their secret: all of the cocktails are mixed before the bar opens, put into temperature-controlled tanks, and then served via a tap, like beer would be. That means that cocktails can be served far faster than they would be in a regular bar; the increased volume allows management to cut prices. And wonders of wonders: these pre-fab cocktails are truly fab. I'm especially fond of the one that mimics the flavors of a Manhattan by using raisin-infused bourbon. Despite the fact that drinks are served in hokey laboratory beakers (we get it! You used science to pre-make your cocktails), the scene here is quite hip, the bar attracting a range of attractive 20- and 30-somethings, the space looking a bit like an old West saloon (with chandeliers and old-timey floral wallpaper on the ceiling). 47 Wilson Ave (near Melrose St.), Bushwick, Brooklyn. www.yourssincerely.co. ⓒ **929/234-2344.** Subway: L to Morgan.

Zombie Hut ★ Tiki time! This tropical bar in Carroll Gardens is not only the best antidote to NYC's sometimes frigid weather, it serves up affordable tipples to a mellow soundtrack (lots of Bob Marley) in a classic woven-grass and carved mask setting. An array of loaner board games keep the crowd entertained, as does (in good weather) the tiki torch-lit back garden. 273 Smith St., Carroll Gardens, Brooklyn. ⓒ **718/875-3433.** Subway: F, G to Carroll St.

Dance Clubs

No New York trends fluctuate quite as much as the club scene. So remember: Finding and going to the latest hot spot is not worth agonizing over. Clubgoers spend their lives obsessing over "the Scene." But this is New York, and there are so many choices, no one club is the empirical best. Instead of giving you a random list of the clubs that were hot at the moment, I'm going to suggest picking up a copy of *Time Out New York,* which will list the best parties of the week. Go to the one that most intrigues you.

To score reduced admissions or place yourself on a guest list for select clubs try the website **www.clubplanet.com**. Many clubs offer guest-list sign-up services directly on their websites, too. No matter what, call ahead, because schedules change constantly and can do so at the last minute.

Note: New York nightlife starts late, of course. With the exception of places that have scheduled performances, dance floors stay almost empty until midnight.

THE GAY & LESBIAN SCENE

Though the stats are shaky, most experts estimate that New York City is home to the largest gay population in North America, if not the world. All in all, there are about 70 major bars and nightclubs to suit every taste, wardrobe, and fetish, but the party only starts there. I'd recommend that you check out such publications as *Next* (www.nextmagazine.com), the lesbian-centric *GO* (www.gomag.com), and the more mainstream *Time Out New York* magazine (given out free on Wednesdays at subway stations and elsewhere) for listings of these clubs as well as the innumerable dance parties, go-go and drag shows, gay knitting circles (yes, really), and other happenings that take place at dozens of venues around the city. Of course, many New York bars, clubs, and cabarets are mixed with both gay and straight clientele (especially in 'hoods like the Village, Chelsea, and Hell's Kitchen).

sing out lou (OR LOUISE)

The "Church of Show Tunes" is in joyous session 7 nights a week at **Marie's Crisis,** a basement piano bar that has a pedigree and an atmosphere like no other. In a low-ceilinged room, covered with Christmas lights, dozens of men (and some women) gather each evening to belt out Sondheim, Porter, Loesser, and Rodgers and Hammerstein. A few times an evening the roving bartenders will take a solo, but for the most part the crowd sings in a booming chorus, usually while grinning ear to ear. The drinks are cheap, the crowd friendly, and the voices darn good.

Marie's Crisis has been in business a good 40 years now, but the history of the building goes back to the 1800s (legend has it the ceiling beams were taken from old ships). Thomas Paine, author of *Common Sense and The Crisis,* lived and died in this house, which explains the "crisis" part of the name. And after serving as a brothel from the 1850s to the late 1880s, it became a "boy bar" in the 1890s called "Marie's." The mural behind the piano was created by the Works Progress Administration, under President Franklin Delano Roosevelt (lord knows why it's here!); it portrays both the French and the American revolutions.

59 Grove St. (at Seventh Ave.). No website. ✆ **212/243-9323.** Subway: 1 to Christopher St.

Boxers ★ Yes, that's the outfit the bartender was wearing the night I visited, but the name of the joint also refers to the fact that this is a sports bar, with 11 massive TVs lining the walls and huge photos of ripped men engaged in all sorts of games on the walls. Hell's Kitchen is the latest hot spot for gay nightlife, so expect a toned, young crowd here, up for a party. A big perk: the lovely roof bar. 742 Ninth Ave. (at 50th St.). www.boxersnyc.com. ✆ **212/942-1518.** Subway: C, E to 50th St.

Cubby Hole ★★ Early in the evening, the Cubby Hole gets a mixed crowd from the neighborhood of men and even straight women, but by 11pm it's strictly "lipstick lesbians" and club girls rocking out to the jukebox. It's a fun scene and the decor is hilarious, with hundreds of paper animals and fish, Chinese lanterns, and plastic flying pigs dangling from the ceiling. 281 W. 12th St. (at W. 4th St.). www.cubbyholebar.com. ✆ **212/243-9041.** Subway: A, C, E, or L to 14th St.

The Eagle ★★ For "bears," "cubs," and the boys who love them, this dungeonlike club is the epicenter of the leather scene in New York. Forgot your chaps? Not a problem—the Eagle has a tiny "leather goods" store in the elevator for all your codpiece and whipping needs. 554 W. 28th St. (btw. Tenth and Eleventh aves.). www.eaglynyc.com. ✆ **646/473-1866.** Subway: C, E to 28th St.

Flaming Saddles Saloon ★★★ Yeehaw! Welcome to "Coyote Ugly" for gay men (and the many women who show up to watch the hot, shirtless bartenders hoof it on top of the bar every 40 minutes or so). The soundtrack is country-western and the mood exuberant. 739 Ninth Ave. (btw. 52nd and 53rd sts.). www.flamingsaddles.com. ✆ **212/713-0481.** Subway: 1 to Houston.

Henrietta Hudson ★   Dominated by a large pool table (always in use) in the center room and two bars, this divey bar hosts dancing many nights and seems especially popular among Latina and African-American women. See the website for special theme nights (Wednesday is Salsa Night). 438–444 Hudson St. (at Morton St.). www.henriettahudson.com. ✆ **212/924-3347.** Subway: 1 to Houston St.

The Monster ★★★   A fabulous Art Deco space, once home to El Chico (a former flamenco cabaret whose murals still adorn the walls), the Monster has two faces. Upstairs is a piano bar with a crowd of show-tune-crazy regulars; downstairs a groovy discothèque with go-go boys, weekend tea dances, and the most popular Latin Night in the city. The Monster experienced a resurgence of popularity recently, and now is hot, hot, hot! 80 Grove St. at Sheridan Square. www.manhattan-monster.com. ✆ **212/924-3558.** Subway: 1 to Christopher St.

Therapy ★★   A chic, candlelit, two-floor bar that attracts a "pretty boys in Barney's shirts" crowd of buff 20- and 30-somethings for casual cruising. You could come here and meet the love of your life, see a show, or just have a drink. It's where the ladies from RuPaul's Drag Show often perform. 348 W. 52nd St. (btw. Eighth and Ninth aves.). www.therapy-nyc.com. ✆ **212/397-1700.** Subway: C, E to 50th St.

XL ★   Set in the Out Hotel, on many nights this is one of the sweatiest, writhingest dance floors in the city. While some locals sniff that it's too "bridge and tunnel" (that is, filled with non-New Yorkers), others think of it as the hottest party in the city. 512 W. 42nd St. (at Tenth Ave.). www.xlnightclub.com. ✆ **212/239-2999.** Subway: A, C, E, or L to 42nd St.

SPECTATOR SPORTS

For details on the New York City Marathon and the U.S. Open tennis championships, see the "New York City Calendar of Events" in chapter 9.

BASEBALL   With two baseball teams in town, you can catch a game almost any day, from Opening Day in April to the beginning of the playoffs in October (though Yankees tickets can be hard to come by).

For info on pricing and availability of tickets for the Metropolitans, visit http://newyork.mets.mlb.com or call the **Mets Ticket Office** at ✆ **718/507-TIXX** (507-8499).

Yankee Stadium is, as it has always been in every incarnation, in the Bronx. (Subway: C, D, 4 to 161st St./Yankee Stadium). For single-game tickets, contact **Yankee Stadium** (http://newyork.yankees.mlb.com; ✆ **718/293-4300**). You can also buy Mets and Yankees tickets by contacting **Ticketmaster** (www.ticketmaster.com; ✆ **800/745-3000**), visiting the stadium on the day of the game, or trying online resale sites such as **StubHub** (www.stubhub.com).

BASKETBALL   There are two pro hoops teams that play in New York at **Madison Square Garden,** Seventh Avenue, between 31st and 33rd streets (www.thegarden.com or www.ticketmaster.com; ☏ **212/465-6741,** or 800/745-3000 for tickets; subway A, C, E, 1, 2, 3 to 34th St.). The **New York Knicks** (www.nba.com/knicks; ☏ **877/NYK-DUNK** [695-3865] or 212/465-JUMP [5867]) are the NBA team from NYC. They play from November through mid-February. The second is the accomplished WNBA team the **New York Liberty** (www.wnba.com/liberty; ☏ **212/564-9622**); its season falls in the summer months, beginning in late May.

FOOTBALL   Both the **New York Giants** (www.giants.com) and the **New York Jets** (www.newyorkjets.com) play in the Meadowlands Stadium. It's located not in New York City, but in East Rutherford, New Jersey, and tickets are VERY difficult to get. Tickets are available from Ticketmaster.com and, if price is no object, StubHub.com.

ICE HOCKEY   NHL hockey is represented in Manhattan by the **New York Rangers,** who play at Madison Square Garden (http://rangers.nhl.com or www.thegarden.com; ☏ **212/465-6741;** subway A, C, E, 1, 2, 3 to 34th St.). Rangers tickets are hard to get, so plan well ahead; visit **www.ticketmaster. com** for online orders or call ☏ **800/745-3000.**

PLANNING YOUR VISIT

As with any trip, a little preparation is essential before you start your journey to NYC. This chapter provides a variety of planning tools, including information on how to get there, how to get around within the city once there, and when to come. And then, in a mainly alphabetical listing, I deal with the dozens of miscellaneous resources and organizations that you can turn to for help.

GETTING THERE
By Plane

Three major airports serve New York City: **John F. Kennedy International Airport** (JFK, www.panynj.gov/airports/jfk.html; © **718/244-4444**) in Queens, about 15 miles from midtown Manhattan; **LaGuardia Airport** (LGA, www.panynj.gov/airports/laguardia.html; © **718/533-3400**), also in Queens, about 8 miles from Midtown; and **Newark Liberty International Airport** (EWR, www.panynj.gov/airports/newark-liberty.html; © **973/961-6000**) in nearby New Jersey, about 16 miles from midtown New York. Almost every major domestic airline serves at least one of the New York–area airports; most serve two or all three.

GETTING INTO TOWN FROM THE AIRPORT
Since there's no need to rent a car in New York, you're going to have to figure out how you want to get from the airport to your hotel and back.

Generally, travel time between the airports and Midtown by taxi or car is 45 to 60 minutes for JFK or Newark, and 20 to 35 minutes for LaGuardia. Always allow extra time, especially during rush hour or peak holiday travel times, and if you're taking public transportation.

SUBWAYS & PUBLIC BUSES For a major international city, New York's public transit options to and from our airports are pretty crummy, but not impossible to navigate. The subway *can* be more reliable than taking a car or taxi at the height of rush hour, but *a few words of warning:* This isn't the right option for you if you're bringing more than a single piece of luggage or if you have young

FINDING A GOOD airfare INTO NYC

Book at the right time. It sounds odd, but you can often save a good amount by booking domestic airfare 57 days in advance of departure. That figure comes from a study of 23 million airfare transactions that an industry group called the Airlines Reporting Corporation undertook in 2016. Book earlier than that, and you won't have access to the lowest-priced seats, as the airlines only release them when they have an idea of how the plane is selling. Book too close to departure, and the airline knows they've "got you" and will charge more.

Fly when others don't and take an itinerary the business travelers don't want. Those who fly Sunday, Tuesday or Wednesday, and who stay over a Saturday night, generally pay less than those who fly at more popular times.

Do a smart Web search. Such search engines as DoHop.com, Kayak.com, and Momondo.com will search all of the discount sites as well as the airline sites directly, so that you get a broader and more impartial search. The only airline that won't come up is Southwest Airlines, so be sure to search it separately, as it now flies into LaGuardia and Newark airports.

Don't be particular about airports. Go to whatever airport is offering the cheapest fares. None of the three New York City airports are any more or less convenient to the city than the others (although LaGuardia is somewhat closer), and they all have equally lousy records for delays and lost luggage.

children in tow, since there's a good amount of walking, including stairs, and usually a subway car that's too crowded for excess baggage. Also note that, particularly to JFK and LaGuardia, public transport will likely take double the time a car will. That's particularly true during off-peak travel times.

o **LaGuardia Airport:** The M60 bus will take you to or from the city; you'll board (or debark) at either 125th Street in Harlem, or just down the elevated-subway stairs at the N or Q-train Astoria Boulevard station in Queens. The bus isn't very reliable (I've waited over 45 minutes for it), but if you have the patience, this is the cheapest way, at just $2.75, to get to or from the airport and the city.

o **Newark Airport:** Passengers first take the **AirTrain** (www.panynj.gov; © **888/EWR-INFO** [397-4636]) from their terminal to the Newark Airport train station, where they transfer to a **NJ Transit train** (www.njtransit.com; © **973/275-5555**) heading to New York Penn Station at 33rd Street and Seventh Avenue. (DON'T accidentally board a train to Penn Station Newark, a common mistake.) **Amtrak** (www.amtrak.com; © **800/USA-RAIL** [872-7245]) will also connect to this station, but it is far more expensive than New Jersey transit, so I don't recommend it. From there, catch either a cab, an uber, subway, or a bus to your hotel. A one-way trip costs $15 at minimum for most passengers: $12.50 for the New Jersey train and then another $2.50 for the bus or subway in Manhattan to your hotel. Unlike the M60 bus to LaGuardia, service on NJ Transit is relatively frequent, with trains running at least six times an hour from 6am to 9pm and four times an hour from 9pm to midnight (there's no service from 2am–5am). NJ transit tickets can be purchased from vending machines at both the air terminal and the train station. There are discounts for children and seniors.

○ **JFK Airport:** If you take an **AirTrain** from the airport, you have a choice of two options: The cheaper, but slower, method is to take either the A, E, J, or Z subway at Jamaica Station and the Sutphin Blvd.–Archer Ave. Station; or the A subway to Howard Beach. Either way, it's $7.75 total fare; the Howard Beach route is usually the fastest from midtown Manhattan. Complete info on the subway/AirTrain link can be found at web.mta.info/mta/airtrain.htm. You can also take the Long Island Railroad from the AirTrain to Penn Station in NYC (total fare $15), which is less than the cost of a shuttle bus—see p. 260—but not very convenient, unless you're staying close to Penn Station.

TAXIS Despite significant rate hikes in the past few years, taxis are still a quick and convenient way to travel to and from the airports. They're available at designated taxi stands outside the terminals, with uniformed dispatchers on hand during peak hours at JFK and LaGuardia, around the clock at Newark. Follow the GROUND TRANSPORTATION or TAXI signs. There may be a long line, but generally those lines move quickly. Fares, whether fixed or metered, do not include bridge and tunnel tolls ($4–$6, if applicable) or a tip for the cabbie (20% is customary). They do include all passengers in the cab and luggage— never pay more than the metered or flat rate, except for tolls and a tip (8pm–6am, a 50¢ surcharge also applies on New York yellow cabs). **Taxis have a limit of four passengers,** so if there are more in your group, you'll have to take more than one cab or try and hail a minivan taxi. For more, see p. 266.

○ **From JFK:** A flat rate of $52 to Manhattan (plus tolls, tip, and a 50¢ NY state tax) is charged. The meter will not be turned on and the surcharge will not be added.

○ **From LaGuardia:** There's no set fare, but you can expect the meter to run about $35, plus tolls and tip.

○ **From Newark:** The dispatcher for New Jersey taxis gives you a slip of paper with a flat rate ranging from $50 to $75 (toll and tip extra), depending on where you're going in New York City, so be precise about your destination. New York yellow cabs aren't permitted to pick up passengers at Newark. The yellow-cab fare from Manhattan to Newark is the meter amount plus $17.50 and tolls (totaling about $69–$75). New Jersey taxis aren't permitted to take passengers from Manhattan to Newark.

PRIVATE CAR & LIMOUSINE SERVICES Private (or "livery") car and limousine companies range from sedans and vans to limousines, and provide 24-hour door-to-door airport transfers for roughly the same cost as a taxi. Or at least that's the case for those who choose curbside pickup at the airport. Being greeted by a driver holding a sign with your name on it as you exit the baggage area is a service that comes at a premium (costs will vary by car company). The advantage of indoor pickup is that you'll avoid the hassles of taxi lines. Frankly, I don't see much advantage to arranging for curbside pickup from the airport as the wait can be up to 30 minutes (you'll call the dispatcher when you arrive) and the taxi line is never that long. **My advice:** Use car services to get *to* the airport, but simply hop a cab when coming into the city.

The companies with the best reputations are **Carmel** (www.carmellimo. com; ✆ **866/666-6666**), **Allstate** (www.allstatelimo.com; ✆ **800/453-4099** or 212/333-3333), and **Tel-Aviv** (www.telavivlimo.com; ✆ **800/222-9888**). (Keep in mind, though, that these services are only as good as the individual drivers. If you have a problem, report it immediately to the main office.) Ask when booking what the fare will be. There may be waiting charges tacked on if the driver has to wait an excessive amount of time due to flight delays, but the car companies will usually check on your flight to get an accurate landing time. Many travelers now also use the apps **Uber** and **Lyft** for airport pickups. Uber has a sharing setting that can cut the cost of getting into the city, if others are also using it at the time you arrive.

Warning: When you leave the terminal, you may be approached by a private car driver trying to get a fare back to Manhattan, or a driver without a taxi/livery license looking to make extra money. It's illegal, as well as more expensive than doing Uber, taking a taxi, or using one of the services listed above. And you may be taken advantage of if the driver thinks you're a NYC newbie. Don't negotiate with them. Grab a cab, order a car, or take a bus or shuttle.

PRIVATE BUSES & SHUTTLES   Buses and shuttle services provide a comfortable and less expensive (but usually more time-consuming) option for airport transfers than do taxis and car services.

The familiar blue vans of **SuperShuttle** (www.supershuttle.com; ✆ **800/258-3826**) serve all three area airports, providing door-to-door service to Manhattan and points on Long Island every 15 to 30 minutes around the clock. You don't need to reserve your airport-to-Manhattan ride; just go to the ground-transportation desk or use the courtesy phone in baggage claim and ask for SuperShuttle. Hotel pickups for your return trip require 24 to 48 hours notice; you can make your reservations online. Fares run from about $16 to $28 per person, depending on the airport and location of your hotel.

NYC Airporter (www.nycairporter.com; ✆ **718/777-5111**) buses travel from JFK and LaGuardia to the Port Authority Bus Terminal (42nd Street and Eighth Avenue), Grand Central Terminal (Park Avenue between 41st and 42nd streets), Bryant Park (on 42nd Street near Fifth Avenue), and Penn Station (Seventh Avenue between 31st and 32nd streets). Look for the airport's ground transportation desk (there's one in every terminal) or the uniformed personnel of the Airporter outside. Buses depart the airport every 20 to 30 minutes (depending on your departure point and destination) between 5am and 11:30pm. Fare from JFK to Manhattan is $16 one-way and $30 round-trip; from LaGuardia it's $14 one-way and $27 round-trip. For round-trip

Getting There

PLANNING YOUR VISIT

If you're traveling to a borough other than Manhattan, contact **ETS Air Service** (www.etsairportshuttle.com; ℂ **718/221-5341**) for shared door-to-door service. For service to Westchester County or Connecticut, contact **Connecticut Limousine** (www.ctlimo.com; ℂ **800/472-5466** or 203/974-4700). If you're traveling to points in New Jersey from Newark Airport, contact **State Shuttle** (www.stateshuttle.com; ℂ **800/427-3207**) for destinations throughout New Jersey.

Additionally, **New York Airport Service** express buses (www.nyairportservice.com; ℂ **212/812-2702**) serve the entire New York metropolitan region from JFK, Newark, and LaGuardia, offering connections to the Long Island Rail Road; the Metro-North Railroad to Westchester County, upstate New York, and Connecticut; and New York's Port Authority terminal, where you head for New Jersey.

ticket holders *only* there's a free shuttle bus from Bryant Park to midtown hotels, but no pickup service from hotels on the way back to the airport.

Olympia Airport Express (www.coachusa.com/olympia/ss.newarkairport. asp; ℂ **877/863-9275**) provides service every 30 minutes (between 6:45am–11:15pm) from Newark Airport to Bryant Park (at 42nd Street and Fifth Avenue), the Port Authority Bus Terminal (on 42nd Street between Eighth and Ninth avenues), and Grand Central Terminal (on 41st Street between Park and Lexington avenues). Call for the exact schedule for your return trip to the airport. The one-way fare runs $16, $28 round-trip; $5 one-way for members of the military.

By Bus

Busing to and from New York City from major East Coast cities has become the single most cost-effective way to get into town. A number of companies offer frequent, regular service between most of the major cities in the East (and as far west as Buffalo and Toronto) for a fraction of what you'd pay by train or plane. From Philadelphia, the average ride might range from $10 to $20; for the other two cities you'll pay $15 to $30, but occasional specials reduce the fares to just $1. The website GoToBus.com provides a comprehensive list of options, but I've had good personal experiences with the following bus lines:

o **Megabus** (www.megabus.com; ℂ **877/GO2-MEGA** [462-6342])
o **Boltbus** (www.boltbus.com; ℂ **877/BOLTBUS** [265-8287])
o **Vamoose** (www.vamoosebus.com; ℂ **212/695-6766**)

By Train

Amtrak (www.amtrak.com; ℂ **800/USA-RAIL** [872-7245]) runs frequent service to New York City's Penn Station, on Seventh Avenue between 31st and 33rd streets, where you can get a taxi, subway, or bus to your hotel.

9

PLANNING YOUR VISIT | Getting There

If you're traveling to New York from a city along Amtrak's Northeast Corridor—such as Boston, Philadelphia, Baltimore, or Washington, D.C.—Amtrak may end up being faster than flying (when you factor in time getting to the airport and getting through security), especially on the high-speed Acela trains. The Acela Express trains cut travel time from D.C. down to 2½ hours, and travel time from Boston to a lightning-quick 3 hours.

GETTING AROUND THE CITY

Because most travelers confine themselves to Manhattan, I will as well in this section. Those traveling to the outer boroughs can be confident, however, that public transportation—subways, buses, ferries, or some combination of the three—can get you anywhere you wish to go in the city proper, whether it be the sandy shores of Brighton Beach, Brooklyn, or Yankee Stadium in the Bronx. The city's transportation network is run by the Metropolitan Transportation Authority (aka the MTA); maps and schedules for NYC's myriad transportation options can be found at www.mta.info.

Subway

I wish I could confine my transportation advice to just three words—"**take the subway**"—and be done with it. To my mind, the NYC subways, 113 years young in 2017, are the single most efficient, rapid, easy, and affordable way to get just about anywhere you'd want to go in Manhattan, with the exception of some of the far eastern sections of the Upper East Side, or crosstown journeys above 59th Street. They run 24 hours a day, 7 days a week, and yes, they get crowded at rush hour (roughly from 8 to 9:30am and from 5 to 6:30pm on weekdays), but even then they're still the fastest way to get from point A to point B.

But because of the starring role the subways have played in action films set in New York over the years, with squinty-eyed thugs menacing grandmothers on graffiti-riddled trains, many visitors are scared to go underground. That fear is unwarranted. Not only is the graffiti gone, thanks to the efforts of those invisible transit cops (you rarely see one, but there are 3,000 of them keeping order underground and on the buses, often in plain clothes), the subways are safer than ever. Of course, that doesn't make them Disneyland. Though the cars are heated in winter and air-conditioned in summer, the platforms are not, and they often feel 10 degrees colder than the city streets in winter, and 10 degrees hotter in summer. Pickpockets remain a problem, as they are in Paris, London, and every other big city. So remember to move your wallet to a place where you can keep track of it before boarding the train (if you're wearing pants, the front pocket is usually best).

PAYING YOUR WAY

To use both the city's buses and subways, would-be passengers purchase a MetroCard, which is a credit card-sized plastic pass, with a magnetic strip that records how much money the card holds. It's swiped to get onto both forms of transportation.

A SingleRide subway fare (available only at vending machines) is $3 (half-price for seniors and those with disabilities); however, if you buy more than one ride you'll pay just $2.75 per ride. Children under 44 inches tall ride free (up to three per adult). To these rates, you'll need to add a $1 fee for the subway card itself (add time or money onto your card and there will be no additional fee). Once you're in the system, you can transfer free of charge to any subway line that you can reach without exiting your station. MetroCards also allow you a **free transfer** between bus and subway within a 2-hour period.

MetroCards are purchased at the ATM-style vending machines located in every subway station, which accept cash, credit cards, and debit cards; from a MetroCard merchant, including corner delis and drugstores; and Hudson News, at Penn Station and Grand Central Terminal.

MetroCards come in a few different configurations:

Pay-Per-Ride MetroCards can be used for up to four people by swiping up to four times. You can put any amount from $5.50 to $100 on your card. Every time you put $5.50 or more on your Pay-Per-Ride MetroCard, it's automatically credited 11%—in other words, spend $20 and you get an extra $2.20. You can refill your card at any time until the expiration date on the card, usually about a year from the date of purchase, at any subway station.

Unlimited-Ride MetroCards, which can't be used for more than one person at a time or more frequently than at 18-minute intervals, are available in two values: the **7-Day MetroCard,** which allows you 7 days' worth of unlimited subway and bus rides for $31; and the **30-Day MetroCard,** for $116.50. They go into effect the first time you use them—so if you buy a card on Monday and don't begin to use it until Wednesday, Wednesday is when the

Mass Transit Fares in New York City

SUBWAYS, MTA BUS

Fare Type	Full**	Reduced*
Base Pay-Per-Ride MetroCard Fare	$2.75	$1.35
Minimum purchase for new MetroCard	$5	$5
Cash (Bus only)	$2.75	$1.25
Single-Ride Ticket	$3	N/A
UNLIMITED-RIDE METROCARD		
7-day	$31	$15.50
30-day	$116.50	$58.25

* Reduced-fare customers who do not have a reduced-fare MetroCard pay $2.50 at a subway station booth for a round-trip.

** Reduced fares are available to those over 65 and persons with qualifying disabilities. Both groups must apply in advance for the discount at www.mta.info. Reduced fares are not available during peak periods, 6–10am and 3–7pm weekdays.

clock starts ticking. Seven- and 30-day MetroCards run out at midnight on the last day.

Tips for using your MetroCard: The MetroCard swiping mechanisms at turnstiles are the source of much grousing among subway riders. If you swipe too fast or too slow, the turnstile will ask you to swipe again (as Hillary Clinton discovered when she was campaigning for Prez and trying to look local by taking the subway). If this happens, *do not move to a different turnstile,* or you may end up paying twice. If you've tried repeatedly and really can't make your MetroCard work, tell the token booth clerk; chances are good you'll get the movement down, though.

If you're not sure how much money you have left on your MetroCard or when it expires, use the station's MetroCard Reader, located near the station entrance or the token booth (on buses the fare box also displays this info).

USING THE SYSTEM

As you can see from the subway map on the inside back cover of this book, the subway system basically mimics the lay of the land above ground, with most lines in Manhattan running north and south, like the avenues, and a few lines east and west, like the streets.

To **go up and down the east side of Manhattan** (and to the Bronx and Brooklyn), take the 4, 5, or 6 train.

To travel **up and down the West Side** (and also to the Bronx and Brooklyn), take the 1, 2, or 3 line; the A, C, E, or F line; or the B or D line.

The N, R, and Q lines first **cut diagonally across town** from east to west and then snake under Seventh Avenue before shooting out to Queens.

The **crosstown** S line, called the Shuttle, runs back and forth between Times Square and Grand Central Terminal. Farther downtown, across 14th Street, the L line works its own crosstown magic.

Express trains often skip about three stops for each one they make; express stops are indicated on subway maps with a white (rather than solid) circle. Local stops are usually about nine blocks apart.

Directions are almost always indicated using "uptown" (northbound) and "downtown" (southbound), so be sure to know what direction you want to head. The outsides of some subway entrances are marked UPTOWN ONLY or DOWNTOWN ONLY; read carefully, as it's easy to head in the wrong direction or get stuck on the wrong platform.

By Bus

Since buses can get stuck in traffic and stop every couple of blocks, rather than the eight or nine blocks that local subways traverse between stops (unless you catch a "Limited" bus), they're much less useful than the subway. I recommend using them only if you have to travel east to west; note that you can combine a bus ride with a subway ride at no additional cost (the transfer has to take place within 2 hours of the time you first boarded either the subway or the train).

PAYING YOUR WAY

Like the subway fare, a SingleRide **bus fare** is $3, half-price for seniors and riders with disabilities, and free for children under 44 inches (up to three per adult). The fare is payable with a **MetroCard** or **exact change** (excluding pennies). And they do mean *change:* Bus drivers don't make change, and fare boxes don't accept dollar bills or pennies. You can't purchase MetroCards on the bus, so have them ready before you board.

In recent years, the MTA introduced a sidewalk payment system for **Select Bus Service** on certain routes. This was done, apparently, to speed up the boarding process, but it's mostly served to confuse the heck out of riders. In Manhattan, on buses that go crosstown (east to west and vice versa) on 34th and 86th streets, and on buses that run downtown or uptown on First and Second Avenues, would-be riders must insert coins or MetroCards into a sidewalk stand. You'll receive a receipt, which you should hold on to, as police sometimes board the buses to check receipts (my husband got confused by the system, lost his receipt, and got a $100 ticket). The service is also in place on the buses that serve LaGuardia Airport and a number of bus lines in the outer boroughs.

USING THE SYSTEM

You can't flag down a city bus—you have to meet it at a bus stop. **Bus stops** are located every two or three blocks on the right-side corner of the street (facing the direction of traffic flow). They're marked by a curb painted yellow and a blue-and-white sign with a bus emblem and the route number or numbers, and usually an ad-bedecked bus shelter.

Almost every major avenue has its own **bus route.** They run either north or south: downtown on Fifth, uptown on Madison, downtown on Lexington, uptown on Third, and so on. There are **crosstown buses** at strategic locations all around town, generally at the numbered streets that have the width of avenues (like 14th, 23rd, 34th, and 42nd streets, to name a few). You'll usually find a crosstown bus every 8 to 10 blocks, except in the area below 8th street.

Some bus routes, however, are erratic: The M104, for example, turns at Eighth Avenue and 41st Street and goes up Broadway to West 129th Street.

Most routes operate 24 hours a day, but service is infrequent at night. During rush hour, main routes have "Limited" buses, identifiable by the red card in the front window; they stop only at major cross streets.

Most city buses are equipped with wheelchair lifts, making buses the city's most accessible mode of

> ### Take a Free Ride
>
> The Alliance for Downtown New York's **Downtown Connection (www.down townny.com)** offers free bus service providing easy access to downtown destinations, including Battery Park City, the World Financial Center, and South Street Seaport. The buses run daily every 15 minutes or so from 10am to 7:30pm and make dozens of stops along a 5-mile route from Chambers Street on the west side to Beekman Street on the east side.

public transportation. Buses also "kneel," lowering down to the curb to make boarding easier.

By Taxi

Cabs can be hailed on any street, provided you find an empty one—often simple, yet nearly impossible at 5pm when the taxi drivers change shifts. They're pricey, but can be convenient if you're tired or are not sure how to find an address. Don't assume they'll be quicker than the subway or walking, though. In traffic-clogged Midtown at midday, you can often walk to where you're going more quickly.

Official New York City taxis, licensed by the Taxi and Limousine Commission (TLC), are yellow, with the rates printed on the door and a light with a medallion number on the roof. *Note:* In 2013, a city law was passed creating a new fleet of apple-green taxis, which pick up passengers in the outer boroughs and upper Manhattan. Like yellow cabs, they are hailable, but unlike the yellow ones they are not allowed to pick up passengers in Manhattan below West 110th Street or East 96th Street (though they are allowed to drop off passengers there).

The **base fare** on entering the cab is $2.50. The **cost** is 50¢ for every ⅕ mile and for every 60 seconds in stopped or slow-moving traffic (or for waiting time). There's no extra charge for each passenger or for luggage. However, you must pay **bridge or tunnel tolls.** You'll also pay a **$1 surcharge** between 4 and 8pm and a **50¢ surcharge** between 8pm and 6am. A 15% to 20% tip is customary. All taxis are now equipped with a device that allows you to pay by credit card.

Drivers are required by law to take you anywhere in the five boroughs, to Nassau or Westchester counties, and to the major airports. They are supposed to know how to get to any address in the city. They are also required to provide A/C and turn off the radio on demand. Smoking in the cab is not allowed.

You are allowed to dictate the route that is taken. It's a good idea to look at a map before you get in a taxi. Taxi drivers have been known to jack up the fare on visitors who don't know better by taking a circuitous route between points A and B. Don't be afraid to speak up.

On the other hand, listen to drivers who propose an alternate route. These guys spend 8 or 10 hours a day on these streets, and they know where the worst traffic is, or where Con Ed has dug up an intersection that should be avoided. A knowledgeable driver will know how to get you to your destination efficiently.

Another important tip: **Always make sure the meter is turned on**

Taxi-Hailing Tips

When you're waiting on the street for an available taxi, look at the **medallion light** on the top of the coming cabs. If the light is out, the taxi is in use. When the center part (the number) is lit, the taxi is available—this is when you raise your hand to flag the cab. If all the lights are on, the driver is off-duty. Taxi regulations limit the number of people permitted to take a cab to four, so split up if your group is larger.

at the start of the ride. You'll see the red LED readout register the initial $2.50 and start calculating the fare as you go. I've witnessed unscrupulous drivers buzzing visitors around the city with the meter off, then overcharging them at drop-off.

For all driver complaints, including the one above, and to report lost property, call ℭ **311** or 212/NEW-YORK (212/639-9675; outside the metro area).

By Uber, Lyft & Via

These three services have become so ubiquitous that the value of a taxi medallion (the official license necessary to own a yellow cab) plummeted from several hundred thousand dollars to well under half that amount in 2015. All three services are accessible through apps you can download to a smartphone. With Lyft and Uber, you key in your pick-up and drop-off locations and receive a price for the ride. They are often cheaper than a taxi, though when "surge pricing" takes effect, rates can increase threefold. The credit card that you register when you get the app is charged for the ride; no tipping necessary.

Via is a ride-sharing service. As with the other two, you input your desired pick-up and drop-off, but because you'll be sharing the van with others, you may have to trek a few blocks to an appointed spot to catch the ride (and you may be dropped a few blocks from where you're going). Because of this, few tourists are using Via (perhaps because they're nervous about finding their way to and from the van), but boy is it affordable. A ride for one person costs just $5 usually, no matter how far you're traveling. If you have a companion, they'll be charged just $2.50 (less than the subway!) and tipping isn't allowed. The hidden perk: you get into the most wonderful conversations with other passengers on Via. There's something about the intimacy of sharing a car with just a few others that encourages socializing. *Note*: Uber also has a ride-sharing feature, but I've never been able to make it work. The wait times for pick-up are always too long.

I only recommend using Uber or Lyft when they give you a wait time of 4 minutes or less. When the wait is longer, except in the most deserted areas of town, it will likely be more convenient to simply hail a taxi. Via might be worth the wait, as it will be significantly cheaper for long distances.

By Bicycle

Believe it or not, New York is in the process of becoming a great bicycling city. It boasts a number of designated bike routes and lanes, including some protected bike lanes painted green and with their own traffic signals.

And you don't have to bring your own wheels to ride, thanks to the **Citibike** system (www.citibikenyc.com). Following the successful examples set by cities like Paris, Montreal, and Washington D.C., the city's program charges $12 a day ($24 for 3 days), with an unlimited number of 30-minute-long rides (if your ride lasts longer, you pay $4 for every additional 15 minutes). The freestanding, solar-powered racks dot many streets across the five boroughs, each holding around a dozen sturdy bikes outfitted with lights and tough tires. Download the Citibike App to find the rack nearest to you.

For a current map of the ever-expanding city bike-lane network, visit the NYC DOT webpage at **www.nyc.gov** or **www.nycbikemaps.com**. Alas, helmets are not provided at these stands; it's a smart idea to bring your own.

By Car

Forget driving yourself around the city. It's not worth the headache. Traffic is horrendous, and parking even more problematic.

If you do arrive in New York City by car, park it in a garage (expect to pay at least $25–$45 per day) and leave it there for the duration of your stay. If you drive a rental car in, return it as soon as you arrive and rent another when you leave. All of the major car-rental companies have multiple Manhattan locations.

Traveling from the City to the Suburbs

Along with taking the bus (see p. 257), many use the **PATH system** (www.panynj.gov/path; ✆ **800/234-7284**) which connects Manhattan with cities in New Jersey, including Hoboken and Newark, by subway-style trains. Stops in Manhattan are at the World Trade Center, Christopher and 9th streets, and along Sixth Avenue at 14th, 23rd, and 33rd streets. The fare is $2.75.

New Jersey Transit (www.njtransit.com; ✆ **973/275-5555**) operates commuter trains from Penn Station, and buses from the Port Authority at Eighth Avenue and 42nd Street, to points throughout New Jersey.

The **Long Island Rail Road** (www.mta.info/lirr; ✆ **511**) runs from Penn Station, at Seventh Avenue between 31st and 33rd streets, to Queens (ocean beaches, Citi Field [home of the New York Mets], Belmont Park) and points beyond on Long Island, to even better beaches and summer hot spots such as the Hamptons. You can also connect to the Fire Island ferry from the LIRR.

Metro-North Railroad (www.mta.info/mnr; ✆ **212/532-4900**) departs from Grand Central, at 42nd Street and Lexington Avenue, for areas north of the city, including Westchester County, the Hudson Valley, and Connecticut.

Perhaps the most common side trip from NYC is to **Woodbury Commons**, a shopping outlet that offers real savings on over 220 brands, everything from Nike and Banana Republic to Tory Burch and Armani. The mall is located approximately 45 minutes outside the city; it's reachable via bus and a number of shuttles (some of which pick up at Manhattan hotels). To see a full list of transportation options, with pricing, go to www. premiumoutlets.com/outlet/woodbury-common.

WHEN TO GO

"Anytime you like" is the short answer. New York is a 12-month, 24-hour destination, and there's always something exciting going on here.

Significantly, New York does not experience the real extremes of temperature of a Minneapolis or Phoenix. Yes, we get snowstorms and 10° weather, but rarely for more than a day or two, with the snow usually scooped into graying piles overnight. We also have heat waves, but it's unusual for the

New York's Average Temperature & Rainfall

	JAN	FEB	MAR	APR	MAY	JUNE	JULY	AUG	SEPT	OCT	NOV	DEC
Daily Temp. (°F)	38	42	50	61	71	79	84	83	75	64	54	43
Daily Temp. (°C)	3	6	10	16	22	26	29	28	24	18	12	6
Days of Precipitation	11	10	11	11	11	10	11	10	8	8	9	10

temperature to break 100°F for more than 4 or 5 days each summer, though it will be a sticky heat when it hits and none too pleasant. In general, this type of extreme heat occurs only in late July and August, with the most blustery and bitterly cold days falling in January and February, and occasionally December. (Of course, in this age of climate change, you never know what will happen.)

If you want to know what to pack just before you go, check the Weather Channel's online 10-day forecast at **www.weather.com**.

Culture, too, is a year-round exercise. Most of the major plays, musicals, and art shows debut between September and May, so those who like to be on culture's cutting edge visit then. In the summer months NYC teems with arts events as the city transforms itself into an outdoor theater/concert hall, with dozens of free shows—from Shakespeare in the Park to Shakespeare in the Parking Lot—crowding the calendar. All of the major art institutions participate in this summer free-for-all, with the Museum of Modern Art sponsoring concerts in its sculpture garden, the Metropolitan Opera bringing music to the parks, and dozens of other institutions, large and small, established and unknown, jumping on the alfresco bandwagon.

So what it all comes down to, in my mind, is cost, and here there is a *major* difference between seasons. People who visit in the slower months pay the right amount for their lodging, and those who come when the city is crowded—and here I'm going to sound like the clichéd New Yorker—get screwed.

So when are prices the most moderate? Deep winter, in the months of January (after the 4th) and February, it's not at all unusual to find a lovely room for as little as $109 a night. Visit in the fall, especially October and November, or around the December holidays, and that same room, in the same hotel, could cost upward of $300 a night. Spring is also pricey, albeit slightly less so than the fall, and prices drop into a middle range in the summer. Room rates over Christmas, New Year's, the New York Marathon, and Thanksgiving reach their pinnacles for the year. If you must visit at those times, get ready to pay a good $50 more than even the pricey fall rates.

New York City Calendar of Events

I've included a very limited sampling below of what I consider "visit-worthy" events. As I can make no claims to psychic abilities, I can't include all of the nifty happenings that haven't yet been announced. To get a complete picture, pick up a copy of *Time Out New York* magazine when you arrive. The "Around Town" section will leave you dizzy—usually there are upward of 150 interesting events happening any week. For a more selective listing, buy the current *New Yorker* magazine, which devotes the first tenth of its pages to its picks for the most intellectually stimulating or artistically important events. **NewYorkmag.com**, the website of New York Magazine, is another swell resource. For the most complete listings, go to the NYC Convention & Visitors Bureau's site: **www.nycgo.com**.

JANUARY

New York Boat Show. Yachts to pontoon boats to canoes are all on display at the **Jacob K. Javits Convention Center**, from January 25–29, 2017. **www.nyboatshow. com**.

Winter Restaurant Week. A misnomer, because this gourmet shindig actually lasts 2 weeks. This is the time of year when cheap foodies can try out the city's best restaurants for as little as $25 at lunch or $38 at dinner for three courses. Visit **www.nycgo.com** for the 2017 dates. You can make reservations starting 2 weeks in advance. Late January/ early February.

Chinese New Year. Two weeks of parades, festive meals, and special performances staged throughout Chinatown's streets, and along East Broadway. Visit **www.explore chinatown.com**. Chinese New Year falls on January 28 in 2017.

FEBRUARY

Fashion Week. Early February is when American designers parade their new lines for the press and big department store buyers. It's impossible to get tickets to the runway shows (they go to the likes of Kim Kardashian and Katie Holmes). I only mention Fashion Week here because the event can tie up rooms at the Midtown hotels (and at the more fashionable ones uptown and down).

Westminster Kennel Club Dog Show. I've always found it funny that Fashion Week— that parade of "Best in Breed" women— should be followed directly by a dog show. At least at the dog show, they're upfront about the purpose of the spectacle. The winnowing from just cute to anatomically awesome takes place the second weekend of the month at **Madison Square Garden**. With over 2,500 pooches appearing, it's quite the scene. Check the website **www. westminsterkennelclub.org** for further info. Tickets are available starting in mid-October via **Ticketmaster** (www.ticketmaster.com). Mid-February.

MARCH

The Pier Antiques Show. Never heard of it? Then you obviously aren't into antiques and collectibles, as this is one of the largest shows in the world for folks who care about old stuff. Taking place on the Passenger Ship Terminal Piers for a weekend, the show draws hundreds of treasure seekers. Visit **www.pierantiqueshow.com** for this year's dates. Usually late March, and again in mid-November.

St. Patrick's Day Parade. Thanks to one of the largest Irish-American populations in the United States, St. Paddy's is an enormous event in NYC, rivaling only New Year's Eve for its displays of public inebriation. Every pub in town throws a party, and in the afternoon, all of 150,000 marchers parade down Fifth Avenue from 44th to 86th streets, starting at 11am. For more info: **www.nycst patricksparade.org**. March 17.

APRIL

New York International Auto Show. Here's the irony: You don't need a car in New York, yet this is the largest car show in the U.S. Held at the Javits Center, many concept cars show up that will never roll off the assembly line but are fun to dream about. To learn more: **www.autoshowny.com**. Mid-April.

Easter Parade. No floats, no marching bands—just ordinary people strolling in extraordinary hats mark Easter in one of the city's most low-key but charming celebrations. Fifth Avenue from 57th Street all the way down to 45th is closed to traffic from 11am to 4pm, with the greatest number of chapeaus in evidence around noon. Easter is March 16, 2017.

Tribeca Film Festival. Founded by Robert DeNiro and Jane Rosenthal in 2002, this little film festival has quickly grown into one of the most influential in the nation. You'll see films from all over the world, from big studio pictures to tiny independent productions. And unlike other film fests, this one is truly for all ages, with a nifty street fair on the second weekend (usually featuring a zoo and rides), as well as children's films. Mid-April. To learn more, visit **www.tribecafilm. com/festival**.

MAY

Fleet Week. About 10,000 Navy and Coast Guard personnel are "at liberty" in New York for the annual Fleet Week at the end of May. Usually from 1 to 4pm daily, you can watch the ships and aircraft carriers as they dock at the piers on the west side of Manhattan, tour them with on-duty personnel, and watch dramatic exhibitions by the U.S. Marines. Even if you don't take in any of the events, you'll know it's Fleet Week because those 10,000 sailors invade NYC in their starched white uniforms. It's wonderful—just like *On the Town* come to life. Late May.

Frieze New York. An off-shoot of the London original, this artapalooza brings hundreds of international galleries to tents on Randall's Island. Big money is spent and made here, but even if you're not a buyer, the chance to see art this cutting-edge is exciting. Early May.

JUNE

Belmont Stakes. The final event in horse racing's grand trifecta of events (the Kentucky Derby and the Preakness are the first two). Any horse able to win all three instantly enters the record books and his owner becomes a multi-millionaire, thanks to the breeding fees he'll be able to collect for the rest of that horse's life. For information, visit **www.nyra.com**. Early June.

Gay Pride Weekend. More than just a parade (though the naughty, outrageous, rambunctious parade is still at the heart of the festivities), NY's pride weekend draws men and women from across the U.S. for a weekend of lectures, dances, and rallies. Learn more at **www.nycpride.org**.

Mermaid Parade. A smaller, nautically-themed, daytime version of Greenwich Village's Halloween Parade, the Mermaid Parade takes place toward the end of June each year in Coney Island. Founded in 1983, the parade has the same kind of homegrown ambience and raunch as its Greenwich Village counterpart. Along with the ball

that follows, featuring performances by local burlesque acts, the event is a heckuva a lot of fun. Get details at **www.coneyisland.com**.

JULY

Macy's Fourth of July Fireworks. Catch Macy's fireworks extravaganza over New York Harbor. It's the country's largest pyrotechnic show on Independence Day. **www. macys.com/fireworks**.

Summer Restaurant Week. Mid-July (see "January," above).

Several Festivals at Lincoln Center. The **Lincoln Center Festival** celebrates the best of the performing arts from all over—theater, ballet, contemporary dance, opera, nouveau circus performances, and even puppet- and media-based art. Recent editions have featured performances by the Bolshoi Ballet, Anne Teresa de Keersmaeker's Rosas company, and actors Cate Blanchett and Isabelle Huppert. Schedules are available in the spring, and tickets go on sale in May or early June. Visit **www.lincolncenterfestival.org** or call ✆ **212/875-5000**. An outdoor festival of artists at Lincoln Center, with free performances, runs through the end of August. The **Mostly Mozart Concert**, an indoor offering, brings master musicians from all over the world to play the music of the 18th-century master. Also part of the fun outdoors at Lincoln Center at this time of year is **Midsummer Night's Swing:** evenings of big-band swing, salsa, and tango under the stars to the sounds of top-flight bands. Dance lessons are offered with the purchase of a ticket.

AUGUST

Harlem Week. The world's largest black and Hispanic cultural festival actually spans almost the entire month, to include the Harlem Jazz and Music Festival and the New York City Children's Festival. Expect a full slate of music, from gospel to hip-hop, and lots of other festivities. Visit **http://harlem week.com**. Throughout August.

New York International Fringe Festival (FringeNYC). Held in a variety of downtown venues and park spaces for a crowd looking for the next underground hit (as in *Urinetown*, which went from the Fringe to

Broadway in 2001), this arts festival presents alternative as well as traditional theater. Hundreds of events are held at all hours over about 10 days. Suffice it to say that the quality can vary wildly Visit **www.fringenyc.org**. Mid- to late August.

U.S. Open Tennis Championships. For one brief, bright-tennis-whites moment each year at the end of August (and into September), the city becomes a center for international sport with the start of the U.S. Open, one of tennis' four Grand Slam events. For full information, visit **www.usopen.org** or **www.usta.com** for information. Two weeks around Labor Day.

SEPTEMBER

Fashion Week. Part 2 of the event mentioned above (see "February"), and yes, it sends hotel rates soaring. See details on dates at **www.mbfashionweek.com**.

New York Film Festival. Legendary hits like *Pulp Fiction* and *Mean Streets* both had their U.S. premieres at the Film Society of Lincoln Center's 2-week festival, a major stop on the film-fest circuit. Screenings are held in various Lincoln Center venues; advance tickets are always a good bet, and a necessity for certain events (especially evening and weekend screenings). Check out **www.filmlinc.com/nyff**. Two weeks from late September to early October.

OCTOBER

Greenwich Village Halloween Parade. This is New York's most outrageous event and the largest Halloween parade in the world. Some locals spend all year working on their costumes; if you dress up, you can march, too. For information on how to do that, and for the parade routing (which changes), visit **www.halloween-nyc.com**. To snag a viewing spot in Greenwich Village along the parade route, you'll need to show up at about 5pm (2 hours before the parade starts) . . . or have a nice dinner and show up at 9pm to view the second half. The crowd will have thinned by then, and because the event usually doesn't end until close to 11pm, you'll have more than enough time to enjoy it. October 31.

Open House New York. The doors are thrown open at dozens of homes and buildings around the city, all of which are usually off limits to the public and feature notable architecture. Mid-October. Exact dates at www.ohny.org

NOVEMBER

New York City Marathon. Some 30,000 runners from around the world participate in the largest U.S. marathon, and more than a million fans cheer them on as they follow a route that touches all five New York boroughs and finishes at Central Park. Go to **www.nyrr.org** for applications. First Sunday in November.

Holiday Trimmings. Starting the day after Thanksgiving (and often even before that), the entire city dresses up for Christmas, stringing lights, hanging tinsel, and inserting the computer chips into all of the moving figurines that have, of late, hijacked the windows of the city's large department stores. The best street to see the trimmings, by far, is **Fifth Avenue, between 39th and 59th streets.** Along with the spectacular windows at the big department stores— **Saks Fifth Avenue, Lord & Taylor, Bergdorf Goodman,** and **Tiffany's**—you'll also want to admire the massive fir tree at Rockefeller Center (off Fifth Avenue, at 51st Street, lit in late November; go to www.rockefeller center.com for details). The windows at **Macy's** (34th Street at Broadway) are also deservedly famous, as is the indoor winter wonderland display at the heart of which is a Santa, waiting to hear your tots' Christmas wishes (just like in *Miracle on 34th Street*). **Madison Avenue, between 55th and 60th streets,** is also worth a stroll, and if you have the time, drop by **Bloomingdales** (Lexington Avenue, between 59th and 60th streets) for its yearly display.

Chanukah is also a big deal in this city, with the largest Jewish population outside of Israel. On Fifth Avenue at 59th Street, a giant menorah—at 32 feet it's the largest in the world—is lit each year on the first night of Chanukah and for 7 nights thereafter. On the first and final evenings, steaming *latkes* (potato pancakes) are distributed at sunset, and live music accompanies the electric candle-lighting. December 24 will be the first night of Chanukah in 2016; it will fall on December 12 in 2017.

Radio City Christmas Spectacular. This New York tradition now starts well before Thanksgiving, and it's still as extravagantly kitschy as ever, with laser-light shows, onstage ice-skating, horses, camels, and, of course, the fabulous Rockettes executing their 300-plus kicks per show. Shows run approximately 7 days a week, with six daily performances (on many dates) starting at 9am and going until 10pm. For information, go to **www.radiocity christmas.com**; you can also buy tickets at the box office or via Ticketmaster's **Radio City Hot Line** (✆ **866/858-0007**), or visit **www. ticketmaster.com**. Throughout November and December.

The Pier Antiques Show. Mid-November (see "March," above).

Macy's Thanksgiving Day Parade. The procession of this much-beloved national tradition starts at Central Park West and 77th Street and finishes at Herald Square at 34th Street. Huge hot-air balloons in the forms of Minions, Snoopy, and other cartoon favorites are the best part. The night before, you can see the big blow-up on Columbus Avenue at West 77th and 81st streets. Thanksgiving Day.

The Nutcracker. Ballet impresario George Balanchine's masterpiece. The music is by Tchaikovsky, and half the cast is under 15, culled from New York City Ballet's famous dance school at Juilliard. Your children will love it, though it's an expensive treat. The show sells out early, so make your reservations in October if you can, when the seats first go on sale. Go online to **www.nycbal let.com**. Late November through early January.

Christmas Traditions. In addition to the *Radio City Christmas Spectacular* and the New York City Ballet's staging of *The Nutcracker* (see "November," above), traditional holiday events include the National Chorale's singalong performances of Handel's *Messiah* at **Avery Fisher Hall** (www.lincolncenter.org). The *Messiah* is also staged in many churches and other venues throughout the city during December. Check local listings.

New Year's Eve. The biggest party of all is in Times Square, where raucous revelers count down the year's final seconds until the ball drops at midnight at 1 Times Square. Standing in the cold, surrounded by thousands of tipsy revelers, all penned in by NYPD barricades, is a masochist's delight. Use the restroom before you wedge yourself in. More info at **www.timessquarenyc.org**. December 31.

Runner's World Midnight Run. Enjoy **fireworks** followed by the New York Road Runners Club's annual run in **Central Park,** which is fun for runners and spectators alike; go to **www.nyrr.org**. December 31.

Brooklyn's Fireworks Celebration. Head to Brooklyn for the city's largest New Year's Eve **fireworks** celebration inside Prospect Park. Visit **www.prospectpark.org**. December 31.

New Year's Eve Concert for Peace. The Cathedral of St. John the Divine is known for its annual concert, whose past performances have included singer Judy Collins, Forces of Nature Dance Company, and the world premiere of *Songs of War, Remembrance, and Hope* by Glen Cortese. The evening culminates in the passing of a candle flame while the audience of thousands sings *This Little Light of Mine*. For tickets, go to **www. stjohndivine.org**. December 31.

Public Holidays

Banks, government offices, post offices, and many stores, restaurants, and museums are closed on the following legal national holidays: January 1 (New Year's Day), the third Monday in January (Martin Luther King, Jr., Day), the third Monday in February (Presidents' Day), the last Monday in May

(Memorial Day), July 4 (Independence Day), the first Monday in September (Labor Day), the second Monday in October (Columbus Day), November 11 (Veterans Day/Armistice Day), the fourth Thursday in November (Thanksgiving Day), and December 25 (Christmas). The Tuesday after the first Monday in November is Election Day, a government holiday.

[FastFACTS] NEW YORK CITY

Area Codes There are five area codes in NYC: two in Manhattan, the original **212** plus **646;** and three in the outer boroughs, the original **718,** plus **929** and **347.** Also common is the **917** area code for cellphones. All calls between these area codes are local calls, but you'll have to dial 1 + the area code + the seven digits for all calls, even those made within your area code.

Business Hours In general, **retail stores** are open Monday through Saturday from 10am to 6 or 7pm, Thursday from 10am to 8:30 or 9pm, and Sunday from 11am to 5pm. **Banks** tend to be open Monday through Friday from 9am to 5pm, with many open Saturday mornings, and some on Sundays.

Customs What You Can Bring into the U.S. It is forbidden to bring into the country almost any meat products. Generally, condiments including vinegars, oils, spices, coffee, tea, and some cheeses and baked goods are permitted. Avoid rice products, as rice can often harbor insects. Fruits and vegetables are prohibited as well. International visitors may carry in or out up to $10,000 in U.S.

or foreign currency with no formalities; larger sums must be declared to U.S. Customs on entering or leaving. For more details regarding U.S. Customs and Border Protection, consult your nearest U.S. embassy or consulate, or **U.S. Customs and Border Protection (www.cbp.gov).**

Disabled Travelers New York is more accessible than ever to travelers with disabilities. The city's bus system is wheelchair-friendly, and most of the major sightseeing attractions are accessible. Even so, call first to be sure that the places you want to go to are fully accessible and lifts are operational.

Most hotels are ADA-compliant, with suitable rooms for travelers who use wheelchairs as well as those with other disabilities. But before you book, **ask lots of questions based on your needs.** Many city hotels are in older buildings that have been modified to meet requirements; still, elevators and bathrooms can be on the small side, and other impediments may exist. If you have mobility issues, you'll probably do best to book one of the city's newer hotels, which tend to be

more accommodating. Some Broadway theaters and other performance venues provide total wheelchair accessibility; others provide partial accessibility. Many also offer lower-priced tickets for theatergoers with disabilities and their companions, though you'll need to check individual policies and reserve in advance.

Hospital Audiences, Inc. (www.hainyc.org) arranges attendance and provides details about accessibility at cultural institutions as well as cultural events adapted for people with disabilities. Services include "Describe!," which allows visually impaired theatergoers to enjoy theater events.

Museums: In New York, the general rule is: The larger the museum, the more extensive its facilities for persons with disabilities. For example, the Metropolitan Museum of Art offers free rental of standard and extra-wide wheelchairs at all of its coat-check stands, regular sign-language and touch tours for the deaf and blind, attended elevators, and accessible bathrooms and water fountains. In smaller museums you'll find fewer such amenities, so call first for information.

Doctors If you get sick, consider asking your hotel concierge to recommend a local doctor—even his or her own. This will probably yield a better recommendation than any toll-free telephone number would.

There are also many walk-in medical centers, like **City MD** (www.citymd.com), which offers 17 clinics in Manhattan and dozens in the other boroughs. Hours vary widely. Their midtown office is at 944 Second Ave. (at 50th Street).

New York Presbyterian Hospital offers physician referrals at ℂ **877/697-9355.** Because of a shortage of hospitals in New York City, I don't recommend emergency room visits except in, well, dire emergencies.

Pack **prescription medications** in their original containers in your carry-on luggage. Also bring along copies of your prescriptions in case you lose your pills or run out.

If you have dental problems on the road, a service known as **1-800-DENTIST** (ℂ **800/336-8422**) will provide the name of a local dentist.

Drinking Laws The legal age for purchase and consumption of alcoholic beverages is 21; proof of age can be requested at bars, nightclubs, and restaurants, especially if you're graced with youthful looks. Liquor and wine are sold only in licensed stores, most of which are now open 7 days a week. Beer can be purchased in grocery stores and delis 24 hours a day. Last call in bars is at 4am, though many close earlier. Do not carry open containers of alcohol in any public area that isn't zoned for alcohol consumption. The police can fine you on the spot.

Electricity Like Canada, the United States uses 110 to 120 volts AC (60 cycles), compared to 220 to 240 volts AC (50 cycles) in most of Europe, Australia, and New Zealand.

Embassies & Consulates All embassies are in the nation's capital, Washington, D.C. Some consulates are in New York, and most nations have a mission to the United Nations here. To find where your embassy is, check **www.embassy.org/embassies**.

Emergencies For all emergencies—a fire, police, or health emergency—call **911.**

Family Travel Good bets for the most timely information include the "Weekend" section of Friday's *New York Times,* which has a section dedicated to kid-friendly activities; and the weekly *New York* magazine, which has a full calendar of children's events.

The first place to look for babysitting is in your hotel (better yet, ask about babysitting when you reserve). Many hotels have babysitting services or will provide you with lists of reliable sitters. If this doesn't pan out, call the **Baby Sitters' Guild** (ℂ **212/682-0227;** www.babysittersguild.com). The sitters are licensed, insured, and bonded, and can even take your child on outings.

Hospitals The following hospitals have 24 hour emergency rooms. Don't forget your insurance card.

Downtown: New York Presbyterian Hospital, 170 William St. between Beekman and Spruce streets (ℂ **212/312-5106** or 212/312-5000), and **Beth Israel Medical Center,** First Avenue and 16th Street (ℂ **212/420-2000**).

Midtown: Bellevue Hospital Center, 462 First Ave. at 27th Street (ℂ **212/562-4141**); **New York University Langone Medical Center,** 550 First Ave. at 33rd Street (ℂ **212/263-7300**); and **Roosevelt Hospital,** 425 W. 59th St. between Ninth and Tenth avenues (ℂ **212/523-4000**).

Upper West Side: St. Luke's Hospital Center, 1111 Amsterdam Ave. at 114th Street (ℂ **212/523-4000**); and **Columbia Presbyterian Medical Center,** 630 W. 168th St., between Broadway and Fort Washington Avenue (ℂ **212/305-2500**).

Upper East Side: New York Presbyterian Hospital, 525 E. 68th St. at York Avenue (ℂ **212/746-5454**); **Lenox Hill Hospital,** 100 E. 77th St. between Park and Lexington avenues (ℂ **212/434-2000**); and **Mount Sinai Medical Center,** 1190 Fifth Ave. at 100th Street (ℂ **212/241-6500**).

Internet & Wi-Fi New York is rife with Wi-Fi "hotspots" that offer free Wi-Fi access or charge a small fee for usage. A good directory of free hotspots in the city can be found at **www.openwifispots.com**. Many of the city's parks and major plazas offer free Wi-Fi through various sponsors. Many subway stops also offer Wi-Fi, as do all Starbucks and all public libraries.

Your hotel will likely also provide Wi-Fi in your room, usually for free.

Legal Aid If accused of a serious offense, say and do nothing before consulting a lawyer. In the U.S., the burden is on the state to prove a person's guilt beyond a reasonable doubt, and everyone has the right to remain silent, whether he or she is suspected of a crime or actually arrested. Once arrested, a person can make one telephone call to a party of his or her choice. The international visitor should call his or her embassy or consulate.

LGBT Travelers In truth, gay and lesbian travelers need very little special advice when it comes to New York City. With one of the largest and most politically active gay populations in the world, and dozens of gay bars and clubs (see chapter 8), you should feel welcomed and accepted in the Big Apple. After all, this is where the Broadway musical was born, right?

Traditionally, the gay community of New York has been centered around Christopher Street in the West Village, but in the last decade it's expanded to Chelsea and Hell's Kitchen. If you're a bar-hopper, these are the three areas you'll want to explore, though there are gay bars in every neighborhood of the city, just as there are gay people in every neighborhood. For more complete listings of bars and special events than you'll find in this tome, surf to *Gay City News* (www. gaycitynews.com), **Next** (www.nextmagazine.com) and *GO* magazine (www. gomag.com), which is lesbian-oriented. Another good resource is *Time Out* (available for free every Wednesday at subway stations and at www.timeout.com/newyork), which has a large section devoted to gay and lesbian events and festivities.

Mail At press time, domestic postage rates were 35¢ for a postcard and 49¢ for a letter. For more information go to **www. usps.com**.

Medical Requirements Unless you're arriving from an area known to be suffering from an epidemic (particularly cholera or yellow fever), inoculations or vaccinations are not required for entry into the United States.

Money & Costs In terms of how much to bring: not that much in cash. You never have to carry too much cash in New York, and while the city's pretty safe, it's best not to overstuff your wallet (although always make sure you have at least $20 in cash for small purchases).

ATMs In most Manhattan neighborhoods, you can find a bank with *ATMs* (automated teller machines) every few blocks. Most delis and other stores have an ATM on premises, so if you need cash quickly, you're probably never more than about 100 feet away from one.

Newspapers & Magazines There are three major daily newspapers: the *New York Times*, the *Daily News*, and the *New York Post*. There are several weekly and biweekly newspapers and magazines (such as the glossies *New York Magazine* and *Time Out New York*), as well as the *Village Voice* and *Gay City News*, which are excellent sources of info about events.

Packing The most important item in your suitcase will be a pair of very comfortable shoes, because your dogs are gonna be barking! This is a walking city, and what with getting from place to place and trudging through the marble halls of the Metropolitan Museum of Art or the American Museum of Natural History, a springy, supportive pair of shoes is essential (you may want to bring two pairs to increase your feet ease). Other than that, fill your suitcase with what pleases you most at home: Very few actual New Yorkers have the budget or time to dress like the socialites of

WHAT THINGS COST IN NEW YORK CITY

	US $
Cab from JFK Airport to Manhattan (plus tolls)	52.00
Single full-fare subway or bus ride	3.00
7-Day Unlimited-Ride MetroCard for bus or subway	31.00
Ticket to a NY Yankees game (Terrace)	85.00
Pint of beer (draft pilsner or lager)	7.00
Cup of coffee in a cafe or bar	4.00
Coca-Cola in a cafe or bar	3.00
Cocktail in a bar	15.00
Bottle of water	1.00–2.00
Tube of toothpaste	5.99
Admission to Museum of Modern Art	25.00
Movie ticket	14.00
Walking tour	15.00
Discount ticket to a Broadway show	65.00–85.00
Full-price ticket to a Broadway show (orchestra)	135.00

Gossip Girl, and unless you plan on going to the opera or a fancy restaurant, smart casual clothes should suffice.

Dressing appropriately for the weather is also key, so be sure to check the chart on p. 269 for the average temperatures at various times of the year. If you're visiting in the fall or spring (mid-September to mid-November, and mid-March to mid-May) bring clothes that you can layer, as a balmy afternoon can turn chilly once the sun goes down.

Police Dial ☏ **911** in an emergency; otherwise, call ☏ **646/610-5000** (NYPD Switchboard) for the number of the nearest precinct. For nonemergency matters, call ☏ **311.**

Safety The FBI consistently rates New York City as one of the safest large cities in the United States, but it is still a large city and crime most definitely exists. So trust your instincts and take the same precautions you'd take in any large city (don't flash your money or carry too much of it at one time; stay in well-lit, crowded areas).

In general, the subways are safe, especially in Manhattan. There are questionable characters like anywhere else in the city, but subway crime has gone down to 1960s levels. Still, always keep a hand on your belongings.

When using the subway, **don't wait for trains near the edge of the platform** or on extreme ends of a station. During non-rush hours, wait for the train in view of the token-booth clerk or under the yellow DURING OFF HOURS TRAINS STOP HERE signs,

and ride in the train conductor's car (usually in the center of the train; you'll see his or her head stick out of the window when the doors open). Choose crowded cars over empty ones—there's safety in numbers.

Senior Travel New York subway and bus fares are half-price ($1.35) for people 65 and older. Many museums and sights (and some theaters and performance halls) offer discounted admittance and tickets to seniors; ask!

Many hotels offer senior discounts, but they may not be as good as the regular discounts one gets through bargain websites, so always check before pulling out your AARP card.

Smoking Smoking is prohibited on all public transportation; in the lobbies of hotels and office buildings; in taxis, bars, parks, beaches, and restaurants; and in most shops.

Student Travel   There are student discounts at almost every museum in New York, so student travelers should bring their school IDs with them.

Taxes   **Sales tax** is 8.875% on meals, most goods, and some services. **Hotel tax** is 5.875%. **Parking garage tax** is 18.375%. The United States has no value-added tax (VAT) or other indirect tax at the national level.

Telephones   Generally, hotel surcharges on long-distance and local calls are astronomical, so you're better off using your **cellphone.**

To make a **local call** in one of the five boroughs, **dial 1,** followed by the area code and the seven-digit number. **To make calls within the United States and to Canada,** dial 1. **For other international calls,** dial 011, followed by the country code, city code, and the number you are calling.

Calls to area codes **800, 888, 855, 877,** and **866** are toll-free. However, calls to area code **900** (chat lines, bulletin boards, "dating" services, and so on) can be expensive—charges of 95¢ to $3 or more per minute.

For **directory assistance** ("Information"), dial **411** for numbers across the U.S. and Canada.

Mobile Phones: It's a good bet that your phone

will work in New York City, but take a look at your wireless company's coverage map on its website before heading out. There's also the savvy option of using your smartphone's **Skype** app at Wi-Fi hotspots for free and very cheap calling.

Time   The continental United States is divided into **four time zones:** Eastern Standard Time (EST), Central Standard Time (CST), Mountain Standard Time (MST), and Pacific Standard Time (PST). Alaska and Hawaii have their own zones. For example, when it's noon in New York City (EST), it's 5pm in London (GMT), 11am in Chicago (CST), 10am in Denver (MST), 9am in Los Angeles (PST), 7am in Honolulu (HST), and 2am the next day in Sydney.

Daylight saving time (summer time) is in effect from 1am on the second Sunday in March to 1am on the first Sunday in November. Daylight saving time moves the clock 1 hour ahead of standard time.

Tipping   In hotels, tip **bellhops** at least $1 per bag and tip the **chamber staff** $1 to $2 per day (more if you've left a big mess). Tip the **doorman** or **concierge** only if he or she has provided you with some specific service (for example, calling a cab for you or obtaining difficult-to-get theater tickets). Tip the **valet-parking attendant** $1 every time you get your car.

In restaurants, bars, and nightclubs, tip **service staff** and **bartenders** 15% to 20% of the check (or you can simply double the tax on the check, which will be 16%). Tip **checkroom attendants** $1 per garment, and tip **valet-parking attendants** $1 per vehicle.

As for other service personnel, tip **cab drivers** 15% to 20% of the fare; tip **skycaps** at airports at least $1 per bag ($2–$3 if you have a lot of luggage); and tip **hairdressers, barbers,** and **massage therapists** 15% to 20%.

Toilets   You won't find any public toilets on the streets in New York City, but they can be found in hotel lobbies, bars, restaurants, museums, department stores, and railway and bus stations. Large hotels and fast-food restaurants are often the best bet for clean facilities.

You can find relief at the New York Public Library's main building on Fifth Avenue just south of 42nd Street. Grand Central Terminal, at 42nd Street between Park and Lexington avenues, also has clean restrooms. Your best bet in other areas is Starbucks or another city java chain—you can't go more than a few blocks without seeing one.

Visitor Information NYC & Company is the city's megaphone and its website, **www.nycgo.com**, holds a wealth of free and ever-changing information.

Index

Map List

Photo Credits

Frommer's EasyGuide to New York City, 4th Edition

Published by
FROMMER MEDIA LLC

ISBN 978-1-62887-276-7 (paper), 978-1-62887-277-4 (e-book)

Editorial Director: Pauline Frommer
Editor: Holly Hughes
Production Editor: Lindsay Conner
Cartographer: Roberta Stockwell
Cover Design: Howard Grossman

Front cover photo: Statue of Liberty © Usa-Pyon / Shutterstock.com

For information on our other products or services, see www.frommers.com.

FrommerMedia LLC also publishes its books in a variety of electronic formats. Some content that appears in print may not be available in electronic formats.

Manufactured in the United States of America

5 4 3 2 1

ABOUT THE AUTHOR

Pauline Frommer started traveling with her guidebook-writing parents at the age of four months and hasn't stopped since. Her first job in travel was on the website Frommers.com, and eventually she worked her way up to Editor in Chief. Pauline also served as Travel Editor for MSNBC.com for several years, before working with John Wiley & Sons to create the award-winning Pauline *Frommer Guidebooks*, a 14-book series that won the coveted "Best Guidebook of the Year" title 3 years in a row from the North American Travel Journalists Association and once from the Society of American Travel Writers.

For 4 years, Pauline created weekly travel segments for CNN's Headline News and CNN's Pipeline. You may also have seen her talking travel on *The Today Show, Live with Regis and Kelly, The O'Reilly Factor, NBC Nightly News* and *ABC World News, Good Morning America, FOX News* and every local news station you can name. On weekends, she hosts a nationally syndicated radio show on travel. Her writings have been widely published in everything from *Budget Travel Magazine* to the *Newsweek* to *Nick, Jr.* magazine; she also pens an internationally syndicated newspaper column for King Features. Frommer resides in New York City with her husband and two daughters.

ABOUT THE FROMMER TRAVEL GUIDES

For most of the past 50 years, Frommer's has been the leading series of travel guides in North America, accounting for as many as 24% of all guidebooks sold. I think I know why.

Though we hope our books are entertaining, we nevertheless deal with travel in a serious fashion. Our guidebooks have never looked on such journeys as a mere recreation, but as a far more important human function, a time of learning and introspection, an essential part of a civilized life. We stress the culture, lifestyle, history, and beliefs of the destinations we cover, and urge our readers to seek out people and new ideas as the chief rewards of travel.

We have never shied from controversy. We have, from the beginning, encouraged our authors to be intensely judgmental, critical—both pro and con—in their comments, and wholly independent. Our only clients are our readers, and we have triggered the ire of countless prominent sorts, from a tourist newspaper we called "practically worthless" (it unsuccessfully sued us) to the many rip-offs we've condemned.

And because we believe that travel should be available to everyone regardless of their incomes, we have always been cost-conscious at every level of expenditure. Though we have broadened our recommendations beyond the budget category, we insist that every lodging we include be sensibly priced. We use every form of media to assist our readers, and are particularly proud of our feisty daily website, the award-winning Frommers.com.

I have high hopes for the future of Frommer's. May these guidebooks, in all the years ahead, continue to reflect the joy of travel and the freedom that travel represents. May they always pursue a cost-conscious path, so that people of all incomes can enjoy the rewards of travel. And may they create, for both the traveler and the persons among whom we travel, a community of friends, where all human beings live in harmony and peace.

Arthur Frommer